Practical Reverse Engineering

x86, x64, ARM, Windows® Kernel, Reversing Tools, and Obfuscation

Bruce Dang
Alexandre Gazet
Elias Bachaalany

with contributions from Sébastien Josse

WILEY

Practical Reverse Engineering: x86, x64, ARM, Windows® Kernel, Reversing Tools, and Obfuscation

Published by
John Wiley & Sons, Inc.
10475 Crosspoint Boulevard
Indianapolis, IN 46256
www.wiley.com

Copyright © 2014 by Bruce Dang
Published by John Wiley & Sons, Inc., Indianapolis, Indiana
Published simultaneously in Canada

ISBN: 978-1-118-78731-1
ISBN: 978-1-118-78725-0 (ebk)
ISBN: 978-1-118-78739-7 (ebk)

Manufactured in the United States of America

SKY10079411_071124

For general information on our other products and services please contact our Customer Care Department within the United States at (877) 762-2974, outside the United States at (317) 572-3993 or fax (317) 572-4002.

Wiley publishes in a variety of print and electronic formats and by print-on-demand. Some material included with standard print versions of this book may not be included in e-books or in print-on-demand. If this book refers to media such as a CD or DVD that is not included in the version you purchased, you may download this material at http://booksupport.wiley.com. For more information about Wiley products, visit www.wiley.com.

Library of Congress Control Number: 2013954099

This book is dedicated to those who relentlessly pursue knowledge and selflessly share it with others.

About the Authors

Bruce Dang is a senior security development engineering lead at Microsoft working on security technologies in unreleased Microsoft products. Previously, he worked on security vulnerabilities reported to Microsoft and was the first to publicly share analytical techniques for targeted attacks with Office documents. He and his team analyzed the famous Stuxnet malware, which supposedly attacked the Iranian uranium enrichment process. He has spoken at RSA, BlackHat Vegas, BlackHat Tokyo, Chaos Computer Club, REcon, and many other industry conferences.

Alexandre Gazet is a security researcher at Quarkslab. His interests focus on reverse engineering, software protections, and vulnerability research. Alexandre has presented at several conferences, including HITB Kuala Lumpur (2009) and REcon Montreal (2010 and 2011).

Elias Bachaalany has been a computer programmer, reverse engineer, freelance technical writer, and an occasional reverse engineering trainer for the past 14 years. Over his long career, Elias has worked with various technologies, including writing scripts, doing extensive web development, working with database design and programming, writing device drivers and low-level code such as boot loaders or minimal operating systems, writing managed code, assessing software protections, and writing reverse engineering and desktop security tools. Elias has also presented twice at REcon Montreal (2012 and 2013).

While working for Hex-Rays SA in Belgium, Elias helped to improve and add new features to IDA Pro. During that period, he authored various technical blog posts, provided IDA Pro training, developed various debugger plugins, amped up IDA Pro's scripting facilities, and contributed to the IDAPython project since version 1.2.0 and onwards. Elias currently works at Microsoft with a talented team of software security engineers.

Sébastien Josse is a security researcher at the French Ministry of Defense (Direction Générale de l'Armement). He has more than ten years of experience as an instructor, researcher, and consultant in the field of information systems security, in both the civilian and defense sectors. He dedicated his PhD dissertation (École Polytechnique, 2009) to the dynamic analysis of protected programs, focusing mainly on cryptographic mechanisms resistant to reverse engineering and on the use of a virtualization system to carry through analysis of protected programs. He has published in the journal *JICV* and several conferences proceedings, including ECRYPT (2004), EICAR (2006, 2008, 2011), AVAR (2007) and HICSS (2012, 2013 and 2014).

About the Technical Editor

Matt Miller is a principal security engineer in Microsoft's Trustworthy Computing organization, where he currently focuses on researching and developing exploit-mitigation technology. Prior to joining Microsoft, Matt was core developer for the Metasploit framework and a contributor to the journal *Uninformed*, where he wrote about topics related to exploitation, reverse engineering, program analysis, and operating system internals.

Credits

Executive Editor
Carol Long

Project Editor
John Sleeva

Technical Editor
Matt Miller

Production Editor
Daniel Scribner

Copy Editor
Luann Rouff

Editorial Manager
Mary Beth Wakefield

Freelancer Editorial Manager
Rosemarie Graham

Associate Director of Marketing
David Mayhew

Marketing Manager
Ashley Zurcher

Business Manager
Amy Knies

Vice President and Executive Group Publisher
Richard Swadley

Associate Publisher
Jim Minatel

Project Coordinator, Cover
Todd Klemme

Proofreader
Josh Chase, Word One New York

Indexer
Ron Strauss

Cover Designer
Ryan Sneed

Acknowledgments

Writing this book has been one of the most interesting and time-consuming endeavors we have ever gone through. The book represents something that we wish we had when we started learning about reverse engineering more than 15 years ago. At the time, there was a dearth of books and online resources (there were no blogs back then); we learned the art primarily through friends and independent trial-and-error experiments. The information security "industry" was also non-existent back then. Today, the world is different. We now have decompilers, web scanners, static source scanners, cloud (?), and APTs (unthinkable!). Numerous blogs, forums, books, and in-person classes aim to teach reverse engineering. These resources vary greatly in quality. Some are sub-standard but shamelessly published or offered to take advantage of the rise in demand for computer security; some are of extremely high quality but not well attended/read due to lack of advertising, specialization or because they are simply "too esoteric." There is not a unifying resource that people can use as the foundation for learning reverse engineering. We hope this book is that foundation.

Now for the best part, acknowledging the people who helped us arrive at where we are today. All of the authors would like to acknowledge Rolf Rolles for his contributions to the obfuscation chapter. Rolf is a real pioneer in the field of reverse engineering. His seminal work on virtual machine deobfuscation, applying program analysis to reverse engineering, and binary analysis education influenced and inspired a new generation of reverse engineers. We hope that he will continue to contribute to the field and inspire others to do the same. Next, we would also like to thank Matt Miller, our comrade and technical reviewer. Matt is another true pioneer in our field and has made seminal contributions to exploit mitigations in Windows. His dedication to details and helping others learn should be a model for all. Finally, we would like to thank Carol Long, John Sleeva, Luann Rouff, and the staff at John Wiley & Sons for putting up with us through the publishing process.

— The authors

I would like to thank my parents for their sacrifices to give me better opportunities in life; my sister and brother, Ivy Dang and Donald Dang, for being a constant source of support and inspiration; and Rolf Rolles for being a good friend and source of reason all these years. I did not have many role models growing up, but the following people directly helped shape my perspectives: Le Thanh Sang, Vint Cerf, and Douglas Comer. At university, I learned the joy of Chinese literature from David Knetchges, Buddhist studies from Kyoko Tokuno, Indian history from Richard Salomon (who would have thought so much can be learned from rocks and coins!), Central Asian history from Daniel Waugh, and Chinese language from Nyan-Ping Bi. While they are not reverse engineers, their enthusiasm and dedication forever inspired and made me a better human being and engineer. If I had met them earlier, my career path would probably be very different.

Through the journey of professional life, I was fortunate enough to meet intelligent people who influenced me (in no particular order): Alex Carp, rebel, Navin Pai, Jonathan Ness, Felix Domke, Karl J., Julien Tinnes, Josh Phillips, Daniel Radu, Maarten Boone, Yoann Guillot, Ivanlef0u (thanks for hosting us), Richard van Eeden, Dan Ho, Andy Renk, Elia Florio, Ilfak Guilfanov, Matt Miller, David Probert, Damian Hasse, Matt Thomlinson, Shawn Hoffman, David Dittrich, Eloi Vanderbeken, LMH, Ali Rahbar, Fermin Serna, Otto Kivling, Damien Aumaitre, Tavis Ormandy, Ali Pezeshk, Gynvael Coldwind, anakata (a rare genius), Richard van Eeden, Noah W., Ken Johnson, Chengyun Yu, Elias Bachaalany, Felix von Leitner, Michal Chmielewski, sectorx, Son Pho Nguyen, Nicolas Pouvesle, Kostya Kortchinsky, Peter Viscerola, Torbjorn L., Gustavo di Scotti, Sergiusz Fonrobert, Peter W., Ilja van Sprundel, Brian Cavenah, upb, Maarten Van Horenbeeck, Robert Hensing, Cristian Craioveanu, Claes Nyberg, Igor Skorchinsky, John Lambert, Mark Wodrich (role model Buddhist), David Midturi, Gavin Thomas, Sebastian Porst, Peter Vel, Kevin Broas, Michael Sandy, Christer Oberg, Mateusz "j00ru" Jurczyk, David Ross, and Raphael Rigo. Jonathan Ness and Damian Hasse were always supportive of me doing things differently and constantly gave me opportunities to fail/succeed. If I forgot you, please forgive me.

The following people directly provided feedback and improved the initial drafts of my chapters: Michal Chmielewski, Shawn Hoffman, Nicolas Pouvesle, Matt Miller, Alex Ionescu, Mark Wodrich, Ben Byer, Felix Domke, Ange Albertini, Igor Skorchinsky, Peter Ferrie, Lien Duong, iZsh, Frank Boldewin, Michael Hale Ligh, Sebastien Renaud, Billy McCourt, Peter Viscerola, Dennis Elser, Thai Duong, Eloi Vanderbeken, Raphael Rigo, Peter Vel, and Bradley Spengler (a true overachiever). Without their insightful comments and suggestions, most of the book would be unreadable. Of course, you can blame me for the remaining mistakes.

There are numerous other unnamed people that contributed to my knowledge and therefore this book.

I also want to thank Molly Reed and Tami Needham from The Omni Group for giving us a license of OmniGraffle to make illustrations in the earlier drafts.

Last but not least, I want to thank Alex, Elias, and Sébastien for helping me with this book. Without them, the book would have never seen the light of day.

— Bruce

First, I would like to thank Bruce Dang for inviting me to take part in this great project. It has been a long and enriching journey. Rolf Rolles was there at first, and I personally thank him for the countless hours we spent together imagining the obfuscation chapter and collecting material. Sébastien Josse then agreed to joined us; his contribution is invaluable and our chapter wouldn't be the same without him. Thank you, Seb.

I also want to thank my friends Fabrice Desclaux, Yoann Guillot, and Jean-Philippe Luyten for their invaluable feedback.

Finally, thanks to Carol Long for making this book possible, and to John Sleeva for keeping us on track.

— Alexandre

I want to start by thanking Bruce Dang, my friend and colleague, for giving me the chance to participate in this endeavor. I also want to thank all my friends and colleagues for their support and help. In particular, I would like to thank Daniel Pistelli (CEO of Cerbero GmbH), Michal Chmielewski, Swamy Shivaganga Nagaraju, and Alexandre Gazet for their technical input and feedback during the writing of the book.

I want to thank Mr. Ilfak Guilfanov (CEO of Hex-Rays SA). I learned a lot from him while working at Hex-Rays. His hard work, patience, and perseverance to create IDA Pro will always be an inspiration to me.

A big thanks to John Wiley & Sons for giving us the opportunity to publish this book. Thanks also to the acquisition editor Carol Long for her prompt and professional assistance, and to the project editor John Sleeva and copy editor Luann Rouff for their energy, patience, and hard work.

— Elias

I want to thank Alexandre, Elias, and Bruce for giving me the opportunity to contribute to this book. I also want to thank Jean-Philippe Luyten for putting us in touch. Finally, thanks to Carol Long and John Sleeva for their help and professionalism in the realization of this project.

— Sébastien

Contents at a Glance

Contents

Introduction

The reverse engineering learning process is similar to that of foreign language acquisition for adults. The first phase of learning a foreign language begins with an introduction to letters in the alphabet, which are used to construct words with well-defined semantics. The next phase involves understanding the grammatical rules governing how words are glued together to produce a proper sentence. After being accustomed to these rules, one then learns how to stitch multiple sentences together to articulate complex thoughts. Eventually it reaches the point where the learner can read large books written in different styles and still understand the thoughts therein. At this point, one can read reference books on the more esoteric aspects of the language—historical syntax, phonology, and so on.

In reverse engineering, the language is the architecture and assembly language. A word is an assembly instruction. Paragraphs are sequences of assembly instructions. A book is a program. However, to fully understand a book, the reader needs to know more than just vocabulary and grammar. These additional elements include structure and style of prose, unwritten rules of writing, and others. Understanding computer programs also requires a mastery of concepts beyond assembly instructions.

It can be somewhat intimidating to start learning an entirely new technical subject from a book. However, we would be misleading you if we were to claim that reverse engineering is a simple learning endeavor and that it can be completely mastered by reading this book. The learning process is quite involved because it requires knowledge from several disparate domains of knowledge. For example, an effective reverse engineer needs to be knowledgeable in computer architecture, systems programming, operating systems, compilers, and so on; for certain areas, a strong mathematical background is necessary. So how do you know where to start? The answer depends on your experience and skills. Because we cannot accommodate everyone's background, this introduction outlines the learning and reading methods for those without any programming background. You should find your "position" in the spectrum and start from there.

For the sake of discussion, we loosely define reverse engineering as the process of understanding a system. It is a problem-solving process. A system can be a hardware device, a software program, a physical or chemical process, and so on. For the purposes of the book, the system is a software program. To understand a program, you must first understand how software is written. Hence, the first requirement is knowing how to program a computer through a language such as C, C++, Java, and others. We suggest first learning C due to its simplicity, effectiveness, and ubiquity. Some excellent references to consider are *The C Programming Language*, by Brian Kernighan and Dennis Ritchie (Prentice Hall, 1988) and *C: A Reference Manual*, by Samuel Harbison (Prentice Hall, 2002). After becoming comfortable with writing, compiling, and debugging basic programs, consider reading *Expert C Programming: Deep C Secrets*, by Peter van der Linden (Prentice Hall, 1994). At this point, you should be familiar with high-level concepts such as variables, scopes, functions, pointers, conditionals, loops, call stacks, and libraries. Knowledge of data structures such as stacks, queues, linked lists, and trees might be useful, but they are not entirely necessary for now. To top it off, you might skim through *Compilers: Principles, Techniques, and Tools*, by Alfred Aho, Ravi Sethi, and Jeffrey Ullman, (Prentice Hall, 1994) and *Linkers and Loaders*, by John Levine (Morgan Kaufmann, 1999), to get a better understanding of how a program is really put together. The key purpose of reading these books is to gain exposure to basic concepts; you do not have to understand every page for now (there will be time for that later). Overachievers should consider *Advanced Compiler Design and Implementation*, by Steven Muchnick (Morgan Kaufmann, 1997).

Once you have a good understanding of how programs are generally written, executed, and debugged, you should begin to explore the program's execution environment, which includes the processor and operating system. We suggest first learning about the Intel processor by skimming through *Intel 64 and IA-32 Architectures Software Developer's Manual, Volume 1: Basic Architecture* by Intel, with special attention to Chapters 2–7. These chapters explain the basic elements of a modern computer. Readers interested in ARM should consider *Cortex-A Series Programmer's Guide* and *ARM Architecture Reference Manual ARMv7-A and ARMv7-R Edition* by ARM. While our book covers x86/x64/ARM, we do not discuss every architectural detail. (We assume that the reader will refer to these manuals, as necessary.) In skimming through these manuals, you should have a basic appreciation of the technical building blocks of a computing system. For a more conceptual understanding, consider *Structured Computer Organization* by Andrew Tanenbaum (Prentice Hall, 1998). All readers should also consult the *Microsoft PE and COFF Specification.* At this point, you will have all the necessary background to read and understand Chapter 1, "x86 and x64," and Chapter 2, "ARM."

Next, you should explore the operating system. There are many different operating systems, but they share many common concepts including processes, threads, virtual memory, privilege separation, multi-tasking, and so on. The best way to understand these concepts is to read *Modern Operating Systems*, by Andrew Tanenbaum (Prentice Hall, 2005). Although Tanenbaum's text is excellent for concepts, it does not discuss important technical details for real-life operating systems. For Windows, you should consider skimming through *Windows NT Device Driver Development*, by Peter Viscarola and Anthony Mason (New Riders Press, 1998); although it is a book on driver development, the background chapters provide an excellent and concrete introduction to Windows. (It is also excellent supplementary material for the Windows kernel chapter in this book.) For additional inspiration (and an excellent treatment of the Windows memory manager), you should also read *What Makes It Page? The Windows 7 (x64) Virtual Memory Manager*, by Enrico Martignetti (CreateSpace Independent Publishing Platform, 2012).

At this point, you would have all the necessary background to read and understand Chapter 3 "The Windows Kernel." You should also consider learning Win32 programming. *Windows System Programming*, by Johnson Hart (Addison-Wesley Professional, 2010), and *Windows via C/C++*, by Jeffrey Richter and Christophe Nasarre (Microsoft Press, 2007), are excellent references.

For Chapter 4, "Debugging and Automation," consider *Inside Windows Debugging: A Practical Guide to Debugging and Tracing Strategies in Windows*, by Tarik Soulami (Microsoft Press, 2012), and *Advanced Windows Debugging*, by Mario Hewardt and Daniel Pravat (Addison-Wesley Professional, 2007).

Chapter 5, "Obfuscation," requires a good understanding of assembly language and should be read after the x86/x64/ARM chapters. For background knowledge, consider *Surreptitious Software: Obfuscation, Watermarking, and Tamperproofing for Software Protection*, by Christian Collberg and Jasvir Nagra (Addison-Wesley Professional, 2009).

NOTE This book includes exercises and walk-throughs with real, malicious viruses and rootkits. We intentionally did this to ensure that readers can immediately apply their newly learned skills. The malware samples are referenced in alphabetical order (Sample A, B, C, …), and you can find the corresponding SHA1 hashes in the Appendix. Because there may be legal concerns about distributing such samples with the book, we decided not to do so; however, you can download these samples by searching various malware repositories, such as www.malware.lu, or request them from the forums at http://kernelmode.info. Many of the samples are from famous hacking incidents that made worldwide news, so they should be interesting. Perhaps some enthusiastic readers will gather all the samples in a package and share them on BitTorrent.

If none of those options work for you, please feel free to email the authors. Make sure that you analyze these in a safe environment to prevent accidental self-infection.

In addition, to familiarize you with Metasm, we've prepared two exercise scripts: `symbolic-execution-lvl1.rb` and `symbolic-execution-lvl2.rb`. Answering the questions will lead you to a journey in Metasm internals. You can find the scripts at `www.wiley.com/go/practicalreverseengineering`.

It is important to realize that the exercises are a vital component of the book. The book was intentionally written in this way. If you simply read the book without doing the exercises, you will not understand or retain much. You should feel free to blog or write about your answers so that others can learn from them; you can post them on the Reverse Engineering reddit (`www.reddit.com/r/ReverseEngineering`) and get feedback from the community (and maybe the authors). If you successfully complete all of the exercises, pat yourself on the back and then send Bruce your resume.

The journey of becoming an effective reverse engineer is long and time consuming, requiring patience and endurance. You may fail many times along the way (by not understanding concepts or by failing to complete exercises in this book), but don't give up. Remember: Failing is part of success. With this guidance and the subsequent chapters, you should be well prepared for the learning journey.

We, the authors, would love to hear about your learning experience so that we can further adjust our material and improve the book. Your feedback will be invaluable to us and, potentially, future publications. You can send feedback and questions to Bruce Dang (`bruce.dang@gmail.com`), Alexandre Gazet (`agazet@quarkslab.com`), or Elias Bachaalany (`elias.bachaalany@gmail.com`).

x86 and x64

The x86 is little-endian architecture based on the Intel 8086 processor. For the purpose of our chapter, x86 is the 32-bit implementation of the Intel architecture (IA-32) as defined in the *Intel Software Development Manual*. Generally speaking, it can operate in two modes: *real* and *protected*. Real mode is the processor state when it is first powered on and only supports a 16-bit instruction set. Protected mode is the processor state supporting virtual memory, paging, and other features; it is the state in which modern operating systems execute. The 64-bit extension of the architecture is called x64 or x86-64. This chapter discusses the x86 architecture operating in protected mode.

x86 supports the concept of privilege separation through an abstraction called *ring level*. The processor supports four ring levels, numbered from 0 to 3. (Rings 1 and 2 are not commonly used so they are not discussed here.) Ring 0 is the highest privilege level and can modify all system settings. Ring 3 is the lowest privileged level and can only read/modify a subset of system settings. Hence, modern operating systems typically implement user/kernel privilege separation by having user-mode applications run in ring 3, and the kernel in ring 0. The ring level is encoded in the cs register and sometimes referred to as the *current privilege level* (CPL) in official documentation.

This chapter discusses the x86/IA-32 architecture as defined in the *Intel 64 and IA-32 Architectures Software Developer's Manual, Volumes 1–3* (www.intel .com/content/www/us/en/processors/architectures-software-developer-manuals.html).

Register Set and Data Types

When operating in protected mode, the x86 architecture has eight 32-bit general-purpose registers (GPRs): EAX, EBX, ECX, EDX, EDI, ESI, EBP, and ESP. Some of them can be further divided into 8- and 16-bit registers. The instruction pointer is stored in the EIP register. The register set is illustrated in Figure 1-1. Table 1-1 describes some of these GPRs and how they are used.

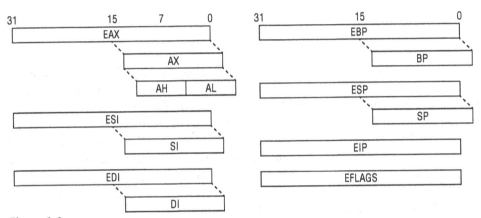

Figure 1-1

Table 1-1: Some GPRs and Their Usage

REGISTER	PURPOSE
ECX	Counter in loops
ESI	Source in string/memory operations
EDI	Destination in string/memory operations
EBP	Base frame pointer
ESP	Stack pointer

The common data types are as follows:

- **Bytes**—8 bits. Examples: AL, BL, CL
- **Word**—16 bits. Examples: AX, BX, CX
- **Double word**—32 bits. Examples: EAX, EBX, ECX
- **Quad word**—64 bits. While x86 does not have 64-bit GPRs, it can combine two registers, usually EDX:EAX, and treat them as 64-bit values in some scenarios. For example, the RDTSC instruction writes a 64-bit value to EDX:EAX.

The 32-bit EFLAGS register is used to store the status of arithmetic operations and other execution states (e.g., trap flag). For example, if the previous "add" operation resulted in a zero, the ZF flag will be set to 1. The flags in EFLAGS are primarily used to implement conditional branching.

In addition to the GPRs, EIP, and EFLAGS, there are also registers that control important low-level system mechanisms such as virtual memory, interrupts, and debugging. For example, CR0 controls whether paging is on or off, CR2 contains the linear address that caused a page fault, CR3 is the base address of a paging data structure, and CR4 controls the hardware virtualization settings. DR0–DR7 are used to set memory breakpoints. We will come back to these registers later in the "System Mechanism" section.

> **NOTE** Although there are eight debug registers, the system allows only four memory breakpoints (DR0–DR3). The remaining registers are used for status.

There are also model-specific registers (MSRs). As the name implies, these registers may vary between different processors by Intel and AMD. Each MSR is identified by name and a 32-bit number, and read/written to through the RDMSR/WRMSR instructions. They are accessible only to code running in ring 0 and typically used to store special counters and implement low-level functionality. For example, the SYSENTER instruction transfers execution to the address stored in the IA32_SYSENTER_EIP MSR (0x176), which is usually the operating system's system call handler. MSRs are discussed throughout the book as they come up.

Instruction Set

The x86 instruction set allows a high level of flexibility in terms of data movement between registers and memory. The movement can be classified into five general methods:

- Immediate to register
- Register to register
- Immediate to memory

- Register to memory and vice versa
- Memory to memory

The first four methods are supported by all modern architectures, but the last one is specific to x86. A classical RISC architecture like ARM can *only* read/write data from/to memory with load/store instructions (LDR and STR, respectively); for example, a simple operation like incrementing a value in memory requires three instructions:

1. Read the data from memory to a register (LDR).

2. Add one to the register (ADD).

3. Write the register to memory (STR).

On x86, such an operation would require only one instruction (either INC or ADD) because it can directly access memory. The MOVS instruction can read and write memory at the same time.

ARM

```
01: 1A 68     LDR    R2, [R3]
; read the value at address R3 and save it in R2
02: 52 1C     ADDS   R2, R2, #1
; add 1 to it
03: 1A 60         STR      R2, [R3]
; write updated value back to address R3
```

x86

```
01: FF 00         inc      dword ptr [eax]
; directly increment value at address EAX
```

Another important characteristic is that x86 uses variable-length instruction size: the instruction length can range from 1 to 15 bytes. On ARM, instructions are either 2 or 4 bytes in length.

Syntax

Depending on the assembler/disassembler, there are two syntax notations for x86 assembly code, Intel and AT&T:

Intel

```
mov ecx, AABBCCDDh
mov ecx, [eax]
mov ecx, eax
```

AT&T

```
movl $0xAABBCCDD, %ecx
movl (%eax), %ecx
movl %eax, %ecx
```

It is important to note that these are the same instructions but written differently. There are several differences between Intel and AT&T notation, but the most notable ones are as follows:

- AT&T prefixes the register with %, and immediates with $. Intel does not do this.

- AT&T adds a suffix to the instruction to indicate operation width. For example, MOVL (long), MOVB (byte), etc. Intel does not do this.

- AT&T puts the source operand before the destination. Intel reverses the order.

Disassemblers/assemblers and other reverse-engineering tools (IDA Pro, OllyDbg, MASM, etc.) on Windows typically use Intel notation, whereas those on UNIX frequently follow AT&T notation (GCC). In practice, Intel notation is the dominant form and is used throughout this book.

Data Movement

Instructions operate on values that come from registers or main memory. The most common instruction for moving data is MOV. The simplest usage is to move a register or immediate to register. For example:

```
01: BE 3F 00 0F 00    mov    esi, 0F003Fh ; set ESI = 0xF003
02: 8B F1             mov    esi, ecx     ; set ESI = ECX
```

The next common usage is to move data to/from memory. Similar to other assembly language conventions, x86 uses square brackets ([]) to indicate memory access. (The only exception to this is the LEA instruction, which uses [] but does not actually reference memory.) Memory access can be specified in several different ways, so we will begin with the simplest case:

Assembly

```
01: C7 00 01 00 00+   mov    dword ptr [eax], 1
; set the memory at address EAX to 1
02: 8B 08             mov    ecx, [eax]
; set ECX to the value at address EAX
03: 89 18             mov    [eax], ebx
; set the memory at address EAX to EBX
04: 89 46 34          mov    [esi+34h], eax
; set the memory address at (ESI+34) to EAX
05: 8B 46 34          mov    eax, [esi+34h]
; set EAX to the value at address (ESI+0x34)
06: 8B 14 01          mov    edx, [ecx+eax]
; set EDX to the value at address (ECX+EAX)
```

Pseudo C

```
01: *eax = 1;
02: ecx = *eax;
03: *eax = ebx;
04: *(esi+0x34) = eax;
05: eax = *(esi+0x34);
06: edx = *(ecx+eax);
```

These examples demonstrate memory access through a base register and offset, where offset can be a register or immediate. This form is commonly used to access structure members or data buffers at a location computed at runtime. For example, suppose that ecx points to a structure of type KDPC with the layout

```
kd> dt nt!_KDPC
   +0x000 Type             : UChar
   +0x001 Importance       : UChar
   +0x002 Number           : Uint2B
   +0x004 DpcListEntry     : _LIST_ENTRY
   +0x00c DeferredRoutine  : Ptr32     void
   +0x010 DeferredContext  : Ptr32 Void
   +0x014 SystemArgument1  : Ptr32 Void
   +0x018 SystemArgument2  : Ptr32 Void
   +0x01c DpcData          : Ptr32 Void
```

and used in the following context:

Assembly

```
01: 8B 45 0C        mov   eax, [ebp+0Ch]
02: 83 61 1C 00     and   dword ptr [ecx+1Ch], 0
03: 89 41 0C        mov   [ecx+0Ch], eax
04: 8B 45 10        mov   eax, [ebp+10h]
05: C7 01 13 01 00+ mov   dword ptr [ecx], 113h
06: 89 41 10        mov   [ecx+10h], eax
```

Pseudo C

```
KDPC *p = ...;
p->DpcData = NULL;
p->DeferredRoutine = ...;
*(int *)p = 0x113;
p->DeferredContext = ...;
```

Line 1 reads a value from memory and stores it in EAX. The DeferredRoutine field is set to this value in line 3. Line 2 clears the DpcData field by AND'ing it with 0. Line 4 reads another value from memory and stores it in EAX. The DeferredContext field is set to this value in line 6.

Line 5 writes the double-word value 0x113 to the base of the structure. Why does it write a double-word value at the base if the first field is only 1 byte in size? Wouldn't that implicitly set the Importance and Number fields as well? The answer is yes. Figure 1-2 shows the result of converting 0x113 to binary.

00000000 00000000 *00000001* 00010011		
00000000 00000000	*00000001*	00010011
Number	Importance	Type

Figure 1-2

The Type field is set to 0x13 (bold bits), Importance is set to 0x1 (italicized bits), and Number is set to 0x0 (the remaining bits). By writing one value, the code managed to initialize three fields with a single instruction! The code could have been written as follows:

```
01: 8B 45 0C        mov    eax, [ebp+0Ch]
02: 83 61 1C 00     and    dword ptr [ecx+1Ch], 0
03: 89 41 0C        mov    [ecx+0Ch], eax
04: 8B 45 10        mov    eax, [ebp+10h]
05: C6 01 13        mov    byte ptr [ecx],13h
06: C6 41 01 01     mov    byte ptr [ecx+1],1
07: 66 C7 41 02 00+ mov    word ptr [ecx+2],0
08: 89 41 10        mov    [ecx+10h], eax
```

The compiler decided to fold three instructions into one because it knew the constants ahead of time and wants to save space. The three-instruction version occupies 13 bytes (the extra byte in line 7 is not shown), whereas the one-instruction version occupies 6 bytes. Another interesting observation is that memory access can be done at three granularity levels: byte (line 5–6), word (line 6), and double-word (line 1–4, 8). The default granularity is 4 bytes, which can be changed to 1 or 2 bytes with an override prefix. In the example, the override prefix byte is 66 (italicized). Other prefixes are discussed as they come up.

The next memory access form is commonly used to access array-type objects. Generally, the format is as follows: [Base + Index * scale]. This is best understood through examples:

```
01: 8B 34 B5 40 05+ mov    esi, _KdLogBuffer[esi*4]
; always written as  mov    esi, [_KdLogBuffer + esi * 4]
; _KdLogBuffer is the base address of a global array and
; ESI is the index; we know that each element in the array
; is 4 bytes in length (hence the scaling factor)
```

```
02: 89 04 F7        mov    [edi+esi*8], eax
; here is EDI is the array base address; ESI is the array
; index; element size is 8.
```

In practice, this is observed in code looping over an array. For example:

```
01:                 loop_start:
02: 8B 47 04        mov    eax, [edi+4]
03: 8B 04 98        mov    eax, [eax+ebx*4]
04: 85 C0           test   eax, eax
...
05: 74 14           jz     short loc_7F627F
06:                 loc_7F627F:
07: 43              inc    ebx
08: 3B 1F           cmp    ebx, [edi]
09: 7C DD           jl     short loop_start
```

Line 2 reads a double-word from offset +4 from EDI and then uses it as the base address into an array in line 3; hence, you know that EDI is likely a structure that has an array at +4. Line 7 increments the index. Line 8 compares the index against a value at offset +0 in the same structure. Given this info, this small loop can be decompiled as follows:

```
typedef struct _FOO
{
    DWORD size;         // +0x00
    DWORD array[...];   // +0x04
} FOO, *PFOO;

PFOO bar = ...;
for (i = ...; i < bar->size; i++) {
    if (bar->array[i] != 0) {
        ...
    }
}
```

The MOVSB/MOVSW/MOVSD instructions move data with 1-, 2-, or 4-byte granularity between two memory addresses. They implicitly use EDI/ESI as the destination/source address, respectively. In addition, they also automatically update the source/destination address depending on the direction flag (DF) flag in EFLAGS. If DF is 1, the addresses are decremented; otherwise, they are incremented. These instructions are typically used to implement string or memory copy functions when the length is known at compile time. In some cases, they are accompanied by the REP prefix, which repeats an instruction up to ECX times. Consider the following example:

Assembly

```
01: BE 28 B5 41 00    mov    esi, offset _RamdiskBootDiskGuid
; ESI = pointer to RamdiskBootDiskGuid
02: 8D BD 40 FF FF+   lea    edi, [ebp-0C0h]
; EDI is an address somewhere on the stack
03: A5                movsd
; copies 4 bytes from ESI to EDI ; increment each by 4
04: A5                movsd
; same as above
05: A5                movsd
; save as above
06: A5                movsd
; same as above
```

Pseudo C

```
/* a GUID is 16-byte structure */
GUID RamDiskBootDiskGuid = ...; // global
...
GUID foo;
memcpy(&foo, &RamdiskBootDiskGuid, sizeof(GUID));
```

Line 2 deserves some special attention. Although the LEA instruction uses
[], it actually does not read from a memory address; it simply evaluates the
expression in square brackets and puts the result in the destination register.
For example, if EBP were 0x1000, then EDI would be 0xF40 (=0x1000 – 0xC0)
after executing line 2. The point is that LEA does not access memory, despite
the misleading syntax.

The following example, from nt!KiInitSystem, uses the REP prefix:

```
01: 6A 08            push   8    ; push 8 on the stack (will explain stacks
                                 ; later)
02: ...
03: 59               pop    ecx  ; pop the stack. Basically sets ECX to 8.
04: ...
05: BE 00 44 61 00   mov    esi, offset _KeServiceDescriptorTable
06: BF C0 43 61 00   mov    edi, offset _KeServiceDescriptorTableShadow
07: F3 A5            rep movsd   ; copy 32 bytes (movsd repeated 8 times)
; from this we can deduce that whatever these two objects are, they are
;   likely to be 32 bytes in size.
```

The rough C equivalent of this would be as follows:

```
memcpy(&KeServiceDescriptorTableShadow, &KeServiceDescriptorTable, 32);
```

The final example, nt!MmInitializeProcessAddressSpace, uses a combination of these instructions because the copy size is not a multiple of 4:

```
01: 8D B0 70 01 00+  lea   esi, [eax+170h]
; EAX is likely the base address of a structure. Remember what we said
; about LEA ...
02: 8D BB 70 01 00+  lea   edi, [ebx+170h]
; EBX is likely to be base address of another structure of the same type
03: A5                     movsd
04: A5                     movsd
05: A5                     movsd
06: 66 A5                  movsw
07: A4                     movsb
```

After lines 1–2, you know that EAX and EBX are likely to be of the same type because they are being used as source/destination and the offset is identical. This code snippet simply copies 15 bytes from one structure field to another. Note that the code could also have been written using the MOVSB instruction with a REP prefix and ECX set to 15; however, that would be inefficient because it results in 15 reads instead of only five.

Another class of data movement instructions with implicit source and destination includes the SCAS and STOS instructions. Similar to MOVS, these instructions can operate at 1-, 2-, or 4-byte granularity. SCAS implicitly compares AL/AX/EAX with data starting at the memory address EDI; EDI is automatically incremented/decremented depending on the DF bit in EFLAGS. Given its semantic, SCAS is commonly used along with the REP prefix to find a byte, word, or double-word in a buffer. For example, the C strlen() function can be implemented as follows:

```
01: 30 C0              xor    al, al
; set AL to 0 (NUL byte).  You will frequently observe the XOR reg, reg
;  pattern in code.
02: 89 FB              mov    ebx, edi
; save the original pointer to the string
03: F2 AE              repne  scasb
; repeatedly scan forward one byte at a time as long as AL does not match the
; byte at EDI when this instruction ends, it means we reached the NUL byte in
; the string buffer
04: 29 DF              sub    edi, ebx
; edi is now the NUL byte location. Subtract that from the original pointer
; to the length.
```

STOS is the same as SCAS except that it writes the value AL/AX/EAX to EDI. It is commonly used to initialize a buffer to a constant value (such as memset()). Here is an example:

```
01: 33 C0              xor    eax, eax
; set EAX to 0
02: 6A 09              push   9
; push 9 on the stack
03: 59                 pop    ecx
; pop it back in ECX. Now ECX = 9.
```

```
04: 8B FE              mov     edi, esi
; set the destination address
05: F3 AB              rep stosd
; write 36 bytes of zero to the destination buffer (STOSD repeated 9 times)
; this is equivalent lent to memset(edi, 0, 36)
```

LODS is another instruction from the same family. It reads a 1-, 2-, or 4-byte value from ESI and stores it in AL, AX, or EAX.

Exercise

1. This function uses a combination SCAS and STOS to do its work. First, explain what is the type of the [EBP+8] and [EBP+C] in line 1 and 8, respectively. Next, explain what this snippet does.

```
01: 8B 7D 08           mov     edi, [ebp+8]
02: 8B D7              mov     edx, edi
03: 33 C0              xor     eax, eax
04: 83 C9 FF           or      ecx, 0FFFFFFFFh
05: F2 AE              repne scasb
06: 83 C1 02           add     ecx, 2
07: F7 D9              neg     ecx
08: 8A 45 0C           mov     al, [ebp+0Ch]
09: 8B FA              mov     edi, edx
10: F3 AA              rep stosb
11: 8B C2              mov     eax, edx
```

Arithmetic Operations

Fundamental arithmetic operations such as addition, subtraction, multiplication, and division are natively supported by the instruction set. Bit-level operations such as AND, OR, XOR, NOT, and left and right shift also have native corresponding instructions. With the exception of multiplication and division, the remaining instructions are straightforward in terms of usage. These operations are explained with the following examples:

```
01: 83 C4 14           add     esp, 14h        ; esp = esp + 0x14
02: 2B C8              sub     ecx, eax        ; ecx = ecx - eax
03: 83 EC 0C           sub     esp, 0Ch        ; esp = esp - 0xC
04: 41                 inc     ecx             ; ecx = ecx + 1
05: 4F                 dec     edi             ; edi = edi - 1
06: 83 C8 FF           or      eax, 0FFFFFFFFh ; eax = eax | 0xFFFFFFFF
07: 83 E1 07           and     ecx, 7          ; ecx = ecx & 7
08: 33 C0              xor     eax, eax        ; eax = eax ^ eax
09: F7 D7              not     edi             ; edi = ~edi
10: C0 E1 04           shl     cl, 4           ; cl = cl << 4
11: D1 E9              shr     ecx, 1          ; ecx = ecx >> 1
12: C0 C0 03           rol     al, 3           ; rotate AL left 3 positions
13: D0 C8              ror     al, 1           ; rotate AL right 1 position
```

The left and right shift instructions (lines 11–12) merit some explanation, as they are frequently observed in real-life code. These instructions are typically used to optimize multiplication and division operations where the multiplicand and divisor are a power of two. This type of optimization is sometimes known as *strength reduction* because it replaces a computationally expensive operation with a cheaper one. For example, integer division is relatively a slow operation, but when the divisor is a power of two, it can be reduced to shifting bits to the right; 100/2 is the same as 100>>1. Similarly, multiplication by a power of two can be reduced to shifting bits to the left; 100*2 is the same as 100<<1.

Unsigned and signed multiplication is done through the MUL and IMUL instructions, respectively. The MUL instruction has the following general form: MUL reg/memory. That is, it can only operate on register or memory values. The register is multiplied with AL, AX, or EAX and the result is stored in AX, DX:AX, or EDX:EAX, depending on the operand width. For example:

```
01: F7 E1          mul    ecx                   ; EDX:EAX = EAX * ECX
02: F7 66 04       mul    dword ptr [esi+4]     ; EDX:EAX = EAX * dword_at(ESI+4)
03: F6 E1          mul    cl                    ; AX = AL * CL
04: 66 F7 E2       mul    dx                    ; DX:AX = AX * DX
```

Consider a few other concrete examples:

```
01: B8 03 00 00 00    mov    eax,3              ; set EAX=3
02: B9 22 22 22 22    mov    ecx,22222222h      ; set ECX=0x22222222
03: F7 E1             mul    ecx                ; EDX:EAX = 3 * 0x22222222 =
                                                ; 0x66666666
                                                ; hence, EDX=0, EAX=0x66666666

04: B8 03 00 00 00    mov    eax,3              ; set EAX=3
05: B9 00 00 00 80    mov    ecx,80000000h      ; set ECX=0x80000000
06: F7 E1             mul    ecx                ; EDX:EAX = 3 * 0x80000000 =
                                                ; 0x180000000
                                                ; hence, EDX=1, EAX=0x80000000
```

The reason why the result is stored in EDX:EAX for 32-bit multiplication is because the result potentially may not fit in one 32-bit register (as demonstrated in lines 4–6).

IMUL has three forms:

- **IMUL reg/mem** — Same as MUL
- **IMUL reg1, reg2/mem** — reg1 = reg1 * reg2/mem
- **IMUL reg1, reg2/mem, imm** — reg1 = reg2 * imm

Some disassemblers shorten the parameters. For example:

```
01: F7 E9               imul  ecx         ; EDX:EAX = EAX * ECX
02: 69 F6 A0 01 00+     imul  esi, 1A0h   ; ESI = ESI * 0x1A0
```

```
03: 0F AF CE          imul  ecx, esi   ; ECX = ECX * ESI
```

Unsigned and signed division is done through the DIV and IDIV instructions, respectively. They take only one parameter (divisor) and have the following form: DIV/IDIV reg/mem. Depending on the divisor's size, DIV will use either AX, DX:AX, or EDX:EAX as the dividend, and the resulting quotient/remainder pair are stored in AL/AH, AX/DX, or EAX/EDX. For example:

```
01: F7 F1             div   ecx        ; EDX:EAX / ECX, quotient in EAX,
02: F6 F1             div   cl         ; AX / CL, quotient in AL, remainder in AH
03: F7 76 24          div   dword ptr [esi+24h] ; see line 1

04: B1 02             mov   cl,2       ; set CL = 2
05: B8 0A 00 00 00    mov   eax,0Ah    ; set EAX = 0xA
06: F6 F1             div   cl         ; AX/CL = A/2 = 5 in AL (quotient),
                                       ; AH = 0 (remainder)
07: B1 02             mov   cl,2       ; set CL = 2
08: B8 09 00 00 00    mov   eax,09h    ; set EAX = 0x9
09: F6 F1             div   cl         ; AX/CL = 9/2 = 4 in AL (quotient),
                                       ; AH = 1 (remainder)
```

Stack Operations and Function Invocation

The stack is a fundamental data structure in programming languages and operating systems. For example, local variables in C are stored on the functions' stack space. When the operating system transitions from ring 3 to ring 0, it saves state information on the stack. Conceptually, a stack is a last-in first-out data structure supporting two operations: push and pop. Push means to put something on top of the stack; pop means to remove an item from the top. Concretely speaking, on x86, a stack is a contiguous memory region pointed to by ESP and it grows downwards. Push/pop operations are done through the PUSH/POP instructions and they implicitly modify ESP. The PUSH instruction decrements ESP and then writes data at the location pointed to by ESP; POP reads the data and increments ESP. The default auto-increment/decrement value is 4, but it can be changed to 1 or 2 with a prefix override. In practice, the value is almost always 4 because the OS requires the stack to be double-word aligned.

Suppose that ESP initially points to 0xb20000 and you have the following code:

```
; initial ESP = 0xb20000
01: B8 AA AA AA AA    mov   eax,0AAAAAAAAh
02: BB BB BB BB BB    mov   ebx,0BBBBBBBBh
03: B9 CC CC CC CC    mov   ecx,0CCCCCCCCh
04: BA DD DD DD DD    mov   edx,0DDDDDDDDh
05: 50                push  eax
; address 0xb1fffc will contain the value 0xAAAAAAAA and ESP
; will be 0xb1fffc (=0xb20000-4)
```

```
06: 53                  push    ebx
; address 0xb1fff8 will contain the value 0xBBBBBBBB and ESP
; will be 0xb1fff8 (=0xb1fffc-4)
07: 5E                  pop     esi
; ESI will contain the value 0xBBBBBBBB and ESP will be 0xb1fffc
; (=0xb1fff8+4)
08: 5F                  pop     edi
; EDI will contain the value 0xAAAAAAAA and ESP will be 0xb20000
; (=0xb1fffc+4)
```

Figure 1-3 illustrates the stack layout.

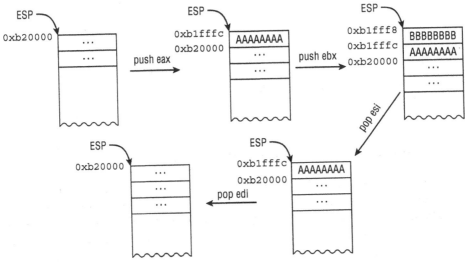

Figure 1-3

ESP can also be directly modified by other instructions, such as ADD and SUB.

While high-level programming languages have the concept of functions that can be called and returned from, the processor does not provide such abstraction. At the lowest level, the processor operates only on concrete objects, such as registers or data coming from memory. How are functions translated at the machine level? They are implemented through the stack data structure! Consider the following function:

C

```c
int
__cdecl addme(short a, short b)
{
    return a+b;
}
```

Assembly

```
01: 004113A0 55            push    ebp
```

```
02: 004113A1 8B EC          mov     ebp, esp
03: ...
04: 004113BE 0F BF 45 08    movsx   eax, word ptr [ebp+8]
05: 004113C2 0F BF 4D 0C    movsx   ecx, word ptr [ebp+0Ch]
06: 004113C6 03 C1          add     eax, ecx
07: ...
08: 004113CB 8B E5          mov     esp, ebp
09: 004113CD 5D             pop     ebp
10: 004113CE C3             retn
```

The function is invoked with the following code:

C

```
sum = addme(x, y);
```

Assembly

```
01: 004129F3 50                push   eax
02: ...
03: 004129F8 51                push   ecx
04: 004129F9 E8 F1 E7 FF FF    call   addme
05: 004129FE 83 C4 08          add    esp, 8
```

Before going into the details, first consider the CALL/RET instructions and calling conventions. The CALL instruction performs two operations:

1. It pushes the return address (address immediately after the CALL instruction) on the stack.

2. It changes EIP to the call destination. This effectively transfers control to the call target and begins execution there.

RET simply pops the address stored on the top of the stack into EIP and transfers control to it (literally like a "POP EIP" but such instruction sequence does not exist on x86). For example, if you want to begin execution at 0x12345678, you can just do the following:

```
01: 68 78 56 34 12    push   0x12345678
02: C3                ret
```

A *calling convention* is a set of rules dictating how function calls work at the machine level. It is defined by the Application Binary Interface (ABI) for a particular system. For example, should the parameters be passed through the stack, in registers, or both? Should the parameters be passed in from left-to-right or right-to-left? Should the return value be stored on the stack, in registers, or both? There are many calling conventions, but the popular ones are CDECL, STDCALL, THISCALL, and FASTCALL. (The compiler can also generate its own custom calling convention, but those will not be discussed here.) Table 1-2 summarizes their semantic.

Table 1-2: Calling Conventions

	CDECL	STDCALL	FASTCALL
Parameters	Pushed on the stack from right-to-left. Caller must clean up the stack after the call.	Same as CDECL except that the callee must clean the stack.	First two parameters are passed in ECX and EDX. The rest are on the stack.
Return value	Stored in EAX.	Stored in EAX.	Stored in EAX.
Non-volatile registers	EBP, ESP, EBX, ESI, EDI.	EBP, ESP, EBX, ESI, EDI.	EBP, ESP, EBX, ESI, EDI.

We now return to the code snippet to discuss how the function addme is invoked. In line 1 and 3, the two parameters are pushed on the stack; ECX and EAX are the first and second parameter, respectively. Line 4 invokes the addme function with the CALL instruction. This immediately pushes the return address, 0x4129FE, on the stack and begins execution at 0x4113A0. Figure 1-4 illustrates the stack layout after line 4 is executed.

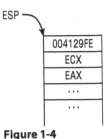

Figure 1-4

After line 4 executes, we are now in the addme function body. Line 1 pushes EBP on the stack. Line 2 sets EBP to the current stack pointer. This two-instruction sequence is typically known as the *function prologue* because it establishes a new function frame. Line 4 reads the value at address EBP+8, which is the first parameter on the stack; line 5 reads the second parameter. Note that the parameters are accessed using EBP as the base register. When used in this context, EBP is known as the *base frame pointer* (see line 2) because it points to the stack frame for the current function, and parameters/locals can be accessed relative to it. The compiler can also be instructed to generate code that does not use EBP as the base frame pointer through an optimization called *frame pointer omission*. With such optimization, access to local variables and parameters is done relative to ESP, and EBP can be used as a general register like EAX, EBX, ECX, and so on. Line 6 adds the numbers and saves the result in EAX. Line 8 sets the stack pointer to the base frame pointer. Line 9 pops the saved EBP from line 1 into

EBP. This two-instruction sequence is commonly referred to as the *function epilogue* because it is at the end of the function and restores the previous function frame. At this point, the top of the stack contains the return address saved by the CALL instruction at 0x4129F9. Line 10 performs a RET, which pops the stack and resumes execution at 0x4129FE. Line 5 in the snippet shrinks the stack by 8 because the caller must clean up the stack per CDECL's calling convention.

If the function addme had local variables, the code would need to grow the stack by subtracting ESP after line 2. All local variables would then be accessible through a negative offset from EBP.

Exercises

1. Given what you learned about CALL and RET, explain how you would read the value of EIP? Why can't you just do MOV EAX, EIP?

2. Come up with at least two code sequences to set EIP to 0xAABBCCDD.

3. In the example function, addme, what would happen if the stack pointer were not properly restored before executing RET?

4. In all of the calling conventions explained, the return value is stored in a 32-bit register (EAX). What happens when the return value does not fit in a 32-bit register? Write a program to experiment and evaluate your answer. Does the mechanism change from compiler to compiler?

Control Flow

This section describes how the system implements conditional execution for higher-level constructs like if/else, switch/case, and while/for. All of these are implemented through the CMP, TEST, JMP, and Jcc instructions and EFLAGS register. The following list summarizes the common flags in EFLAGS:

- **ZF/Zero flag**—Set if the result of the previous arithmetic operation is zero.
- **SF/Sign flag**—Set to the most significant bit of the result.
- **CF/Carry flag**—Set when the result requires a carry. It applies to unsigned numbers.
- **OF/Overflow flag**—Set if the result overflows the max size. It applies to signed numbers.

Arithmetic instructions update these flags based on the result. For example, the instruction SUB EAX, EAX would cause ZF to be set. The Jcc instructions, where "cc" is a conditional code, changes control flow depending on these flags. There can be up to 16 conditional codes, but the most common ones are described in Table 1-3.

Table 1-3: Common Conditional Codes

CONDITIONAL CODE	ENGLISH DESCRIPTION	MACHINE DESCRIPTION
B/NAE	Below/Neither Above nor Equal. Used for unsigned operations.	CF=1
NB/AE	Not Below/Above or Equal. Used for unsigned operations.	CF=0
E/Z	Equal/Zero	ZF=1
NE/NZ	Not Equal/Not Zero	ZF=0
L	Less than/Neither Greater nor Equal. Used for signed operations.	$(SF \wedge OF) = 1$
GE/NL	Greater or Equal/Not Less than. Used for signed operations.	$(SF \wedge OF) = 0$
G/NLE	Greater/Not Less nor Equal. Used for signed operations.	$((SF \wedge OF) \mid ZF) = 0$

Because assembly language does not have a defined type system, one of the few ways to recognize signed/unsigned types is through these conditional codes.

The CMP instruction compares two operands and sets the appropriate conditional code in EFLAGS; it compares two numbers by subtracting one from another without updating the result. The TEST instruction does the same thing except it performs a logical AND between the two operands.

If-Else

If-else constructs are quite simple to recognize because they involve a compare/test followed by a Jcc. For example:

Assembly

```
01:   mov   esi, [ebp+8]
02:   mov   edx, [esi]
03:   test  edx, edx
04:   jz    short loc_4E31F9
05:   mov   ecx, offset _FsRtlFastMutexLookasideList
06:   call  _ExFreeToNPagedLookasideList@8
07:   and   dword ptr [esi], 0
08:   lea   eax, [esi+4]
09:   push  eax
10:   call  _FsRtlUninitializeBaseMcb@4
11: loc_4E31F9:
```

```
12:    pop    esi
13:    pop    ebp
14:    retn   4
15: _FsRtlUninitializeLargeMcb@4 endp
```

Pseudo C

```
if (*esi == 0) {
  return;
}
ExFreeToNPagedLookasideList(...);
*esi = 0;
...
return;

OR

if (*esi != 0) {
  ...
  ExFreeToNPagedLookasideList(...);
  *esi = 0;
  ...
}
return;
```

Line 2 reads a value at location ESI and stores it in EDX. Line 3 ANDs EDX with itself and sets the appropriate flags in EFLAGS. Note that this pattern is commonly used to determine whether a register is zero. Line 4 jumps to loc_4E31F9 (line 12) if ZF=1. If ZF=0, then it executes line 5 and continues until the function returns.

Note that there are two slightly different but logically equivalent C translations for this snippet.

Switch-Case

A switch-case block is a sequence of if/else statements. For example:

Switch-Case

```
switch(ch) {
    case 'c':
        handle_C();
        break;
    case 'h':
        handle_H();
        break;
    default:
        break;
}
domore();
...
```

If-Else

```
if (ch == 'c') {
    handle_C();
} else
if (ch == 'h') {
    handle_H();
}
domore();
...
```

Hence, the machine code translation will be a series if/else. The following simple example illustrates the idea:

Assembly

```
01:    push    ebp
02:    mov     ebp, esp
03:    mov     eax, [ebp+8]
04:    sub     eax, 41h
05:    jz      short loc_caseA
06:    dec     eax
07:    jz      short loc_caseB
08:    dec     eax
09:    jz      short loc_caseC
10:    mov     al, 5Ah
11:    movzx   eax, al
12:    pop     ebp
13:    retn
14: loc_caseC:
15:    mov     al, 43h
16:    movzx   eax, al
17:    pop     ebp
18:    retn
19: loc_caseB:
20:    mov     al, 42h
21:    movzx   eax, al
22:    pop     ebp
23:    retn
24: loc_caseA:
25:    mov     al, 41h
26:    movzx   eax, al
27:    pop     ebp
28:    retn
```

C

```
unsigned char switchme(int a)
{
    unsigned char res;
```

```
switch(a) {
case 0x41:
    res = 'A';
    break;
case 0x42:
    res = 'B';
    break;
case 0x43:
    res = 'C';
    break;
default:
    res = 'Z';
    break;
}
return res;
}
```

Real-life switch-case statements can be more complex, and compilers commonly build a *jump table* to reduce the number of comparisons and conditional jumps. The jump table is essentially an array of addresses, each pointing to the handler for a specific case. This pattern can be observed in Sample J in sub_10001110:

Assembly

```
01:   cmp      edi, 5
02:   ja       short loc_10001141
03:   jmp      ds:off_100011A4[edi*4]
04: loc_10001125:
05:   mov      esi, 40h
06:   jmp      short loc_10001145
07: loc_1000112C:
08:   mov      esi, 20h
09:   jmp      short loc_10001145
10: loc_10001133:
11:   mov      esi, 38h
12:   jmp      short loc_10001145
13: loc_1000113A:
14:   mov      esi, 30h
15:   jmp      short loc_10001145
16: loc_10001141:
17:   mov      esi, [esp+0Ch]
18: ...
19: off_100011A4 dd offset loc_10001125
20:    dd offset loc_10001125
21:    dd offset loc_1000113A
22:    dd offset loc_1000112C
23:    dd offset loc_10001133
24:    dd offset loc_1000113A
```

Pseudo C

```
switch(edi) {
  case 0:
  case 1:
    // goto loc_10001125;
    esi = 0x40;
    break;
  case 2:
  case 5:
    // goto loc_1000113A;
    esi = 0x30;
    break;
  case 3:
    // goto loc_1000112C;
    esi = 0x20;
    break;
  case 4:
    // goto loc_10001133;
    esi = 0x38;
    break;
  default:
    // goto loc_10001141;
    esi = *(esp+0xC)
    break;
}
...
```

Here, the compiler knows that there are only five cases and the case value is consecutive; hence, it can construct the jump table and index into it directly (line 3). Without the jump table, there would be 10 additional instructions to test each case and branch to the handler. (There are other forms of switch/case optimizations, but we will not cover them here.)

Loops

At the machine level, loops are implemented using a combination of Jcc and JMP instructions. In other words, they are implemented using if/else and goto constructs. The best way to understand this is to rewrite a loop using only if/else and goto. Consider the following example:

Using for

```
for (int i=0; i<10; i++) {
    printf("%d\n", i);
}
printf("done!\n");
```

Using if/else and goto

```
int i = 0;
loop_start:
    if (i < 10) {
        printf("%d\n", i);
        i++;
        goto loop_start;
    }
printf("done!n");
```

When compiled, both versions are identical at the machine-code level:

```
01: 00401002    mov     edi, ds:__imp__printf
02: 00401008    xor     esi, esi
03: 0040100A    lea     ebx, [ebx+0]
04: 00401010 loc_401010:
05: 00401010    push    esi
06: 00401011    push    offset Format                 ; "%d\n"
07: 00401016    call    edi ; __imp__printf
08: 00401018    inc     esi
09: 00401019    add     esp, 8
10: 0040101C    cmp     esi, 0Ah
11: 0040101F    jl      short loc_401010
12: 00401021    push    offset aDone                  ; "done!\n"
13: 00401026    call    edi ; __imp__printf
14: 00401028    add     esp, 4
```

Line 1 sets EDI to the printf function. Line 2 sets ESI to 0. Line 4 begins the loop; however, note that it does not begin with a comparison. There is no comparison here because the compiler knows that the counter was initialized to 0 (see line 2) and is obviously going to be less than 10 so it skips the check. Lines 5–7 call the printf function with the right parameters (format specifier and our number). Line 8 increments the number. Line 9 cleans up the stack because printf uses the CDECL calling convention. Line 10 checks to see if the counter is less than 0xA. If it is, it jumps back to loc_401010. If the counter is not less than 0xA, it continues execution at line 12 and finishes with a printf.

One important observation to make is that the disassembly allowed us to infer that the counter is a signed integer. Line 11 uses the "less than" conditional code (JL), so we immediately know that the comparison was done on signed integers. Remember: If "above/below," it is unsigned; if "less than/greater than," it is signed. Sample L has a small function, sub_1000AE3B, with the following interesting loop:

Assembly

```
01: sub_1000AE3B proc near
02:    push    edi
```

```
03:    push    esi
04:    call    ds:lstrlenA
05:    mov     edi, eax
06:    xor     ecx, ecx
07:    xor     edx, edx
08:    test    edi, edi
09:    jle     short loc_1000AE5B
10: loc_1000AE4D:
11:    mov     al, [edx+esi]
12:    mov     [ecx+esi], al
13:    add     edx, 3
14:    inc     ecx
15:    cmp     edx, edi
16:    jl      short loc_1000AE4D
17: loc_1000AE5B:
18:    mov     byte ptr [ecx+esi], 0
19:    mov     eax, esi
20:    pop     edi
21:    retn
22: sub_1000AE3B endp
```

C

```c
char *sub_1000AE3B (char *str)
{
  int len, i=0, j=0;
  len = lstrlenA(str);
  if (len <= 0) {
    str[j] = 0;
    return str;
  }
  while (j < len) {
    str[i] = str[j];
    j = j+3;
    i = i+1;
  }
  str[i] = 0;
  return str;
}
```

The sub_1000AE3B function has one parameter passed using a custom calling convention (ESI holds the parameter). Line 2 saves EDI. Line 3 calls lstrlenA with the parameter; hence, you immediately know that ESI is of type char *. Line 5 saves the return value (string length) in EDI. Lines 6–7 clear ECX and EDX. Lines 8–9 check to see if the string length is less than or equal to zero. If it is, control is transferred to line 18, which sets the value at ECX+ESI to 0. If it is not, then execution is continued at line 11, which is the start of a loop. First, it reads the character at ESI+EDX (line 11), and then it stores it at ESI+ECX (line 12).

Next, it increments the EDX and ECX by three and one, respectively. Lines 15–16 check to see if EDX is less than the string length; if so, execution goes back to the loop start. If not, execution is continued at line 18.

It may seem convoluted at first, but this function takes an obfuscated string whose deobfuscated value is every third character. For example, the string SX] OTYFKPTY^W\\aAFKRW\\E is actually SOFTWARE. The purpose of this function is to prevent naïve string scanners and evade detection. As an exercise, you should decompile this function so that it looks more "natural" (as opposed to our literal translation).

Outside of the normal Jcc constructs, certain loops can be implemented using the LOOP instruction. The LOOP instruction executes a block of code up to ECX time. For example:

Assembly

```
01: 8B CA          mov     ecx, edx
02:             loc_CFB8F:
03: AD              lodsd
04: F7 D0           not     eax
05: AB              stosd
06: E2 FA           loop    loc_CFB8F
```

Rough C

```
while (ecx != 0) {
    eax = *esi;
    esi++;
    *edi = ~eax;
    edi++;
    ecx--;
}
```

Line 1 reads the counter from EDX. Line 3 is the loop start; it reads in a double-word at the memory address ESI and saves that in EAX; it also increments EDI by 4. Line 4 performs the NOT operator on the value just read. Line 5 writes the modified value to the memory address EDI and increments ESI by 4. Line 6 checks to see if ECX is 0; if not, execution is continued at the loop start.

System Mechanism

The previous sections explain mechanisms and instructions that are available to code running at all privilege levels. To get a better appreciation of the architecture, this section discusses two fundamental system-level mechanisms: *virtual address translation* and *exception/interrupt handling*. You may skip this section on a first read.

Address Translation

The physical memory on a computer system is divided into 4KB units called *pages*. (A page can be more than 4KB, but we will not discuss the other sizes here.) Memory addresses are divided into two categories: virtual and physical. Virtual addresses are those used by instructions executed in the processor when paging is enabled. For example:

```
01: A1 78 56 34 12  mov   eax, [0x12345678]; read memory at the virtual
                                           ; address 0x12345678
01: 89 08          mov   [eax], ecx      ; write ECX at the virtual
                                           ; address EAX
```

Physical addresses are the actual memory locations used by the processor when accessing memory. The processor's memory management unit (MMU) transparently translates every virtual address into a physical address before accessing it. While a virtual address may seem like just another number to the user, there is a structure to it when viewed by the MMU. On x86 systems with physical address extension (PAE) support, a virtual memory address can be divided into indices into three tables and offset: page directory pointer table (PDPT), page directory (PD), page table (PT), and page table entry (PTE). A PDPT is an array of four 8-byte elements, each pointing to a PD. A PD is an array of 512 8-byte elements, each pointing to a PT. A PT is an array of 512 8-byte elements each containing a PTE. For example, the virtual address 0xBF80EE6B can be understood as shown in Figure 1-5.

0xBF80EE6B			
10111111 10000000 11101110 01101011			
10 (0x2)	111111 100 (0x1FC)	00000 1110 (0xE)	1110 01101011 (0xE6B)
2 bits	9 bits	9 bits	12 bits
Index into PDPT	Index into PD	Index into PT	Page offset

Figure 1-5

The 8-byte elements in these tables contain data about the tables, memory permission, and other memory characteristics. For example, there are bits that determine whether the page is read-only or readable/writable, executable or non-executable, accessible by user or not, and so on.

The address translation process revolves around these three tables and the CR3 register. CR3 holds the physical base address of the PDPT. The rest of this section walks through the translation of the virtual address 0xBF80EE6B on a real system (refer to Figure 1-5):

```
kd> r @cr3          ; CR3 is the physical address for the base of a PDPT
cr3=085c01e0
kd> !dq @cr3+2*8 L1  ; read the PDPT entry at index 2
# 85c01f0 00000000`0d66e001
```

Per the documentation, the bottom 12 bits of a PDPT entry are flags/reserved bits, and the remaining ones are used as the physical address of the PD base. Bit 63 is the NX flag in PAE, so you will also need to clear that as well. In this particular example, we did not clear it because it is already 0. (We are looking at code pages that are executable.)

```
; 0x00000000`0d66e001 = 00001101 01100110 11100000 00000001
; after clearing the bottom 12 bits, we have
; 0x0d66e000          = 00001101 01100110 11100000 00000000
; This tells us that the PD base is at physical address 0x0d66e000
kd> !dq 0d66e000+0x1fc*8 L1    ; read the PD entry at index 0x1FC
# d66efe0 00000000`0964b063
```

Again, per the documentation, the bottom 12 bits of a PD entry are used for flags/reserved bits, and the remaining ones are used as the base for the PT:

```
; 0x0964b063 = 00001001 01100100 10110000 01100011
; after clearing the bottom 12 bits, we get
; 0x0964b000 = 00001001 01100100 10110000 00000000
; This tells us that the PT base is at 0x0964b000
kd> !dq 0964b000+e*8 L1        ; read the PT entry at index 0xE
# 964b070 00000000`06694021
```

Again, the bottom 12 bits can be cleared to get to the base of a page entry:

```
; 0x06694021 = 00000110 01101001 01000000 00100001
; after clearing bottom 12 bits, we get
; 0x06694000 = 00000110 01101001 01000000 00000000
; This tells us that the page entry base is at 0x06694000
kd> !db 06694000+e6b L8        ; read 8 bytes from the page entry at offset
0xE6B
# 6694e6b 8b ff 55 8b ec 83 ec 0c ..U.....[).t....    ; our data at that
                                                      ; physical page
kd> db bf80ee6b L8             ; read 8 bytes from the virtual address
bf80ee6b  8b ff 55 8b ec 83 ec ..U.....[).t....       ; same data!
```

After the entire process, it is determined that the virtual address 0xBF80EE6B translates to the physical address 0x6694E6B.

Modern operating systems implement process address space separation using this mechanism. Every process is associated with a different CR3, resulting in process-specific virtual address translation. It is the magic behind each process's illusion that it has its own address space. Hopefully you will have more appreciation for the processor the next time your program accesses memory!

Interrupts and Exceptions

This section briefly discusses interrupts and exceptions, as complete implementation details can be found in Chapter 3, "The Windows Kernel."

In contemporary computing systems, the processor is typically connected to peripheral devices through a data bus such as PCI Express, FireWire, or USB.

When a device requires the processor's attention, it causes an interrupt that forces the processor to pause whatever it is doing and handle the device's request. How does the processor know how to handle the request? At the highest level, one can think of an interrupt as being associated with a number that is then used to index into an array of function pointers. When the processor receives the interrupt, it executes the function at the index associated with the interrupt and resumes execution at wherever it was before the interrupt occurred. These are called *hardware interrupts* because they are generated by hardware devices. They are asynchronous by nature.

When the processor is executing an instruction, it may run into exceptions. For example, an instruction could generate a divide-by-zero error, reference an invalid address, or trigger a privilege level transition. For the purpose of this discussion, exceptions can be classified into two categories: *faults* and *traps*. A fault is a correctable exception. For example, when the processor executes an instruction that references a valid memory address but the data is not present in main memory (it was paged out), a page fault exception is generated. The processor handles this by saving the current execution state, calling the page fault handler to correct this exception (by paging in the data), and re-executing the same instruction (which should no longer cause a page fault). A trap is an exception caused by executing special kinds of instructions. For example, the instruction SYSENTER causes the processor to begin executing the generic system call handler; after the handler is done, execution is resumed at the instruction immediately after SYSENTER. Hence, the major difference between a fault and a trap is where execution resumes. Operating systems commonly implement system calls through the interrupt and exception mechanism.

Walk-Through

We finish the chapter with a walk-through of a function with fewer than 100 instructions. It is Sample J's `DllMain` routine. This exercise has two objectives. First, it applies almost every concept covered in the chapter (except for switch-case). Second, it teaches an important requirement in the practice of reverse engineering: reading technical manuals and online documentation. Here is the function:

```
01:     ; BOOL __stdcall DllMain(HINSTANCE hinstDLL, DWORD fdwReason,
        ; LPVOID lpvReserved)
02:                     _DllMain@12 proc near
03: 55                  push    ebp
04: 8B EC               mov     ebp, esp
05: 81 EC 30 01 00+     sub     esp, 130h
06: 57                  push    edi
07: 0F 01 4D F8         sidt    fword ptr [ebp-8]
08: 8B 45 FA            mov     eax, [ebp-6]
09: 3D 00 F4 03 80      cmp     eax, 8003F400h
```

```
10: 76 10                   jbe       short loc_10001C88 (line 18)
11: 3D 00 74 04 80          cmp       eax, 80047400h
12: 73 09                   jnb       short loc_10001C88 (line 18)
13: 33 C0                   xor       eax, eax
14: 5F                      pop       edi
15: 8B E5                   mov       esp, ebp
16: 5D                      pop       ebp
17: C2 0C 00                retn      0Ch
18:                         loc_10001C88:
19: 33 C0                   xor       eax, eax
20: B9 49 00 00 00          mov       ecx, 49h
21: 8D BD D4 FE FF+         lea       edi, [ebp-12Ch]
22: C7 85 D0 FE FF+         mov       dword ptr [ebp-130h], 0
23: 50                      push      eax
24: 6A 02                   push      2
25: F3 AB                   rep stosd
26: E8 2D 2F 00 00          call      CreateToolhelp32Snapshot
27: 8B F8                   mov       edi, eax
28: 83 FF FF                cmp       edi, 0FFFFFFFFh
29: 75 09                   jnz       short loc_10001CB9 (line 35)
30: 33 C0                   xor       eax, eax
31: 5F                      pop       edi
32: 8B E5                   mov       esp, ebp
33: 5D                      pop       ebp
34: C2 0C 00                retn      0Ch
35:                         loc_10001CB9:
36: 8D 85 D0 FE FF+         lea       eax, [ebp-130h]
37: 56                      push      esi
38: 50                      push      eax
39: 57                      push      edi
40: C7 85 D0 FE FF+         mov       dword ptr [ebp-130h], 128h
41: E8 FF 2E 00 00          call      Process32First
42: 85 C0                   test      eax, eax
43: 74 4F                   jz        short loc_10001D24 (line 70)
44: 8B 35 C0 50 00+         mov       esi, ds:_stricmp
45: 8D 8D F4 FE FF+         lea       ecx, [ebp-10Ch]
46: 68 50 7C 00 10          push      10007C50h
47: 51                      push      ecx
48: FF D6                   call      esi ; _stricmp
49: 83 C4 08                add       esp, 8
50: 85 C0                   test      eax, eax
51: 74 26                   jz        short loc_10001D16 (line 66)
52:                         loc_10001CF0:
53: 8D 95 D0 FE FF+         lea       edx, [ebp-130h]
54: 52                      push      edx
55: 57                      push      edi
56: E8 CD 2E 00 00          call      Process32Next
57: 85 C0                   test      eax, eax
58: 74 23                   jz        short loc_10001D24 (line 70)
59: 8D 85 F4 FE FF+         lea       eax, [ebp-10Ch]
60: 68 50 7C 00 10          push      10007C50h
61: 50                      push      eax
62: FF D6                   call      esi ; _stricmp
63: 83 C4 08                add       esp, 8
```

```
64: 85 C0              test    eax, eax
65: 75 DA              jnz     short loc_10001CF0 (line 52)
66:              loc_10001D16:
67: 8B 85 E8 FE FF+    mov     eax, [ebp-118h]
68: 8B 8D D8 FE FF+    mov     ecx, [ebp-128h]
69: EB 06              jmp     short loc_10001D2A (line 73)
70:              loc_10001D24:
71: 8B 45 0C           mov     eax, [ebp+0Ch]
72: 8B 4D 0C           mov     ecx, [ebp+0Ch]
73:              loc_10001D2A:
74: 3B C1              cmp     eax, ecx
75: 5E                 pop     esi
76: 75 09              jnz     short loc_10001D38 (line 82)
77: 33 C0              xor     eax, eax
78: 5F                 pop     edi
79: 8B E5              mov     esp, ebp
80: 5D                 pop     ebp
81: C2 0C 00           retn    0Ch
82:              loc_10001D38:
83: 8B 45 0C           mov     eax, [ebp+0Ch]
84: 48                 dec     eax
85: 75 15              jnz     short loc_10001D53 (line 93)
86: 6A 00              push    0
87: 6A 00              push    0
88: 6A 00              push    0
89: 68 D0 32 00 10     push    100032D0h
90: 6A 00              push    0
91: 6A 00              push    0
92: FF 15 20 50 00+    call    ds:CreateThread
93:              loc_10001D53:
94: B8 01 00 00 00     mov     eax, 1
95: 5F                 pop     edi
96: 8B E5              mov     esp, ebp
97: 5D                 pop     ebp
98: C2 0C 00           retn    0Ch
99:              _DllMain@12 endp
```

Lines 3–4 set up the function prologue, which saves the previous base frame pointer and establishes a new one. Line 5 reserves 0x130 bytes of stack space. Line 6 saves EDI. Line 7 executes the SIDT instruction, which writes the 6-byte IDT register to a specified memory region. Line 8 reads a double-word at EBP-6 and saves it in EAX. Lines 9–10 check if EAX is below-or-equal to 0x8003F400. If it is, execution is transferred to line 18; otherwise, it continues executing at line 11. Lines 11–12 do a similar check except that the condition is not-below 0x80047400. If it is, execution is transferred to line 18; otherwise, it continues executing at line 13. Line 13 clears EAX. Line 14 restores the saved EDI register in line 6. Lines 15–16 restore the previous base frame and stack pointer. Line 17 adds 0xC bytes to the stack pointer and then returns to the caller.

Before discussing the next area, note a few things about these first 17 lines. The SIDT instruction (line 7) writes the content of the IDT register to a 6-byte memory location. What is the IDT register? The Intel/AMD reference manual states that IDT is an array of 256 8-byte entries, each containing a pointer to an interrupt handler, segment selector, and offset. When an interrupt or exception occurs, the processor uses the interrupt number as an index into the IDT and calls the entry's specified handler. The IDT register is a 6-byte register; the top 4 bytes contain the base of the IDT array/table and the bottom 2 bytes store the table limit. With this in mind, you now know that line 8 is actually reading the IDT base address. Lines 9 and 11 check whether the base address is in the range (0x8003F400, 0x80047400). What is special about these seemingly random constants? If you search the Internet, you will note that 0x8003F400 is an IDT base address on Windows XP on x86. This can be verified in the kernel debugger:

```
0: kd> vertarget
Windows XP Kernel Version 2600 (Service Pack 3) MP (2 procs) Free x86 compat-
ible
Built by: 2600.xpsp.080413-2111
...
0: kd> r @idtr
idtr=8003f400
0: kd> ~1
1: kd> r @idtr
idtr=bab3c590
```

Why does the code check for this behavior? One possible explanation is that the developer assumed that an IDT base address falling in that range is considered "invalid" or may be the result of being virtualized. The function automatically returns zero if the IDTR is "invalid." You can decompile this code to C as follows:

```
typedef struct _IDTR {
    DWORD base;
    SHORT limit;
} IDTR, *PIDTR;
BOOL __stdcall DllMain (HINSTANCE hinstDLL, DWORD fdwReason, LPVOID lpvRe-
served)
{
    IDTR idtr;
    __sidt(&idtr);
    if (idtr.base > 0x8003F400 && idtr.base < 0x80047400h) { return FALSE; }
    //line 18
    ...

}
```

> **NOTE** If you read the manual closely, you'll note that each processor has its own IDT and hence IDTR. Therefore, on a multi-core system, IDTR will be different for each core. Clearly, 0x8003F400 is valid only for core 0 on Windows XP. If the instruction were to be scheduled to run on another core, the IDTR would be 0xBAB3C590. On later versions of Windows, the IDT base addresses change between reboots; hence, the practice of hardcoding base addresses will not work.

If the IDT base seems valid, the code continues execution at line 18. Lines 19–20 clear EAX and set ECX to 0x49. Line 21 uses sets EDI to whatever EBP-0x12C is; since EBP is the base frame pointer, EBP-0x12C is the address of a local variable. Line 22 writes zero at the location pointed to by EBP-0x130. Lines 23–24 push EAX and 2 on the stack. Line 25 zeroes a 0x124-byte buffer starting from EBP-0x12C. Line 26 calls CreateToolhelp32Snapshot:

```
HANDLE WINAPI CreateToolhelp32Snapshot(
  _In_   DWORD dwFlags,
  _In_   DWORD th32ProcessID
);
```

This Win32 API function takes two integer parameters. As a general rule, Win32 API functions follow STDCALL calling convention. Hence, the dwFlags and th32ProcessId parameters are 0x2 (line 24) and 0x0 (line 23). This function enumerates all processes on the system and returns a handle to be used in Process32Next. Lines 27–28 save the return value in EDI and check if it is -1. If it is, the return value is set to 0 and it returns (lines 30–34); otherwise, execution continues at line 35. Line 36 sets EAX to the address of the local variable previously initialized to 0 in line 22; line 40 initializes it to 0x128. Lines 37–39 push ESI, EAX, and EDI on the stack. Line 41 calls Process32First:

Function prototype

```
BOOL WINAPI Process32First(
  _In_      HANDLE hSnapshot,
  _Inout_   LPPROCESSENTRY32 lppe
);
```

Relevant structure definition

```
typedef struct tagPROCESSENTRY32 {
  DWORD      dwSize;
  DWORD      cntUsage;
  DWORD      th32ProcessID;
  ULONG_PTR  th32DefaultHeapID;
  DWORD      th32ModuleID;
  DWORD      cntThreads;
  DWORD      th32ParentProcessID;
  LONG       pcPriClassBase;
  DWORD      dwFlags;
  TCHAR      szExeFile[MAX_PATH];
} PROCESSENTRY32, *PPROCESSENTRY32;

00000000 PROCESSENTRY32 struc ; (sizeof=0x128)
00000000 dwSize dd ?
00000004 cntUsage dd ?
00000008 th32ProcessID dd ?
```

```
0000000C th32DefaultHeapID dd ?
00000010 th32ModuleID dd ?
00000014 cntThreads dd ?
00000018 th32ParentProcessID dd ?
0000001C pcPriClassBase dd ?
00000020 dwFlags dd ?
00000024 szExeFile db 260 dup(?)
00000128 PROCESSENTRY32 ends
```

Because this API takes two parameters, hSnapshot is EDI (line 39, previously the returned handle from CreateToolhelp32Snapshot in line 27), and lppe is the address of a local variable (EBP-0x130). Because lppe points to a PROCESSENTRY32 structure, we immediately know that the local variable at EBP-0x130 is of the same type. It also makes sense because the documentation for Process32First states that before calling the function, the dwSize field must be set to the size of a PROCESSENTRY32 structure (which is 0x128). We now know that lines 19–25 were simply initializing this structure to 0. In addition, we can say that this local variable starts at EBP-0x130 and ends at EBP-0x8.

Line 42 tests the return value of Process32Next. If it is zero, execution begins at line 70; otherwise, it continues at line 43. Line 44 saves the address of the stricmp function in ESI. Line 45 sets ECX to the address of a local variable (EBP-0x10C), which happens to be a field in PROCESSENTRY32 (see the previous paragraph). Lines 46–48 push 0x10007C50/ECX on the stack and call stricmp. We know that stricmp takes two character strings as arguments; hence, ECX must be the szExeFile field in PROCESSENTRY32 and 0x10007C50 is the address of a string:

```
.data:10007C50 65 78 70 6C 6F+Str2 db 'explorer.exe',0
```

Line 49 cleans up the stack because stricmp uses CDECL calling convention. Line 50 checks stricmp's return value. If it is zero, meaning that the string matched "explorer.exe", execution begins at line 66; otherwise, it continues execution at line 52. We can now decompile lines 18–51 as follows:

```
HANDLE h;
PROCESSENTRY32 procentry;
h = CreateToolhelp32Snapshot(TH32CS_SNAPPROCESS, 0);
if (h == INVALID_HANDLE_VALUE) { return FALSE; }

memset(&procentry, 0, sizeof(PROCESSENTRY32));
procentry.dwSize = sizeof(procentry); // 0x128
if (Process32Next(h, &procentry) == FALSE) {
    // line 70
    ...
}
if (stricmp(procentry.szExeFile, "explorer.exe") == 0) {
    // line 66
    ...
}
// line 52
```

Lines 52–65 are nearly identical to the previous block except that they form a loop with two exit conditions. The first exit condition is when `Process32Next` returns `FALSE` (line 58) and the second is when `stricmp` returns zero. We can decompile lines 52–65 as follows:

```
while (Process32Next(h, &procentry) != FALSE) {
    if (stricmp(procentry.szExeFile, "explorer".exe") == 0)
        break;
}
```

After the loop exits, execution resumes at line 66. Lines 67–68 save the matching `PROCESSENTRY32`'s `th32ParentProcessID`/`th32ProcessID` in `EAX`/`ECX` and continue execution at 37. Notice that Line 66 is also a jump target in line 43.

Lines 70–74 read the `fdwReason` parameter of `DllMain` (`EBP+C`) and check whether it is 0 (`DLL_PROCESS_DETACH`). If it is, the return value is set to 0 and it returns; otherwise, it goes to line 82. Lines 82–85 check if the `fdwReason` is greater than 1 (i.e., `DLL_THREAD_ATTACH`, `DLL_THREAD_DETACH`). If it is, the return value is set to 1 and it returns; otherwise, execution continues at line 86. Lines 86–92 call `CreateThread`:

```
HANDLE WINAPI CreateThread(
    _In_opt_    LPSECURITY_ATTRIBUTES lpThreadAttributes,
    _In_        SIZE_T dwStackSize,
    _In_        LPTHREAD_START_ROUTINE lpStartAddress,
    _In_opt_    LPVOID lpParameter,
    _In_        DWORD dwCreationFlags,
    _Out_opt_   LPDWORD lpThreadId
);
```

with `lpStartAddress` as 0x100032D0. This block can be decompiled as follows:

```
if (fdwReason == DLL_PROCESS_DETACH) { return FALSE; }
if (fdwReason == DLL_THREAD_ATTACH || fdwReason == DLL_THREAD_DETACH) {
    return TRUE; }
CreateThread(0, 0, (LPTHREAD_START_ROUTINE) 0x100032D0, 0, 0, 0);
return TRUE;
```

Having analyzed the function, we can deduce that the developer's original intention was this:

1. Detect whether the target machine has a "sane" IDT.

2. Check whether "explorer.exe" is running on the system—i.e., someone logged on.

3. Create a main thread that infects the target machine.

Exercises

1. Repeat the walk-through by yourself. Draw the stack layout, including parameters and local variables.

2. In the example walk-through, we did a nearly one-to-one translation of the assembly code to C. As an exercise, re-decompile this whole function so that it looks more natural. What can you say about the developer's skill level/experience? Explain your reasons. Can you do a better job?

3. In some of the assembly listings, the function name has a @ prefix followed by a number. Explain when and why this decoration exists.

4. Implement the following functions in x86 assembly: strlen, strchr, memcpy, memset, strcmp, strset.

5. Decompile the following kernel routines in Windows:

   ■ KeInitializeDpc

   ■ KeInitializeApc

   ■ ObFastDereferenceObject (and explain its calling convention)

   ■ KeInitializeQueue

   ■ KxWaitForLockChainValid

   ■ KeReadyThread

   ■ KiInitializeTSS

   ■ RtlValidateUnicodeString

6. *Sample H*. The function sub_13846 references several structures whose types are not entirely clear. Your task is to first recover the function prototype and then try to reconstruct the structure fields. After reading Chapter 3, return to this exercise to see if your understanding has changed. (Note: This sample is targeting Windows XP x86.)

7. *Sample H*. The function sub_10BB6 has a loop searching for something. First recover the function prototype and then infer the types based on the context. Hint: You should probably have a copy of the PE specification nearby.

8. *Sample H*. Decompile sub_11732 and explain the most likely programming construct used in the original code.

9. *Sample L*. Explain what function sub_1000CEA0 does and then decompile it back to C.

10. If the current privilege level is encoded in CS, which is modifiable by user-mode code, why can't user-mode code modify CS to change CPL?

11. Read the Virtual Memory chapter in *Intel Software Developer Manual, Volume 3* and *AMD64 Architecture Programmer's Manual, Volume 2: System Programming*. Perform a few virtual address to physical address translations yourself and verify the result with a kernel debugger. Explain how data execution prevention (DEP) works.

12. Bruce's favorite x86/x64 disassembly library is BeaEngine by BeatriX (www.beaengine.org). Experiment with it by writing a program to disassemble a binary at its entry point.

x64

x64 is an extension of x86, so most of the architecture properties are the same, with minor differences such as register size and some instructions are unavailable (like PUSHAD). The following sections discuss the relevant differences.

Register Set and Data Types

The register set has 18 64-bit GPRs, and can be illustrated as shown in Figure 1-6. Note that 64-bit registers have the "R" prefix.

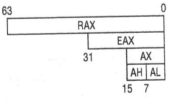 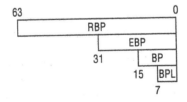

Figure 1-6

While RBP can still be used as the base frame pointer, it is rarely used for that purpose in real-life compiler-generated code. Most x64 compilers simply treat RBP as another GPR, and reference local variables relative to RSP.

Data Movement

x64 supports a concept referred to as *RIP-relative addressing*, which allows instructions to reference data at a relative position to RIP. For example:

```
01: 0000000000000000 48 8B 05 00 00+  mov     rax, qword ptr cs:loc_A
02:                                    ; originally written as "mov rax,
[rip]"
03: 0000000000000007                   loc_A:
```

```
04: 0000000000000007 48 31 C0        xor     rax, rax
05: 000000000000000A 90              nop
```

Line 1 reads the address of `loc_A` (which is 0x7) and saves it in RAX. RIP-relative addressing is primarily used to facilitate position-independent code.

Most arithmetic instructions are automatically promoted to 64 bits even though the operands are only 32 bits. For example:

```
48 B8 88 77 66+ mov   rax, 1122334455667788h
31 C0           xor   eax, eax  ; will also clear the upper 32bits of RAX.
                                 ; i.e., RAX=0 after this
48 C7 C0 FF FF+ mov   rax,0FFFFFFFFFFFFFFFFh
FF C0           inc   eax  ; RAX=0 after this
```

Canonical Address

On x64, virtual addresses are 64 bits in width, but most processors do not support a full 64-bit virtual address space. Current Intel/AMD processors only use 48 bits for the address space. All virtual memory addresses must be in canonical form. A virtual address is in canonical form if bits 63 to the most significant implemented bit are either all 1s or 0s. In practical terms, it means that bits 48–63 need to match bit 47. For example:

```
0xfffff801`c9c11000 = 11111111 11111111 11111000 00000001 11001001 11000001
    00010000 00000000 ; canonical
0x000007f7`bdb67000 = 00000000 00000000 00000111 11110111 10111101 10110110
    01110000 00000000 ; canonical
0xffff0800`00000000 = 11111111 11111111 00001000 00000000 00000000 00000000
    00000000 00000000 ; non-canonical
0xffff8000`00000000 = 11111111 11111111 10000000 00000000 00000000 00000000
    00000000 00000000 ; canonical
0xfffff960`000989f0 = 11111111 11111111 11111001 01100000 00000000 00001001
    10001001 11110000 ; canonical
```

If code tries to dereference a non-canonical address, the system will cause an exception.

Function Invocation

Recall that some calling conventions require parameters to be passed on the stack on x86. On x64, most calling conventions pass parameters through registers. For example, on Windows x64, there is only one calling convention and the first four parameters are passed through RCX, RDX, R8, and R9; the remaining are pushed on the stack from right to left. On Linux, the first six parameters are passed on RDI, RSI, RDX, RCX, R8, and R9.

NOTE For more information regarding x64 ABI on Windows, see the "x64 Software Conventions" section on MSDN (http://msdn.microsoft.com/en-us/library/7kcdt6fy.aspx).

Exercises

1. Explain two methods to get the instruction pointer on x64. At least one of the methods must use RIP addressing.

2. Perform a virtual-to-physical address translation on x64. Were there any major differences compared to x86?

A company named Acorn Computers developed a 32-bit RISC architecture named the Acorn RISC Machine (later renamed to Advanced RISC Machine) in the late 1980s. This architecture proved to be useful beyond their limited product line, so a company named ARM Holdings was formed to license the architecture for use in a wide variety of products. It is commonly found in embedded devices such as cell phones, automobile electronics, MP3 players, televisions, and so on. The first version of the architecture was introduced in 1985, and at the time of this writing it is at version 7 (ARMv7). ARM has developed a number of specific cores (e.g., ARM7, ARM7TDMI, ARM926EJS, Cortex)—not to be confused with the different architecture specifications, which are numbered ARMv1–ARMv7. While there are several versions, most devices are either on ARMv4, 5, 6, or 7. ARMv4 and v5 are relatively "old," but they are also the most dominant and common versions of the processor ("more than 10 billion" cores in existence, according to ARM marketing). Popular consumer electronic products typically use more recent versions of the architecture. For example, the third-generation Apple iPod Touch and iPhone run on an ARMv6 chip, and later iPhone/iPad and Windows Phone 7 devices are all on ARMv7.

Whereas companies such as Intel and AMD design and manufacture their processors, ARM follows a slightly different model. ARM designs the architecture and licenses it to other companies, which then manufacture and integrate the processors into their devices. Companies such as Apple, NVIDIA, Qualcomm, and Texas Instruments market their own processors (A, Tegra, Snapdragon, and OMAP, respectively), but their core architecture is licensed from ARM. They all implement the base instruction set and memory model defined in the ARM architecture reference manual. Additional extensions can be added to the processor; for example, the Jazelle extension enables Java bytecode to be executed natively on the processor. The Thumb extension adds instructions that can be 16 or 32 bits wide, thus allowing higher code density (native ARM instructions are always 32 bits in width). The Debug extension allows engineers to analyze the physical processor using special debugging hardware. Each extension is typically represented by a letter (J, T, D, etc.). Depending on their requirements, manufacturers can decide whether they need to license these additional extensions. This is why ARMv6 and earlier processors have letters after them (e.g., ARM1156T2 means ARMv6 with Thumb-2 extension). These conventions are no longer used in ARMv7, which instead uses three profiles (Application, Real-time, and Microcontroller) and model name (Cortex) with different features. For example, ARMv7 Cortex-A series are processors with the application profile; and Cortex-M are meant for microcontrollers and only support Thumb mode execution.

This chapter covers the ARMv7 architecture as defined in the *ARM Architecture Reference Manual: ARMv7-A and ARMv7-R Edition* (ARM DDI 0406B).

Basic Features

Because ARM is a RISC architecture, there are a few basic differences between ARM and CISC architectures (x86/x64). (From a practical perspective, new versions of Intel processors have some RISC features as well—i.e., they are not "purely" CISC.) First, the ARM instruction set is very small compared to x86, but it offers more general-purpose registers. Second, the instruction length is fixed width (16 bits or 32 bits, depending on the state). Third, ARM uses a load-store model for memory access. This means data must be moved from memory into registers before being operated on, and only load/store instructions can access memory. On ARM, this translates to the LDR and STR instructions. If you want to increment a 32-bit value at a particular memory address, you must first load the value at that address to a register, increment it, and store it back. In contrast with x86, which allows most instructions to directly operate on data in memory, such a simple operation on ARM would require three instructions (one load, one increment, one store). This may imply that there is more code to read for the reverse engineer, but in practice it does not really matter much once you are used to it.

ARM also offers several different privilege levels to implement privilege isolation. In x86, privileges are defined by four rings, with ring 0 having the highest privilege and ring 3 having the lowest. In ARM, privileges are defined by eight different modes:

■ User (USR)

■ Fast interrupt request (FIQ)

■ Interrupt request (IRQ)

■ Supervisor (SVC)

■ Monitor (MON)

■ Abort (ABT)

■ Undefined (UND)

■ System (SYS)

Code running in a given mode has access to certain privileges and registers that others may not; for example, code running in USR mode is not allowed to modify system registers (which are typically modified only in SVC mode). USR is the least privileged mode. While there are many technical differences, for the sake of simplicity you can make the analogy that USR is like ring 3 and SVC is like ring 0. Most operating systems implement kernel mode in SVC and user mode in USR. Both Windows and Linux do this.

If you recall from Chapter 1, x64 processors can execute in 32-bit, 64-bit, or both interchangeably. ARM processors are similar in that they can also operate in two states: ARM and Thumb. ARM/Thumb state determines only the instruction set, not the privilege level. For example, code running in SVC mode can be either ARM or Thumb. In ARM state, instructions are always 32 bits wide; in Thumb state, instructions can be either 16 bits or 32 bits wide. Which state the processor executes in depends on two conditions:

■ When branching with the BX and BLX instruction, if the destination register's least significant bit is 1, then it will switch to Thumb state. (Although instructions are either 2- or 4-byte aligned, the processor will ignore the least significant bit so there won't be alignment issues.)

■ If the T bit in the current program status register (CPSR) is set, then it is in Thumb mode. The semantic of CPSR is explained in the following section, but for now you can think of it as an extended EFLAGS register in x86.

When an ARM core boots up, most of the time it enters ARM state and remains that way until there is an explicit or implicit change to Thumb. In practice, many recent operating system code mainly uses Thumb code because higher code density is wanted (a mixture of 16/32-bit wide instructions may be smaller in size than all 32-bit ones); applications can operate in whatever mode they want.

While most Thumb and ARM instructions have the same mnemonic, 32-bit Thumb instructions have a .w suffix.

> **NOTE** It is a common misconception to think that Thumb is like real mode and ARM is like protected mode on x86/x64. Do not think of it this way. Most operating systems on the x86/x64 platform run in protected mode and rarely, if ever, switch back to real mode. Operating systems and applications on the ARM platform can execute both in ARM and Thumb state interchangeably. Note also that these states are completely different from the privilege modes explained in the previous paragraph (USR, SVC, etc.).
>
> There are two versions of Thumb: Thumb-1 and Thumb-2. Thumb-1 was used in ARMv6 and earlier architectures, and its instructions are always 16 bits in width. Thumb-2 extends that by adding more instructions and allowing them to be either 16 or 32 bits in width. ARMv7 requires Thumb-2, so whenever we talk about Thumb, we are referring to Thumb-2.
>
> There are several other differences between ARM and Thumb states but we cannot cover them all here. For example, some instructions are available in ARM state but not Thumb state, and vice versa. You can consult the official ARM documentation for more details.

In addition to having different states of execution, ARM also supports conditional execution. This means that an instruction encodes certain arithmetic conditions that must be met in order for it to be executed. For example, an instruction can specify that it will only be executed if the result of the previous instruction is zero. Contrast this with x86, for which almost every single instruction is executed unconditionally. (Intel has a couple of instructions directly supporting conditional execution: CMOV and SETNE.) Conditional execution is useful because it cuts down on branch instructions (which are very expensive) and reduces the number of instructions to be executed (which leads to higher code density). All instructions in ARM state support conditional execution, but by default they execute unconditionally. In Thumb state, a special instruction IT is required to enable conditional execution.

Another unique ARM feature is the barrel shifter. Certain instructions can "contain" another arithmetic instruction that shifts or rotates a register. This is useful because it can shrink multiple instructions into one; for example, you want to multiply a register by 2 and then store the result in another register. Normally, this would require two instructions (a multiply followed by a move), but with the barrel shifter you can include the multiply (shift left by 1) inside the MOV instruction. The instruction would be something like the following:

```
MOV R1, R0, LSL #1              ; R1 = R0 * 2
```

Data Types and Registers

Similar to high-level languages, ARM supports operations on different data types. The supported data types are: 8-bit (byte), 16-bit (half-word), 32-bit (word), and 64-bit (double-word).

The ARM architecture defines sixteen 32-bit general-purpose registers, numbered R0, R1, R2, . . . , R15. While all of them are available to the application programmer, in practice the first 12 registers are for general-purpose usage (such as EAX, EBX, etc., in x86) and the last three have special meaning in the architecture:

- R13 is denoted as the stack pointer (SP). It is the equivalent of ESP/RSP in x86/x64. It points to the top of the program stack.

- R14 is denoted as the link register (LR). It normally holds the return address during a function call. Certain instructions implicitly use this register. For example, BL always stores the return address in LR before branching to the destination. x86/x64 does not have an equivalent register because it always stores the return address on the stack. In code that does not use LR to store the return address, it can be used as a general-purpose register.

- R15 is denoted as the program counter (PC). When executing in ARM state, PC is the address of the current instruction plus 8 (two ARM instructions ahead); in Thumb state, it is the address of the current instruction plus 4 (two 16-bit Thumb instructions ahead). It is analogous to EIP/RIP in x86/x64 except that they always point to the address of the next instruction to be executed. Another major difference is that code can directly read from and write to the PC register. Writing an address to PC will immediately cause execution to start at that address. This can be elaborated upon a bit further to avoid confusion. Consider the following snippet in Thumb state:

```
1: 0x00008344 push    {lr}
2: 0x00008346 mov     r0, pc
3: 0x00008348 mov.w   r2, r1, lsl #31
4: 0x0000834c pop     {pc}
```

After line 2 is executed, R0 will hold the value 0x0000834a (=0x00008346+4):

```
(gdb) br main

Breakpoint 1 at 0x8348
...
Breakpoint 1, 0x00008348 in main ()
(gdb) disas main
```

```
Dump of assembler code for function main:
   0x00008344 <+0>:     push    {lr}
   0x00008346 <+2>:     mov     r0, pc
=> 0x00008348 <+4>:     mov.w   r2, r1, lsl #31
   0x0000834c <+8>:     pop     {pc}
   0x0000834e <+10>:    lsls    r0, r0, #0
End of assembler dump.
(gdb) info register pc
pc              0x8348   0x8348 <main+4>
(gdb) info register r0
r0              0x834a   33610
```

Here we set a breakpoint at 0x00008348. When it hits, we show the PC and
R0 register; as shown, PC points to the third instruction at 0x00008348 (about
to be executed) and R0 shows the previously read PC value. From this example,
you can see that when directly reading PC, it follows the definition; but when
debugging, PC points to the instruction that is to be executed.

The reason for this peculiarity is due to legacy pipelining from older ARM
processors, which always fetched two instructions ahead of the currently executing instruction. Nowadays, the pipelines are much more complicated so this does
not really matter much, but ARM retains this definition to ensure compatibility
with earlier processors.

Similar to other architectures, ARM stores information about the current
execution state in the current program status register (CPSR). From an application programmer's perspective, CPSR is similar to the EFLAGS/RFLAG register
in x86/x64. Some documentation may discuss the application program status
register (APSR), which is an alias for certain fields in the CPSR. There are many
flags in the CPSR, some of which are illustrated in Figure 2-1 (others are covered
in later sections).

- E (Endianness bit)—ARM can operate in either big or little endian mode.
  This bit is set to 0 or 1 for little or big endian, respectively. Most of the
  time, little endian is used, so this bit will be 0.

- T (Thumb bit)—This is set if you are in Thumb state; otherwise, it is ARM
  state. One way to explicitly transition from Thumb to ARM (and vice
  versa) is to modify this bit.

- M (Mode bits)—These bits specify the current privilege mode (USR, SVC, etc.)

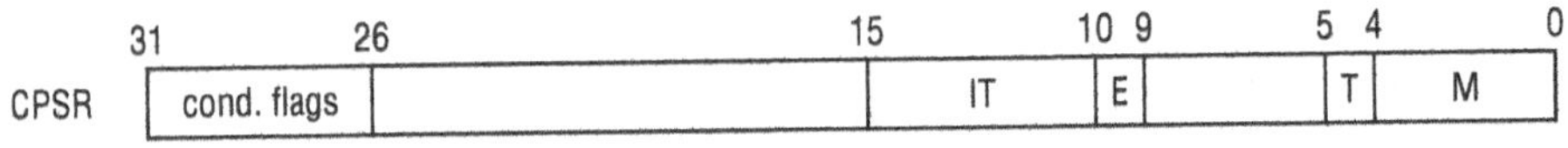

	31	26		15	10 9	5 4	0
CPSR	cond. flags			IT	E	T	M

Figure 2-1

System-Level Controls and Settings

ARM offers the concept of coprocessors to support additional instructions and system-level settings. For example, if the system supports a memory management unit (MMU), then its settings must be exposed to boot or kernel code. On x86/x64, these settings are stored in CR0 and CR4; on ARM, they are stored in coprocessor 15. There are 16 coprocessors in the ARM architecture, each identified by a number: CP0, CP1, . . . , CP15. (When used in code, these are referred to as P0, . . . , P15.) The first 13 are either optional or reserved by ARM; the optional ones can be used by manufacturers to implement manufacturer-specific instructions or features. For example, CP10 and CP11 are usually used for floating-point and NEON support. Each coprocessor contains additional "opcodes" and registers that can be controlled through special ARM instructions. CP14 and CP15 are used for debug and system settings; CP15, usually known as the *system control coprocessor*, stores most of the system settings (caching, paging, exceptions, and so forth).

> **NOTE** NEON provides the single-instruction multiple data (SIMD) instruction set that is commonly used in multimedia applications. It is similar to SSE/MMX instructions in x86-based architectures.

Each coprocessor has 16 registers and eight corresponding opcodes. The semantic of these registers and opcodes is specific to the coprocessor. Accessing coprocessors can only be done through the MRC (read) and MCR (write) instructions; they take a coprocessor number, register number, and opcodes. For example, to read the translation base register (similar to CR3 in x86/x64) and save it in R0, you use the following:

```
MRC p15, 0, r0, c2, c0, 0 ; save TTBR in r0
```

This says, "read coprocessor 15's C2/C0 register using opcode 0/0 and store the result in the general-purpose register R0." Because there are so many registers and opcodes within each coprocessor, you must read the documentation to determine the precise meaning of each. Some registers (C13/C0) are reserved for operating systems in order to store process- or thread-specific data.

While the MRC and MCR instructions do not require high privilege (i.e., they can be executed in USR mode), some of the coprocessor registers and opcodes are only accessible in SVC mode. Attempts to read certain registers without sufficient privilege will result in an exception. In practice, you will infrequently see these instructions in user-mode code; they are commonly found in very low-level code such as ROM, boot loaders, firmware, or kernel-mode code.

Introduction to the Instruction Set

At this point, you are ready to look at the important ARM instructions. Besides conditional execution and barrel shifters, there are several other peculiarities about the instructions that are not found in x86. First, some instructions can operate on a range of registers in sequence. For example, to store five registers, R6–R10, at a particular memory location referenced by R1, you would write STM R1, {R6-R10}. R6 would be stored at memory address R1, R7 at R1+4, R8 at R1+8, and so on. Nonconsecutive registers can also be specified via comma separation (e.g., {R1,R5,R8}). In ARM assembly syntax, the register ranges are usually specified inside curly brackets. Second, some instructions can optionally update the base register after a read/write operation. This is usually done by affixing an exclamation mark (!) after the register name. For example, if you were to rewrite the previous instruction as STM R1!, {R6-R10} and execute it, then R1 will be updated with the address immediately after where R10 was stored. To make it clearer, here is an example:

```
01: (gdb) disas main
02: Dump of assembler code for function main:
03: => 0x00008344 <+0>:     mov    r6,  #10
04:    0x00008348 <+4>:     mov    r7,  #11
05:    0x0000834c <+8>:     mov    r8,  #12
06:    0x00008350 <+12>:    mov    r9,  #13
07:    0x00008354 <+16>:    mov    r10, #14
08:    0x00008358 <+20>:    stmia  sp!, {r6, r7, r8, r9, r10}
09:    0x0000835c <+24>:    bx     lr
10: End of assembler dump.
11: (gdb) si
12: 0x00008348 in main ()
13: ...
14: 0x00008358 in main ()
15: (gdb) info reg sp
16: sp              0xbedf5848     0xbedf5848
17: (gdb) si
18: 0x0000835c in main ()
19: (gdb) info reg sp
20: sp              0xbedf585c     0xbedf585c
21: (gdb) x/6x 0xbedf5848
22: 0xbedf5848:     0x0000000a     0x0000000b     0x0000000c
0x0000000d
23: 0xbedf5858:     0x0000000e     0x00000000
```

Line 15 displays the value of SP (0xbedf5848) before executing the STM instruction; lines 17 and 19 execute the STM instruction and display the updated value of SP. Line 21 dumps six words starting at the old value of SP. Note that R6 was stored at the old SP, R7 at SP+0x4, R8 at SP+0x8, R9 at SP+0xc, and R10 at SP+0x10. The new SP (0xbedf585c) is immediately after where R10 was stored.

> **NOTE** STMIA and STMEA are pseudo-instructions for STM—that is, they have the same meaning. Disassemblers can pick either one to display. Some will show STMEA if the base register is SP, and STMIA for other registers; some always use STM; and some always use STMIA. There is no strict rule, so you have to get used to this if you are using multiple disassemblers.

Loading and Storing Data

The preceding section mentions that ARM is a load-store architecture, which means that data must be loaded into registers before it can be operated on. The only instructions that can touch memory are load and store; all other instructions can operate only on registers. To load means to read data from memory and save it in a register; to store means to write the content of a register to a memory location. On ARM, the load/store instructions are LDR/STR, LDM/STM, and PUSH/POP.

LDR and STR

These instructions can load and store 1, 2, or 4 bytes to and from memory. Their full syntax is somewhat complicated because there are several different ways to specify the offset and side effects for updating the base register. Consider the simplest case:

```
01:  03 68        LDR         R3, [R0] ; R3 = *R0
02:  23 60        STR         R3, [R4] ; *R4 = R3;
```

For the instruction in line 1, R0 is the base register and R3 is the destination; it loads the word value at address R0 into R3. In line 2, R4 is the base register and R3 is the destination; it takes the value in R3 and stores at the memory address R4. This example is simple because the memory address is specified by the base register.

At a fundamental level, the LDR/STR instructions take a base register and an offset; there are three offset forms and three addressing modes for each form. We begin by discussing the offset forms: immediate, register, and scaled register.

The first offset form uses an immediate as the offset. An immediate is simply an integer. It is added to or subtracted from the base register to access data at an offset known at compile time. The most common usage is to access a particular field in a structure or vtable. The general format is as follows:

- STR Ra, [Rb, imm]
- LDR Ra, [Rc, imm]

Rb is the base register, and imm is the offset to be added to Rb.

For example, suppose that R0 holds a pointer to a KDPC structure and the following code:

Structure Definition

```
0:000> dt ntkrnlmp!_KDPC
    +0x000 Type             : UChar
    +0x001 Importance       : UChar
    +0x002 Number           : Uint2B
    +0x004 DpcListEntry      : _LIST_ENTRY
    +0x00c DeferredRoutine   : Ptr32     void
    +0x010 DeferredContext   : Ptr32 Void
    +0x014 SystemArgument1   : Ptr32 Void
    +0x018 SystemArgument2   : Ptr32 Void
    +0x01c DpcData           : Ptr32 Void
```

Code

```
01: 13 23        MOVS    R3, #0x13
02: 03 70        STRB    R3, [R0]
03: 01 23        MOVS    R3, #1
04: 43 70        STRB    R3, [R0,#1]
05: 00 23        MOVS    R3, #0
06: 43 80        STRH    R3, [R0,#2]
07: C3 61        STR     R3, [R0,#0x1C]
08: C1 60        STR     R1, [R0,#0xC]
09: 02 61        STR     R2, [R0,#0x10]
```

In this case, R0 is the base register and the immediates are 0x1, 0x2, 0xC, 0x10, and 0x1C. The snippet can be translated into C as follows:

```
KDPC *obj = ...;              /* R0 is obj */
obj->Type = 0x13;
obj->Importance = 0x1;
obj->Number = 0x0;
obj->DpcData = NULL;
obj->DeferredRoutine = R1;    /* R1 is unknown to us */
obj->DeferredContext = R2;    /* R2 is unknown to us */
```

This offset form is similar to the MOV Reg, [Reg + Imm] on the x86/x64.

The second offset form uses a register as the offset. It is commonly used in code that needs to access an array but the index is computed at runtime. The general format is as follows:

- STR Ra, [Rb, Rc]
- LDR Ra, [Rb, Rc]

Depending on the context, either Rb or Rc can be the base/offset. Consider the following two examples:

Example 1

```
01: 03 F0 F2 FA    BL    strlen
02: 06 46          MOV R6, R0
; R0 is strlen's return value
03: ...
04: BB 57          LDRSB R3, [R7,R6]
; in this case, R6 is the offset
```

Example 2

```
01: B3 EB 05 08    SUBS.W  R8, R3, R5
02: 2F 78          LDRB    R7, [R5]
03: 18 F8 05 30    LDRB.W  R3, [R8,R5]
; here, R5 is the base and R8 is the offset
04: 9F 42          CMP     R7, R3
```

This is similar to the MOV Reg, [Reg + Reg] form on x86/x64.

The third offset form uses a scaled register as the offset. It is commonly used in a loop to iterate over an array. The barrel shifter is used to scale the offset. The general format is as follows:

- LDR Ra, [Rb, Rc, <shifter>]
- STR Ra, [Rb, Rc, <shifter>]

Rb is the base register; Rc is an immediate; and <shifter> is the operation performed on the immediate—typically, a left/right shift to scale the immediate. For example:

```
01: 0E 4B          LDR     R3, =KeNumberNodes
02: ...
03: 00 24          MOVS    R4, #0
04: 19 88          LDRH    R1, [R3]
05: 09 48          LDR     R0, =KeNodeBlock
06: 00 23          MOVS    R3, #0
07:                loop_start
08: 50 F8 23 20    LDR.W   R2, [R0,R3,LSL#2]
09: 00 23          MOVS    R3, #0
10: A2 F8 90 30    STRH.W  R3, [R2,#0x90]
11: 92 F8 89 30    LDRB.W  R3, [R2,#0x89]
12: 53 F0 02 03    ORRS.W  R3, R3, #2
13: 82 F8 89 30    STRB.W  R3, [R2,#0x89]
14: 63 1C          ADDS    R3, R4, #1
15: 9C B2          UXTH    R4, R3
16: 23 46          MOV     R3, R4
17: 8C 42          CMP     R4, R1
18: EF DB          BLT     loop_start
```

`KeNumberNodes` and `KeNodeBlock` are a global integer and an array of `KNODE` pointers, respectively.

Lines 1 and 5 simply load those globals into a register (we explain this syntax later). Line 8 iterates over the `KeNodeBlock` array (`R0` is the base), `R3` is the index multiplied by 4 (because it is an array of pointers; pointers are 4 bytes in size on this platform). Lines 10–13 initialize some fields of the `KNODE` element. Line 14 increments the index. Line 17 compares the index against the size of the array (`R1` is the size; see line 4) and if it is less than the size then continues the loop.

This snippet can be roughly translated to C as follows:

```
int KeNumberNodes = …;
KNODE *KeNodeBlock[KeNumberNodes] = …;
for (int i=0; i < KeNumberNodes; i++) {
    KeNodeBlock[i].x = …;
    KeNodeBlock[i].y = …;
    …
}
```

This is similar to the `MOV, Reg, [Reg + idx * scale]` form on x86/x64.

Having covered the three offset forms, the rest of this section discusses addressing modes: offset, pre-indexed, and post-indexed. The only distinction among them is whether the base register is modified and, if so, in what way. All the preceding offset examples use offset addressing mode, which means that the base register is never modified. This is the simplest and most common mode. You can quickly recognize it because it does not contain an exclamation mark (!) anywhere and the immediate is inside the square brackets. (Some publications categorize these modes as pre-index, pre-index with writeback, and post-index. The terminology used here reflects the official ARM documentation.) The general syntax for the offset mode is `LDR Rd, [Rn, offset]`.

Pre-indexed address mode means that the base register will be updated with the final memory address used in the reference operation. The semantic is very similar to the prefix form of the unary `++` and `--` operator in C. The syntax for this mode is `LDR Rd, [Rn, offset]!`. For example:

```
12 F9 01 3D   LDRSB.W R3, [R2 ,#-1]! ; R3 = *(R2-1)
                                     ; R2 = R2-1
```

Post-indexed address mode means that the base register is used as the final address, then updated with the offset calculated. This is very similar to the postfix form of the unary `++` and `--` operator in C. The syntax for this mode is `LDR Rd, [Rn], offset`. For example:

```
10 F9 01 6B   LDRSB.W R6, [R0],#1  ; R6 = *R0
                                   ; R0 = R0+1
```

The pre- and post-index forms are normally observed in code that accesses an offset in the same buffer multiple times. For example, suppose the code needs to loop and check whether a character in a string matches one of five characters; the compiler may update the base pointer so that it can shave off an increment instruction.

NOTE Here's a tip to recognize and remember the different address modes in LDR/ STR: If there is a !, then it is prefix; if the base register is in brackets by itself, then it is postfix; anything else is offset mode.

Other Usage for LDR

As explained earlier, LDR is used to load data from memory into a register; however, sometimes you see it in these forms:

```
01: DF F8 50 82    LDR.W    R8, =0x2932E00 ; LDR R8, [PC, x]
02: 80 4A          LDR      R2, =a04d ; "%04d" ; LDR R2, [PC, y]
03: 0E 4B          LDR      R3, =__imp_realloc ; LDR R3, [PC, z]
```

Clearly, this is not valid syntax according to the previous section. Technically, these are called *pseudo-instructions* and they are used by disassemblers to make manual inspection easier. Internally, they use the immediate form of LDR with PC as a base register; sometimes, this is called *PC-relative addressing* (or *RIP-relative addressing* on x64). ARM binaries usually have a literal pool that is a memory area in a section to store constants, strings, or offsets that others can reference in a position-independent manner. (The literal pool is part of the code, so it will be in the same section.) In the preceding snippet, the code is referencing a 32-bit constant, a string, and an offset to an imported function stored in the literal pool. This particular pseudo-instruction is useful because it allows a 32-bit constant to be moved into a register in one instruction. To make it clearer, consider the following snippet:

```
01: .text:0100B134 35 4B    LDR    R3, =0x68DB8BAD
                  ; actually LDR R3, [PC, #0xD4]
                  ; at this point, PC = 0x0100B138
02: ...
03: .text:0100B20C AD 8B DB 68 dword_100B20C DCD 0x68DB8BAD
```

How did the disassembler shorten the first instruction from LDR R3, [PC, #0xD4] to the alternate form? Because the code is in Thumb state, PC is the current instruction plus 4, which is 0x0100B138; it is using the immediate form of PC, so it is trying to read the word at 0x0100B20C (=0x100B138+0xD4), which happens to be the constant we want to load.

Another related instruction is ADR, which gets the address for a label/function and puts it in a register. For example:

```
01: 00009390 65 A5          ADR     R5, dword_9528
02: 00009392 D5 E9 00 45    LDRD.W  R4, R5, [R5]
03: ...
04: 00009528 00 CE 22 A9+dword_9528 DCD 0xA922CE00 , 0xC0A4
```

This instruction is typically used to implement jump tables or callbacks where you need to pass the address of a function to another. Internally, this instruction just calculates an offset from PC and saves it in the destination register.

LDM and STM

LDM and STM are similar to LDR/STR except that they load and store multiple words at a given base register. They are useful when moving multiple data blocks to and from memory. The general syntax is as follows:

- LDM<mode> Rn[!], {Rm}
- STM<mode> Rn[!], {Rm}

Rn is the base register and it holds the memory address to load/store from; the optional exclamation mark (!) means that the base register should be updated with the new address (writeback). Rm is the range of register to load/store. There are four modes:

- IA (Increment After)—Stores data starting at the memory location specified by the base address. If there is writeback, then the address 4 bytes above the last location is written back. This is the default mode if nothing is specified.

- IB (Increment Before)—Stores data starting at the memory location 4 bytes above the base address. If there is writeback, then the address of the last location is written back.

- DA (Decrement After)—Stores data such that the last location is the base address. If there is writeback, then the address 4 bytes below the lowest location is written back.

- DB (Decrement Before)—Stores data such that the last location is 4 bytes below the base address. If there is writeback, then the address of the first location is written back.

This may sound a bit confusing at first, so let's walk through an example with the debugger:

```
01: (gdb) br main
02: Breakpoint 1 at 0x8344
03: (gdb) disas main
04: Dump of assembler code for function main:
```

```
05:      0x00008344 <+0>:      ldr     r6, =mem  ; edited a bit
06:      0x00008348 <+4>:      mov     r0, #10
07:      0x0000834c <+8>:      mov     r1, #11
08:      0x00008350 <+12>:     mov     r2, #12
09:      0x00008354 <+16>:     ldm     r6, {r3, r4, r5}  ; IA mode
10:      0x00008358 <+20>:     stm     r6, {r0, r1, r2}  ; IA mode
11: ...
12: (gdb) r
13: Breakpoint 1, 0x00008344 in main ()
14: (gdb) si
15: 0x00008348 in main ()
16: (gdb) x/3x $r6
17: 0x1050c <mem>:   0x00000001       0x00000002       0x00000003
18: (gdb) si
19: 0x0000834c in main ()
20: ...
21: (gdb)
22: 0x00008358 in main ()
23: (gdb) info reg r3 r4 r5
24: r3               0x1       1
25: r4               0x2       2
26: r5               0x3       3
27: (gdb) si
28: 0x0000835c in main ()
29: (gdb) x/3x $r6
30: 0x1050c <mem>:   0x0000000a       0x0000000b       0x0000000c
```

Line 5 stores a memory address in R6; the content of this memory address (0x1050c) is three words (line 17). Lines 6–8 set R0–R2 with some constants. Line 9 loads three words into R3–R5, starting at the memory location specified by R6. As shown in lines 24–26, R3–R5 contain the expected value. Line 10 stores R0–R2, starting at the memory location specified by R6. Line 29 shows that the expected values were written. Figure 2-2 illustrates the result of the preceding operations.

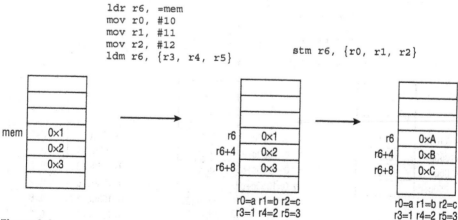

Figure 2-2

Here's the same experiment with writeback:

```
01: (gdb) br main
02: Breakpoint 1 at 0x8344
03: (gdb) disas main
04: Dump of assembler code for function main:
05:     0x00008344 <+0>:    ldr    r6, =mem    ; edited a bit
06:     0x00008348 <+4>:    mov    r0, #10
07:     0x0000834c <+8>:    mov    r1, #11
08:     0x00008350 <+12>:   mov    r2, #12
09:     0x00008354 <+16>:   ldm    r6!, {r3, r4, r5} ; IA mode w/ writeback
10:     0x00008358 <+20>:   stmia  r6!, {r0, r1, r2} ; IA mode w/ writeback
11: ...
12: (gdb) r
13: Breakpoint 1, 0x00008344 in main ()
14: (gdb) si
15: 0x00008348 in main ()
16: ...
17: (gdb)
18: 0x00008354 in main ()
19: (gdb) x/3x $r6
20: 0x1050c <mem>:  0x00000001    0x00000002    0x00000003
21: (gdb) si
22: 0x00008358 in main ()
23: (gdb) info reg r6
24: r6              0x10518    66840
25: (gdb) si
26: 0x0000835c in main ()
27: (gdb) info reg $r6
28: r6              0x10524    66852
29: (gdb) x/4x $r6-12
30: 0x10518 :       0x0000000a    0x0000000b    0x0000000c
0x00000000
```

Line 9 uses IA mode with writeback, so the r6 is updated with an address 4 bytes above the last location (line 23). The same can be observed in lines 10, 27, and 30. Figure 2-3 shows the result of the preceding snippet.

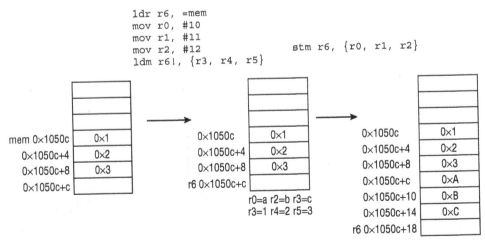

Figure 2-3

Because LDM and STM can move multiple words at a time, they are typically used in block- copy or move operations. For example, they are sometimes used to inline memcpy when the copy length is known at compile time. They are similar to the MOVS instruction with the REP prefix on x86. Consider the following blobs of code generated by two different compilers from the same source file:

Compiler A

```
01: A4 46          MOV     R12, R4
02: 35 46          MOV     R5, R6
03: BC E8 0F 00    LDMIA.W R12!, {R0-R3}
04: 0F C5          STMIA   R5!, {R0-R3}
05: BC E8 0F 00    LDMIA.W R12!, {R0-R3}
06: 0F C5          STMIA   R5!, {R0-R3}
07: 9C E8 0F 00    LDMIA.W R12, {R0-R3}
08: 85 E8 0F 00    STMIA.W R5, {R0-R3}
```

Compiler B

```
01: 30 22          MOVS    R2, #0x30
02: 21 46          MOV     R1, R4
03: 30 46          MOV     R0, R6
04: 23 F0 17 FA    BL      memcpy
```

All this does is copy 48 bytes from one buffer to another; the first compiler uses LDM/STM with writebacks to load/store 16 bytes at a time, while the second simply calls into its implementation of memcpy. When reverse engineering code, you can spot the inlined memcpy form by recognizing that the same source and destination pointers are being used by LDM/STM with the same register set. This is a good trick to keep in mind because you will see it often.

Another common place where LDM/STM can be seen is at the beginning and end of functions in ARM state. In this context, they are used as the prologue and epilogue. For example:

```
01: F0 4F 2D E9    STMFD   SP!, {R4-R11,LR}  ; save regs + return address
02: ...
03: F0 8F BD E8    LDMFD   SP!, {R4-R11,PC}  ; restore regs and return
```

STMFD and LDMFD are pseudo-instructions for STMDB and LMDIA/LDM, respectively.

NOTE You will often see the suffixes FD, FA, ED, or EA after STM/LDM. They are simply pseudo-instructions for the LDM/STM instructions in different modes (IA, IB, etc.). The association is STMFD/STMDB, STMFA/STMIB, STMED/STMDA, STMEA/STMIA, LDMFD/LDMIA, LDMFA/LDMDA, and LDMEA/LDMDB. It can be somewhat challenging to memorize these associations—the most effective way is to draw pictures for each instruction.

PUSH and POP

The final set of load/store instructions is PUSH and POP. They are similar to LDM/ STM except for two characteristics:

- They implicitly use SP as the base address.
- SP is automatically updated.

The stack grows downward to lower addresses as it does in the x86/x64 architecture. The general syntax is PUSH/POP {Rn}, where Rn can be a range of registers.

PUSH stores the registers on the stack such that the last location is 4 bytes below the current stack pointer, and updates SP with the address of the first location. POP loads the registers starting from the current stack pointer and updates SP with the address 4 bytes above the last location. PUSH/POP are actually the same as STMDB/LDMIA with writeback and SP as the base pointer. Here is a short walk-through demonstrating the instructions:

```
01: (gdb) disas main
02: Dump of assembler code for function main:
03:    0x00008344 <+0>:     mov.w   r0, #10
04:    0x00008348 <+4>:     mov.w   r1, #11
05:    0x0000834c <+8>:     mov.w   r2, #12
06:    0x00008350 <+12>:    push    {r0, r1, r2}
07:    0x00008352 <+14>:    pop     {r3, r4, r5}
08: ...
09: (gdb) br main
10: Breakpoint 1 at 0x8344
11: (gdb) r
12: Breakpoint 1, 0x00008344 in main ()
13: (gdb) si
14: 0x00008348 in main ()
15: ...
16: (gdb)
17: 0x00008350 in main ()
18: (gdb) info reg sp        ; current stack pointer
19: sp              0xbee56848      0xbee56848
20: (gdb) si
21: 0x00008352 in main ()
22: (gdb) x/3x $sp           ; sp is updated after the push
23: 0xbee5683c:     0x0000000a      0x0000000b      0x0000000c
24: (gdb) si                ; pop into the registers
25: 0x00008354 in main ()
26: (gdb) info reg r3 r4 r5  ; new registers
27: r3              0xa     10
28: r4              0xb     11
29: r5              0xc     12
30: (gdb) info reg sp        ; new sp (4 bytes above the last location)
31: sp              0xbee56848      0xbee56848
32: (gdb) x/3x $sp-12
33: 0xbee5683c:     0x0000000a      0x0000000b      0x0000000c
```

Figure 2-4 illustrates the preceding snippet.

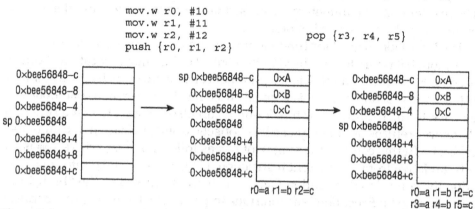

```
mov.w r0, #10
mov.w r1, #11
mov.w r2, #12                    pop {r3, r4, r5}
push {r0, r1, r2}
```

Figure 2-4

The most common place for PUSH/POP is at the beginning and end of functions. In this context, they are used as the prologue and epilogue (like STMFD/LDMFD in ARM state). For example:

```
01: 2D E9 F0 4F   PUSH.W  {R4-R11,LR} ; save registers + return address
02: ...
03: BD E8 F0 8F   POP.W   {R4-R11,PC} ; restore registers and return
```

Some disassemblers actually use this pattern as a heuristic to determine function boundaries.

Functions and Function Invocation

Unlike x86/x64, which has only one instruction for function invocation (CALL) and branching (JMP), ARM offers several depending on how the destination is encoded. When you call a function, the processor needs to know where to resume execution after the function returns; this location is typically referred to as the *return address*. In x86, the CALL instruction implicitly pushes the return address on the stack before jumping to the target function; when it is done executing, the target function resumes execution at the return address by popping it off the stack into EIP.

The mechanism on ARM is essentially the same with a few minor differences. First, the return address can be stored on the stack or in the link register (LR); to resume execution after the call, the return address is explicitly popped off the stack into PC or there will be an unconditional branch to LR. Second, a branch can switch between ARM and Thumb state, depending on the destination address's LSB. Third, a standard calling convention is defined by ARM: The first four 32-bit parameters are passed via registers (R0-R3) and the rest are on the stack. Return value is stored in R0.

The instructions used for function invocations are B, BX, BL, and BLX.

Although it is rare to see B used in the context of function invocation, it can be used for transfer of control. It is simply an unconditional branch and is identical to the JMP instruction in x86. It is normally used inside of loops and conditionals to go back to the beginning or break out; it can also be used to call a function that never returns. B can only use label offsets as its destination; it cannot use registers. In this context, the syntax of B is as follows: B imm, where imm is an offset relative from the current instruction. (This does not take into consideration the conditional execution flags, which are discussed in the "Branching and Conditional Execution" section.) One important fact to note is that because ARM and Thumb instructions are 4- and 2-byte aligned, the target offset needs to be an even number. Here is a snippet showing the usage of B:

```
01: 0001C788    B          loc_1C7A8
02: 0001C78A
03: 0001C78A loc_1C78A
04: 0001C78A    LDRB       R7, [R6,R2]
05: ...
06: 0001C7A4    STRB.W     R7, [R3,#-1]
07: 0001C7A8
08: 0001C7A8 loc_1C7A8
09: 0001C7A8    MOV        R7, R3
10: 0001C7AA    ADDS       R3, #2
11: 0001C7AC    CMP        R2, R4
12: 0001C7AE    BLT        loc_1C78A
```

In line 1, you see B being used as an unconditional jump to start off a loop. You can ignore the other instructions for now.

BX is Branch and Exchange. It is similar to B in that it transfers control to a target, but it has the ability to switch between ARM/Thumb state, and the target address is stored in a register. Branching instructions that end with X indicate that they are capable of switching between states. If the LSB of the target address is 1, then the processor automatically switches to Thumb state; otherwise, it executes in ARM state. The instruction format is BX <register>, where register holds the destination address. The two most common uses of this instruction are returning from a function by branching to LR (i.e., BX LR) and transferring of control to code in a different mode (i.e., going from ARM to Thumb or vice versa). In compiled code, you will almost always see BX LR at the end of functions; it is basically the same as RET in x86.

BL is Branch with Link. It is similar to B except that it also stores the return address in LR before transferring control to the target offset. This is probably the closest equivalence to the CALL instruction in x86 and you will often see it used to invoke functions. The instruction format is the same as B (that is, it takes only offsets). Here is a short snippet demonstrating function invocation and returning:

```
01: 00014350    BL              foo ; LR = 0x00014354
02: 00014354    MOVS            R4, #0x15
03: ...
04: 0001B224 foo
05: 0001B224    PUSH            {R1-R3}
06: 0001B226    MOV             R3, 0x61240
07: ...
08: 0001B24C    BX              LR  ; return to 0x00014354
```

Line 1 calls the function foo using BL; before transferring control to the destination, BL stores the return address (0x000014354) in LR. foo does some work and returns to the caller (BX LR).

BLX is Branch with Link and Exchange. It is like BL with the option to switch state. The major difference is that BLX can take either a register or an offset as its branch destination; in the case where BLX uses an offset, the processor always swaps state (ARM to Thumb and vice versa). Because it shares the same characteristics as BL, you can also think of it as the equivalent of the CALL instruction in x86. In practice, both BL and BLX are used to call functions. BL is typically used if the function is within a 32MB range, and BLX is used whenever the target range is undetermined (like a function pointer). When operating in Thumb state, BLX is usually used to call library routines; in ARM state, BL is used instead.

Having explored all instructions related to unconditional branching and direct function invocation, and how to return from a function (BX LR), you can consolidate your knowledge by looking at a full routine:

```
01: 0100C388                    ; void *__cdecl mystery(int)
02: 0100C388                    mystery
03: 0100C388 2D E9 30 48    PUSH.W  {R4,R5,R11,LR}
04: 0100C38C 0D F2 08 0B    ADDW    R11, SP, #8
05: 0100C390 0C 4B          LDR     R3, =__imp_malloc
06: 0100C392 C5 1D          ADDS    R5, R0, #7
07: 0100C394 6F F3 02 05    BFC.W   R5, #0, #3
08: 0100C398 1B 68          LDR     R3, [R3]
09: 0100C39A 15 F1 08 00    ADDS.W  R0, R5, #8
10: 0100C39E 98 47          BLX     R3
11: 0100C3A0 04 46          MOV     R4, R0
12: 0100C3A2 24 B1          CBZ     R4, loc_100C3AE
13: 0100C3A4 EB 17          ASRS    R3, R5, #0x1F
14: 0100C3A6 63 60          STR     R3, [R4,#4]
15: 0100C3A8 25 60          STR     R5, [R4]
16: 0100C3AA 08 34          ADDS    R4, #8
17: 0100C3AC 04 E0          B       loc_100C3B8
18: 0100C3AE               loc_100C3AE
19: 0100C3AE 04 49          LDR     R1, =aFailed ; "failed..."
20: 0100C3B0 2A 46          MOV     R2, R5
21: 0100C3B2 07 20          MOVS    R0, #7
```

```
22: 0100C3B4 01 F0 14 FC    BL        foo
23: 0100C3B8
24: 0100C3B8                  loc_100C3B8
25: 0100C3B8 20 46             MOV     R0, R4
26: 0100C3BA BD E8 30 88     POP.W   {R4,R5,R11,PC}
27: 0100C3BA                 ; End of function mystery
```

This function covers several of the ideas discussed earlier (ignore the other instructions for now):

- Line 3 is the prologue, using the PUSH {..., LR} sequence; L26 is the epilogue.
- Line 10 calls malloc via BLX.
- Line 22 calls foo via BL.
- Line 26 returns, using the POP {..., PC} sequence.

Arithmetic Operations

After loading a value from memory into a register, the code can move it around and perform operations on it. The simplest operation is to move it to another register with the MOV instruction. The source can be a constant, a register, or something processed by the barrel shifter. Here are examples of its usage:

```
01: 4F F0 0A 00    MOV.W   R0, #0xA   ; r0 = 0xa
02: 38 46          MOV     R0, R7     ; r0 = r7
03: A4 4A A0 E1    MOV     R4, R4, LSR #21 ; r4 = (r4>>21)
```

Line 3 shows the source operand being processed by the barrel shifter before being moved to the destination. The barrel shifter's operations include left shift (LSL), right shift (LSR, ASR), and rotate (ROR, RRX). The barrel shifter is useful because it allows the instruction to work on constants that cannot normally be encoded in immediate form. ARM and Thumb instructions can be either 16 or 32 bits wide, so they cannot directly have 32-bit constants as a parameter; with the barrel shifter, an immediate can be transformed into a larger value and moved to another register. Another way to move a 32-bit constant into a register is to split the constant into two 16-bit halves and move them one a time; this is normally done with the MOVW and MOVT instructions. MOVT sets the top 16 bits of a register, and MOVW sets the bottom 16 bits.

The basic arithmetic and logical operations are ADD, SUB, MUL, AND, ORR, and EOR. Here are examples of their usage:

```
01: 4B 44          ADD     R3, R9              ; r3 = r3+r9
02: 0D F2 08 0B    ADDW    R11, SP, #8         ; r11 = sp+8
03: 04 EB 80 00    ADD.W   R0, R4, R0,LSL#2 ; r0 = r4 + (r0<<2)
04: EA B0          SUB     SP, SP, #0x1A8   ; sp = sp-0x1a8
```

```
05: 03 FB 05 F2    MUL.W     R2, R3, R5         ; r2 = r3*r5 (32bit result)
06: 14 F0 07 02    ANDS.W    R2, R4, #7         ; r2 = r4 & 7 (flag)
07: 83 EA C1 03    EOR.W     R3, R3, R1,LSL#3   ; r3 = r3 ^ (r1<<3)
08: 53 40          EORS      R3, R2             ; r3 = r3 ^ r2 (flag)
09: 43 EA 02 23    ORR.W     R3, R3, R2,LSL#8   ; r3 = r3 | (r2<<8)
10: 53 F0 02 03    ORRS.W    R3, R3, #2         ; r3 = r3 | 2 (flag)
11: 13 43          ORRS      R3, R2             ; r3 = r3 | r2 (flag)
```

Note the "S" after some of these instructions. Unlike x86, ARM arithmetic instructions do not set the conditional flag by default. The "S" suffix indicates that the instruction should set arithmetic conditional flags (zero, negative, etc.) depending on its result. Note that the MUL instruction truncates the result such that only the bottom 32 bits are stored in the destination register; for full 64-bit multiplication, use the SMULL and UMULL instructions (see ARM TRM for the details).

Where is the divide instruction? ARM does not have a native divide instruction. (ARMv7-R and ARMv7-M cores have SDIV and UDIV, but they are not discussed here.) In practice, the runtime will have a software implementation for division and code simply call into it when needed. Here is an example with the Windows C runtime:

```
01: 41 46          MOV       R1, R8
02: 30 46          MOV       R0, R6
03: 35 F0 9E FF    BL        __rt_udiv ; software implementation of udiv
```

Branching and Conditional Execution

Every example discussed so far has been executed in a linear manner. Most programs will have conditionals and loops. At the assembly level, these constructs are implemented using conditional flags, which are stored in the application program status register (APSR). The APSR is an alias of the CPSR and is similar to the EFLAG in x86. Figure 2-5 illustrates the relevant flags, described as follows:

- N (Negative flag)—It is set when the result of an operation is negative (the result's most significant bit is 1).

- Z (Zero flag)—It is set when the result of an operation is zero.

- C (Carry flag)—It is set when the result of an operation between two unsigned values overflows.

- V (Overflow flag)—It is set when the result of an operation between two signed values overflows.

- IT (If-then bits)—These encode various conditions for the Thumb instruction IT. They are discussed later.

The N, Z, C, and V bits are identical to the SF, ZF, CF, and OF bits in the EFLAG register on x86. They are used to implement conditionals and loops in higher-level languages; they are also used to support conditional execution at the instruction level. Equality is described in terms of these flags. Table 2-1 shows common relationships and corresponding flags.

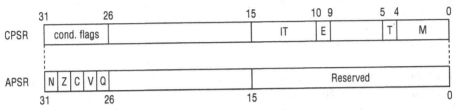

Figure 2-5

Table 2-1: Conditional code and meaning

SUFFIX/CODE	MEANING	FLAGS
EQ	Equal	Z==1
NE	Not equal	Z==0
MI	Minus, negative	N==1
PL	Plus, positive, or zero	N==0
HI	Unsigned higher/above	C==1 and Z==0
LS	Unsigned lower/below	C==0 or Z==1
GE	Signed greater than or equal	N==V
LT	Signed less than	N!=V
GT	Signed greater than	Z==0 and N==V
LE	Signed less than or equal	Z==1 or N!=V

Instructions can be conditionally executed by adding one of these suffixes at the end. For example, BLT means to branch if the LT condition is true. (This is the same as JL in x86.) By default, instructions do not update conditional flags unless the "S" suffix is used; the comparison instructions (CBZ, CMP, TST, CMN, and TEQ) update the flags automatically because they are usually used before branch instructions.

The most common comparison instruction is probably CMP. Its syntax is CMP Rn, X, where Rn is a register and X can be an immediate, a register, or a barrel shift operation. Its semantic is identical to that in x86: It performs Rn - X, sets the appropriate flags, and discards the result. It is usually followed by a conditional branch. Here is an example of its usage and pseudo-code:

ARM

```
01: B3 EB E7 7F    CMP.W    R3, R7, ASR #31
02: 05 DB          BLT      loc_less
03: 01 DC          BGT      loc_greater
04: BD 42          CMP      R5, R7
05: 02 D9          BLS      loc_less
```

```
06:                    loc_greater
07: 07 3D              SUBS        R5, #7
08: 6E F1 00 0E        SBC.W       LR, LR, #0
09:                    loc_less
10: A5 FB 08 12        UMULL.W     R1, R2, R5, R8
11: 87 FB 08 04        SMULL.W     R0, R4, R7, R8
12: 0E FB 08 23        MLA.W       R3, LR, R8, R2
```

Pseudo C

```
if (r3 < r7) { goto loc_less; }
else if ( r3 > r7) { goto loc_greater; }
else if ( r5 < r7) { goto loc_less; }
```

The next most common comparison instruction is TST; its syntax is identical to that of CMP. Its semantic is identical to TEST in x86: It performs Rn & X, sets the appropriate flags, and discards the result. It is usually used to test whether a value is equal to another or to test for flags. Like most compare instructions, it is typically followed by a conditional branch. Here is an example:

```
01: AB 8A              LDRH        R3, [R5,#0x14]
02: 13 F0 02 0F        TST.W       R3, #2
03: 09 D0              BEQ         loc_10179DA
04: ...
05:                loc_10179BE
06: AA 8A              LDRH        R2, [R5,#0x14]
07: 12 F0 04 0F        TST.W       R2, #4
08: 02 D0              BEQ         loc_10179E8
```

In Thumb-2 state, there are two popular comparison instructions: CBZ and CBNZ. Their syntax is simple: CBZ/CBNZ Rn, label, where Rn is a register and label is an offset to branch to if the condition is true. CBZ then branches to label if the register is zero. CBNZ is same except that it checks for a non-zero condition. These instructions are usually used to determine whether a number is 0 or a pointer is NULL. Here is a typical usage:

ARM

```
01: 10 F0 48 FF    BL          foo
                   ; foo returns a pointer in r0
02: 28 B1              CBZ         R0, loc_100BC8E
03: ...
04:                loc_100BC8E
05: 01 20              MOVS        R0, #1
06: 28 E0              B           locret_100BCE4
07: ...
08:                locret_100BCE4
09: BD E8 F8 89        POP.W       {R3-R8,R11,PC}
```

Pseudo C

```
type *a;
a = foo(...);
if (a == NULL) { return 1; }
```

The other comparison instructions are CMN/TEQ, which performs addition/exclusive-or on the operands. Because they are not commonly used they are not covered here.

You have seen that the branch instruction (B) can be made to do conditional branches by adding a suffix (BEQ, BLE, BLT, BLS, etc.). In fact, most ARM instructions can be conditionally executed in the same way. If the condition is not met, the instruction can be seen as a no-op. Instruction-level conditional execution can reduce branches, which may speed up execution time. Here is an example:

ARM

```
01: 00 00 50 E3    CMP      R0, #0
02: 01 00 A0 03    MOVEQ    R0, #1
03: 68 00 D0 15    LDRNEB   R0, [R0,#0x68]
04: 1E FF 2F E1    BX       LR
```

Pseudo C

```
unk_type *a = ...;
if (a == NULL) { return 1; }
else { return a->off_48; }
```

You immediately know that R0 is a pointer because of the LDR instruction in line 3. Line 1 checks whether R0 is NULL. If true (EQ), then line 2 sets R0 to 1; otherwise, NEQ loads the value at R0+0x68 into R0 (line 3) and then returns. Because EQ and NEQ cannot be true at the same time, only one of the instructions will be executed. Note that there are no branch instructions.

Thumb State

Unlike most ARM instructions, Thumb instructions cannot be conditionally executed (with the exception of B) without the IT (if-then) instruction. This is a Thumb-2-specific instruction that allows up to four instructions after it to be conditionally executed. The general syntax is as follows: ITxyz cc, where cc is the conditional code for the first instruction; x, y, and z describe the condition for the second, third, and fourth instruction, respectively. Conditions for instructions after the first are described by one of two letters: T or E. T means that the condition must match cc to be executed; E means to execute only if the condition is the inverse of cc. Consider the following example:

ARM

```
01: 00 2B         CMP      R3, #0
             ; check and set condition
02: 12 BF            ITEE NE
             ; begin IT block
03: BC FA 8C F0   CLZNE.W R0, R12
             ; first instruction
```

```
04: B6 FA 86 F0    CLZEQ.W R0, R6
              ; second instruction
05: 20 30          ADDEQ   R0, #0x20
              ; third instruction
```

Pseudo C

```
if (R3 != 0) {
 R0 = countleadzeros(R12);
} else {
 R0 = countleadzeros(R6);
 R0 += 0x20
}
```

Line 1 performs a comparison and sets a conditional flag. Line 2 specifies the conditions and start the if-then block. NE is the execution condition for the first instruction; the first E (after IT) indicates that the execution condition for the second instruction is the inverse of the first. (EQ is the inverse of NE.) The second E indicates the same for the third instruction. Lines 3–5 are instructions inside the IT block.

Due to its flexibility, the IT instruction can be used to reduce the number of instructions required to implement short conditionals in Thumb state.

Switch-Case

Switch-case statements can be understood as many if-else statements bundled together. Because the test expression and target label are known at compile time, compilers usually construct a jump table to store addresses (ARM) or offsets (Thumb) for each case handler. After determining the index into the jump table, the compiler indirectly branches to the destination by loading the destination address into PC. In ARM state, this is normally done by LDR with PC as the destination and base register. Consider the following example:

```
01:  ; R1 is the case
02: 0B 00 51 E3    CMP      R1, #0xB   ; is it within range?
03: 01 F1 9F 97    LDRLS    PC, [PC,R1,LSL#2] ; yes, switch by
                                       ; indexing into the table
04: 14 00 00 EA    B        loc_DD10   ; no, break
05: 3C DD 00 00+   DCD loc_DD3C   ; begin of jump table
06: 4C DD 00 00+   DCD loc_DD4C
07: 68 DD 00 00+   DCD loc_DD68
08: 8C DD 00 00+   DCD loc_DD8C
09: BC DD 00 00+   DCD loc_DDBC
10: F0 DD 00 00+   DCD loc_DDF0
11: 38 DE 00 00+   DCD loc_DE38
12: 38 DE 00 00+   DCD loc_DE38
13: EC DC 00 00+   DCD loc_DCEC  ; case/index 8
14: EC DC 00 00+   DCD loc_DCEC  ; case/index 9
15: 3C DD 00 00+   DCD loc_DD3C
```

```
16: 3C DD 00 00     DCD loc_DD3C
17:                  loc_DCEC   ; handler for case 8,9
18: 00 00 A0 E3     MOV    R0, #0
19: 08 10 41 E2     SUB    R1, R1, #8
20: 04 30 A0 E3     MOV    R3, #4
21: 14 00 82 E5     STR    R0, [R2,#0x14]
22: BC 31 C2 E1     STRH   R3, [R2,#0x1C]
23: 10 10 82 E5     STR    R1, [R2,#0x10]
```

Line 2 checks whether the case is within range; if not, then it executes the default handler (line 4). Line 3 conditionally executes if R1 is within range; it branches to the case-handler by indexing into the jump table and loads the destination address in PC. Recall that PC is 8 bytes after the current instruction (in ARM state), so the jump table is usually stored 8 bytes from the LDR instruction.

In Thumb mode, the same concept applies except that the jump table contains offsets instead of addresses. ARM added new instructions to support table-branching with byte or half-word offsets: TBB and TBH. For TBB, the table entries are byte values; for TBH, they are half-words. The table entries must be multiplied by two and added to PC to get the final branch destination. Here is the preceding example using TBB:

```
01: 0101E600 0B 29         CMP    R1, #0xB ; is it within range?
02: 0101E602 76 D8         BHI    loc_101E6F2 ; no, break
03: 0101E604 04 26         MOVS   R6, #4
04: 0101E606 DF E8 01 F0   TBB.W  [PC,R1] ; branch using table offset
05: 0101E60A 06            jpt_101E606 DCB 6 ; begin of jump table
06: 0101E60B 09            DCB 9
07: 0101E60C 0F            DCB 0xF
08: 0101E60D 18            DCB 0x18
09: 0101E60E 24            DCB 0x24
10: 0101E60F 32            DCB 0x32
11: 0101E610 45            DCB 0x45
12: 0101E611 45            DCB 0x45
13: 0101E612 6D            DCB 0x6D ; offset for 8
14: 0101E613 6D            DCB 0x6D ; offset for 9
15: 0101E614 06            DCB 6
16: 0101E615 06            DCB 6
17: ...
18: 0101E6E4               loc_101E6E4   ; handler for case 8,9
19: 0101E6E4 B1 F1 08 03   SUBS.W R3, R1, #8
20: 0101E6E8 00 20         MOVS   R0, #0
21: 0101E6EA 60 61         STR    R0, [R4,#0x14]
```

Because it is in Thumb state, PC is 4 bytes after the current instruction; hence, for case 8, the table entry would be at address 0x0101E612 (=0x0101E60A+8), which is 0x6d, and the handler is at 0x101E6E4 (=PC+(0x6d*2)). Similar to the previous example, the jump table is usually placed after the TBB/TBH instruction. Note that the TBB/TBH are used only in Thumb state.

Miscellaneous

This section briefly discusses concepts that are not directly related to the process of reverse engineering. However, in practice, they are important to know because they may contribute to your overall knowledge. More knowledge is always good. You can skip this section on a first read.

Just-in-Time and Self-Modifying Code

ARM supports the concept of just-in-time (JIT) and self-modifying code (SMC). JIT code is native code that is dynamically generated by a JIT compiler; for example, the Microsoft .NET languages compile to an intermediate language (MSIL) that is converted into native machine code (x86, x64, ARM, etc.) for execution on the CPU core. SMC is code that is generated or modified by the current instruction stream. A common example of SMC is encoded shellcode that is decoded and executed at run-time. Both JIT and SMC code require writing to memory new data that is then later fetched by execution.

The ARM core has two separate cache lines for instruction (i-cache) and data (d-cache); instructions are executed from the i-cache, and memory access is through the d-cache. These cache lines are not guaranteed to be coherent, which means that data written to one cache may not be immediately visible to the other. For example, suppose the i-cache holds four instructions from the instruction stream and the user generates new or modified instructions at the same spot (which updates the d-cache). Because they are not coherent, the i-cache may not know about the recent modification, so it executes stale instructions (which may lead to mysterious crashes or incorrect results). If you are writing JIT systems or shellcode, this is clearly not a desirable situation. The solution is to explicitly force the i-cache to be refreshed (also known as *flushing the cache*). On ARM, this is done by updating a register in the system control coprocessor (CP15):

```
01: 4F F0 00 00    MOV.W    R0, #0
02: 07 EE 15 0F    MCR      p15, 0, R0,c7,c5, 0
```

Most operating systems provide an interface for this operation, so you do not have to write it yourself. On Linux, use __clear_cache; on Windows, use FlushInstructionCache.

Synchronization Primitives

ARM does not have an instruction similar to cmpxchg (compare-and-exchange) in x86; instead, two instructions are used: LDREX and STREX. These instructions are just like LDR/STR, except that they acquire exclusive access to the memory address before loading/storing. Together, they are typically used to implement compare-and-exchange intrinsics. For example:

ARM

```
01: 01 21           MOVS        R1, #1
02:                 loc_100C4B0
03: 54 E8 00 2F     LDREX.W     R2, [R4]
04: 1A B9           CBNZ        R2, loc_100C4BE
05: 44 E8 00 13     STREX.W     R3, R1, [R4] ; r3 is the result
06: 00 2B           CMP         R3, #0
07: F8 D1           BNE         loc_100C4B0
```

Pseudo C

```
if (InterlockedCompareExchange(&r4, 1, 0) == 0) { do stuff; }
```

Line 3 performs an atomic load into R2 and compares it against 0; if it is zero, then it is exchanged with zero and the result is returned in R3. This is actually the implementation of `InterlockedCompareExchange` in Windows.

From time to time, you will run into code using the DMB, DSB, and ISB instructions. These are barrier instructions that ensure that memory access and instruction fetches are synchronized before executing subsequent instructions. This is necessary in some cases because memory access and instructions can be executed out of order (i.e., the CPU might execute the instructions in a different order than what appears in the assembly code), and other executing threads may not see the updated result and consequently have an inconsistent view of the data. For this reason, you will often see these instructions used in code that implements locks.

System Services and Mechanisms

When an ARM core boots up, it starts executing code in the ARM state at the memory address 0x00000000 or 0xFFFF0000, depending on a setting in coprocessor 15. This is determined by the vector (V) bit in the system control register (CP15, C1/C0). If it is 0, then the exception vector is at 0x00000000; otherwise, it is at 0xFFFF0000. This address is usually in flash memory (RAM has not been initialized yet so it cannot be used), and the content therein is commonly known as the *exception vectors*. ARM has a list of predefined vectors starting at the base address. The RESET exception handler is first in the table so it is executed after a reset event. Because it is the first code to be executed, it usually begins by performing basic hardware configuration and starts the boot process. Here is an exception vector taken from a real device:

```
01: 00000000 1A 00 00 EA    B  vect_RESET
02: 00000004 12 00 00 EA    B  vect_UNDEFINED_INSTRUCTION
```

```
03: 00000008 12 00 00 EA    B    vect_SUPERVISOR_CALL ; (for SWI/SVC)
04: 0000000C 12 00 00 EA    B    vect_PREFETCHABORT
05: ...
06: 00000054                    vect_UNDEFINED_INSTRUCTION
07: 00000054 FE FF FF EA    B    vect_UNDEFINED_INSTRUCTION
08: 00000058                    vect_SUPERVISOR_CALL
09: 00000058 FE FF FF EA    B    vect_SUPERVISOR_CALL
10: 0000005C                    vect_PREFETCHABORT
11: 0000005C FE FF FF EA    B    vect_PREFETCHABORT
12: ...
13: 00000070                    vect_RESET
14: 00000070 1C F1 9F E5    LDR PC, =0x10000078
15:              ; code has been mapped at 0x10000078
16:              ; begin executing there
17: ...
18: 10000078 18 01 9F E5    LDR R0, =0x2001
19: 1000007C 11 0F 0F EE    MCR p15, 0, R0,c15,c1, 0
20:              ; initializes a vendor-specific register
21: 10000080 00 00 A0 E1    NOP
22: 10000084 00 00 A0 E1    NOP
23: 10000088 00 00 A0 E1    NOP
24: 1000008C 78 00 A0 E3    MOV R0, #0x78
25: 10000090 10 0F 01 EE    MCR p15, 0, R0,c1,c0, 0
26:              ; initializes system control register
```

After initializing hardware, the reset exception code jumps to a bootloader that is typically located in flash memory, removable media (MMC, SD card, etc.), or some other form of storage. Some devices use U-Boot, a popular, open-source bootloader. The bootloader performs more hardware initialization, reads an OS image from storage and maps it into main memory, and transfers control there. After that, the operating system boots up and the system is ready for use.

An operating system manages hardware resources and provides services to users. Because user code (usually in USR mode) runs at a lower privilege than kernel/OS code (usually SVC mode), it has to use an interface to request service from the OS. In practice, the interface is provided through a software interrupt or special trap instruction provided by the processor; the service is commonly implemented as system calls. (For example, on Linux x86, you can use interrupt 0x80 or the special instruction SYSENTER to issue a system call; on x64, this is provided by the SYSCALL instruction.) On ARM, there is no dedicated system-call instruction, so software interrupt is used to implement syscalls. When a software interrupt happens, the processor switches to supervisor mode to handle the interrupt. Software interrupts can be triggered by the SWI/SVC instruction. (These instructions are identical except they are named differently.)

Both instructions take an immediate as the parameter—some operating systems use this parameter as an index into a system call table; and some do not use the parameter but require the system call number to be in a register (for example, Windows uses R12 for this purpose). On some Linux systems, the syscall number is put in R7 and arguments are passed via R0-R2. For example:

Linux (Ubuntu)

```
01: 05 20 A0 E1    MOV    R2, R5     ; 3rd arg
02: 06 10 A0 E1    MOV    R1, R6     ; 2nd arg
03: 09 00 A0 E1    MOV    R0, R9     ; 1st arg
04: 92 70 A0 E3    MOV    R7, #0x92
; syscall number
05: 00 00 00 EF    SVC    0 ; make the syscall
06: 04 00 70 E3    CMN    R0, #4
; check return value
07: 00 30 A0 13    MOVNE  R3, #0
; condition move based on return value
```

Windows RT

```
ZwCreateFile (in ntdll)
4F F0 53 0C    MOV.W    R12, #0x53
01 DF          SVC      1
70 47          BX       LR
           ; End of function ZwCreateFile
```

SVC transitions to supervisor mode, copies the relevant user registers into their own space, performs whatever function is requested, and returns when it is done. How does the SVC know where to return? Normally, it returns to the instruction after SVC. Before processing the exception, SVC mode copies the return address to R14_svc, which is a banked register in SVC mode. Banked registers are those that have meaning only in the context of a particular processor mode. For example, R13_svc and R14_svc are banked registers in SVC mode so they will have different values than R13-14 in USR mode.

While there is a dedicated instruction for software breakpoint BKPT, there are a few ways that it can be implemented. The first is through the BKPT instruction, which triggers the prefetch abort exception handler; the handler can then pass control to a debugger. Another common method is to trigger the undefined instruction exception handler via an undefined instruction. The ARM instruction encoding has a reserved range that is guaranteed to be undefined.

Instructions

Every instruction in ARM state encodes an arithmetic condition to support conditional execution. By default, the condition is AL (always execute). This condition is encoded in the four most significant bits in the opcode (bits 28–31); AL is defined as 0b1110, which is 0xE. If you pay close attention to the assembly snippets (in ARM state), you will notice that the byte code usually has an 0xE* pattern at the end. In fact, if you look at the instructions in a hex editor, you will notice that 0xE* commonly occurs every four bytes. For example:

```
FE FF FF EA FE FF FF EA FE FF FF EA FE FF FF EA
FE FF FF EA 1C F1 9F E5 00 00 A0 E1 18 01 9F E5
11 0F 0F EE 00 00 A0 E1 00 00 A0 E1 00 00 A0 E1
78 00 A0 E3 10 0F 01 EE 00 00 A0 E1 00 00 A0 E1
00 00 A0 E1 00 00 A0 E3 17 0F 08 EE 17 0F 07 EE
```

Why is it important to know this pattern? Because ARM code is sometimes embedded in ROM or flash memory and may not follow a specific file format. In your reverse engineering journey, sometimes you will just be given a raw memory dump without much context, so it can be useful to guess the architecture by looking at the opcodes. The other reason is related to exploits. Shellcode can be embedded inside an exploit delivered over the network or in a document; to analyze it, you must extract the shellcode from the rest of the network traffic. Sometimes it is straightforward and the shellcode boundary is obvious, other times it is not. However, if you can recognize the pattern, you can quickly guess the start/end of code. The ability to recognize instruction boundaries in a seemingly random blob of data is important. Maybe you will appreciate it later.

Walk-Through

Having learned all the fundamentals, you can apply them in this section by fully decompiling an unknown function. This function encompasses many concepts and techniques covered in this chapter, so it is an excellent way to put your knowledge to the test. Along the way, you will also learn new skills that were only hinted at in the early sections. Because the function is somewhat long, we put it in graph form to save space and improve readability. The function body is shown in Figure 2-6, and all the code line numbers discussed in this section refer to this figure.

Following is the context in which it is called:

```
01: 17 9B          LDR          R3, [SP,#0x5c]
02: 16 9A          LDR          R2, [SP,#0x58]
03: 51 46          MOV          R1, R10
04: 20 46          MOV          R0, R4
05: FF F7 98 FF    BL           unk_function
```

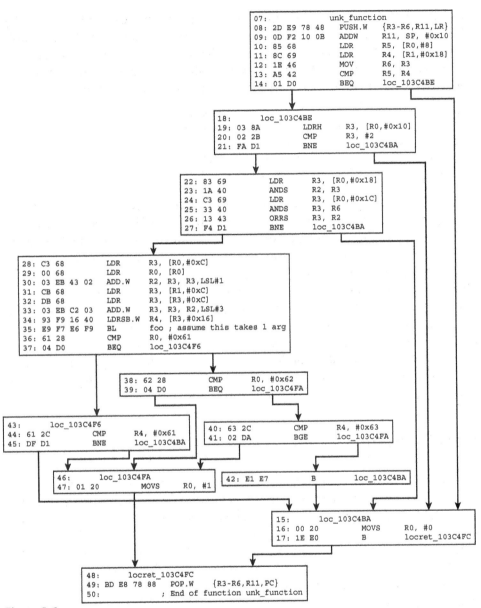

Figure 2-6

When approaching an unknown function (or any block of code), the first step is to determine what you know for certain about it. The following list enumerates these facts and how you know them:

- The code is Thumb state and the instruction set is Thumb-2. You know this because: 1) prologue and epilogue (lines 1 and 49) use the PUSH/POP pattern; 2) instruction size is either 16 or 32 bits in width; 3) the disassembler shows the .w prefix for some instructions, indicating that they are using the 32-bit encoding.

- The function preserves R3–R6 and R11. You know this because they are saved and restored in the prologue (line 1) and epilogue (line 49), respectively.
- The function takes at most four arguments (R0–R3) and returns a Boolean (R0). You know this because according to the ARM ABI (Application Binary Interface), the first four parameters are passed in R0–R3 (the rest are pushed on the stack) and the return value is in R0. It is "at most four" in this case because you saw that before calling the function in line 5, R0–R3 are initialized with some values and you do not see any other instructions writing to the stack (for additional arguments). At this point, the function prototype is as follows:

  ```
  BOOL unk_function(int, int, int, int)
  ```

- The first two arguments' type is "pointer to an object." You know this because R0 and R1 are the base address in a load instruction (lines 10–11). The types are most likely structures because there is access to offset 0x10, 0x18, 0x1c, and so on (line 10, 11, 19, 22, 24, 28, etc.). You can be nearly certain that they are not arrays because the access/load pattern is not sequential. It is uncertain whether R0 and R1 are pointers to one or two different structure types without further context. For now, you can assume that they are two different types. You update the prototype as follows:

  ```
  BOOL unk_function(struct1 *, struct2 *, int, int)
  ```

- loc_103C4BA is the exit path to return 0; loc_103C4FA is the exit path to return 1; and locret_103C4FC returns from the function. Hence, branches to these locations indicate that you are done with the function.
- The third and fourth arguments are of type integer. You know this because R2 and R3 are being used in AND/ORR operations (lines 23, 25, and 26). While there is indeed a possibility that they can be pointers, it is unlikely to be the case unless they were encoding/decoding pointers; and even if they were pointers, you should see them being used in load/store operations but you don't.
- Even though R11 is adjusted to be 0x10 bytes above the stack pointer, it is never used after that instruction. Hence, it can be ignored.
- The function foo (line 35) takes one argument. Its entire body is not included here due to space constraints. Just assume this is a given for the sake of simplicity.

Having enumerated known facts, you now need to use them to logically derive other useful facts. The next important task is to delve into the two unknown structures identified. Obviously you cannot recover its entire layout because only some of its elements are referenced in the function; however, you can still infer the field type information.

R0 is of type struct1 *. In line 10, it loads a field member at offset 0x8 and then compares it with R4 (line 13). R4 is a field member at offset 0x18 in the structure struct2 (R1). Because they are being compared to each other, you know that they are of the same type. Line 13 compares these two fields. If they are equal, then execution proceeds to `loc_103C4BE`; otherwise, 0 is returned (line 15). Because of the equality compare, you can infer that these two fields are integers.

Line 19 loads another field member from `struct1` and compares it against 2; if it is not equal, then 0 is returned (line 21). You can infer that the field type is a short because of the `LDRH` instruction (loads a half-word).

Lines 22–23 load another field member from `struct1` and `AND`s it against the third argument (which is assumed to be an integer). Lines 25–27 do something similar with the fourth argument. Because of these operations, you can infer that field members at offset `0x18` and `0x1c` are integers.

The structure definitions so far are as follows:

```
struct1
...
    +0x008 field08_i ; same type as struct2.field18_i
...
    +0x010 field10_s ; short
...
    +0x018 field18_i ; int
    +0x01c field1c_i ; int

struct2
...
    +0x018 field18_i ; same type as struct1.field08_i
```

> **NOTE** For struct field names, you might follow the habit of indicating the offset and the "type." For example, an "I" suffix means integer (or some generic 32-bit type), "s" means short (16-bit), "c" means char (1 byte), and "p" means pointer of some type. This enables you to quickly remember what their types are. When you determine their true purpose, you can then rename them to something more meaningful.

Given these types, you can already recover the pseudo-code of everything from line 1 to 27. It is as follows:

```
struct1 *arg1 = ...;
struct1 *arg2 = ...;
int arg3 = ...;
int arg4 = ...;

BOOL result = unk_function(arg1, arg2, arg3, arg4);
if (arg1->field08_i == arg2->field18_i) {
  if (arg1->field10_s != 2) return 0;
  if ( ((arg1->field18_i & arg3) |
        (arg1->field1c_i & arg4)
       ) != 0
     ) return 0;
...
} else {
```

```
    return 0;
}
```

NOTE   It is a bit suspicious that the AND operation is being used on two adjacent integer fields. This usually means that they are actually 64-bit integers split into two registers/memory locations. This is a common pattern used to access 64-bit constants on 32-bit architectures.

Astute readers will notice that lines 25–27 may seem a bit redundant. ANDS sets the condition flags, ORRS immediately overwrites it, and BNE takes the flag from ORRS; hence, the conditions set by ANDS are really not necessary. The compiler generates this redundancy because it is optimizing for code density: AND will be 4 bytes long, but ANDS is only 2 bytes. MOV and MOVS are also subjected to the same optimization. You will often see this pattern in code optimized for Thumb.

Line 28 loads another field from struct1 into R3; line 29 loads from offset zero of the same structure into R0; and line 30 sets R2 to R3*3 (=R3+(R3<<1)). Line 31 loads a field from struct2 into R3 and then accesses another field using that as a base pointer. This implies that you have a pointer to another structure inside struct2 at offset 0xC. Line 32 loads a field from that new structure into R3; line 33 updates it to be R3+R2*8; and line 34 uses that as a base address and loads a signed short value at offset 0x16 of another structure into R4.

Let's update the structure definition before continuing:

```
struct1
    +0x000 field00_i ; int
...
    +0x008 field08_i ; same type as struct2.field18_i
    +0x00c field0c_i ; integer
...
    +0x010 field10_s ; short
...
    +0x018 field18_i ; int
    +0x01c field1c_i ; int
...

struct2
...
    +0x00c field0c_p ; struct3 *
...
    +0x018 field18_i ; same type as struct1.field08_i
...

struct3
...
    +0x00c field0c_p ; struct4 *
...

struct4 (size=0x18=24) // why?
```

```
...
    +0x016 field16_c; char
    +0x017 end
```

You could deduce that there was an array involved because of the multiplication/scaling factor (lines 30 and 33); there were not two arrays because R2–R3 in line 30 is not a base address but an index. Also, it does not make sense for a base address to be multiplied by 3. The base address of the array is R3 in line 33 because it is being indexed with R2. You inferred that each array element must be 0x18 (24) because after simplification, it was R2*3*8, where R2 is the index and 24 is the scale.

Figure 2-7 illustrates the relationships between the four structures.

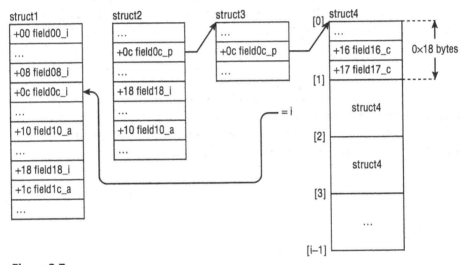

Figure 2-7

Here is the pseudo-code for lines 28–35:

```
r3 = arg1->field0c_i;
r2 = r3 + r3<<1
   = arg1->field0c_i*3;
r3 = arg2->field0c_p;
r3 = arg2->field0c_p->field0c_p;
r3 = arg2->field0c_p->field0c_p + r2*8
   = arg2->field0c_p->field0c_p + arg1->field0c_i*24;
   = arg2->field0c_p->field0c_p[arg1->field0c_i];
r4 = arg2->field0c_p->field0c_p[arg1->field0c_i].field16_c;
r0 = foo(arg1->field00_i);
```

The rest of the function is simply comparing the return value from foo and r4. The full pseudo-code now looks like this:

```
struct1 *arg1 = ...;
struct2 *arg2 = ...;
```

```
int arg3 = ...;
int arg4 = ...;

BOOL result = unk_function(arg1, arg2, arg3, arg4);

BOOL unk_function(struct1 *arg1, struct2 *arg2, int arg3, int arg4)
{
  char a;
  int b;
  if (arg1->field08_i == arg2->field18_i) {
    if (arg1->field10_s != 2) return 0;
    if ( ((arg1->field18_i & arg3) |
          (arg1->field1c_i & arg4)
         ) != 0
       ) return 0;
    b = foo(arg1->field00_i);
    a = arg2->field0c_p->field0c_p[arg1->field0c_i].field16_c;
    if (b == 0x61 && a != 0x61) {
      return 0;
    } else { return 1;}
    if (b == 0x62 && a >= 0x63) {
      return 1;
    } else { return 0;}
  } else {
   return 0;
  }
}
```

While this function used multiple, interconnected data structures whose full layout is unclear, you can see how you were still able to recover some of the field types and their relationship with others. You also learned how to recognize a type's width and signedness by considering the instruction and conditional code associated with them.

Next Steps

This chapter provided the fundamental skills required to statically reverse engineer ARM code. We intentionally avoided writing an instruction manual and left out many details; to improve your skills, you will need to do the exercises, practice, and read the ARM manuals (these activities go together). The technical reference manual can be somewhat dense, but the knowledge acquired from this chapter will make it much easier to understand.

Your next step should be to buy an ARM device and experiment with it. There are many ARM devices to choose from, but perhaps the two most conducive to learning are the BeagleBoard and the PandaBoard. These are development boards intended to introduce people to embedded development on the ARM platform; they are relatively powerful, cheap ($150–$170), well-documented, and have a large user community. (You may not run into many people who understand ARM assembly, but that's okay because you already read this chapter. The areas for which you may need help are usually related to the onboard peripherals and how they are programmed/controlled.) You can install Linux with a full development environment on these boards, so it is very simple to test your knowledge of ARM.

Exercises

The exercises are included to ensure that you have a good understanding of the concepts and to raise your motivation. Some of the exercises were intentionally selected to include instructions that were not covered in the chapter so that you get used to reading the manual (a very important habit); calling context is also omitted to make you think more. Every function is self-contained to facilitate complete decompilation; some are selected such that you can verify your answer if you have done enough of them. It is recommended that you write comments and notes, and draw connections between branches/labels, on the exercise themselves.

For the code in each exercise, do the following in order (whenever possible):

- Determine whether it is in Thumb or ARM state.
- Explain each instruction's semantic. If the instruction is LDR/STR, explain the addressing mode as well.
- Identify the types (width and signedness) for every possible object. For structures, recover field size, type, and friendly name whenever possible. Not all structure fields will be recoverable because the function may only access a few fields. For each type recovered, explain to yourself (or someone else) how you inferred it.
- Recover the function prototype.
- Identify the function prologue and epilogue.
- Explain what the function does and then write pseudo-code for it.
- Decompile the function back to C and give it a meaningful name.

1. Figure 2-8 shows a function that takes two arguments. It may seem somewhat challenging at first, but its functionality is very common. Have patience.

2. Figure 2-9 shows a function that was found in the export table.

3. Here is a simple function:

```
01:                     mystery3
02: 83 68               LDR          R3, [R0,#8]
03: 0B 60               STR          R3, [R1]
04: C3 68               LDR          R3, [R0,#0xC]
05: 00 20               MOVS         R0, #0
06: 4B 60               STR          R3, [R1,#4]
07: 70 47               BX           LR
08:                     ; End of function mystery3
```

4. Figure 2-10 shows another easy function.

5. Figure 2-11 is simple as well. The actual string names have been removed so you cannot cheat by searching the Internet.

6. Figure 2-12 involves some twiddling.

7. Figure 2-13 illustrates a common routine, but you may not have seen it implemented this way.

8. In Figure 2-14, byteArray is a 256-character array whose content is byte-Array[] = {0, 1, …, 0xff}.

9. What does the function shown in Figure 2-15 do?

10. Figure 2-16 is a function from Windows RT. Read MSDN if needed. Ignore the security PUSH/POP cookie routines.

11. In Figure 2-17, sub_101651C takes three arguments and returns nothing. If you complete this exercise, you should pat yourself on the back.

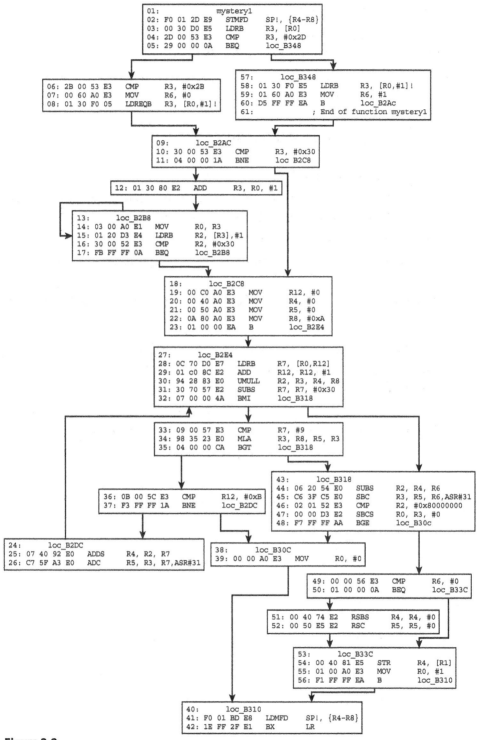

Figure 2-8

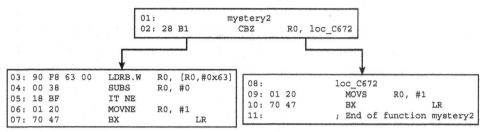

Figure 2-9

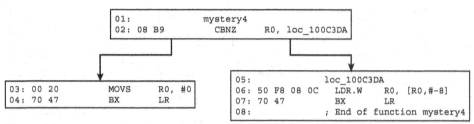

Figure 2-10

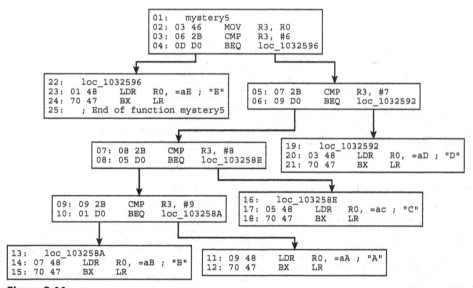

Figure 2-11

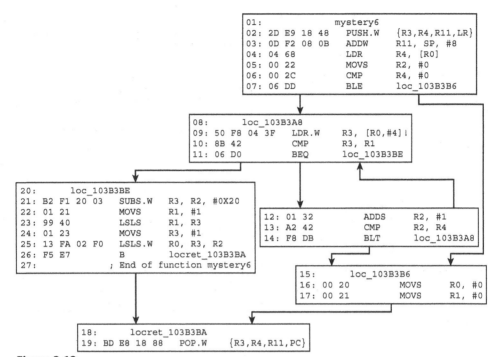

Figure 2-12

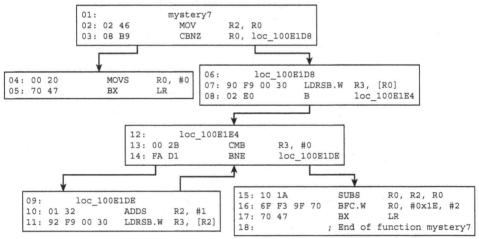

Figure 2-13

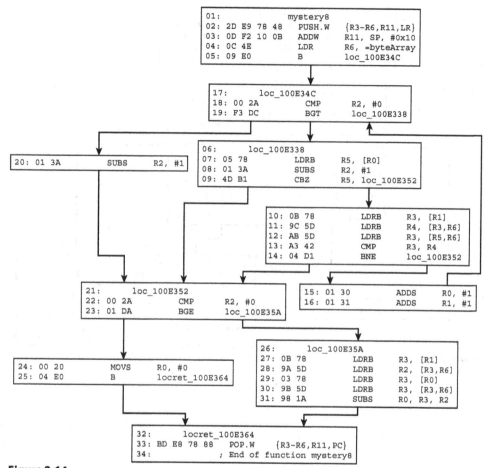

Figure 2-14

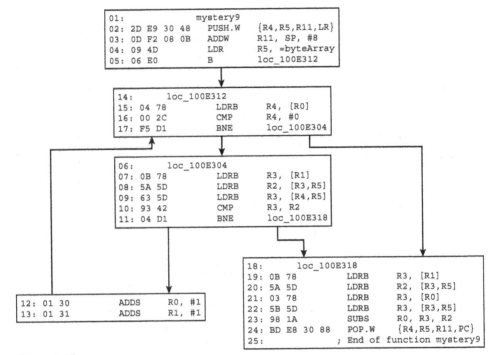

```
01:                 mystery9
02: 2D E9 30 48     PUSH.W      {R4,R5,R11,LR}
03: 0D F2 08 0B     ADDW        R11, SP, #8
04: 09 4D           LDR         R5, =byteArray
05: 06 E0           B           loc_100E312


14:       loc_100E312
15: 04 78           LDRB        R4, [R0]
16: 00 2C           CMP         R4, #0
17: F5 D1           BNE         loc_100E304


06:       loc_100E304
07: 0B 78           LDRB        R3, [R1]
08: 5A 5D           LDRB        R2, [R3,R5]
09: 63 5D           LDRB        R3, [R4,R5]
10: 93 42           CMP         R3, R2
11: 04 D1           BNE         loc_100E318


12: 01 30           ADDS        R0, #1
13: 01 31           ADDS        R1, #1


18:       loc_100E318
19: 0B 78           LDRB        R3, [R1]
20: 5A 5D           LDRB        R2, [R3,R5]
21: 03 78           LDRB        R3, [R0]
22: 5B 5D           LDRB        R3, [R3,R5]
23: 98 1A           SUBS        R0, R3, R2
24: BD E8 30 88     POP.W       {R4,R5,R11,PC}
25:                             ; End of function mystery9
```

Figure 2-15

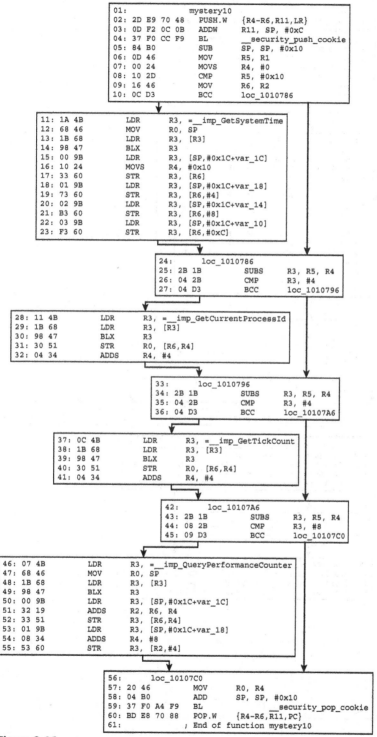

```
01:                 mystery10
02: 2D E9 70 48     PUSH.W    {R4-R6,R11,LR}
03: 0D F2 0C 0B     ADDW      R11, SP, #0xC
04: 37 F0 CC F9     BL        __security_push_cookie
05: 84 B0           SUB       SP, SP, #0x10
06: 0D 46           MOV       R5, R1
07: 00 24           MOVS      R4, #0
08: 10 2D           CMP       R5, #0x10
09: 16 46           MOV       R6, R2
10: 0C D3           BCC       loc_1010786
```

```
11: 1A 4B           LDR       R3, =__imp_GetSystemTime
12: 68 46           MOV       R0, SP
13: 1B 68           LDR       R3, [R3]
14: 98 47           BLX       R3
15: 00 9B           LDR       R3, [SP,#0x1C+var_1C]
16: 10 24           MOVS      R4, #0x10
17: 33 60           STR       R3, [R6]
18: 01 9B           LDR       R3, [SP,#0x1C+var_18]
19: 73 60           STR       R3, [R6,#4]
20: 02 9B           LDR       R3, [SP,#0x1C+var_14]
21: B3 60           STR       R3, [R6,#8]
22: 03 9B           LDR       R3, [SP,#0x1C+var_10]
23: F3 60           STR       R3, [R6,#0xC]
```

```
24:         loc_1010786
25: 2B 1B           SUBS      R3, R5, R4
26: 04 2B           CMP       R3, #4
27: 04 D3           BCC       loc_1010796
```

```
28: 11 4B           LDR       R3, =__imp_GetCurrentProcessId
29: 1B 68           LDR       R3, [R3]
30: 98 47           BLX       R3
31: 30 51           STR       R0, [R6,R4]
32: 04 34           ADDS      R4, #4
```

```
33:         loc_1010796
34: 2B 1B           SUBS      R3, R5, R4
35: 04 2B           CMP       R3, #4
36: 04 D3           BCC       loc_10107A6
```

```
37: 0C 4B           LDR       R3, =__imp_GetTickCount
38: 1B 68           LDR       R3, [R3]
39: 98 47           BLX       R3
40: 30 51           STR       R0, [R6,R4]
41: 04 34           ADDS      R4, #4
```

```
42:         loc_10107A6
43: 2B 1B           SUBS      R3, R5, R4
44: 08 2B           CMP       R3, #8
45: 09 D3           BCC       loc_10107C0
```

```
46: 07 4B           LDR       R3, =__imp_QueryPerformanceCounter
47: 68 46           MOV       R0, SP
48: 1B 68           LDR       R3, [R3]
49: 98 47           BLX       R3
50: 00 9B           LDR       R3, [SP,#0x1C+var_1C]
51: 32 19           ADDS      R2, R6, R4
52: 33 51           STR       R3, [R6,R4]
53: 01 9B           LDR       R3, [SP,#0x1C+var_18]
54: 08 34           ADDS      R4, #8
55: 53 60           STR       R3, [R2,#4]
```

```
56:         loc_10107C0
57: 20 46           MOV       R0, R4
58: 04 B0           ADD       SP, SP, #0x10
59: 37 F0 A4 F9     BL        __security_pop_cookie
60: BD E8 70 88     POP.W     {R4-R6,R11,PC}
61:                 ; End of function mystery10
```

Figure 2-16

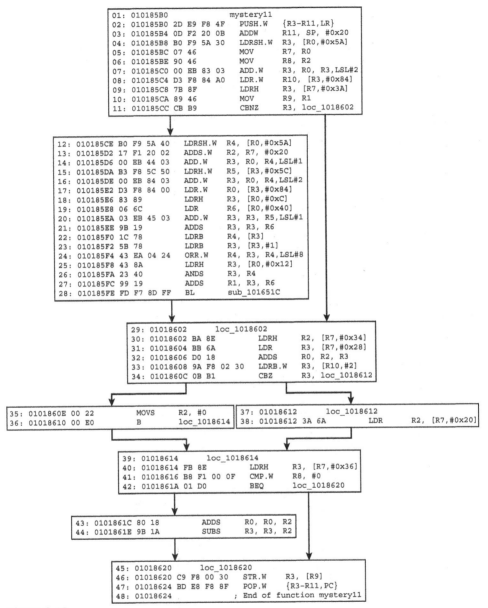

```
01: 010185B0                     mystery11
02: 010185B0 2D E9 F8 4F    PUSH.W    {R3-R11,LR}
03: 010185B4 0D F2 20 0B    ADDW      R11, SP, #0x20
04: 010185B8 B0 F9 5A 30    LDRSH.W   R3, [R0,#0x5A]
05: 010185BC 07 46          MOV       R7, R0
06: 010185BE 90 46          MOV       R8, R2
07: 010185C0 00 EB 83 03    ADD.W     R3, R0, R3,LSL#2
08: 010185C4 D3 F8 84 A0    LDR.W     R10, [R3,#0x84]
09: 010185C8 7B 8F          LDRH      R3, [R7,#0x3A]
10: 010185CA 89 46          MOV       R9, R1
11: 010185CC CB B9          CBNZ      R3, loc_1018602
```

```
12: 010185CE B0 F9 5A 40    LDRSH.W   R4, [R0,#0x5A]
13: 010185D2 17 F1 20 02    ADDS.W    R2, R7, #0x20
14: 010185D6 00 EB 44 03    ADD.W     R3, R0, R4,LSL#1
15: 010185DA B3 F8 5C 50    LDRH.W    R5, [R3,#0x5C]
16: 010185DE 00 EB 84 03    ADD.W     R3, R0, R4,LSL#2
17: 010185E2 D3 F8 84 00    LDR.W     R0, [R3,#0x84]
18: 010185E6 83 89          LDRH      R3, [R0,#0xC]
19: 010185E8 06 6C          LDR       R6, [R0,#0x40]
20: 010185EA 03 EB 45 03    ADD.W     R3, R3, R5,LSL#1
21: 010185EE 9B 19          ADDS      R3, R3, R6
22: 010185F0 1C 78          LDRB      R4, [R3]
23: 010185F2 5B 78          LDRB      R3, [R3,#1]
24: 010185F4 43 EA 04 24    ORR.W     R4, R3, R4,LSL#8
25: 010185F8 43 8A          LDRH      R3, [R0,#0x12]
26: 010185FA 23 40          ANDS      R3, R4
27: 010185FC 99 19          ADDS      R1, R3, R6
28: 010185FE FD F7 8D FF    BL        sub_101651C
```

```
29: 01018602              loc_1018602
30: 01018602 BA 8E        LDRH      R2, [R7,#0x34]
31: 01018604 BB 6A        LDR       R3, [R7,#0x28]
32: 01018606 D0 18        ADDS      R0, R2, R3
33: 01018608 9A F8 02 30  LDRB.W    R3, [R10,#2]
34: 0101860C 0B B1        CBZ       R3, loc_1018612
```

```
35: 0101860E 00 22    MOVS    R2, #0
36: 01018610 00 E0    B       loc_1018614
```

```
37: 01018612          loc_1018612
38: 01018612 3A 6A    LDR    R2, [R7,#0x20]
```

```
39: 01018614          loc_1018614
40: 01018614 FB 8E        LDRH    R3, [R7,#0x36]
41: 01018616 B8 F1 00 0F  CMP.W   R8, #0
42: 0101861A 01 D0        BEQ     loc_1018620
```

```
43: 0101861C 80 18    ADDS    R0, R0, R2
44: 0101861E 9B 1A    SUBS    R3, R3, R2
```

```
45: 01018620              loc_1018620
46: 01018620 C9 F8 00 30  STR.W    R3, [R9]
47: 01018624 BD E8 F8 8F  POP.W    {R3-R11,PC}
48: 01018624             ; End of function mystery11
```

Figure 2-17

The Windows Kernel

This chapter discusses the principles and techniques necessary for analyzing kernel-mode driver code, such as rootkits, on the Windows platform. Because drivers interact with the OS through well-defined interfaces, the analytical task can be decomposed into the following general objectives:

- Understand how core OS components are implemented
- Understand the structure of a driver
- Understand the user-driver and driver-OS interfaces and how Windows implements them
- Understand how certain driver software constructs are manifested in binary form
- Systematically apply knowledge from the previous steps in the general reverse engineering process

If the process of reverse engineering Windows drivers could be modeled as a discrete task, 90% would be understanding how Windows works and 10% would be understanding assembly code. Hence, the chapter is written as an introduction to the Windows kernel for reverse engineers. It begins with a discussion of the user-kernel interfaces and their implementation. Next, it discusses linked lists and how they are used in Windows. Then it explains concepts such as threads, processes, memory, interrupts, and how they are used in the kernel and drivers. After that it goes into the architecture of a kernel-mode driver and the driver-kernel programming interface. It concludes by applying these concepts to the reverse engineering of a rootkit.

Unless specified otherwise, every example in this chapter is taken from Windows 8 RTM.

Windows Fundamentals

We begin with a discussion of core Windows kernel concepts, including fundamental data structures and kernel objects relevant to driver programming and reverse engineering.

Memory Layout

Like many operating systems, Windows divides the virtual address space into two portions: kernel and user space. On x86 and ARM, the upper 2GB is reserved for the kernel and the bottom 2GB is for user processes. Hence, virtual addresses from 0 to 0x7fffffff are in user space, 0x80000000 and above are in kernel space. On x64, the same concept applies except that user space is from 0 to 0x000007ff`ffffffff and kernel space is 0xffff0800`00000000 and above. Figure 3-1 illustrates the general layout on x86 and x64. The kernel memory space is mostly the same in all processes. However, running processes only have access to their user address space; kernel-mode code can access both. (Some kernel address ranges, such as those in session and hyper space, vary from process to process.) This is an important fact to keep in mind because we will come back to it later when discussing execution context. Kernel- and user-mode pages are distinguished by a special bit in their page table entry.

When a thread in a process is scheduled for execution, the OS changes a processor-specific register to point to the page directory for that particular process. This is so that all virtual-to-physical address translations are specific to the process and not others. This is how the OS can have multiple processes and each one has the illusion that it owns the entire user-mode address space. On x86 and x64 architectures, the page directory base register is CR3; on ARM it is the translation table base register (TTBR).

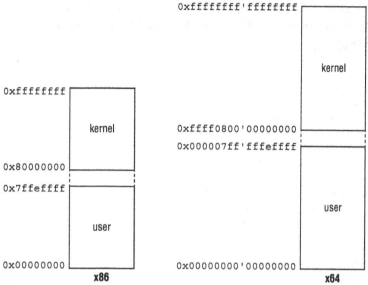

Figure 3-1

It is possible to change this default behavior by specifying the /3GB switch in the boot options. With /3GB, the user address space increases to 3GB and the remaining 1GB is for the kernel.

The user/kernel address ranges are stored in two symbols in the kernel: MmSystemRangeStart (kernel) and MmHighestUserAddress (user). These symbols can be viewed with a kernel debugger. You may notice that there is a 64KB gap between user/kernel space on x86/ARM. This region, usually referred to as the *no-access region*, is there so that the kernel does not accidentally cross the address boundary and corrupt user-mode memory. On x64, the astute reader may notice that 0xffff0800`00000000 is a non-canonical address and hence unusable by the operating system. This address is really only used as a separator between user/kernel space. The first usable address in kernel space starts at 0xffff8000`00000000.

Processor Initialization

When the kernel boots up, it performs some basic initialization for each processor. Most of the initialization details are not vital for daily reverse engineering tasks, but it is important to know a few of the core structures.

The *processor control region* (PCR) is a per-processor structure that stores critical CPU information and state. For example, on x86 it contains the base address of the IDT and current IRQL. Inside the PCR is another data structure called the *processor region control block* (PRCB). It is a per-processor structure that contains information about the processor—i.e., CPU type, model, speed, current thread

that it is running, next thread to run, queue of DPCs to run, and so on. Like
the PCR, this structure is undocumented, but you can still view its definition
with the kernel debugger:

x64 (x86 is similar)

PCR

```
0: kd> dt nt!_KPCR
   +0x000 NtTib              : _NT_TIB
   +0x000 GdtBase            : Ptr64 _KGDTENTRY64
   +0x008 TssBase            : Ptr64 _KTSS64
   +0x010 UserRsp            : Uint8B
   +0x018 Self               : Ptr64 _KPCR
   +0x020 CurrentPrcb        : Ptr64 _KPRCB
...
   +0x180 Prcb               : _KPRCB
```

PRCB

```
0: kd> dt nt!_KPRCB
   +0x000 MxCsr              : Uint4B
   +0x004 LegacyNumber       : UChar
   +0x005 ReservedMustBeZero : UChar
   +0x006 InterruptRequest   : UChar
   +0x007 IdleHalt           : UChar
   +0x008 CurrentThread      : Ptr64 _KTHREAD
   +0x010 NextThread         : Ptr64 _KTHREAD
   +0x018 IdleThread         : Ptr64 _KTHREAD
...
   +0x040 ProcessorState     : _KPROCESSOR_STATE
   +0x5f0 CpuType            : Char
   +0x5f1 CpuID              : Char
   +0x5f2 CpuStep            : Uint2B
   +0x5f2 CpuStepping        : UChar
   +0x5f3 CpuModel           : UChar
   +0x5f4 MHz                : Uint4B
...
   +0x2d80 DpcData           : [2] _KDPC_DATA
   +0x2dc0 DpcStack          : Ptr64 Void
   +0x2dc8 MaximumDpcQueueDepth : Int4B
...
```

ARM

PCR

```
0: kd> dt nt!_KPCR
   +0x000 NtTib              : _NT_TIB
   +0x000 TibPad0            : [2] Uint4B
   +0x008 Spare1             : Ptr32 Void
   +0x00c Self               : Ptr32 _KPCR
   +0x010 CurrentPrcb        : Ptr32 _KPRCB
...
```

PRCB

```
0: kd> dt nt!_KPCR
   +0x000 NtTib            : _NT_TIB
   +0x000 TibPad0          : [2] Uint4B
   +0x008 Spare1           : Ptr32 Void
   +0x00c Self             : Ptr32 _KPCR
   +0x010 CurrentPrcb      : Ptr32 _KPRCB
...
0: kd> dt nt!_KPRCB
   +0x000 LegacyNumber        : UChar
   +0x001 ReservedMustBeZero  : UChar
   +0x002 IdleHalt            : UChar
   +0x004 CurrentThread       : Ptr32 _KTHREAD
   +0x008 NextThread          : Ptr32 _KTHREAD
   +0x00c IdleThread          : Ptr32 _KTHREAD
...
   +0x020 ProcessorState      : _KPROCESSOR_STATE
   +0x3c0 ProcessorModel      : Uint2B
   +0x3c2 ProcessorRevision   : Uint2B
   +0x3c4 MHz                 : Uint4B
...
   +0x690 DpcData             : [2] _KDPC_DATA
   +0x6b8 DpcStack            : Ptr32 Void
...
   +0x900 InterruptCount      : Uint4B
   +0x904 KernelTime          : Uint4B
   +0x908 UserTime            : Uint4B
   +0x90c DpcTime             : Uint4B
   +0x910 InterruptTime       : Uint4B
...
```

The PCR for a current processor is always accessible from kernel-mode through special registers. It is stored in the FS segment (x86), GS segment (x64), or one of the system coprocessor registers (ARM). For example, the Windows kernel exports two routines to get the current EPROCESS and ETHREAD: PsGetCurrentProcess and PsGetCurrentThread. These routines work by querying the PCR/PRCB:

```
PsGetCurrentThread proc near
   mov    rax, gs:188h   ; gs:[0] is the PCR, offset 0x180 is the PRCB,
                         ; offset 0x8 into the PRCB is the CurrentThread
field
   retn
PsGetCurrentThread endp

PsGetCurrentProcess proc near
   mov    rax, gs:188h     ; get current thread (see above)
   mov    rax, [rax+0B8h]  ; offset 0x70 into the ETHREAD is the associated
                           ; process(actually ETHREAD.ApcState.Process)
   retn
PsGetCurrentProcess endp
```

System Calls

An operating system manages hardware resources and provides interfaces through which users can request them. The most commonly used interface is the system call. A system call is typically a function in the kernel that services I/O requests from users; it is implemented in the kernel because only high-privilege code can manage such resources. For example, when a word processor saves a file to disk, it first needs to request a file handle from the kernel, writes to the file, and then commits the file content to the hard disk; the OS provides system calls to acquire a file handle and write bytes to it. While these appear to be simple operations, the system calls must perform many important tasks in the kernel to service the request. For example, to get a file handle, it must interact with the file system (to determine whether the path is valid or not) and then ask the security manager to determine whether the user has sufficient rights to access the file; to write bytes to the file, the kernel needs to figure out which hard drive volume the file is on, send the request to the volume, and package the data into a structure understood by the underlying hard-drive controller. All these operations are done with complete transparency to the user.

The Windows system call implementation details are officially undocumented, so it is worth exploring for intellectual and pedagogical reasons. While the implementation varies between processors, the concepts remain the same. We will first explain the concepts and then discuss the implementation details on x86, x64, and ARM.

Windows describes and stores system call information with two data structures: a service table descriptor and an array of function pointers/offsets. The service table descriptor is a structure that holds metadata about system calls supported by the OS; its definition is officially undocumented, but many people have reverse engineered its important field members as follows. (You can also figure out these fields by analyzing the `KiSystemCall64` or `KiSystemService` routines.)

```
typedef struct _KSERVICE_TABLE_DESCRIPTOR
{
  PULONG Base; // array of addresses or offsets
  PULONG Count;
  ULONG Limit; // size of the array
  PUCHAR Number;
  ...
} KSERVICE_TABLE_DESCRIPTOR, *PKSERVICE_TABLE_DESCRIPTOR;
```

`Base` is a pointer to an array of function pointers or offsets (depending on the processor); a system call number is an index into this array. `Limit` is the number of entries in the array. The kernel keeps two global arrays of `KSERVICE_DESCRIPTOR_DESCRIPTOR`: `KeServiceDescriptorTable` and `KeServiceDescriptorTableShadow`. The former contains the native syscall table; the latter contains the same data, in addition to the syscall table for GUI threads. The kernel also keeps two global pointers to the arrays of addresses/offsets: KiServiceTable points to the non-GUI syscall table and W32pServiceTable points to the GUI one. Figure 3-2 illustrates how these data structures are related to each other on x86.

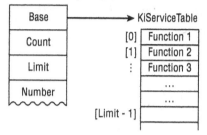

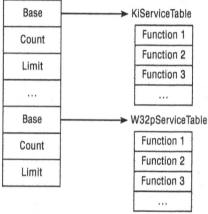

Figure 3-2

On x86, the Base field is an array of function pointers for the syscalls:

```
0: kd> dps nt!KeServiceDescriptorTable
81472400    813564d0 nt!KiServiceTable      ; Base
81472404    00000000
81472408    000001ad
8147240c    81356b88 nt!KiArgumentTable
0: kd> dd nt!KiServiceTable
813564d0    81330901 812cf1e2 81581540 816090af
813564e0    815be478 814b048f 8164e434 8164e3cb
813564f0    812dfa09 814e303f 814a0830 81613a9f
81356500    814e5b65 815b9e3a 815e0c4e 8158ce33
...
0: kd> dps nt!KiServiceTable
813564d0    81330901 nt!NtWorkerFactoryWorkerReady
813564d4    812cf1e2 nt!NtYieldExecution
813564d8    81581540 nt!NtWriteVirtualMemory
813564dc    816090af nt!NtWriteRequestData
```

```
813564e0   815be478 nt|NtWriteFileGather
813564e4   814b048f nt|NtWriteFile
```

However, on x64 and ARM, it is an array of 32-bit integers which encodes the system call offset and number of arguments passed on the stack. The offset is contained in the top 20 bits, and the number of arguments on the stack is contained in the bottom 4 bits. The offset is added to the base of `KiServiceTable` to get the real address of the syscall. For example:

```
0: kd> dps nt!KeServiceDescriptorTable
fffff803`955cd900  fffff803`952ed200 nt!KiServiceTable  ; Base
fffff803`955cd908  00000000`00000000
fffff803`955cd910  00000000`000001ad
fffff803`955cd918  fffff803`952edf6c nt!KiArgumentTable
0: kd> u ntdll!NtCreateFile
ntdll!NtCreateFile:
000007f8`34f23130 mov     r10,rcx
000007f8`34f23133 mov     eax,53h ; syscall number
000007f8`34f23138 syscall
...
0: kd> x nt!KiServiceTable
fffff803`952ed200 nt!KiServiceTable (<no parameter info>)
0: kd> dd nt!KiServiceTable + (0x53*4) L1
fffff803`952ed34c 03ea2c07        ; encoded offset and number of arguments
0: kd> u nt!KiServiceTable + (0x03ea2c07>>4) ; get the offset and add it to
Base
nt!NtCreateFile:
fffff803`956d74c0 sub     rsp,88h
fffff803`956d74c7 xor     eax,eax
fffff803`956d74c9 mov     qword ptr [rsp+78h],rax
fffff803`956d74ce mov     dword ptr [rsp+70h],20h
0: kd> ? 0x03ea2c07 & 0xf        ; number of arguments
Evaluate expression: 7 = 00000000`00000007
; NtCreateFile takes 11 arguments. The first 4 are passed via registers and
; the last 7 are passed on the stack
```

As demonstrated, every system call is identified by a number that is an index into `KiServiceTable` or `W32pServiceTable`. At the lowest level, user-mode APIs decompose to one or more system calls.

Conceptually, this is how system calls work on Windows. The implementation details vary depending on processor architecture and platform. System calls are typically implemented through software interrupts or architecture-specific instructions, the details of which are covered in the following sections.

Faults, Traps, and Interrupts

In preparation for the next sections, we need to introduce some basic terminology to explain how peripheral devices and software interact with the processor. In contemporary computing systems, the processor is typically connected to peripheral devices through a data bus such as PCI Express, FireWire, or USB. When a device requires the processor's attention, it causes an *interrupt* that forces the processor to pause whatever it is doing and handle the device's request. How does the processor know how to handle the request? At the highest level, one can think of an interrupt as being associated with a number that is then used to index into an array of function pointers. When the processor receives the interrupt, it executes the function at the index associated with the request and resumes execution wherever it was before the interrupt occurred. These are called *hardware interrupts* because they are generated by hardware devices. They are asynchronous by nature.

When the processor is executing an instruction, it may run into *exceptions*. For example, the instruction causes a divide-by-zero error, references an invalid address, or triggers privilege-level transition. For the purpose of this discussion, exceptions can be classified into two categories: faults and traps. A *fault* is a correctable exception. For example, when the processor executes an instruction that references a valid memory address but the data is not present in main memory (it was paged out), a *page fault* exception is generated. The processor handles this by saving the current execution state, calls the page fault handler to correct this exception (by paging in the data), and re-executes the same instruction (which should no longer cause a page fault). A *trap* is an exception caused by executing special kinds of instructions. For example, on x64, the instruction SYSCALL causes the processor to begin executing at an address specified by an MSR; after the handler is done, execution is resumed at the instruction immediately after SYSCALL. Hence, the major difference between a fault and a trap is where execution resumes. System calls are commonly implemented through special exceptions or trap instructions.

Interrupts

The Intel architecture defines an interrupt descriptor table (IDT) with 256 entries; each entry is a structure with information defining the interrupt handler. The base address of the IDT is stored in a special register called IDTR. An interrupt is associated with an index into this table. There are predefined interrupts reserved by the architecture. For example, 0x0 is for division exception, 0x3 is for software breakpoint, and 0xe is for page faults. Interrupts 32–255 are user-defined.

On x86, each entry in the IDT table is an 8-byte structure defined as follows:

```
1: kd> dt nt!_KIDTENTRY
    +0x000 Offset            : Uint2B
    +0x002 Selector          : Uint2B
    +0x004 Access            : Uint2B
    +0x006 ExtendedOffset    : Uint2B
```

(On x64, the IDT entry structure is mostly the same except that the interrupt handler's address is divided into three members. You can see it by dumping the nt!_KIDTENTRY64 structure. Also note that the IDTR is 48 bits in width and divided into two parts: IDT base address and limit. WinDBG displays only the base address.)

The interrupt handler's address is split between the Offset and ExtendedOffset fields. Here is an example decoding the IDT and disassembling the divide-by-zero interrupt handler (0x0):

```
1: kd> r @idtr
idtr=8b409d50
1: kd> dt nt!_KIDTENTRY 8b409d50
    +0x000 Offset          : 0xa284
    +0x002 Selector        : 8
    +0x004 Access          : 0x8e00
    +0x006 ExtendedOffset  : 0x813c
1: kd> u 0x813ca284
nt!KiTrap00:
813ca284 push    0
813ca286 mov     word ptr [esp+2],0
813ca28d push    ebp
813ca28e push    ebx
```

Figure 3-3 illustrates the IDT on x86.

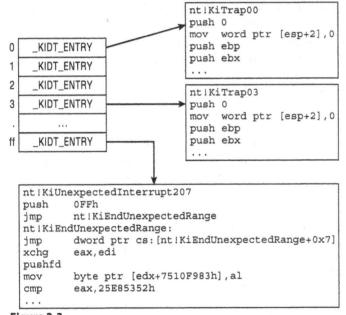

Figure 3-3

On pre-Pentium 2 processors, Windows uses interrupt 0x2e to implement system calls. User-mode programs call APIs in kernel32.dll (or kernelbase.dll), which eventually resolve to short stubs in ntdll.dll that trigger interrupt 0x2e. To illustrate, consider the following snippet from the kernelbase!CreateFileW API routine on Windows 7:

```
[inside kernelbase!CreateFileW]
...
.text:0DCE9C87 mov ecx, [ebp+dwFlagsAndAttributes]
.text:0DCE9C8A push [ebp+lpSecurityAttributes]
.text:0DCE9C8D mov eax, [ebp+dwDesiredAccess]
.text:0DCE9C90 push [ebp+lpFileName]
.text:0DCE9C93 mov esi, ds:__imp__NtCreateFile@44
.text:0DCE9C99 push [ebp+var_4]
.text:0DCE9C9C and ecx, 7FA7h
.text:0DCE9CA2 push [ebp+dwShareMode]
.text:0DCE9CA5 mov [ebp+dwFlagsAndAttributes], ecx
.text:0DCE9CA8 push ecx
.text:0DCE9CA9 push ebx
.text:0DCE9CAA lea ecx, [ebp+var_20]
.text:0DCE9CAD push ecx
.text:0DCE9CAE or eax, 100080h
.text:0DCE9CB3 lea ecx, [ebp+var_64]
.text:0DCE9CB6 push ecx
.text:0DCE9CB7 push eax
.text:0DCE9CB8 mov [ebp+dwDesiredAccess], eax
.text:0DCE9CBB lea eax, [ebp+var_8]
.text:0DCE9CBE push eax
.text:0DCE9CBF call esi ; NtCreateFile(...)
```

It does some preliminary validation (not shown here) and then calls ntdll!NtCreateFile. The implementation for that is as follows:

```
[ntdll!NtCreateFile]
.text:77F04A10 _NtCreateFile@44 proc near
.text:77F04A10 mov eax, 42h ; syscall #
.text:77F04A15 mov edx, 7FFE0300h ; KUSER_SHARED_DATA.SystemCall
; the symbol for 0x7ffe0300 is SharedUserData!SystemCallStub
.text:77F04A1A call dword ptr [edx] ; call handler
.text:77F04A1C retn 2Ch ; return back to caller
.text:77F04A1C _NtCreateFile@44 endp
```

NtCreateFile sets EAX to 0x42 because that's the system call number for NtCreateFile in the kernel. Next, it reads a pointer at 0x7ffe0300 and calls it. What is special about 0x7ffe0300? On all architectures, there is a per-process structure called KUSER_SHARED_DATA that is always mapped at 0x7ffe0000. It contains some generic information about the system and a field called SystemCall:

```
0:000> dt ntdll!_KUSER_SHARED_DATA
   +0x000 TickCountLowDeprecated : Uint4B
   +0x004 TickCountMultiplier : Uint4B
   +0x008 InterruptTime : _KSYSTEM_TIME
   +0x014 SystemTime : _KSYSTEM_TIME
```

```
+0x020 TimeZoneBias : _KSYSTEM_TIME
...
+0x2f8 TestRetInstruction : Uint8B
+0x300 SystemCall : Uint4B ; syscall handler
+0x304 SystemCallReturn : Uint4B
...
```

When disassembling the system call stub, you see this:

```
0:000> u poi(SharedUserData!SystemCallStub)
ntdll!KiIntSystemCall:
76e46500 lea edx,[esp+8]
76e46504 int 2Eh
76e46506 ret
76e46507 nop
```

Dumping the IDT entry at index `0x2e` shows that `KiSystemService` is the system call dispatcher:

```
0: kd> !idt 0x2e
Dumping IDT: ...
2e: 8284b22e nt!KiSystemService
0: kd> u nt!KiSystemService
nt!KiSystemService:
8284b22e push 0
8284b230 push ebp
8284b231 push ebx
8284b232 push esi
8284b233 push edi
8284b234 push fs
8284b236 mov ebx,30h
...
```

The details of the system call dispatcher are covered in the next section.

Traps

The previous section explains how system calls are implemented with the built-in interrupt processing mechanism. This section explains how they are implemented through trap instructions on x64, x86, and ARM.

Beginning with the implementation on x64, consider the system call stub `ntdll!NtCreateFile`:

```
01: .text:00000001800030F0   public ZwCreateFile
02: .text:00000001800030F0 ZwCreateFile proc near
03: .text:00000001800030F0   mov     r10, rcx
04: .text:00000001800030F3   mov     eax, 53h
05: .text:00000001800030F8   syscall
06: .text:00000001800030FA   retn
07: .text:00000001800030FA ZwCreateFile endp
```

Line 3 saves the first argument to R10; it has to do this because SYSCALL's semantic dictates that the return address (line 6) must be stored in RCX. Line 4 saves the system call number in EAX; once SYSCALL transitions to kernel mode, it will use this as an index into the KiServiceTable array. Line 5 executes SYSCALL which transitions to kernel mode. How does it do this? The documentation for SYSCALL specifies that RIP will be loaded with a value defined by the IA32_LSTAR MSR (0xc0000082), and you can observe it in the debugger:

```
1: kd> rdmsr 0xC0000082
msr[c0000082] = fffff800`89e96dc0
1: kd> u fffff800`89e96dc0
nt!KiSystemCall64:
fffff800`89e96dc0 swapgs
fffff800`89e96dc3 mov      qword ptr gs:[10h],rsp
fffff800`89e96dcc mov      rsp,qword ptr gs:[1A8h]
fffff800`89e96dd5 push     2Bh
fffff800`89e96dd7 push     qword ptr gs:[10h]
fffff800`89e96ddf push     r11
```

This kernel debugger output indicates that SYSCALL will always end up executing KiSystemCall64 in the kernel. In fact, KiSystemCall64 is the main system call dispatcher in x64 Windows. Windows sets the IA32 LSTAR MSR to KiSystemCall64 early in the processor initialization process (see KiInitializeBootStructures). It is primarily responsible for saving the user-mode context, setting up a kernel stack, copying the user-mode arguments to the kernel stack, determining the system call in KiServiceTable (or W32pServiceTable) using the index passed in from EAX, invoking the system call, and returning to user mode. How does the syscall dispatcher know where to return in user mode? Recall that SYSCALL saves the return address in RCX. After the system call finishes its work and returns, the system call dispatcher uses the SYSRET instruction, which sets RIP to RCX so it goes back to user mode.

While KiSystemCall64 supports many functionalities (syscall profiling, user-mode scheduling, debugging, etc.), its primary responsibility is to dispatch system call requests. In the previous section, we stated that each value in the KiServiceTable array encodes an offset to the system call and the number of arguments passed on the stack. This can be observed in the following code snippet from KiSystemCall64:

```
01: KiSystemCall64 proc near
02:
03: var_110= byte ptr -110h
04:
05:     swapgs
06:     mov      gs:10h, rsp      ; KPCR->UserRsp
07:     mov      rsp, gs:1A8h     ; KPCR->KPRCB->RspBase
08:                               ; setup a new kernel stack
```

```
09:   push    2Bh
10:   push    qword ptr gs:10h ; KPCR->UserRsp
11:   push    r11
12:
13:   sti                     ; enable interrupts
14:   mov     [rbx+88h], rcx  ; KTHREAD->FirstArgument
15:   mov     [rbx+80h], eax  ; KTHREAD->SystemCallNumber
16: KiSystemServiceStart proc near
17:   mov     [rbx+90h], rsp  ; KTHREAD->TrapFrame
18:   mov     edi, eax        ; eax = syscall #
19:   shr     edi, 7          ; determine which syscall table
20:   and     edi, 20h
21:   and     eax, 0FFFh      ; index into table (recall 64bit syscall
encoding)
22: KiSystemServiceRepeat proc near
23:   lea     r10, KeServiceDescriptorTable
24:   lea     r11, KeServiceDescriptorTableShadow
25:   test    dword ptr [rbx+78h], 40h ; determines if it is a GUI thread
26:   cmovnz  r10, r11            ; which table to use?
27:   cmp     eax, [rdi+r10+10h] ; is that syscall table within the table
Limit?
28:                              ; i.e., KSERVICE_TABLE_DESCRIPTOR.Limit
29:   jnb     case_invalidcallnumber
30:   mov     r10, [rdi+r10]     ; select the right table
31:   movsxd  r11, dword ptr [r10+rax*4] ; get the syscall offset
32:   mov     rax, r11
33:   sar     r11, 4
34:   add     r10, r11    ; add it to the base of the table to get syscall VA
35:   cmp     edi, 20h    ; edi determines which table. here it is used to
                          ; determined if it is a GUI
36:   jnz     short case_nonguirequest
37:   mov     r11, [rbx+0F0h]
38:
39: KiSystemServiceCopyEnd proc near
40:   test    cs:dword_140356088, 40h
41:   jnz     case_loggingenabled
42:   call    r10         ; invoke the system call
```

Walking through `KiSystemCall64` can be an instructional experience and is left as an exercise.

On x86, Windows uses the `SYSENTER` instruction to implement system calls. The mechanics is similar to that of `SYSCALL` on x64 processors. Before going into the implementation, let's look at the system call stub for `ntdll!NtQueryInformationProcess`:

```
01: _ZwQueryInformationProcess@20 proc near
02:   mov     eax, 0B0h           ; system call number
03:   call    sub_6A214FCD        ; stub
04:   retn    14h         ; clean stack and return. NtQueryInformationProcess
takes
05:                       ; 5 parameters and they are passed on the stack
                          ; SYSENTER will return here (see next
example)
```

```
06:  _ZwQueryInformationProcess@20 endp
07:
08:  sub_6A214FCD proc near
09:     mov      edx, esp
10:     sysenter
11:     retn
12:  sub_6A214FCD endp
```

`ntdll!NtCreateFile` sets the system call number and calls another routine that saves the stack pointer in `EDX`, followed by the `SYSENTER` instruction. Intel documentation states that `SYSENTER` sets `EIP` to the value stored in MSR `0x176`:

```
0: kd> rdmsr 0x176
msr[176] = 00000000`80f7d1d0
0: kd> u 00000000`80f7d1d0
nt!KiFastCallEntry:
80f7d1d0 mov      ecx,23h
80f7d1d5 push     30h
80f7d1d7 pop      fs
80f7d1d9 mov      ds,cx
80f7d1db mov      es,cx
80f7d1dd mov      ecx,dword ptr fs:[40h]
```

The debugger output shows that when the instruction `SYSENTER` executes, it transitions to kernel mode and starts executing `KiFastCallEntry`. `KiFastCallEntry` is the main system call dispatcher on x86 Windows using `SYSENTER` (think of it like `KiSystemCall64` on x64). One peculiar characteristic of `SYSENTER` is that it does not save the return address in a register as `SYSCALL` does. Once the system call is complete, how does the kernel know where to return? The answer consists of two parts. Using `NtQueryInformationProcess` again as an example, before calling `SYSENTER` to enter kernel mode, first the sequence of calls looks like this:

```
       kernel32!GetLogicalDrives ->
  ntdll!NtQueryInformationProcess ->
                     stub -> SYSENTER
```

This means that the return address is already set up on the stack before `SYSENTER` is executed. Immediately before `SYSENTER`, `KiFastSystemCall` saves the stack pointer in `EDX`. Second, after `SYSENTER`, the code transitions to `KiFastCallEntry`, which saves this stack pointer. Once the system call is complete, the syscall dispatcher executes the `SYSEXIT` instruction. By definition, `SYSEXIT` sets `EIP` to `EDX`, and ESP to ECX; in practice, the kernel sets `EDX` to `ntdll!KiSystemCallRet` and ECX to the stack pointer before entering the kernel. You can observe this in action by setting a breakpoint at the `SYSEXIT` instruction inside `KiSystemCallExit2` and then viewing the stack from there:

```
1: kd> r
eax=00000000 ebx=00000000 ecx=029af304 edx=77586954 esi=029af3c0 edi=029afa04
eip=815d0458 esp=a08f7c8c ebp=029af3a8 iopl=0         nv up ei ng nz na pe cy
cs=0008  ss=0010  ds=0023  es=0023  fs=0030  gs=0000         efl=00000287
```

```
nt!KiSystemCallExit2+0x18:
815d0458 sysexit
1: kd> dps @ecx L5   # SYSEXIT will set ESP to ECX (note the return address)
029af304  77584fca ntdll!NtQueryInformationProcess+0xa   # return address
029af308  775a9628 ntdll!RtlDispatchException+0x7c
029af30c  ffffffff
029af310  00000022
029af314  029af348
1: kd> u 77584fca
ntdll!NtQueryInformationProcess+0xa:
77584fca ret     14h              # this is line 4 in the last snippet
1: kd> u @edx                     # SYSEXIT will set EIP to EDX
ntdll!KiFastSystemCallRet:
77586954 ret                      # return to 77584fca
```

After executing `KiFastSystemCallRet` (which has only one instruction: RET), you return to `NtQueryInformationProcess`.

It is instructive to compare the SYSENTER implementation on Windows 7 and 8. You will be asked to do this as an exercise.

Windows on ARM uses the `svc` instruction to implement system calls. In older documentation, `svc` may be referred to as `SWI`, but they are the same opcode. Recall that ARM does not have an IDT like x86/x64 but its exception vector table has similar functionality:

```
.text:004D0E00 KiArmExceptionVectors
.text:004D0E00    LDR.W          PC, =0xFFFFFFFF
.text:004D0E04    LDR.W          PC, =(KiUndefinedInstructionException+1)
.text:004D0E08    LDR.W          PC, =(KiSWIException+1)
.text:004D0E0C    LDR.W          PC, =(KiPrefetchAbortException+1)
.text:004D0E10    LDR.W          PC, =(KiDataAbortException+1)
.text:004D0E14    LDR.W          PC, =0xFFFFFFFF
.text:004D0E18    LDR.W          PC, =(KiInterruptException+1)
.text:004D0E1C    LDR.W          PC, =(KiFIQException+1)
```

Whenever the `svc` instruction is executed, the processor switches to supervisor mode and calls `KiSWIException` to handle the exception. This function can be viewed as the ARM equivalent of `KiSystemCall64` on x64. Again, to understand the whole system call process on ARM, consider the user-mode function `ntdll!NtQueryInformationProcess`:

```
01: NtQueryInformationProcess
02:    MOV.W           R12, #0x17                 ; NtQueryInformationProcess
03:    SVC             1
04:    BX              LR
```

The system call number is first put in `R12` and followed by `svc`. When `svc` is executed, you go into the handler `KiSWIException`:

```
01: KiSWIException
02: trapframe= -0x1A0
03:    SUB             SP, SP, #0x1A0
04:    STRD.W          R0, R1, [SP,#0x1A0+trapframe._R0]
```

```
05:    STRD.W       R2, R3, [SP,#0x1A0+trapframe._R2]
06:    STR.W        R12, [SP,#0x1A0+trapframe._R12]
07:    STR.W        R11, [SP,#0x1A0+trapframe._R11]
08:    ORR.W        LR, LR, #1
09:    MOVS         R0, #0x30
10:    MRC          p15, 0, R12,c13,c0, 3 ; get the current thread
11:    STRD.W       LR, R0, [SP,#0x1A0+trapframe._Pc] ; LR is the return
                                             ; address after the
                                             ; SVC instruction. It
                                             ; saved here so the
                                             ; system knows where to
                                             ; return after the
                                             ; syscall is done
12:    LDRB.W       R1, [R12,#_ETHREAD.Tcb.Header.__u0.__s3.DebugActive]
13:    MOVS         R3, #2
14:    STR          R3, [SP,#0x1A0+trapframe.ExceptionActive]
15:    ADD.W        R11, SP, #0x1A0+trapframe._R11
16:    CMP          R1, #0
17:    BNE          case_DebugMode
18: loc_4D00D0
19:    MRC          p15, 0, R0,c1,c0, 2
20:    MOVS         R1, #0
21:    TST.W        R0, #0xF00000
22:    BEQ          loc_4D00F2
23:    ADD          R3, SP, #0x1A0+var_C8
24:    VMRS         R2, FPSCR
25:    ADD          R1, SP, #sizeof(_KTRAP_FRAME)
26:    STR          R2, [SP,#0x1A0+var_114]
27:    VSTMIA       R3, {D8-D15}
28:    BIC.W        R2, R2, #0x370000
29:    VMSR         FPSCR, R2
30:
31: loc_4D00F2
32:    STR          R1, [SP,#0x1A0+trapframe.VfpState]
33:    LDR          R0, [SP,#0x1A0+trapframe._R12]    ; retrieve saved
syscall
                                             ; from line 6
34:    LDR          R1, [SP,#0x1A0+trapframe._R0]
35:    MOV          R2, SP
36:    CPS.W        #0x1F
37:    STR.W        SP, [R2,#0x1A0+trapframe._Sp]
38:    STR.W        LR, [R2,#0x1A0+trapframe._Lr]
39:    CPSIE.W      I, #0x13
40:    STRD.W       R0, R1, [R12,#_ETHREAD.Tcb.SystemCallNumber]
                                             ; write syscall# to the
                                             ; thread
41:    MRC          p15, 0, R0,c13,c0, 4
42:    BFC.W        R0, #0, #0xC
43:    LDR.W        R1, [R0,#0x594]
44:    MOV          R2, #0x5CF300
45:    MOV          R12, #KiTrapFrameLog
46:    CMP          R1, #4
```

```
47:    BCS                loc_4D0178
48:
49:
50: loc_4D0178
51:    MRC                p15, 0, R12,c13,c0, 3
52:    LDR.W              R0, [R12,#_ETHREAD.Tcb.SystemCallNumber]
53:    BL                 KiSystemService       ; dispatch the system call
54:    B                  KiSystemServiceExit   ; return back to usermode
```

This function does many things, but the main points are that it constructs a trap frame (nt!_KTRAP_FRAME) to save some registers, saves the user-mode return address (svc automatically puts the return address in LR), saves the system call number in the current thread object, and dispatches the system call (same mechanism as x64). The return back to user mode is done through KiSystemServiceExit:

```
01: KiSystemServiceExit
02: ...
03:    BIC.W              R0, R0, #1
04:    MOV                R3, SP
05:    ADD                SP, SP, #0x1A0
06:    CPS.W              #0x1F
07:    LDR.W              SP, [R3,#_KTRAP_FRAME._Sp]
08:    LDRD.W             LR, R11, [R3,#_KTRAP_FRAME._Lr]
09:    CPS.W              #0x12
10:    STRD.W             R0, R1, [SP]
11:    LDR                R0, [R3,#_KTRAP_FRAME._R0]
12:    MOVS               R1, #0
13:    MOVS               R2, #0
14:    MOVS               R3, #0
15:    MOV                R12, R1
16:    RFEFD.W            SP          ; return back to usermode
```

Interrupt Request Level

The Windows kernel uses an abstract concept called *interrupt request level (IRQL)* to manage system interruptability. Interrupts can be divided into two general categories: software and hardware. Software interrupts are synchronous events that are triggered by conditions in the running code (divide by 0, execution of an INT instruction, page fault, etc.); hardware interrupts are asynchronous events that are triggered by devices connected to the CPU. Hardware interrupts are asynchronous because they can happen at any time; they are typically used to indicate I/O operations to the processor. The details of how hardware interrupts work are hardware-specific and hence abstracted away by the hardware abstraction layer (HAL) component of Windows.

Concretely speaking, an IRQL is simply a number (defined by the type KIRQL, which is actually a UCHAR) assigned to a processor. Windows associates an IRQL with an interrupt and defines the order in which it is handled. The exact number associated with each IRQL may vary from platform to platform, so we will reference them only by name. The general rule is that interrupts at IRQL X will mask all interrupts that are less than X. Once the interrupt is handled, the kernel lowers the IRQL so that it can run other tasks. Because IRQL is a per-processor value, multiple processors can simultaneously operate at different IRQLs.

There are several different IRQLs, but the most important ones to remember are as follows:

- **PASSIVE LEVEL (0)**—This is the lowest IRQL in the system. All user-mode code and most kernel code executes at this IRQL.

- **APC LEVEL (1)** —This is the IRQL at which asynchronous procedure calls (APCs) are executed. (See the section "Asynchronous Procedure Calls.")

- **DISPATCH LEVEL (2)** —This is the highest software IRQL in the system. The thread dispatcher and deferred procedure calls (DPCs) run at this IRQL. (See the section "Deferred Procedure Calls.") Code at this IRQL cannot wait.

NOTE IRQLs higher than `DISPATCH_LEVEL` are typically associated with real hardware interrupts or extremely low-level synchronization mechanisms. For example, `IPI_LEVEL` is used for communication between processors.

While it seems like IRQL is a thread-scheduling property, it is not. It is a per-processor property, whereas thread priority is a per-thread property.

Because IRQL is a software abstraction of interrupt priority, the underlying implementation has a direct correlation with the hardware. For example, on x86/x64, the local interrupt controller (LAPIC) in the processor has a programmable task priority register (TPR) and a read-only processor priority register (PPR). The TPR determines the interrupt priority; the PPR represents the current interrupt priority. The processor will deliver only interrupts whose priority is higher than the PPR. In practical terms, when Windows needs to change the interrupt priority, it calls the kernel functions KeRaiseIrql/KeLowerIrql, which program the TPR on the local APIC. This can be observed in the definition on x64 (on x64, CR8 is a shadow register allowing quick access to the LAPIC TPR; x86 systems must program the LAPIC to set the TPR):

KeRaiseIrql

```
01: KzRaiseIrql proc near
02:    mov     rax, cr8
03:    movzx   ecx, cl
04:    mov     cr8, rcx
05:    retn
06: KzRaiseIrql endp
```

KeLowerIrql

```
01: KzLowerIrql proc near
02:    movzx   eax, cl
03:    mov     cr8, rax
04:    retn
05: KzLowerIrql endp
```

The preceding concepts explain why code running at high IRQL cannot be preempted by code at lower IRQL.

Pool Memory

Similar to user-mode applications, kernel-mode code can allocate memory at run-time. The general name for it is *pool memory*; one can think it like the heap in user mode. Pool memory is generally divided into two types: paged pool and non-paged pool. Paged pool memory is memory that can be paged out at any given time by the memory manager. When kernel-mode code touches a buffer that is paged out, it triggers a page-fault exception that causes the memory manager to page in that buffer from disk. Non-paged pool memory is memory that can never be paged out; in other words, accessing such memory never triggers a page fault.

This distinction is important because it has consequences for code running at high IRQLs. Suppose a kernel thread is currently running at DISPATCH_LEVEL and it references memory that has been paged out and needs to be handled by the page-fault handler; because the page fault handler (see MmAccessFault) needs to issue a request to bring the page from disk and the thread dispatcher runs at DISPATCH_LEVEL, it cannot resolve the exception and results in a bugcheck. This is one of the reasons why code running at DISPATCH_LEVEL must only reside in and access non-paged pool memory.

Pool memory is allocated and freed by the ExAllocatePool* and ExFreePool* family of functions. By default, non-paged pool memory (type NonPagedPool) is mapped with read, write, and execute permission on x86/x64, but non-executable on ARM; on Windows 8, one can request non-executable, non-paged pool memory by specifying the NonPagedPoolNX pool type. Paged pool memory is mapped read, write, executable on x86, but non-executable on x64/ARM.

Memory Descriptor Lists

A *memory descriptor list (MDL)* is a data structure used to describe a set of physical pages mapped by a virtual address. Each MDL entry describes one contiguous buffer, and multiple entries can be linked together. Once an MDL is built for an existing buffer, the physical pages can be locked in memory (meaning they will not be reused) and can be mapped into another virtual address.

To be useful, MDLs must be initialized, probed, and locked, and then mapped. To better understand the concept, consider some of the practical uses of MDLs.

Suppose a driver needs to map some memory in kernel space to the user-mode address space of a process or vice versa. In order to achieve this, it would first initialize an MDL to describe the memory buffer (IoAllocateMdl), ensure that the current thread has access to those pages and lock them (MmProbeAndLockPages), and then map those pages in memory (MmMapLockedPagesSpecifyCache) in that process.

Another scenario is when a driver needs to write to some read-only pages (such as those in the code section). One way to achieve this is through MDLs. The driver would initialize the MDL, lock it, and then map it to another virtual address with write permission. In this scenario, the driver can use MDLs to implement a VirtualProtect-like function in kernel mode.

Processes and Threads

A thread is defined by two kernel data structures: ETHREAD and KTHREAD. An ETHREAD structure contains housekeeping information about the thread (i.e., thread id, associated process, debugging enabled/disabled, etc.). A KTHREAD structure stores scheduling information for the thread dispatcher, such as thread stack information, processor on which to run, alertable state, and so on. An ETHREAD contains a KTHREAD.

The Windows scheduler operates on threads.

A process contains at least one thread and is defined by two kernel data structures: EPROCESS and KPROCESS. An EPROCESS structure stores basic information about the process (i.e., process id, security token, list of threads, etc.). A KPROCESS structure stores scheduling information for the process (i.e., page directory table, ideal processor, system/user time, etc.). An EPROCESS contains a KPROCESS. Just like ETHREAD and KTHREAD, these data structures are also opaque and should only be accessed with documented kernel routines. However, you can view their field members through the kernel debugger, as follows:

Processes

```
kd> dt nt!_EPROCESS
    +0x000 Pcb                 : _KPROCESS
    +0x2c8 ProcessLock         : _EX_PUSH_LOCK
    +0x2d0 CreateTime          : _LARGE_INTEGER
    +0x2d8 RundownProtect      : _EX_RUNDOWN_REF
    +0x2e0 UniqueProcessId     : Ptr64 Void
    +0x2e8 ActiveProcessLinks  : _LIST_ENTRY
    +0x2f8 Flags2              : Uint4B
    +0x2f8 JobNotReallyActive  : Pos 0, 1 Bit
    +0x2f8 AccountingFolded    : Pos 1, 1 Bit
    +0x2f8 NewProcessReported  : Pos 2, 1 Bit
...
```

```
        +0x3d0 InheritedFromUniqueProcessId : Ptr64 Void
        +0x3d8 LdtInformation   : Ptr64 Void
        +0x3e0 CreatorProcess   : Ptr64 _EPROCESS
        +0x3e0 ConsoleHostProcess : Uint8B
        +0x3e8 Peb              : Ptr64 _PEB
        +0x3f0 Session          : Ptr64 Void
    ...
0: kd> dt nt!_KPROCESS
        +0x000 Header           : _DISPATCHER_HEADER
        +0x018 ProfileListHead  : _LIST_ENTRY
        +0x028 DirectoryTableBase : Uint8B
        +0x030 ThreadListHead   : _LIST_ENTRY
        +0x040 ProcessLock      : Uint4B
    ...
        +0x0f0 ReadyListHead    : _LIST_ENTRY
        +0x100 SwapListEntry    : _SINGLE_LIST_ENTRY
        +0x108 ActiveProcessors : _KAFFINITY_EX
    ...
```

Threads

```
0: kd> dt nt!_ETHREAD
        +0x000 Tcb              : _KTHREAD
        +0x348 CreateTime       : _LARGE_INTEGER
        +0x350 ExitTime         : _LARGE_INTEGER
    ...
        +0x380 ActiveTimerListLock : Uint8B
        +0x388 ActiveTimerListHead : _LIST_ENTRY
        +0x398 Cid              : _CLIENT_ID
    ...
0: kd> dt nt!_KTHREAD
        +0x000 Header           : _DISPATCHER_HEADER
        +0x018 SListFaultAddress : Ptr64 Void
        +0x020 QuantumTarget    : Uint8B
        +0x028 InitialStack     : Ptr64 Void
        +0x030 StackLimit       : Ptr64 Void
        +0x038 StackBase        : Ptr64 Void
        +0x040 ThreadLock       : Uint8B
    ...
        +0x0d8 WaitListEntry    : _LIST_ENTRY
        +0x0d8 SwapListEntry    : _SINGLE_LIST_ENTRY
        +0x0e8 Queue            : Ptr64 _KQUEUE
        +0x0f0 Teb              : Ptr64 Void
```

NOTE Although we say that these should be accessed only with documented kernel routines, real-world rootkits modify semi-documented or completely undocumented fields in these structures to achieve their objectives. For example, one way to hide a process is to remove it from the `ActiveProcessLinks` field in the EPROCESS structure. However, because they are opaque and undocumented, the field offsets can (and do) change from release to release.

There are also analogous user-mode data structures storing information about processes and threads. For processes, there is the process environment block (PEB/ ntdll!_PEB), which stores basic information such as base load address, loaded modules, process heaps, and so on. For threads, there is the thread environment block (TEB/ntdll!_TEB), which stores thread scheduling data and information for the associated process. User-mode code can always access the TEB through the FS (x86), GS (x64) segment, or coprocessor 15 (ARM). You will frequently see system code accessing these objects, so they are listed here:

Current Thread (Kernel Mode)

x86

```
mov       eax, large fs:124h
```

x64

```
mov       rax, gs:188h
```

ARM

```
MRC               p15, 0, R3,c13,c0, 3
BICS.W            R0, R3, #0x3F
```

TEB (User Mode)

x86

```
mov       edx, large fs:18h
```

x64

```
mov       rax, gs:30h
```

ARM

```
MRC               p15, 0, R4,c13,c0, 2
```

Execution Context

Every running thread has an execution context. An execution context contains the address space, security token, and other important properties of the running thread. At any given time, Windows has hundreds of threads running in different execution contexts. From a kernel perspective, three general execution contexts can be defined:

- **Thread context**—Context of a specific thread (or usually the requestor thread in the case of a user-mode thread requesting service from the kernel)

- **System context**—Context of a thread executing in the System process

- **Arbitrary context**—Context of whatever thread was running before the scheduler took over

Recall that each process has its own address space. While in kernel mode, it is important to know what context your code is running in because that determines the address space you are in and security privileges you own. There is no list of rules to precisely determine the execution context in a given scenario, but the following general tips can help:

- When a driver is loaded, its entry point (DriverEntry) executes in System context.

- When a user-mode application sends a request (IOCTL) to a driver, the driver's IOCTL handler runs in thread context (i.e., the context of the user-mode thread that initiated the request).

- APCs run in thread context (i.e., the context of the thread in which the APC was queued).

- DPCs and timers run in arbitrary context.

- Work items run in System context.

- System threads run in System context if the `ProcessHandle` parameter is `NULL` (common case).

For example, a driver's entry point only has access to the System process address space and hence cannot access any other process space without causing an access violation. If a kernel-mode thread wants to change its execution context to another process, it can use the documented API `KeStackAttachProcess`. This is useful when a driver needs to read/write a specific process' memory.

Kernel Synchronization Primitives

The kernel provides common synchronization primitives to be used by other components. The most common ones are events, spin locks, mutexes, resource locks, and timers. This section explains their interface and discusses their usage.

Event objects are used to indicate the state of an operation. For example, when the system is running low on non-paged pool memory, the kernel can notify a driver through events. An event can be in one of two states: signaled or non-signaled. The meaning of signaled and non-signaled depends on the usage scenario. Internally, an event is an object defined by the `KEVENT` structure and initialized by the `KeInitializeEvent` API. After initializing the event, a thread can wait for it with `KeWaitForSingleObject` or `KeWaitForMultipleObjects`. Events are commonly used in drivers to notify other threads that something is finished processing or a particular condition was satisfied.

Timers are used to indicate that a certain time interval has passed. For example, whenever we enter a new century, the kernel executes some code to update the time; the underlying mechanism for this is timers. Internally, timer objects are defined by the `KTIMER` structure and initialized by the `KeInitializeTimer/Ex` routine. When initializing timers, one can specify an optional DPC routine to be executed when they expire. By definition, each processor has its own timer queue; specifically, the `TimerTable` field in the PRCB is a list of timers for that particular processor. Timers are commonly used to do something in a periodic or time-specific manner. Both timers and DPCs are covered in more detail later in this chapter.

Mutexes are used for exclusive access to a shared resource. For example, if two threads are concurrently modifying a shared linked list without a mutex, they may corrupt the list; the solution is to only access the linked list while holding a mutex. While the core semantic of a mutex does not change, the Windows kernel offers two different kinds of mutexes: *guarded mutex* and *fast mutex*. Guarded mutexes are faster than fast mutexes but are only available on Windows 2003 and higher. Internally, a mutex is defined by either a `FAST_MUTEX` or `GUARDED_MUTEX` structure and initialized by `ExInitialize{Fast,Guarded}Mutex`. After initialization, they can be acquired and released through different APIs; see the Windows Driver Kit documentation for more information.

Spin locks are also used for exclusive access to a shared resource. While they are conceptually similar to mutexes, they are used to protect shared resources that are accessed at `DISPATCH_LEVEL` or higher IRQL. For example, the kernel acquires a spin lock before modifying critical global data structures such as the active process list; it must do this because on a multi-processor system, multiple threads can be accessing and modifying the list at the same time. Internally, spin locks are defined by the `KSPIN_LOCK` structure and initialized with `KeInitializeSpinLock`. After initialization, they can be acquired/released through various documented APIs; see the WDK documentation for more information. Note that code holding on to a spin lock is executing at `DISPATCH_LEVEL` or higher; hence, the executing code and the memory it touches must always be resident.

Lists

Linked lists are the fundamental building blocks of dynamic data structures in the kernel and drivers. Many important kernel data structures (such as those related to processes and threads) are built on top of lists. In fact, lists are so commonly used that the WDK provides a set of functions to create and manipulate them in a generic way. Although lists are conceptually simple and have no direct relationship to the understanding of kernel concepts or the practice of reverse engineering, they are introduced here for two important reasons. First, they are used in practically every Windows kernel data structure discussed in this chapter. The kernel commonly operates on entries from various lists (i.e., loaded module list, active process list, waiting threads list, etc.) contained in these structures, so it's important to understand the mechanics of such operations. Second, while the functions operating on lists, e.g., `InsertHeadList`,

`InsertTailList`, `RemoveHeadList`, `RemoveEntryList`, etc., appear in source form in the WDK headers, they are always inlined by the compiler and consequently will never appear as "functions" at the assembly level in real-life binaries; in other words, they will never appear as a *call* or *branch* destination. Hence, you need to understand their implementation details and usage patterns so that you can recognize them at the assembly level.

Implementation Details

The WDK provides functions supporting three list types:

- **Singly-linked list**—A list whose entries are linked together with one pointer (`Next`).

- **Sequenced singly-linked list**—A singly-linked list with support for atomic operations. For example, you can delete the first entry from the list without worrying about acquiring a lock.

- **Circular doubly-linked list**—A list whose entries are linked together with two pointers, one pointing to the next entry (`Flink`) and one pointing to the previous entry (`Blink`).

All three are conceptually identical in terms of *usage* at the source code level. This chapter covers only doubly-linked lists because they are the most common. In one of the exercises, you will be asked to review the WDK documentation on list operations and write a driver that uses all three list types.

The implementation is built on top of one structure:

```
typedef struct _LIST_ENTRY {
    struct _LIST_ENTRY *Flink;
    struct _LIST_ENTRY *Blink;
} LIST_ENTRY, *PLIST_ENTRY;
```

A `LIST_ENTRY` can represent a list head or a list entry. A list head represents the "head" of the list and usually does not store any data except for the `LIST_ENTRY` structure itself; all list functions require a pointer to the list head. A list entry is the actual entry that stores data; in real life, it is a `LIST_ENTRY` structure embedded inside a larger structure.

Lists must be initialized with `InitializeListHead` before usage. This function simply sets the `Flink` and `Blink` fields to point to the list head. Its code is shown below and illustrated in Figure 3-4:

```
VOID InitializeListHead(PLIST_ENTRY ListHead) {
    ListHead->Flink = ListHead->Blink = ListHead;
    return;
}
```

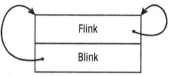

Figure 3-4

In assembly form, this would translate to three instructions: one to retrieve `ListHead` and two to fill out the `Flink` and `Blink` pointers. Consider how `InitializeListHead` manifests itself in x86, x64, and the ARM assembly:

x86

```
lea     eax, [esi+2Ch]
mov     [eax+4], eax
mov     [eax], eax
```

x64

```
lea     r11, [rbx+48h]
mov     [r11+8], r11
mov     [r11], r11
```

ARM

```
ADDS.W      R3, R4, #0x2C
STR         R3, [R3,#4]
STR         R3, [R3]
```

In all three cases, the same pointer and register are used in write-only operations. Another key observation is that the writes at offset +0 and +4/8 from the base register; these offsets correspond to the `Flink` and `Blink` pointers in the structure. Whenever you see this code pattern, you should think of lists.

After initializing the list, entries can be inserted at the head or the tail. As mentioned previously, a list entry is simply a `LIST_ENTRY` inside a larger structure; for example, the kernel KDPC structure (discussed later in the chapter) has a `DpcListEntry` field:

C Definition

```
typedef struct _KDPC {
    UCHAR Type;
    UCHAR Importance;
    volatile USHORT Number;
    LIST_ENTRY DpcListEntry;
    PKDEFERRED_ROUTINE DeferredRoutine;
    PVOID DeferredContext;
    PVOID SystemArgument1;
    PVOID SystemArgument2;
    __volatile PVOID DpcData;
} KDPC, *PKDPC, *PRKDPC;
```

x64

```
0: kd> dt nt!_KDPC
    +0x000 Type              : UChar
    +0x001 Importance        : UChar
    +0x002 Number            : Uint2B
    +0x008 DpcListEntry      : _LIST_ENTRY
    +0x018 DeferredRoutine   : Ptr64     void
    +0x020 DeferredContext   : Ptr64 Void
    +0x028 SystemArgument1   : Ptr64 Void
    +0x030 SystemArgument2   : Ptr64 Void
    +0x038 DpcData           : Ptr64 Void
```

Suppose you have a list with one KDPC entry, as shown in Figure 3-5.

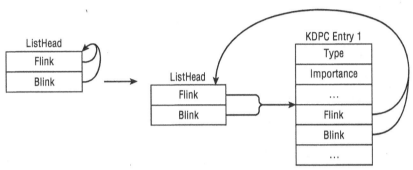

Figure 3-5

Insertion is done with `InsertHeadList` and `InsertTailList`. Consider the insertion of an entry at the head, as shown in Figure 3-6.

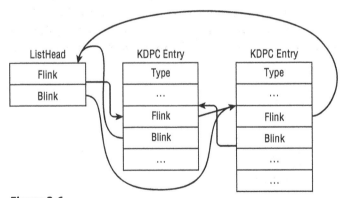

Figure 3-6

The source code for these routines and how they may manifest in assembly form are shown here:

NOTE These snippets are taken from the kernel function `KeInsertQueueDpc` on Windows 8, with a couple of lines removed for clarity. The point here is to observe how the new entry is inserted in the list. Instruction scheduling might change the order of some instructions, but they will be mostly the same.

InsertHeadList

C

```
VOID InsertHeadList(PLIST_ENTRY ListHead, PLIST_ENTRY Entry) {
    PLIST_ENTRY Flink;
    Flink = ListHead->Flink;
    Entry->Flink = Flink;
    Entry->Blink = ListHead;
    Flink->Blink = Entry;
    ListHead->Flink = Entry;
    return;
}
```

ARM

```
LDR     R1, [R5]
STR     R5, [R2,#4]
STR     R1, [R2]
STR     R2, [R1,#4]
STR     R2, [R5]
```

x86

```
mov     edx, [ebx]
mov     [ecx], edx
mov     [ecx+4], ebx
mov     [edx+4], ecx
mov     [ebx], ecx
```

x64

```
mov     rcx, [rdi]
mov     [rax+8], rdi
mov     [rax], rcx
mov     [rcx+8], rax
mov     [rdi], rax
```

InsertTailList

C

```
VOID InsertTailList(PLIST_ENTRY ListHead, PLIST_ENTRY Entry) {
    PLIST_ENTRY Blink;
    Blink = ListHead->Blink;
    Entry->Flink = ListHead;
    Entry->Blink = Blink;
    Blink->Flink = Entry;
    ListHead->Blink = Entry;
    return;
}
```

ARM

```
LDR     R1, [R5,#4]
STR     R5, [R2]
STR     R1, [R2,#4]
STR     R2, [R1]
STR     R2, [R5,#4]
```

x86

```
mov     ecx, [ebx+4]
mov     [eax], ebx
mov     [eax+4], ecx
mov     [ecx], eax
mov     [ebx+4], eax
```

x64

```
mov     rcx, [rdi+8]
mov     [rax], rdi
mov     [rax+8], rcx
mov     [rcx], rax
mov     [rdi+8], rax
```

In the preceding snippets, R5/EBX/RDI point to ListHead, and R2/ECX/RAX point to Entry.

Removal is done with RemoveHeadList, RemoveTailList, and RemoveEntryList. These routines are typically preceded by the IsListEmpty function, which simply checks whether the list head's Flink points to itself:

IsListEmpty

C

```
BOOLEAN IsListEmpty(PLIST_ENTRY ListHead) {
    return (BOOLEAN)(ListHead->Flink == ListHead);
}
```

ARM

```
LDR R2, [R4]
CMP R2, R4
```

x86

```
mov eax, [esi]
cmp eax, esi
```

x64

```
mov rax, [rbx]
cmp rax, rbx
```

RemoveHeadList

C

```
PLIST_ENTRY RemoveHeadList(PLIST_ENTRY ListHead) {
    PLIST_ENTRY Flink;
```

```
    PLIST_ENTRY Entry;
    Entry = ListHead->Flink;
    Flink = Entry->Flink;
    ListHead->Flink = Flink;
    Flink->Blink = ListHead;
    return Entry;
}
```

ARM

```
LDR R2, [R4]
LDR R1, [R2]
STR R1, [R4]
STR R4, [R1,#4]
```

x86

```
mov eax, [esi]
mov ecx, [eax]
mov [esi], ecx
mov [ecx+4], esi
```

x64

```
mov rax, [rbx]
mov rcx, [rax]
mov [rbx], rcx
mov [rcx+8], rbx
```

RemoveTailList

C

```
PLIST_ENTRY RemoveTailList(PLIST_ENTRY ListHead) {
    PLIST_ENTRY Blink;
    PLIST_ENTRY Entry;
    Entry = ListHead->Blink;
    Blink = Entry->Blink;
    ListHead->Blink = Blink;
    Blink->Flink = ListHead;
    return Entry;
}
```

ARM

```
LDR  R6, [R5,#4]
LDR  R2, [R6,#4]
STR  R2, [R5,#4]
STR  R5, [R2]
```

x86

```
mov  ebx, [edi+4]
mov  eax, [ebx+4]
mov  [edi+4], eax
mov  [eax], edi
```

x64

```
mov  rsi, [rdi+8]
mov  rax, [rsi+8]
mov  [rdi+8], rax
mov  [rax], rdi
```

RemoveEntryList

C

```
BOOLEAN RemoveEntryList(PLIST_ENTRY Entry){
    PLIST_ENTRY Blink;
    PLIST_ENTRY Flink;
    Flink = Entry->Flink;
    Blink = Entry->Blink;
    Blink->Flink = Flink;
    Flink->Blink = Blink;
    return (BOOLEAN)(Flink == Blink);
}
```

ARM

```
LDR  R1,[R0]
LDR  R2,[R0,#4]
STR  R1,[R2]
STR  R2,[R1,#4]
```

x86

```
mov  edx, [ecx]
mov  eax, [ecx+4]
mov  [eax], edx
mov  [edx+4], eax
```

x64

```
mov  rdx, [rcx]
mov  rax, [rcx+8]
mov  [rax], rdx
mov  [rdx+8], rax
```

Note that all list manipulation functions operate *solely* on the LIST_ENTRY
structure. In order to do useful things with a list entry, code needs to manipulate the actual data in the entry. How do programs access fields in a list entry?
This is done with the CONTAINING_RECORD macro:

```
#define CONTAINING_RECORD(address, type, field) ((type *)( \
                                    (PCHAR)(address) - \
                                    (ULONG_PTR)(&((type
*)0)->field)))
```

CONTAINING_RECORD returns the base address of a structure using the following
method: It calculates the offset of a field in a structure by casting the structure
pointer to 0, then subtracts that from the real address of the field. In practice,
this macro usually takes the address of the LIST_ENTRY field in the list entry,

the type of the list entry, and the name of that field. For example, suppose you have a list of KDPC entries (see definition earlier) and you want a function to access the DeferredRoutine field; the code would be as follows:

```
PKDEFERRED_ROUTINE ReadEntryDeferredRoutine (PLIST_ENTRY entry) {
        PKDPC p;
        p = CONTAINING_RECORD(entry, KDPC, DpcListEntry);
        return p->DeferredRoutine;
}
```

This macro is commonly used immediately after calling one of the list removal routines or during list entry enumeration.

Walk-Through

Having discussed the concepts and implementation details of the list manipulation functions in kernel mode, we will now apply that to the analysis of Sample C. This walk-through has three objectives:

- Show one common usage of lists in a real-life driver/rootkit
- Demonstrate the uncertainties a reverse engineer faces in practice
- Discuss the problems of undocumented structures and hardcoded offsets

This driver does many things, but we are only interested in two functions: sub_11553 and sub_115DA. Consider the following snippet from sub_115DA:

```
01: .text:000115FF    mov      eax, dword_1436C
02: .text:00011604    mov      edi, ds:wcsncpy
03: .text:0001160A    mov      ebx, [eax]
04: .text:0001160C    mov      esi, ebx
05: .text:0001160E loop_begin:
06: .text:0001160E    cmp      dword ptr [esi+20h], 0
07: .text:00011612    jz       short failed
08: .text:00011614    push     dword ptr [esi+28h]
09: .text:00011617    call     ds:MmIsAddressValid
10: .text:0001161D    test     al, al
11: .text:0001161F    jz       short failed
12: .text:00011621    mov      eax, [esi+28h]
13: .text:00011624    test     eax, eax
14: .text:00011626    jz       short failed
15: .text:00011628    movzx    ecx, word ptr [esi+24h]
16: .text:0001162C    shr      ecx, 1
17: .text:0001162E    push     ecx                          ; size_t
18: .text:0001162F    push     eax                          ; wchar_t *
19: .text:00011630    lea      eax, [ebp+var_208]
20: .text:00011636    push     eax                          ; wchar_t *
21: .text:00011637    call     edi ; wcsncpy
22: .text:00011639    lea      eax, [ebp+var_208]
23: .text:0001163F    push     eax                          ; wchar_t *
24: .text:00011640    call     ds:_wcslwr
25: .text:00011646    lea      eax, [ebp+var_208]
```

```
26: .text:0001164C    push    offset aKrnl          ; "krnl"
27: .text:00011651    push    eax                   ; wchar_t *
28: .text:00011652    call    ds:wcsstr
29: .text:00011658    add     esp, 18h
30: .text:0001165B    test    eax, eax
31: .text:0001165D    jnz     short matched_krnl
32: .text:0001165F    mov     esi, [esi]
33: .text:00011661    cmp     esi, ebx
34: .text:00011663    jz      short loop_end
35: .text:00011665    jmp     short loop_begin
36: .text:00011667 matched_krnl:
37: .text:00011667    lea     eax, [ebp+var_208]
38: .text:0001166D    push    '\'                   ; wchar_t
39: .text:0001166F    push    eax                   ; wchar_t *
40: .text:00011670    call    ds:wcsrchr
41: .text:00011676    pop     ecx
42: .text:00011677    test    eax, eax
```

Lines 1–4 read a pointer from a global variable at `dword_1436C` and save it in EBX and ESI. The loop body references this pointer at offset `0x20` and `0x28`; therefore, you can deduce that it is a pointer to a structure of at least `0x2c` bytes in size. At the end of the loop, it reads another pointer from the structure and compares it against the original pointer (saved in line 3). Note that the pointer is read from offset `0`. Hence, at this point, you can surmise that this loop is iterating over a list in which the "next" pointer is at offset `0`. Can you claim that this structure contains a `LIST_ENTRY` field at offset `0`? No, there is not enough concrete data at the moment to support that. Let's figure out where the global variable `dword_1436C` comes from.

`sub_11553` uses the STDCALL calling convention and takes two parameters: a pointer to a `DRIVER_OBJECT`, and a pointer to a global variable `dword_1436C`. It has the following interesting code snippet:

```
01: .text:00011578    mov     eax, 0FFDFF034h
02: .text:0001157D    mov     eax, [eax]
03: .text:0001157F    mov     eax, [eax+70h]
04: ...
05: .text:0001159E    mov     ecx, [ebp+arg_4]   ; pointer to the global var
06: .text:000115A1    mov     [ecx], eax
```

Line 2 reads a pointer from a hardcoded address, `0xFFDFF034`. On Windows XP, there is a processor control block structure (discussed later in the chapter) at `0xFFDFF000` and offset `0x34` is the `KdVersionBlock` pointer. Lines 3–6 read a pointer value at offset `0x70` into the `KdVersionBlock` and write it back to the global variable; you know it is a pointer because it is used to iterate the list entries in `sub_115DA`. In order to figure out the exact list entry type, you need to determine what is at offset `0x70` of the `KdVersionBlock` structure. Because this is an undocumented OS-specific structure, you have to either reverse engineer the Windows XP kernel or search the Internet to see if other people already figured it out. The results indicate that on Windows XP, offset `0x70` of the `KdVersionBlock` structure is a pointer to a global list head called `PsLoadedModuleList`. Each entry in this list is of type `KLDR_DATA_TABLE_ENTRY` and it stores information about currently loaded kernel modules (name, base address, size, etc.); the first member in this structure is of type `LIST_ENTRY`. This makes sense because we previously deduced that at offset `0` is the "next" pointer (`Flink` to be precise).

> **NOTE** The structure `KLDR_DATA_TABLE_ENTRY` is undocumented, but it is very similar to `LDR_DATA_TABLE_ENTRY`, which is in the public symbols. On Windows XP, the `FullDllName` and `BaseDllName` fields are at the same offset (`0x24` and `0x2c`).

Assuming that the information from the Internet is correct, these two functions can be summarized as follows:

- `sub_11553` reads the `KdVersionBlock` pointer from the processor control block and retrieves the pointer to `PsLoadedModuleList` from there; it saves this pointer to the global variable. `PsLoadedModuleList` is the head of a list whose list entries are of type `KLDR_DATA_TABLE_ENTRY`. This function will be given the friendly name `GetLoadedModuleList`.

- `sub_115DA` uses the list head pointer to iterate over all entries searching for a module name with the substring `"krnl"`. The code searches for the substring `"krnl"` because the author is looking for the NT kernel image name (usually "ntoskrnl.exe"). This function will be given the friendly name `GetKernelName`.

You can briefly translate them back to C:

```
typedef struct _KLDR_DATA_TABLE_ENTRY {
    LIST_ENTRY ListEntry;
    ...
    UNICODE_STRING FullDllName;
    UNICODE_STRING BaseDllName;
    ...
} KLDR_DATA_TABLE_ENTRY, *PKLDR_DATA_TABLE_ENTRY;

BOOL GetLoadedModuleList(PDRIVER_OBJECT drvobj, PLIST_ENTRY g_modlist)
{
    ...
    g_modlist = (PCR->KdVersionBlock) + 0x70
    ...
}

BOOL GetKernelName()
{
    WCHAR fname[...];
    PKLDR_DATA_TABLE_ENTRY entry;
    PLIST_ENTRY p = g_modlist->Flink;
    while (p != g_modlist)
    {
```

```
        entry = CONTAINING_RECORD(p, KLDR_DATA_TABLE_ENTRY, ListEntry);
        ...
        wcsncpy(fname, entry->FullDllName.Buffer, entry->FullDllName
.Length * 2);
        ...
        if (wcsstr(fname, L"krnl") != NULL) { ... }
        p = p->Flink;
    }
    ...
}
```

While this driver may seem to work on a specific version of Windows, there are several problems with it. First, it assumes that the PCR is always located at 0xFFDFF000 and that the KdVersionBlock is always at offset 0x34; these assumptions do not hold for Windows Vista+. Second, the driver assumes that KdVersionBlock always contains a valid value; this is untrue because the value is valid only for the first processor's PCR. Hence, if this code were executed on a multi-processor system and the thread happened to be scheduled on another processor, this code would crash. Third, it assumes that there is a UNICODE_STRING at offset 0x24 in the KLDR_DATA_TABLE_ENTRY structure (which is undocumented itself); this may not always be true because Microsoft may add or remove fields from the structure definition, causing the offset to change. Fourth, this code will certainly fail on an x64 kernel because the offsets are all different. Finally, the loaded module list may change (i.e., drivers being unloaded) while the driver is iterating the list; hence, it may receive stale results or lead to an access violation as a result of accessing a module that is no longer there. Also note that the driver does not use any kind of locking mechanism while iterating a global list. As you analyze more kernel-mode rootkits or third-party drivers, you will frequently encounter code written with these premature assumptions.

For this particular sample, you can tell that the developer just wants to get the kernel image name and base address. This could have been easily achieved using the documented kernel API AuxKlibQueryModuleInformation. (See also the exercise on AuxKlibQueryModuleInformation.)

To conclude, we would like to briefly discuss the thinking process in analyzing these two functions. How were we able to go from seemingly random values such as 0xFFDF034, 0x70, and 0x28 to PCR, KdVersionBlock, PsLoadedModuleList, KLDR_DATA_TABLE_ENTRY, and so on? The truth is that we already have previous kernel knowledge and experience analyzing kernel-mode drivers so we instinctively thought about these structures. For example, we started with a loop that processes each list entry looking for the substring "krnl"; we immediately guessed that they are searching for the kernel image name. The string and length offsets (0x24 and 0x28) alerted us of a UNICODE_STRING; with our kernel knowledge, we guessed that this is the KLDR_DATA_TABLE_ENTRY structure and verified that it is indeed the case using public symbols. Next, we know that PsLoadedModuleList is the global list head for the loaded module list. Because

PsLoadedModuleList is not an exported symbol, we know that the driver must retrieve this from another structure. Going backwards, we see the hardcoded memory address 0xFFDF034 and immediately think of the PCR. We verify this in the debugger:

```
0: kd> dt nt!_KPCR 0xffdff000
   +0x000 NtTib           : _NT_TIB
   +0x01c SelfPcr         : 0xffdff000 _KPCR
   +0x020 Prcb            : 0xffdff120 _KPRCB
   +0x024 Irql            : 0 ''
   +0x028 IRR             : 0
   +0x02c IrrActive       : 0
   +0x030 IDR             : 0xffffffff
   +0x034 KdVersionBlock  : 0x8054d2b8 Void
...
```

From experience, we know that KdVersionBlock is a pointer to a large structure storing interesting information such as the kernel base address and list heads. At that point, we have all the information and data structures to understand the code.

As you can see, there is a systematic thinking process behind the analysis; however, it requires a substantial amount of background knowledge about the operating system, and experience. When you are first starting, you may not have all the knowledge and intuition required to quickly understand kernel-mode drivers. Have no fear! This book attempts to provide a strong foundation by explaining all the major kernel concepts and data structures. With a strong foundation and a lot of practice (see the exercises), you will eventually be able to do it with great ease. Remember: foundational knowledge + intuition + experience + patience = skills.

Exercises

1. On Windows 8 x64, the following kernel functions have InitalizeListHead inlined at least once:

   - CcAllocateInitializeMbcb

   - CmpInitCallbacks

   - ExCreateCallback

   - ExpInitSystemPhase0

   - ExpInitSystemPhase1

   - ExpTimerInitialization

   - InitBootProcessor

   - IoCreateDevice

- `IoInitializeIrp`

- `KeInitThread`

- `KeInitializeMutex`

- `KeInitializeProcess`

- `KeInitializeTimerEx`

- `KeInitializeTimerTable`

- `KiInitializeProcessor`

- `KiInitializeThread`

- `MiInitializeLoadedModuleList`

- `MiInitializePrefetchHead`

- `PspAllocateProcess`

- `PspAllocateThread`

Identify where `InitializeListHead` is inlined in these routines.

2. Repeat the previous exercise for `InsertHeadList` in the following routines:

- `CcSetVacbInFreeList`

- `CmpDoSort`

- `ExBurnMemory`

- `ExFreePoolWithTag`

- `IoPageRead`

- `IovpCallDriver1`

- `KeInitThread`

- `KiInsertQueueApc`

- `KeInsertQueueDpc`

- `KiQueueReadyThread`

- `MiInsertInSystemSpace`

- `MiUpdateWsle`

- `ObpInsertCallbackByAltitude`

3. Repeat the previous exercise for `InsertTailList` in the following routines:

- `AlpcpCreateClientPort`

- `AlpcpCreateSection`

- `AlpcpCreateView`

- `AuthzBasepAddSecurityAttributeToLists`

- `CcFlushCachePriv`

- CcInitializeCacheManager
- CcInsertVacbArray
- CcSetFileSizesEx
- CmRenameKey
- ExAllocatePoolWithTag
- ExFreePoolWithTag
- ExQueueWorkItem
- ExRegisterCallback
- ExpSetTimer
- IoSetIoCompletionEx2
- KeInsertQueueDpc
- KeStartThread
- KiAddThreadToScbQueue
- KiInsertQueueApc
- KiQueueReadyThread
- MiInsertNewProcess
- PnpRequestDeviceAction
- PspInsertProcess
- PspInsertThread

4. Repeat the previous exercise for RemoveHeadList in the following routines:

- AlpcpFlushResourcesPort
- CcDeleteMbcb
- CcGetVacbMiss
- CmpLazyCommitWorker
- ExAllocatePoolWithTag
- FsRtlNotifyCompleteIrpList
- IopInitializeBootDrivers
- KiProcessDisconnectList
- PnpDeviceCompletionQueueGetCompletedRequest
- RtlDestroyAtomTable
- RtlEmptyAtomTable
- RtlpFreeAllAtom

5. Repeat the previous exercise for RemoveTailList in the following routines:

   - BootApplicationPersistentDataProcess
   - CmpCallCallBacks
   - CmpDelayCloseWorker
   - ObpCallPostOperationCallbacks
   - RaspAddCacheEntry

6. Repeat the previous exercise for RemoveEntryList in the following routines:

   - AlpcSectionDeleteProcedure
   - AlpcpDeletePort
   - AlpcpUnregisterCompletionListDatabase
   - AuthzBasepRemoveSecurityAttributeFromLists
   - CcDeleteBcbs
   - CcFindNextWorkQueueEntry
   - CcLazyWriteScan
   - CcSetFileSizesEx
   - CmShutdownSystem
   - CmUnRegisterCallback
   - CmpCallCallBacks
   - CmpPostApc
   - ExFreePoolWithTag
   - ExQueueWorkItem
   - ExTimerRundown
   - ExpDeleteTimer
   - ExpSetTimer
   - IoDeleteDevice
   - IoUnregisterFsRegistrationChange
   - IopfCompleteRequest
   - KeDeregisterBugCheckCallback
   - KeDeregisterObjectNotification
   - KeRegisterObjectNotification
   - KeRemoveQueueApc

- KeRemoveQueueDpc

- KiCancelTimer

- KeTerminateThread

- KiDeliverApc

- KiExecuteAllDpcs

- KiExpireTimerTable

- KiFindReadyThread

- KiFlushQueueApc

- KiInsertTimerTable

- KiProcessExpiredTimerList

- MiDeleteVirtualAddresses

- NtNotifyChangeMultipleKeys

- ObRegisterCallbacks

- ObUnRegisterCallbacks

7. Repeat the previous exercises on Windows 8 x86/ARM and Windows 7 x86/x64. What were the differences (if any)?

8. If you did the exercises for InsertHeadList, InsertTailList, RemoveHeadList, RemoveTailList, and RemoveEntryList on Windows 8, you should have observed a code construct common to all these functions. This construct should also enable you to easily spot the inlined list insertion and removal routines. Explain this code construct and why it is there. Hint: This construct exists only on Windows 8 and it requires you to look at the IDT.

9. In the walk-through, we mentioned that a driver can enumerate all loaded modules with the documented API AuxKlibQueryModuleInformation. Does this API guarantee that the returned module list is always up-to-date? Explain your answer. Next, reverse engineer AuxKlibQueryModuleInformation on Windows 8 and explain how it works. How does it handle the case when multiple threads are requesting access to the loaded module list? Note: The internal function handling this request (and others) is fairly large, so you will need some patience. Alternatively, you can use a debugger to help you trace the interesting code.

10. Explain how the following functions work: KeInsertQueueDpc, KiRetireDpcList, KiExecuteDpc, and KiExecuteAllDpcs. If you feel like an overachiever, decompile those functions from the x86 and x64 assemblies and explain the differences.

Asynchronous and Ad-Hoc Execution

During the lifetime of a driver, it may create system threads, register callbacks for certain events, queue a function to be executed in the future, and so on. This section covers a variety of mechanisms a driver can use to achieve these forms of asynchronous and ad-hoc execution. The mechanisms covered include system threads, work items, APCs, DPCs, timers, and process and thread callbacks.

System Threads

A typical user-mode program may have multiple threads handling different requests. Similarly, a driver may create multiple threads to handle requests from the kernel or user. These threads can be created with the PsCreateSystemThread API:

```
NTSTATUS PsCreateSystemThread(
  _Out_      PHANDLE ThreadHandle,
  _In_       ULONG DesiredAccess,
  _In_opt_   POBJECT_ATTRIBUTES ObjectAttributes,
  _In_opt_   HANDLE ProcessHandle,
  _Out_opt_  PCLIENT_ID ClientId,
  _In_       PKSTART_ROUTINE StartRoutine,
  _In_opt_   PVOID StartContext
);
```

If called with a NULL ProcessHandle parameter, this API will create a new thread in the System process and set its start routine to StartRoutine. The usage of system threads varies according to driver requirement. For example, the driver may decide to create a thread during initialization to handle subsequent I/O requests or wait on some events. One concrete example is the kernel creating a system thread to process DPCs (see also the KiStartDpcThread function).

Exercises

1. After reading some online forums, you notice some people suggesting that PsCreateSystemThread will create a thread in the context of the calling process. In other words, they are suggesting that if you call PsCreateSystemThread in an IOCTL handler, the new thread will be in the context of the requesting user-mode application. Assess the validity of this statement by writing a driver that calls PsCreateSystemThread in the IOCTL handler. Next, experiment with a non-NULL ProcessHandle and determine if the context differs.

2. Cross-reference as many calls to PsCreateSystemThread as possible in the kernel image. Determine whether any of them pass a non-NULL

ProcessHandle parameter. Explain the purpose of these routines. Repeat the exercise for as many functions as possible.

Work Items

Work items are similar to system threads except that no physical thread objects are created for them. A work item is simply an object in a queue processed by a pool of system threads. Concretely speaking, a work item is a structure defined as follows:

```
0: kd> dt nt!_IO_WORKITEM
   +0x000 WorkItem        : _WORK_QUEUE_ITEM
   +0x020 Routine         : Ptr64     void
   +0x028 IoObject        : Ptr64 Void
   +0x030 Context         : Ptr64 Void
   +0x038 Type            : Uint4B
   +0x03c ActivityId      : _GUID
0: kd> dt nt!_WORK_QUEUE_ITEM
   +0x000 List            : _LIST_ENTRY
   +0x010 WorkerRoutine   : Ptr64     void
   +0x018 Parameter       : Ptr64 Void
```

Note that its WorkItem field is actually a list entry containing the worker routine and parameter. This entry will eventually be inserted into a queue later. A driver calls the function IoAllocateWorkItem to get back a pointer to an IO_WORKITEM allocated in non-paged pool. Next, the driver initializes and queues the work item by calling IoQueueWorkItem:

```
PIO_WORKITEM IoAllocateWorkItem(
  _In_  PDEVICE_OBJECT DeviceObject
);

VOID IoQueueWorkItem(
  _In_       PIO_WORKITEM IoWorkItem,
  _In_       PIO_WORKITEM_ROUTINE WorkerRoutine,
  _In_       WORK_QUEUE_TYPE QueueType,
  _In_opt_   PVOID Context
);
```

The initialization part simply fills in the worker routine, parameter/context, and queue priority/type:

```
IO_WORKITEM_ROUTINE WorkItem;

VOID WorkItem(
  _In_       PDEVICE_OBJECT DeviceObject,
  _In_opt_   PVOID Context
)
{ ... }
```

```
typedef enum _WORK_QUEUE_TYPE {
  CriticalWorkQueue       = 0,
  DelayedWorkQueue        = 1,
  HyperCriticalWorkQueue  = 2,
  MaximumWorkQueue        = 3
} WORK_QUEUE_TYPE;
```

Where is it queued? As explained earlier, each processor has an associated KPRCB that contains a field called `ParentNode`, which is a pointer to a `KNODE` structure; when the processor is initialized, this pointer points to an `ENODE` structure that holds the work items queue:

Work items queue

```
0: kd> dt nt!_KPRCB
...
   +0x5338 ParentNode         : Ptr64 _KNODE
0: kd> dt nt!_KNODE
   +0x000 DeepIdleSet        : Uint8B
   +0x040 ProximityId        : Uint4B
   +0x044 NodeNumber         : Uint2B
0: kd> dt nt!_ENODE
   +0x000 Ncb                : _KNODE
   +0x0c0 ExWorkerQueues     : [7] _EX_WORK_QUEUE
   +0x2f0 ExpThreadSetManagerEvent : _KEVENT
   +0x308 ExpWorkerThreadBalanceManagerPtr : Ptr64 _ETHREAD
   +0x310 ExpWorkerSeed      : Uint4B
   +0x314 ExWorkerFullInit : Pos 0, 1 Bit
   +0x314 ExWorkerStructInit : Pos 1, 1 Bit
   +0x314 ExWorkerFlags      : Uint4B
0: kd> dt nt!_EX_WORK_QUEUE
   +0x000 WorkerQueue        : _KQUEUE
   +0x040 WorkItemsProcessed : Uint4B
   +0x044 WorkItemsProcessedLastPass : Uint4B
   +0x048 ThreadCount        : Int4B
   +0x04c TryFailed          : UChar
```

ExQueueWorkItemEx

```
ExQueueWorkItemEx proc near
...
mov      rax, gs:20h
mov      r8, [rax+5338h]      ; enode
movzx    eax, word ptr [r8+44h]
mov      ecx, eax
lea      rax, [rax+rax*2]
shl      rax, 6
add      rax, rbp
...
mov      edx, r9d   ; queue type
mov      rcx, r11   ; workitem passed in
call     ExpQueueWorkItemNode
```

What actually happens is that each processor has several queues to store the work items and there is a system thread dequeueing one item at a time for execution. This system thread responsible for dequeueing is `ExpWorkerThread`.

As previously explained, work items are lightweight because they do not require new thread objects to be created. They also have two important properties:

- They are executed in the context of the System process. The reason is because the `ExpWorkerThread` runs in the System process.

- They are executed at `PASSIVE_LEVEL`.

Due to their lightweight nature, it is a common driver programming pattern to queue work items inside a DPC.

Exercises

1. Explain how we were able to determine that `ExpWorkerThread` is the system thread responsible for dequeueing work items and executing them. Hint: The fastest way is to write a driver.

2. Explore `IoAllocateWorkItem`, `IoInitializeWorkItem`, `IoQueueWorkItem`, `IopQueueWorkItemProlog`, and `ExQueueWorkItem`, and explain how they work.

3. Work items and system threads (i.e., those created by `PsCreateSystemThread`) are mostly identical in terms of functionality, so explain why DPCs frequently queue work items to handle requests but never call `PsCreateSystemThread`.

4. Write a driver to enumerate all work items on the system and explain the problems you had to overcome in the process.

Asynchronous Procedure Calls

Asynchronous procedure calls (APCs) are used to implement many important operations such as asynchronous I/O completion, thread suspension, and process shutdown. Unfortunately, they are undocumented from a kernel perspective. The official driver development documentation simply includes a short section acknowledging that APCs exist and that there are different types. However, for common reverse engineering tasks, it is not necessary to understand all the underlying details. This section explains what APCs are and how they are commonly used.

APC Fundamentals

Generally speaking, APCs are functions that execute in a particular thread context. They can be divided into two types: kernel-mode and user-mode. Kernel-mode

APCs can be either normal or special; normal ones execute at PASSIVE_LEVEL, whereas special ones execute at APC_LEVEL (both execute in kernel mode). User APCs execute at PASSIVE_LEVEL in user mode when the thread is in an alertable state. Because APCs run in thread context, they are always associated with an ETHREAD object.

Concretely speaking, an APC is defined by the KAPC structure:

```
1: kd> dt nt!_KAPC
   +0x000 Type            : UChar
   +0x001 SpareByte0      : UChar
   +0x002 Size            : UChar
   +0x003 SpareByte1      : UChar
   +0x004 SpareLong0      : Uint4B
   +0x008 Thread          : Ptr32 _KTHREAD
   +0x00c ApcListEntry    : _LIST_ENTRY
   +0x014 KernelRoutine   : Ptr32     void
   +0x018 RundownRoutine  : Ptr32     void
   +0x01c NormalRoutine   : Ptr32     void
   +0x014 Reserved        : [3] Ptr32 Void
   +0x020 NormalContext   : Ptr32 Void
   +0x024 SystemArgument1 : Ptr32 Void
   +0x028 SystemArgument2 : Ptr32 Void
   +0x02c ApcStateIndex   : Char
   +0x02d ApcMode         : Char
   +0x02e Inserted        : UChar
```

This structured is initialized by the KeInitializeApc API:

KeInitializeApc

```
NTKERNELAPI VOID KeInitializeApc(
    PKAPC Apc,
    PKTHREAD Thread,
    KAPC_ENVIRONMENT Environment,
    PKKERNEL_ROUTINE KernelRoutine,
    PKRUNDOWN_ROUTINE RundownRoutine,
    PKNORMAL_ROUTINE NormalRoutine,
    KPROCESSOR_MODE ProcessorMode,
    PVOID NormalContext
    );

NTKERNELAPI BOOLEAN KeInsertQueueApc(
    PRKAPC Apc,
    PVOID SystemArgument1,
    PVOID SystemArgument2,
    KPRIORITY Increment
    );
```

Callback prototypes

```
typedef VOID (*PKKERNEL_ROUTINE)(
    PKAPC Apc,
    PKNORMAL_ROUTINE *NormalRoutine,
    PVOID *NormalContext,
    PVOID *SystemArgument1,
    PVOID *SystemArgument2
    );

typedef VOID (*PKRUNDOWN_ROUTINE)(
    PKAPC Apc
    );

typedef VOID (*PKNORMAL_ROUTINE)(
    PVOID NormalContext,
    PVOID SystemArgument1,
    PVOID SystemArgument2
    );

typedef enum _KAPC_ENVIRONMENT {
    OriginalApcEnvironment,
    AttachedApcEnvironment,
    CurrentApcEnvironment,
    InsertApcEnvironment
} KAPC_ENVIRONMENT, *PKAPC_ENVIRONMENT;
```

NOTE This definition is taken from `http://forum.sysinternals.com/howto-capture-kernel-stack-traces_topic19356.html`. While we cannot guarantee its correctness, it has been known to work in experiments.

`Apc` is a caller-allocated buffer of type `KAPC`. In practice, it is usually allocated in non-paged pool by `ExAllocatePool` and freed in the kernel or normal routine. `Thread` is the thread to which this APC should be queued. `Environment` determines the environment in which the APC executes; for example, `OriginalApcEnvironment` means that the APC will run in the thread's process context (if it does not attach to another process). `KernelRoutine` is a function that will be executed at `APC_LEVEL` in kernel mode; `RundownRoutine` is a function that will be executed when the thread is terminating; and `NormalRoutine` is a function that will be executed at `PASSIVE_LEVEL` in `ProcessorMode`. User-mode APCs are those that have a `NormalRoutine` and `ProcessorMode` set to `UserMode`. `NormalContext` is the parameter passed to the `NormalRoutine`.

Once initialized, an APC is queued with the `KeInsertQueueApc` API. `Apc` is the APC initialized by `KeInitializeApc`. `SystemArgument1` and `SystemArgument2` are optional arguments that can be passed to kernel and normal routines. `Increment` is the number to increment the run-time priority; it is similar to the `PriorityBoost` parameter in `IoCompleteRequest`. Where is the APC queued?

Recall that APCs are always associated with a thread. The KTHREAD structure has two APC queues:

```
0: kd> dt nt!_KTHREAD
    +0x000 Header            : _DISPATCHER_HEADER
    +0x018 SListFaultAddress : Ptr64 Void
    +0x020 QuantumTarget     : Uint8B
    ...
    +0x090 TrapFrame         : Ptr64 _KTRAP_FRAME
    +0x098 ApcState          : _KAPC_STATE
    +0x098 ApcStateFill      : [43] UChar
    +0x0c3 Priority          : Char
    +0x288 SchedulerApc      : _KAPC
    ...
    +0x2e0 SuspendEvent      : _KEVENT
0: kd> dt nt!_KAPC_STATE
    +0x000 ApcListHead       : [2] _LIST_ENTRY
    +0x020 Process           : Ptr64 _KPROCESS
    +0x028 KernelApcInProgress : UChar
    +0x029 KernelApcPending  : UChar
    +0x02a UserApcPending    : UChar
```

The ApcState field contains an array of two queues, storing kernel-mode and user-mode APCs, respectively.

Implementing Thread Suspension with APCs

When a program wants to suspend a thread, the kernel queues a kernel APC to the thread. This suspension APC is the SchedulerApc field in the KTHREAD structure; it is initialized in KeInitThread with KiSchedulerApc as the normal routine. KiSchedulerApc simply holds on the thread's SuspendEvent. When the program wants to resume the thread, KeResumeThread releases this event.

Unless you are reverse engineering the Windows kernel or kernel-mode rootkits, it is unlikely that you will run into code using APCs. This is primarily because they are undocumented and hence not commonly used in commercial drivers. However, APCs are frequently used in rootkits because they offer a clean way to inject code into user mode from kernel mode. Rootkits achieve this by queueing a user-mode APC to a thread in the process in which they want to inject code.

Exercises

1. Write a driver using both kernel-mode and user-mode APCs.
2. Write a driver that enumerates all user-mode and kernel-mode APCs for all threads in a process. Hint: You need to take into consideration IRQL level when performing the enumeration.

3. The kernel function `KeSuspendThread` is responsible for suspending a thread. Earlier you learned that APCs are involved in thread suspension in Windows 8. Explain how this function works and how APCs are used to implement the functionality on Windows 7. What is different from Windows 8?

4. APCs are also used in process shutdown. The `KTHREAD` object has a flag called `ApcQueueable` that determines whether an APC may be queued to it. What happens when you disable APC queueing for a thread? Experiment with this by starting up notepad.exe and then manually disable APC queueing to one of its threads (use the kernel debugger to do this).

5. Explain what the following functions do:

   ▪ `KiInsertQueueApc`

   ▪ `PsExitSpecialApc`

   ▪ `PspExitApcRundown`

   ▪ `PspExitNormalApc`

   ▪ `PspQueueApcSpecialApc`

   ▪ `KiDeliverApc`

6. Explain how the function `KeEnumerateQueueApc` works and then recover its prototype. Note: This function is available only on Windows 8.

7. Explain how the kernel dispatches APCs. Write a driver that uses the different kinds of APCs and view the stack when they are executed. Note: We used the same method to figure out how the kernel dispatches work items.

Deferred Procedure Calls

Deferred procedure calls (DPCs) are routines executed at DISPATCH_LEVEL in arbitrary thread context on a particular processor. Hardware drivers use them to process interrupts coming from the device. A typical usage pattern is for the interrupt service routine (ISR) to queue a DPC, which in turn queues a work item to do the processing.

Hardware drivers do this because the ISR usually runs at high IRQLs (above DISPATCH_LEVEL) and if it takes too long, it could reduce the system's overall performance. Hence, the ISR typically queues a DPC and immediately returns so that the system can process other interrupts. Software drivers can use DPCs to quickly execute short tasks.

Internally, a DPC is defined by the KDPC structure:

```
0: kd> dt nt!_KDPC
   +0x000 Type            : UChar
   +0x001 Importance      : UChar
```

```
+0x002 Number           : Uint2B
+0x008 DpcListEntry     : _LIST_ENTRY
+0x018 DeferredRoutine  : Ptr64      void
+0x020 DeferredContext  : Ptr64 Void
+0x028 SystemArgument1  : Ptr64 Void
+0x030 SystemArgument2  : Ptr64 Void
+0x038 DpcData          : Ptr64 Void
```

Each field's semantic is as follows:

- Type—Object type. It indicates the kernel object type for this object (i.e., process, thread, timer, DPC, events, etc.). Recall that kernel objects are defined by the nt!_KOBJECTS enumeration. In this case, you are dealing with DPCs, for which there are two types: normal and threaded.

- Importance—DPC importance. It determines where this DPC entry should be in the DPC queue. See also KeSetImportanceDpc.

- Number—Processor number on which the DPC should be queued and executed. See also KeSetTargetProcessorDpc.

- DpcListEntry—LIST_ENTRY for the DPC entry. Internally, the insertion/removal of DPCs from the DPC queue operate on this field. See KeInsertQueueDpc.

- DeferredRoutine—The function associated with this DPC. It will be executed in arbitrary thread context and at DISPATCH_LEVEL. It is defined as follows:

```
KDEFERRED_ROUTINE CustomDpc;
VOID CustomDpc(
  _In_      struct _KDPC *Dpc,
  _In_opt_  PVOID DeferredContext,
  _In_opt_  PVOID SystemArgument1,
  _In_opt_  PVOID SystemArgument2
)
{ ... }
```

- DeferredContext—Parameter to pass to the DPC function.

- SystemArgument1—Custom data to store in the DPC.

- SystemArgument2— Custom data to store in the DPC.

- DpcData—A pointer to a KDPC_DATA structure:

```
0: kd> dt nt!_KDPC_DATA
   +0x000 DpcListHead      : _LIST_ENTRY
   +0x010 DpcLock          : Uint8B
```

```
+0x018 DpcQueueDepth      : Int4B
+0x01c DpcCount           : Uint4B
```

As you can see, it keeps accounting information about DPCs. The data is stored in the DpcData field of the KPRCB structure associated with the DPC. DpcListHead is the head entry in the DPC queue (it is set during KPRCB initialization) and DpcLock is the spinlock protecting this structure; each time a DPC is queued, the DpcCount and DpcQueueDepth are incremented by one. See also KeInsertQueueDpc. It can be instructive to analyze KeInsertQueueDpc in assembly; pay attention to the KPRCB access and head/tail list insertion.

The DPC usage pattern in code is simple: Initialize the KDPC object with KeInitializeDpc and queue it with KeInsertQueueDpc. When the processor IRQL drops to DISPATCH_LEVEL, the kernel processes all DPCs in that queue.

As mentioned earlier, each CPU core keeps its own queue of DPCs. This queue is tracked by the per-core KPRCB structure:

```
0: kd> dt nt!_KPRCB
    +0x000 MxCsr                : Uint4B
    +0x004 LegacyNumber         : UChar
    +0x005 ReservedMustBeZero    : UChar
    +0x006 InterruptRequest      : UChar
    ...
    +0x2d80 DpcData              : [2] _KDPC_DATA
    +0x2dc0 DpcStack             : Ptr64 Void
    +0x2dc8 MaximumDpcQueueDepth : Int4B
    +0x2dcc DpcRequestRate       : Uint4B
    +0x2dd0 MinimumDpcRate       : Uint4B
    +0x2dd4 DpcLastCount         : Uint4B
    +0x2dd8 ThreadDpcEnable      : UChar
    +0x2dd9 QuantumEnd           : UChar
    +0x2dda DpcRoutineActive     : UChar
0: kd> dt nt!_KDPC_DATA
    +0x000 DpcListHead          : _LIST_ENTRY
    +0x010 DpcLock              : Uint8B
    +0x018 DpcQueueDepth        : Int4B
    +0x01c DpcCount             : Uint4B
```

The two notable fields are DpcData and DpcStack. DpcData is an array of KDPC_DATA structures whereby each element tracks a DPC queue; the first element tracks normal DPCs and the second tracks threaded DPCs. The function KeInsertQueueDpc simply inserts the DPC into one of these two queues. The relationship can be illustrated as shown in Figure 3-7.

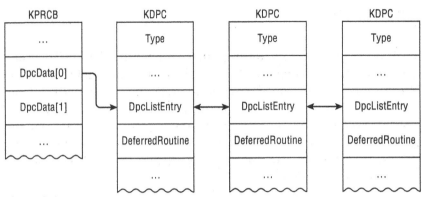

Figure 3-7

DpcStack is a pointer to a block of memory to be used as the DPC routine's stack.

Windows has several mechanisms to process the DPC queue. The first mechanism is through KiIdleLoop. While "idling," it checks the PRCB to determine if DPCs are waiting and if so to call KiRetireDpcList to process all DPCs. This is why sometimes these two functions appear on the stack while executing a DPC. For example:

```
0: kd> kn
 # Child-SP          RetAddr           Call Site
00 fffff800`00b9cc88 fffff800`028db5dc USBPORT!USBPORT_IsrDpc
01 fffff800`00b9cc90 fffff800`028d86fa nt!KiRetireDpcList+0x1bc
02 fffff800`00b9cd40 00000000`00000000 nt!KiIdleLoop+0x5a
```

The second mechanism occurs when the CPU is at DISPATCH_LEVEL. Consider the following stack:

```
0: kd> kn
 # Child-SP          RetAddr           Call Site
00 fffff800`00ba2ef8 fffff800`028db5dc USBPORT!USBPORT_IsrDpc
01 fffff800`00ba2f00 fffff800`028d6065 nt!KiRetireDpcList+0x1bc
02 fffff800`00ba2fb0 fffff800`028d5e7c nt!KyRetireDpcList+0x5
03 fffff880`04ac67a0 fffff800`0291b793 nt!KiDispatchInterruptContinue
04 fffff880`04ac67d0 fffff800`028cbda2 nt!KiDpcInterruptBypass+0x13
05 fffff880`04ac67e0 fffff960`0002992c nt!KiInterruptDispatch+0x212
06 fffff880`04ac6978 fffff960`000363b3 win32k!vAlphaPerPixelOnly+0x7c
07 fffff880`04ac6980 fffff960`00035fa4 win32k!AlphaScanLineBlend+0x303
08 fffff880`04ac6a40 fffff960`001fd4f9 win32k!EngAlphaBlend+0x4f4
09 fffff880`04ac6cf0 fffff960`001fdbaa win32k!NtGdiUpdateTransform+0x112d
0a fffff880`04ac6db0 fffff960`001fdd19 win32k!NtGdiUpdateTransform+0x17de
0b fffff880`04ac6ed0 fffff960`001fded8 win32k!EngNineGrid+0xb1
0c fffff880`04ac6f70 fffff960`001fe395 win32k!EngDrawStream+0x1a0
```

```
0d fffff880`04ac7020 fffff960`001fece7 win32k!NtGdiDrawStreamInternal+0x47d
0e fffff880`04ac70d0 fffff960`0021a480 win32k!GreDrawStream+0x917
0f fffff880`04ac72c0 fffff800`028cf153 win32k!NtGdiDrawStream+0x9c
10 fffff880`04ac7420 000007fe`fd762cda nt!KiSystemServiceCopyEnd+0x13
```

This long stack indicates that win32k.sys was handling some graphics operation request from the user, and then the USB port driver's DPC routine—which has nothing to do with win32k—is executed. What probably happened is that while win32k.sys was handling the request, a device interrupt occurred that caused the CPU to operate at device IRQL; and then the IRQL is eventually lowered to DISPATCH_LEVEL, which causes the DPC queue to be processed.

The third mechanism is through a system thread created during processor initialization. KiStartDpcThread creates a thread (KiExecuteDpc) for each processor, which processes the DPC queue whenever it runs. For example:

```
0: kd> kn
 # Child-SP          RetAddr           Call Site
00 fffff880`03116be8 fffff800`028aadb0 nt!KiDpcWatchdog
01 fffff880`03116bf0 fffff800`028aac4b nt!KiExecuteAllDpcs+0x148
02 fffff880`03116cb0 fffff800`02b73166 nt!KiExecuteDpc+0xcb
03 fffff880`03116d00 fffff800`028ae486 nt!PspSystemThreadStartup+0x5a
04 fffff880`03116d40 00000000`00000000 nt!KiStartSystemThread+0x16
```

Recall that the thread dispatcher runs at DISPATCH_LEVEL, and code running at this IRQL cannot be interrupted by other software IRQLs (i.e., those below DISPATCH_LEVEL). In other words, if there is an infinite loop in the DPC routine, the processor associated with it will spin forever and the system will practically "freeze"; in a multi-processor system, it may not freeze but the processor executing the DPC will not be usable by the thread dispatcher. In addition, the DPC routine cannot wait on any kind of dispatcher objects because the dispatcher itself operates at DISPATCH_LEVEL; this is why functions such as KeWaitForSingleObject and KeDelayExecutionThread cannot be called in DPC routines.

> **NOTE** Windows has a DPC watchdog routine that detects DPCs running over a certain time period and bugchecks with code DPC_WATCHDOG_VIOLATION (0x133). You can query the watchdog timer value by calling KeQueryDpcWatchdogInformation.

Some rootkits use DPCs to synchronize access to global linked lists. For example, they may remove an entry from the ActiveProcessLinks list to hide processes; because this list can be modified at any time by any processor, some rootkit authors use a DPC along with another synchronization mechanism to safely operate on it. In one of the exercises, you will be asked to explain why some authors succeed at this while others fail (machine bugchecks).

Exercises

1. Where and when is the `DpcData` field in KPRCB initialized?

2. Write a driver to enumerate all DPCs on the entire system. Make sure you support multi-processor systems! Explain the difficulties and how you solved them.

3. Explain how the `KiDpcWatchdog` routine works.

Timers

Timers are used to signal the expiration of a certain amount of time, which can be periodically or at some time in the future. Optionally, the timer can also be associated with a DPC. For example, if a driver wants to check the status of a device every five minutes or execute a routine 10 minutes in the future, it can achieve this by using timers.

Concretely speaking, a timer is defined by the KTIMER structure:

Timer-related structures

```
0: kd> dt nt!_KPRCB
...
   +0x2dfc InterruptRate     : Uint4B
   +0x2e00 TimerTable        : _KTIMER_TABLE
0: kd> dt nt!_KTIMER_TABLE
   +0x000 TimerExpiry        : [64] Ptr64 _KTIMER
   +0x200 TimerEntries       : [256] _KTIMER_TABLE_ENTRY
0: kd> dt nt!_KTIMER
   +0x000 Header             : _DISPATCHER_HEADER
   +0x018 DueTime            : _ULARGE_INTEGER
   +0x020 TimerListEntry     : _LIST_ENTRY
   +0x030 Dpc                : Ptr64 _KDPC
   +0x038 Processor          : Uint4B
   +0x03c Period             : Uint4B
0: kd> dt nt!_KTIMER_TABLE_ENTRY
   +0x000 Lock               : Uint8B
   +0x008 Entry              : _LIST_ENTRY
   +0x018 Time               : _ULARGE_INTEGER
```

Timer-related routines

```
VOID KeInitializeTimer(
  _Out_  PKTIMER Timer
);

BOOLEAN KeSetTimer(
  _Inout_   PKTIMER Timer,
```

```
  _In_        LARGE_INTEGER DueTime,
  _In_opt_    PKDPC Dpc
);

BOOLEAN KeSetTimerEx(
  _Inout_     PKTIMER Timer,
  _In_        LARGE_INTEGER DueTime,
  _In_        LONG Period,
  _In_opt_    PKDPC Dpc
);
```

It is initialized by calling KeInitializeTimer, which simply fills out some of the basic fields. After initialization, the timer can be set through either KeSetTimer or KeSetTimerEx. The difference between the two is that KeSetTimerEx can be used to set a recurring timer (i.e., expire every X time unit). Note that these functions can optionally take a DPC object, which is executed when the timer expires. When calling these routines, the timer is inserted into a timer table in the PRCB (TimerTable->TimerListEntry). Once set and queued, a timer may be cancelled and hence removed from the timer table. This is done by the KeCancelTimer API.

How does the system know when a timer expires? On every clock interrupt, the system updates its runtime and checks the timer list to see if there are any expiring entries; if there are, it requests a DPC interrupt that will process the entries. Hence, timers are also processed at DISPATCH_LEVEL.

There are many examples showing how timers are used in the operating system. For example, the system has a periodic timer that synchronizes the system time and checks if the license is expiring (see ExpTimeRefreshDpcRoutine). There is even a timer that expires at the end of a century (see ExpCenturyDpcRoutine).

Exercises

1. Write a driver to enumerate the loaded module list every 10 minutes.

2. Write a driver to enumerate all timers on the system. Make sure you support multi-core systems. Explain why the DPC data associated with the timer does not seem to make sense.

3. Explain the DpcWatchDogTimer field in the PRCB.

4. Write a driver that sets a timer with an associated DPC. Explain the sequence of calls leading to DPC execution. You may be interested in the following functions: KeUpdateRuntime, KeAccumulateTicks, KiTimerExpiration, KiRetireDpcList, and KiExpireTimerTable.

5. Explain how timer insertion works. You will need to look at the function KiInsertTimerTable.

Process and Thread Callbacks

A driver can register callbacks for a variety of events. Two of the most common callbacks are related to processes and threads, and they can be registered through documented APIs such as `PsSetCreateProcessNotifyRoutine`, `PsSetCreateThreadNotifyRoutine`, and `PsSetLoadImageNotifyRoutine`. How do they work?

During system initialization, the kernel calls the function `PspInitializeCallbacks` to initialize three global arrays: `PspCreateThreadNotifyRoutine`, `PspCreateProcessNotifyRoutine`, and `PspLoadImageNotifyRoutine`. When the driver registers a process, thread, or image callback, it is stored in one of these arrays. In addition, there is a global flag, `PspNotifyEnableMask`, which determines what notification types are enabled/disabled. In the thread initialization and termination paths (`PspInsertThread` and `PspExitThread`, respectively), it checks whether the `PspNotifyEnableMask` flag is present and invokes the callbacks accordingly.

These callbacks are primarily provided for drivers and hence are not explicitly used by the kernel. For example, many anti-virus software products register these callbacks to monitor system behavior. Kernel-mode rootkits sometimes use them in conjunction with APCs to inject code into new processes.

Exercises

1. This section provided a general explanation of how process, thread, and image notify callbacks are implemented. Investigate the following functions and explain how they work:

   - `PsSetCreateThreadNotifyRoutine`
   - `PsSetCreateProcessNotifyRoutine`
   - `PsSetLoadImageNotifyRoutine`
   - `PspInitializeCallbacks`

2. If you did exercise 1, write a driver that enumerates all process, thread, and image notify routines on the system and remove them.

3. If you did exercise 1, explain two major weaknesses of these notification callbacks. For example, can you create new processes/threads without being detected by these callbacks? Implement your idea and evaluate its effectiveness. Note: It is possible.

4. If you register an image load callback with `PsSetLoadImageNotifyRoutine`, under what condition is it called? Identify one weakness and implement your idea. Hint: You may need to consult the PE specification.

5. The `PsSetCreateThreadNotifyRoutine`, `PsSetCreateProcessNotifyRoutine`, and `PsSetLoadImageNotifyRoutine` APIs are exposed by the process manager. However, the object and configuration managers also expose their own callbacks through `ObRegisterCallbacks` and `CmRegisterCallback`, respectively. Investigate how these callbacks are implemented.

6. Identify other similar callbacks documented in the WDK and investigate how they work (processor, memory, and so on).

Completion Routines

The Windows I/O model is that of a device stack, whereby devices are layered on top of each other, with each layer implementing some specific function. This means that higher-level drivers can pass requests to lower ones for processing. Whichever layer completes the requests marks it done by calling `IoCompleteRequest`. Completion routines are used to notify drivers that their I/O request has been completed (or that it was cancelled or failed). They run in arbitrary thread context and can be set through the `IoSetCompletionRoutine`/Ex APIs. `IoSetCompletionRoutine` is documented in WDK, but it will never appear in an assembly listing or import table because it is forced-inline; one method to identify the `IoSetCompletion` routine is to see the `CompletionRoutine` field in an `IO_STACK_LOCATION` (see the next section) modified:

Structure definition

```
0: kd> dt nt!_IO_STACK_LOCATION
    +0x000 MajorFunction    : UChar
    +0x001 MinorFunction    : UChar
    +0x002 Flags            : UChar
    +0x003 Control          : UChar
    +0x008 Parameters       : <unnamed-tag>
    +0x028 DeviceObject     : Ptr64 _DEVICE_OBJECT
    +0x030 FileObject       : Ptr64 _FILE_OBJECT
    +0x038 CompletionRoutine : Ptr64     long
    +0x040 Context          : Ptr64 Void
```

Function definition

```
VOID
IoSetCompletionRoutine(
    _In_ PIRP Irp,
    _In_opt_ PIO_COMPLETION_ROUTINE CompletionRoutine,
    _In_opt_ __drv_aliasesMem PVOID Context,
    _In_ BOOLEAN InvokeOnSuccess,
    _In_ BOOLEAN InvokeOnError,
    _In_ BOOLEAN InvokeOnCancel
    )
{
    PIO_STACK_LOCATION irpSp;
```

```
irpSp = IoGetNextIrpStackLocation(Irp);
irpSp->CompletionRoutine = CompletionRoutine;
irpSp->Context = Context;
irpSp->Control = 0;
if (InvokeOnSuccess) {
    irpSp->Control = SL_INVOKE_ON_SUCCESS;
}
if (InvokeOnError) {
    irpSp->Control |= SL_INVOKE_ON_ERROR;
}
if (InvokeOnCancel) {
    irpSp->Control |= SL_INVOKE_ON_CANCEL;
}
}
```

The I/O manager calls the registered completion routine as part of
`IopfCompleteRequest`.

Although the legitimate use of completion routines is obvious, rootkits may use
them for nefarious purposes. For example, they can set a completion routine to
modify the return buffer from a lower driver before it is returned to user mode.

Exercise

1. Write a test driver using a completion routine and determine where it is
   called from.

I/O Request Packets

Windows uses I/O request packets (IRPs) to describe I/O requests to kernel-
mode components (like drivers). When a user-mode application calls an API to
request data, the I/O manager builds an IRP to describe the request and determines which device to send the IRP to for processing. From the time an IRP is
created until its completion by a driver, it may have passed through multiple
devices, and additional IRPs could have been created to fulfill the request. One
can think of IRPs as the fundamental unit of communication between devices
for I/O requests. An IRP is defined in WDK headers by the partially opaque IRP
structure, but most fields are undocumented (hence partially opaque):

```
0: kd> dt nt!_IRP
   +0x000 Type            : Int2B
   ...
```

```
    +0x042 StackCount        : Char
    +0x043 CurrentLocation   : Char
...
    +0x058 Overlay           : <unnamed-tag>
    +0x068 CancelRoutine     : Ptr64       void
    +0x070 UserBuffer        : Ptr64 Void
    +0x078 Tail              : <unnamed-tag>
```

From a programming perspective, an IRP can be divided into two areas: static and dynamic. The static part is an IRP structure with basic information about the request such as who requested the operation (kernel or user), requesting thread, and data passed in from the user. The Overlay and Tail fields are unions containing metadata about the request. The dynamic part is immediately after the header; it is an array of IO_STACK_LOCATION structures containing device-specific request information. An IO_STACK_LOCATION contains the IRP's major and minor function, parameters for the request, and an optional completion routine. Similar to IRP, it is a partially opaque structure:

```
0: kd> dt nt!_IO_STACK_LOCATION
    +0x000 MajorFunction     : UChar
    +0x001 MinorFunction     : UChar
    +0x002 Flags             : UChar
    +0x003 Control           : UChar
    +0x008 Parameters        : <unnamed-tag>
    +0x028 DeviceObject      : Ptr64 _DEVICE_OBJECT
    +0x030 FileObject        : Ptr64 _FILE_OBJECT
    +0x038 CompletionRoutine : Ptr64       long
    +0x040 Context           : Ptr64 Void
```

The Parameters field is a union because the parameter depends on the major and minor function number. Windows has a predefined list of generic major and minor functions to describe all request types. For example, a file read request will lead to an IRP created with the major function IRP_MJ_READ; when Windows requests input from the keyboard class driver, it also uses IRP_MJ_READ. When the I/O manager creates an IRP, it determines how many IO_STACK_LOCATION structures to allocate based on how many devices there are in the current device stack. Each device is responsible for preparing the IO_STACK_LOCATION for the next one. Recall that a driver can set a completion routine with the IoSetCompletionRoutine API; this is actually an inlined routine that sets the CompletionRoutine field in the IO_STACK_LOCATION.

Figure 3-8 illustrates the relationship between these two structures in an IRP.

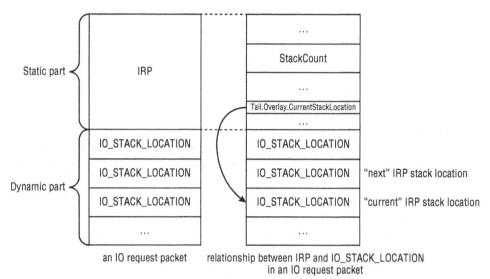

Figure 3-8

Note that the "next" stack location is the element immediately above the "current" one (not after it). This is important to know because stack location routines such as IoGetCurrentIrpStackLocation, IoSkipCurrentIrpStackLocation, IoGetNextIrpStackLocation, and others are simply returning pointers to these array elements using pointer arithmetic.

Although IRPs are typically generated by the I/O manager in response to requests from users or other devices, they may also be created from scratch and sent to other devices for processing. A driver can allocate an IRP with IoAllocateIrp, associate it with a thread, fill out the IRP major and minor code, set up IO_STACK_LOCATION count/size, fill in parameters, and send it to the destination device for processing with IoCallDriver. Some rootkits use this mechanism to directly send requests to the file system driver in order to bypass system call hooking. You will analyze one such rootkit in the exercise.

Structure of a Driver

A *driver* is a piece of software that interacts with the kernel and/or controls hardware resources. While there are many different types of drivers, we are primarily concerned with the following types of kernel-mode drivers:

- **Legacy software driver**—Software that runs in ring 0 and interacts with the kernel through documented and undocumented interfaces. Most rootkits and security drivers are of this type.

- **Legacy filter driver**—Drivers that attach to an existing driver and modify its input.

- **File system minifilter driver**—Drivers that interact with the file system to intercept file I/O requests. Most anti-virus software uses this kind of driver to intercept file writes/reads for scanning purposes; on-disk encryption software is typically implemented through this mechanism.

The standard model for Windows drivers is the Windows Driver Model (WDM). WDM defines both a set of interfaces that drivers must implement and rules to follow in order to safely interact with the kernel. It has been defined since Windows 2000 and all drivers you analyze are based on it. Because writing reliable plug-and-play hardware drivers with full power management and handling all the synchronization idiosyncrasies using pure WDM interfaces is exceedingly difficult, Microsoft introduced the Windows Driver Foundation (WDF) framework. WDF is basically a set of libraries built on top of WDM that simplifies driver development by shielding developers from directly interacting with WDM. WDF is divided into two categories: kernel-mode driver framework (KMDF) and user-mode driver framework (UMDF). KMDF is meant for kernel-mode drivers (such as keyboards and USB devices) and UMDF is for user-mode drivers (such as printer drivers). This book deals only with drivers based on the WDM model.

One can think of a driver as a DLL that is loaded into the kernel address space and executes with the same privilege as the kernel. It has a well-defined entry point and may register dispatch routines to service requests from users or other drivers. Note that a driver does not have a main execution thread; it simply contains code that can be called by the kernel under certain circumstances. This is why drivers usually have to register dispatch routines with the I/O manager (see the next section). When analyzing drivers, the first and most important task is to identify these dispatch routines and understand how they interact with the kernel.

Entry Points

All drivers have an entry point called DriverEntry, which is defined as follows:

DriverEntry

```
NTSTATUS
DriverEntry (
    PDRIVER_OBJECT DriverObject,
    PUNICODE_STRING RegistryPath
);
```

DRIVER_OBJECT

```
typedef struct _DRIVER_OBJECT {
    CSHORT Type;
```

```
    CSHORT Size;
    PDEVICE_OBJECT DeviceObject;
    ULONG Flags;
    PVOID DriverStart;
    ULONG DriverSize;
    PVOID DriverSection;
    PDRIVER_EXTENSION DriverExtension;
    UNICODE_STRING DriverName;
    PUNICODE_STRING HardwareDatabase;
    PFAST_IO_DISPATCH FastIoDispatch;
    PDRIVER_INITIALIZE DriverInit;
    PDRIVER_STARTIO DriverStartIo;
    PDRIVER_UNLOAD DriverUnload;
    PDRIVER_DISPATCH MajorFunction[IRP_MJ_MAXIMUM_FUNCTION + 1];
} DRIVER_OBJECT, *PDRIVER_OBJECT;
```

NOTE Technically, the entry point does not have to be named `DriverEntry`.

When a driver needs to be loaded, its image is mapped into kernel space memory, a driver object is created for it and registered with the object manager, and then the I/O manager calls the entry point. DRIVER_OBJECT is a structure filled out by the I/O manager during the driver loading process; the official documentation indicates that it is a partially opaque structure, but one can view its full definition in the header files. DriverInit is set to the driver's entry point and the I/O manager directly calls this field. The primary responsibility of DriverEntry is to initialize driver-specific settings and register IRP dispatch routines as necessary. These routines are stored in the MajorFunction array. As previously mentioned, Windows has a pre-defined set of IRP major functions to generically describe every I/O request; whenever an I/O request comes in for the driver, the I/O manager calls the appropriate IRP major function handler to process the request. Hence, it is common to see code like the following in DriverEntry:

```
DriverObject->MajorFunction[IRP_MJ_CREATE] = CreateCloseHandler;
DriverObject->MajorFunction[IRP_MJ_CLOSE] = CreateCloseHandler;
DriverObject->MajorFunction[IRP_MJ_DEVICE_CONTROL] = DeviceControlHandler;
...
```

Note that the same dispatch routine can be specified for multiple IRP major functions. Sometimes they will be initialized in a loop:

```
for (i=0; i<IRP_MJ_MAXIMUM; i++) {
    DriverObject->MajorFunction[i] = GenericHandler;
}
DriverObject->MajorFunction[IRP_MJ_CREATE] = CreateHandler;
DriverObject->MajorFunction[IRP_MJ_PNP] = PnpHandler;
...
```

If you do not initialize the MajorFunction table, it will contain the default handler `IopInvalidDeviceRequest`, which simply returns an error to the requestor.

If a driver supports dynamic unloading, it must also fill out the `DriverUnload` field; otherwise, the driver will remain in memory forever (until reboot). A `DriverUnload` routine typically performs driver-specific cleanup tasks. Many rootkits do not register an unload routine.

`RegistryPath` is the registry path for the driver. It is created as part of the normal driver installation process.

Driver and Device Objects

The previous section states that the I/O manager creates a `DRIVER_OBJECT` for every driver loaded in the system. A driver can choose to create one or more device objects. Device objects are defined by the partially opaque `DEVICE_OBJECT` structure:

```
typedef struct _DEVICE_OBJECT {
    CSHORT Type;
    USHORT Size;
    LONG ReferenceCount;
    struct _DRIVER_OBJECT *DriverObject;
    struct _DEVICE_OBJECT *NextDevice;
    struct _DEVICE_OBJECT *AttachedDevice;
    struct _IRP *CurrentIrp;
    ...
    PVOID DeviceExtension;
    DEVICE_TYPE DeviceType;
    CCHAR StackSize;
    ...
    ULONG ActiveThreadCount;
    PSECURITY_DESCRIPTOR SecurityDescriptor;
    ...
    PVOID Reserved;
} DEVICE_OBJECT, *PDEVICE_OBJECT;
```

`DriverObject` is the driver object associated with this device object. If the driver created more than one device object, then `NextDevice` will point to the next device object in the chain. A driver may create multiple device objects to manage different hardware resources it is handling. If no device objects are created, then no one can send requests to the device. Typically, drivers will create device objects in `DriverEntry` through the `IoCreateDevice` API.

`DeviceExtension` is a pointer to device-specific data stored in non-paged pool. Its size is specified as a parameter to `IoCreateDevice`. Developers typically store context information or important data about the driver and other related devices here. Recovering the device extension structure is probably the second most important task in the analysis of drivers.

A driver can "attach" one of its own device objects to another device object so that it receives I/O requests intended for the target device object. For example, if device A attaches to device B, then all IRP requests sent to B will be routed to A first. This attaching mechanism is used to support filter drivers so that they can modify/inspect requests to other drivers. The AttachedDevice field points to the device to which the current device object is attached. Device attaching is done through the IoAttachDevice API family.

IRP Handling

As mentioned earlier, DriverEntry typically registers dispatch routines to handle various IRP major functions. The prototype for these dispatch routines is as follows:

```
NTSTATUS
XXX_Dispatch (
    PDEVICE_OBJECT DeviceObject,
    PIRP Irp
);
```

The first argument is the request's target device object. The second argument is the IRP describing the request.

A dispatch routine typically first determines what IRP major function it received and then determines the request's parameters. It does so by checking the IO_STACK_LOCATION in the IRP. If the dispatch routine successfully completes the request, it calls IoCompleteRequest and returns. If it cannot complete the request, then it has three options: return an error, pass the IRP to another driver, or pend the IRP. For example, a filter driver may choose to process only IRP_MJ_READ requests itself and pass all other requests to the attached device. A driver can pass IRPs to another driver through the IoCallDriver API.

Because IRP parameters for each request are stored in their own IO_STACK_LOCATION, a driver must ensure that it is accessing the right location. This is done through the IoGetCurrentIrpStackLocation API. If the driver wants to pass the same IRP to another driver, it has to either copy the current parameters to the next IO_STACK_LOCATION (IoCopyCurrentIrpStackLocationToNext) or pass the parameter to the next driver (IoSkipCurrentStackLocation).

A Common Mechanism for User-Kernel Communication

Many mechanisms are used to facilitate user-kernel communication. For example, a driver can communicate with user-mode code through a shared memory region double-mapped in user and kernel space. Another method is for the driver to create an event that a user-mode thread can wait on; the event state can be used as a trigger for further action. Yet another (although hackish) method is through interrupt handling. A driver can manually set up a custom interrupt handler in the IDT and user-mode code can trigger it with the `INT` instruction; you will probably never see this technique used in a commercial driver.

While the precise communication mechanism depends on the developer's ultimate goal, a generic documented interface is typically used for user-kernel data exchange. This mechanism is supported by the `IRP_MJ_DEVICE_CONTROL` operation and commonly referred to as device I/O control or simply IOCTL. It works as follows:

1. The driver defines one or more IOCTL codes for each operation it supports.

2. For each supported operation, the driver specifies how it should access the user input and return data to the user. There are three access methods: buffered I/O, direct I/O, and neither. These methods are covered in the next section.

3. Inside the `IRP_MJ_DEVICE_CONTROL` handler, the driver retrieves the IOCTL code from its `IO_STACK_LOCATION` and processes the data based on the input method.

User-mode code can request these IOCTL operations through the `DeviceIoControl` API.

Buffering Methods

A driver can access a user-mode buffer using one of the following three methods:

- **Buffered I/O**—This is referred to as `METHOD_BUFFERED` in the kernel. When using this method, the kernel validates the user buffer to be in accessible user-mode memory, allocates a block of memory in non-paged pool, and copies the user buffer to it. The driver accesses this kernel-mode buffer through the `AssociatedIrp.SystemBuffer` field in the IRP structure. While processing the request, the driver may modify the system buffer (perhaps it needs to return some data back to the user); after completing the request, the kernel copies the system buffer's content back to the user-mode buffer and automatically frees the system buffer.

- **Direct IO**—This is referred to as `METHOD_IN_DIRECT` or `METHOD_OUT_DIRECT` in the kernel. The former is used for passing data to the driver; the latter is used for getting data from the driver. This method is similar to buffered I/O except that the driver gets an MDL describing the user buffer. The I/O manager creates the MDL and locks it in memory before passing it to the driver. Drivers can access this MDL through the `MdlAddress` field of the IRP structure.

- **Neither**—This is referred to as `METHOD_NEITHER` in the kernel. When using this method, the I/O manager does not perform any kind of validation on the user data; it passes the raw data to the driver. Drivers can access the data through the `Parameters.DeviceIoControl.Type3InputBuffer` field in its IO_STACK_LOCATION. While this method may seem the fastest of the three (as there is no validation or mapping of additional buffers), it is certainly the most insecure one. It leaves all the validation to the developer. Without proper validation, a driver using this method may expose itself to security vulnerabilities such as kernel memory corruption or leakage/disclosure.

There is no written rule for determining which method to use in drivers because it depends on the driver's specific requirements. However, in practice, most software drivers use buffered I/O because it provides a good balance between simplicity and security. Direct I/O is common in hardware drivers because it can be used to pass large data chunks without buffering overhead.

I/O Control Code

An IOCTL code is a 32-bit integer that encodes the device type, operation-specific code, buffering method, and security access. Drivers usually define IOCTL codes through the CTL_CODE macro:

```
#define CTL_CODE( DeviceType, Function, Method, Access ) (           \
    ((DeviceType) << 16) | ((Access) << 14) | ((Function) << 2) | (Method) \
    )
```

DeviceType is usually one of the FILE_DEVICE_* constants, but for third-party drivers it can use anything above 0x8000. (This is only the recommended value and there is nothing enforcing it.) Access specifies generic read/write operations allowed by the IOCTL; it can be a combination of FILE_ANY_ACCESS, FILE_READ_ACCESS, and FILE_WRITE_ACCESS. Function is the driver-specific IOCTL code; it can be anything above 0x800. Method specifies one of the buffering methods.

A typical way to define an IOCTL code is as follows:

```
#define FILE_DEVICE_GENIOCTL 0xa000 // our device type
#define GENIOCTL_PROCESS     0x800  // our special IOCTL code

#define IOCTL_PROCESS CTL_CODE(FILE_DEVICE_GENIOCTL, \
                               GENIOCTL_PROCESS, \
                               METHOD_BUFFERED, FILE_READ_DATA)
```

This defines an IOCTL called IOCTL_PROCESS for a custom driver using METHOD_BUFFERED.

When analyzing a driver, it is important to decompose the IOCTL down to its device type, code, access, and buffering method. This can be achieved with a couple of simple documented macros:

```
#define DEVICE_TYPE_FROM_CTL_CODE(ctrlCode) \
                                  (((ULONG)(ctrlCode & 0xffff0000)) >> 16)
#define METHOD_FROM_CTL_CODE(ctrlCode)      ((ULONG)(ctrlCode & 3))
```

Miscellaneous System Mechanisms

This section discusses constructs that—while not essential to understanding kernel drivers—are frequently observed in real-life drivers.

System Control Registers

In order to achieve their goals, many rootkit developers resort to hooking functions in the kernel. However, all kernel code is mapped as read-only, so patching it will result in a bugcheck. On x86/x64, this protection mechanism is actually enforced at the hardware level through a special control register: CR0. CR0 determines several important processor settings, such as whether it is in protected mode and whether paging is enabled; it also determines whether the CPU can write to read-only pages (WP bit). CR0 is only accessible by code running in ring 0. By default, Windows turns on the WP bit, which prohibits writes to pages marked read-only.

> **NOTE** On x64 and ARM, there is a Windows feature called *Kernel Patch Protection*, also known as *PatchGuard*, that tries to detect hooks and modifications to various security-critical data structures and bugchecks the machine. Hence, it is not common to see hooks on these platforms in shipping/production drivers. Nevertheless, hooking is still prevalent because there are many x86 machines out there, so you will frequently run into them.

There are several ways to bypass this restriction and the easiest one is to toggle the WP bit. Hence, you will frequently see this code pattern in rootkits. For example, Sample G:

```
01: .text:0001062F    push    eax
02: .text:00010630    mov     eax, cr0
03: .text:00010633    mov     [esp+8+var_4], eax
04: .text:00010637    and     eax, 0FFFEFFFFh
05: .text:0001063C    mov     cr0, eax
06: .text:0001063F    pop     eax
```

Lines 2–3 copy CR0 to EAX and save it to a local variable. Lines 4–5 turn off the bit 16 in EAX and write it back to CR0. Bit 16 in CR0 is the WP bit.

There are at least two other solutions that do not directly modify CR0. They involve MDLs and knowledge of the platform MMU. You will be required to do this as one of the exercises.

KeServiceDescriptorTable

As previously stated, many rootkits resort to hooking system calls. However, as you learned, system calls are identified by a number that is used as an index into a syscall table. Furthermore, the system call table (KiServiceTable) is not exported, so there is no easy way to access it from a driver. How do rootkit authors get around this?

The kernel exports the KeServiceDescriptorTable symbol, which contains a KSERVICE_TABLE_DESCRIPTOR structure with the system call information. (Recall that on x64, this symbol is not exported.) This is how most rootkits access the system call table. The next step is to identify where the target system call is located. Recall that system calls are identified by a number, not by name. Rootkit authors have several ways to find the right system call. One way is to hardcode the syscall index. Another method is to disassemble the system call stub and get the index from there. Both of these methods have a trade-off: They are simple to implement, but they rely on code or data patterns that may change from service pack to service pack; they may be reliable on some platforms, but will certainly lead to system instability on others. Despite the unreliability, these two methods are frequently used by rootkits in the wild. For example, Sample G has the following code:

```
01: .text:000117D4 sub_117D4 proc near
02: .text:000117D4    push    ebp
03: .text:000117D5    mov     ebp, esp
04: .text:000117D7    push    ecx
05: .text:000117D8    mov     ecx, ds:KeServiceDescriptorTable
06: .text:000117DE    mov     ecx, [ecx]
07: .text:000117E0    push    esi
08: .text:000117E1    mov     esi, ds:ZwQuerySystemInformation
09: ...
10: .text:00011808    call    DisableWP
11: .text:0001180D    mov     ecx, ds:KeServiceDescriptorTable
12: .text:00011813    mov     eax, [esi+1]
13: .text:00011816    mov     ecx, [ecx]
14: .text:00011818    mov     dword ptr [ecx+eax*4], offset sub_1123E
15: ...
16: .text:00011836 sub_117D4 endp
```

Lines 5–10 save the address of KiServiceTable in ECX, save the address of ZwQuerySystemInformation in ESI, and disable the WP bit. Line 12 retrieves the second byte from ZwQuerySystemInformation; it does this because it assumes that the first instruction in the function moves the syscall number to a register and hence the 32-bit value after the opcode contains the actual syscall number (see the following sidebar). Lines 13–14 overwrite that syscall entry in the service table with a new function: sub_1123e. All calls to ZwQuerySystemInformation will now be redirected to sub_1123e.

NOTE We mentioned earlier that line 12 retrieves the second byte from ZwQuerySystemInformation. On 32-bit Windows 7, the first instruction in

`ZwQuerySystemInformation` is `b805010000 mov eax` and `105h`. `b8` is the MOV opcode, while `05010000` (0x105) encodes the immediate, which in this case is the syscall number.

Sections

A *section* is an object used to describe memory backed by some form of storage. The section can be backed by a normal file or a page file. A file-backed section is one for which the memory content is that of a file on disk; if there are modifications to the section, they will be made directly to disk. A page-file-backed section is one whose content is backed by the page file; modifications to such a section will be discarded after it is closed. A driver can create a section with the `ZwCreateSection` API and then map a view of it into another process with `ZwMapViewOfSection`. Each view is basically a virtual address range that can be used to access the memory represented by the associated section object. Hence, there can be multiple views for a section.

Walk-Throughs

Now that you have a strong grasp of Windows kernel and driver concepts, it is time to apply that knowledge by analyzing some real-life rootkits. This section serves two purposes: to explain the thinking process of kernel-mode reverse engineering and to demonstrate the application of driver development techniques to understanding rootkits.

Rootkits come in many different forms. Some hook system calls, some hide files by filtering I/O responses, some intercept network communication, some log keystrokes, and so on. However, like all drivers, they share the same generic structure; for example, they all have a `DriverEntry` function with optional IRP dispatch handlers that interface with the kernel through documented and undocumented interfaces. With this knowledge, you can dissect core components of a driver and systematically analyze them. The general analysis process is as follows:

1. Identify DriverEntry and determine the IRP dispatch handlers, if any.

2. Determine whether the driver attaches to another device to filter/intercept its I/O requests. If so, what is the target device?

3. If the driver creates a device object, determine the name and device extension size.

4. Recover the device extension structure by observing how its field members are used.

5. If the driver supports IOCTL, identify all the IOCTL codes and their corresponding functionality. Determine what buffering method they use.

6. Identify DPCs, work items, APCs, timers, completion routines, callbacks, and system threads.

7. Try to understand how all the pieces fit together.

An x86 Rootkit

The walk-through begins with Sample A.

Its DriverEntry starts at `0x105F0` and ends at `0x106AD`. It first initializes a UNICODE_STRING structure with the strings \Device\fsodhfn2m and \DosDevices\fsodhfn2m. In kernel mode, most strings are described using the UNICODE_STRING structure:

```
typedef struct _UNICODE_STRING {
  USHORT  Length;
  USHORT  MaximumLength;
  PWSTR   Buffer;
} UNICODE_STRING, *PUNICODE_STRING;
```

It is initialized through the RtlInitUnicodeString API. The "Device" string is a device name in the object manager; the "DosDevices" string is used as a symbolic link to the actual device name. The Windows object manager maintains and organizes objects in a filesystem-like structure with the root at "\". There are well-defined directories such as \Devices, \BaseNamedObjects, \ KernelObjects, and so on. \DosDevices is an alias for the \?? directory; it is there because when user-mode applications specify the path to an object they want to access, the \??\ is prepended to it; \?? contains symbolic links pointing to the real object. For example, when a user wants to access "c:\test.txt" through the CreateFile API, the actual path sent to the kernel is "\??\c:\test.txt"; because "c:" is a symbolic link to \Device\HarddiskVolume2 (it may vary on your system), the whole path will eventually resolve to \Device\HarddiskVolume2\test.txt. The symbolic link is necessary because user-mode APIs usually access devices through the \?? directory; if there were no symbolic links there, the device may not be accessible to user-mode apps.

After initializing the two strings, it proceeds to create the actual device object. IoCreateDevice is defined as follows:

```
NTSTATUS
  IoCreateDevice(
    IN PDRIVER_OBJECT  DriverObject,
    IN ULONG  DeviceExtensionSize,
    IN PUNICODE_STRING  DeviceName  OPTIONAL,
    IN DEVICE_TYPE  DeviceType,
    IN ULONG  DeviceCharacteristics,
```

```
   IN BOOLEAN  Exclusive,
   OUT PDEVICE_OBJECT *DeviceObject
   );
```

DriverObject is the caller's DRIVER_OBJECT; it is the driver object that the new device object is associated with. DeviceExtensionSize is how many bytes of non-paged pool memory should be allocated for the driver-specific structure. Because it is a user-defined structure, it is very important to recover its fields. DeviceName is the native device name. DeviceType is one of the pre-defined FILE_DEVICE_* types; if the device does not fall into a generic category, FILE_DEVICE_UNKNOWN is used instead. DeviceCharacteristics refers to the device characteristic; most of the time you will see FILE_DEVICE_SECURE_OPEN. Exclusive determines whether there can be more than one handle to the device. DeviceObject receives the actual device object.

From the disassembly, you can decompile the first basic block and its exiting condition as follows:

```
01: UNICODE_STRING devname;
02: UNICODE_STRING symname;
03:
04: NTSTATUS DriverEntry(PDRIVER_OBJECT DriverObject, \
                         PUNICODE_STRING regpath)
05: {
06:   NTSTATUS status;
07:   PDEVICE_OBJECT devobj;
08:
09:   RtlInitUnicodeString(&devname, L"\\Device\\fsodhfn2m");
10:   RtlInitUnicodeString(&symname, L"\\DosDevices\\fsodhfn2m");
11:   status = IoCreateDevice(
12:              DriverObject,
13:              0,
14:              &devname,
15:              FILE_DEVICE_UNKNOWN,
16:              FILE_DEVICE_SECURE_OPEN,
17:              FALSE,
18:              &devobj);
19:   if (!NT_SUCCESS(status)) {
20:     return status; // loc_106A3
21:   }
22: }
```

NT_SUCCESS() is a common macro that checks if status is greater than or equal to 0. After successfully creating the object, it proceeds to the following:

```
01: .text:00010643    mov     ecx, [ebp+DriverObject]
02: .text:00010646    mov     dword ptr [ecx+38h], offset sub_10300
03: .text:0001064D    mov     edx, [ebp+DriverObject]
04: .text:00010650    mov     dword ptr [edx+40h], offset sub_10300
05: .text:00010657    mov     eax, [ebp+DriverObject]
06: .text:0001065A    mov     dword ptr [eax+70h], offset sub_10300
```

```
07: .text:00010661   mov     ecx, [ebp+DriverObject]
08: .text:00010664   mov     dword ptr [ecx+34h], offset sub_10580
09: .text:0001066B   push    offset SymbolicLinkName  ; SymbolicLinkName
10: .text:00010670   call    ds:IoDeleteSymbolicLink
11: .text:00010676   push    offset DestinationString ; DeviceName
12: .text:0001067B   push    offset SymbolicLinkName  ; SymbolicLinkName
13: .text:00010680   call    ds:IoCreateSymbolicLink
14: .text:00010686   mov     [ebp+var_4], eax
15: .text:00010689   cmp     [ebp+var_4], 0
16: .text:0001068D   jge     short loc_106A1
```

Lines 1–8 set some DRIVER_OBJECT fields to two function pointers. What is at offset 0x38, 0x40, 0x70, and 0x34?

```
0: kd> dt _DRIVER_OBJECT
nt!_DRIVER_OBJECT
   +0x000 Type          : Int2B
   +0x002 Size          : Int2B
   +0x004 DeviceObject  : Ptr32 _DEVICE_OBJECT
...
   +0x034 DriverUnload  : Ptr32       void
   +0x038 MajorFunction : [28] Ptr32       long
```

Offset 0x34 is the DriverUnload routine; now, you know that the driver supports dynamic unloading and sub_10580 is the unload routine. Offset 0x38 is the beginning of the MajorFunction array; recall that this is an array of IRP dispatch handlers. Because there is a maximum of 28 generic IRP major functions, the MajorFunction array has 28 members. The first index is 0, which corresponds to IRP_MJ_CREATE; hence, you know that sub_10300 is the handler for that IRP. Offset 0x40 is the third element in the MajorFunction array (index 2); this corresponds to IRP_MJ_CLOSE, and sub_10300 is reused as the handler. Offset 0x70 is the 16th element in the array (index 0xe), which corresponds to IRP_MJ_DEVICE_CONTROL, and sub_10300 is the handler. At this point, you know that sub_10300 is the handler for the read, close, and device control IRP.

Lines 10–13 delete any existing symbolic link and create a new one to point to the device object previously created.

You can now continue decompiling this block in DriverEntry as follows:

```
01: DriverObject->MajorFunction[IRP_MJ_READ] = sub_10300;
02: DriverObject->MajorFunction[IRP_MJ_CLOSE] = sub_10300;
03: DriverObject->MajorFunction[IRP_MJ_DEVICE_CONTROL] = sub_10300;
04: DriverObject->DriverUnload = sub_10580;
05:
06: IoDeleteSymbolicLink(&symname);
07: status = IoCreateSymbolicLink(&symname, &devname);
08: if (!NT_SUCCESS(status)) {
09:    ... // block .text:0001068F
10:    return status;
```

```
11: }
12: return status;
```

To make life easier, you can rename sub_10300 as IRP_ReadCloseDeviceIo and sub_10580 as DRV_Unload.

The next block at 0x1068F deletes the previously created device object if the symbolic link creation fails. Note that it is getting the device object from the driver object instead of using the pointer passed to IoCreateDevice. You can decompile this block as follows:

```
01: IoDeleteDevice(DriverObject->DeviceObject);
```

That completes decompilation of this rootkit's DriverEntry. To summarize what has been learned so far:

- The driver creates a device object named \Device\fsodhfn2m.

- It supports dynamic unloading and the unload routine is sub_10580 (renamed to DRV_Unload).

- It supports IRP_MJ_READ, IRP_MJ_WRITE, and IRP_MJ_DEVICE_CONTROL operations, and sub_10300 is the handler (renamed to IRP_ReadCloseDeviceIo).

- It creates a symbolic link to the device object. If that fails, the driver returns an error.

The next step is to understand what the DriverUnload routine does. The WDK defines the prototype for the driver unload routine as follows:

```
VOID
Unload(
    PDRIVER_OBJECT  DriverObject
    );
```

After some minor massaging, our unload routine looks like this:

```
01: .text:00010580 ; void __stdcall DRV_Unload(PDRIVER_OBJECT drvobj)
02: .text:00010580 DRV_Unload proc near
03: .text:00010580
04: .text:00010580 drvobj= dword ptr  8
05: .text:00010580
06: .text:00010580    push    ebp
07: .text:00010581    mov     ebp, esp
08: .text:00010583    push    offset SymbolicLinkName  ; SymbolicLinkName
09: .text:00010588    call    ds:IoDeleteSymbolicLink
10: .text:0001058E    mov     eax, [ebp+drvobj]
11: .text:00010591    mov     ecx, [eax+DRIVER_OBJECT.DeviceObject]
12: .text:00010594    push    ecx                          ; DeviceObject
13: .text:00010595    call    ds:IoDeleteDevice
14: .text:0001059B    pop     ebp
15: .text:0001059C    retn    4
16: .text:0001059C DRV_Unload endp
```

The preceding can be decompiled to the following:

```
01: VOID DRV_Unload(PDRIVER_OBJECT drvobj)
02: {
03:   IoDeleteSymbolicLink(&symname);
04:   IoDeleteDevice(drvobj->DeviceObject);
05: }
```

As previously stated, an important key to understanding a driver's functionality is through its IRP dispatch handlers. Analyzing _IRP_ReadCloseDeviceIo, we start at the beginning:

```
01: .text:00010300 ; NTSTATUS __stdcall IRP_ReadCloseDeviceIO(
                        PDEVICE_OBJECT devobj, PIRP Irp)
02: .text:00010300 IRP_ReadCloseDeviceIO proc near
03: .text:00010300 var_14= dword ptr -14h
04: .text:00010300 var_10= dword ptr -10h
05: .text:00010300 var_C= dword ptr -0Ch
06: .text:00010300 var_8= dword ptr -8
07: .text:00010300 var_4= dword ptr -4
08: .text:00010300 devobj= dword ptr  8
09: .text:00010300 Irp= dword ptr  0Ch
10: .text:00010300
11: .text:00010300    push    ebp
12: .text:00010301    mov     ebp, esp
13: .text:00010303    sub     esp, 14h
14: .text:00010306    mov     [ebp+var_4], 0
15: .text:0001030D    mov     eax, [ebp+Irp]
16: .text:00010310    mov     ecx, [ebp+var_4]
17: .text:00010313    mov     [eax+18h], ecx
18: .text:00010316    mov     edx, [ebp+Irp]
19: .text:00010319    mov     dword ptr [edx+1Ch], 0
20: .text:00010320    mov     eax, [ebp+Irp]
21: .text:00010323    mov     ecx, [eax+60h]
22: .text:00010326    mov     [ebp+var_10], ecx
23: .text:00010329    mov     edx, [ebp+var_10]
24: .text:0001032C    movzx   eax, byte ptr [edx]
25: .text:0001032F    cmp     eax, 0Eh
26: .text:00010332    jnz     short loc_1037D
```

We already know its prototype because it is the same for all IRP handlers. When analyzing IRP handlers, you need to be cognizant of a few facts:

- An IRP is a dynamic structure with an array of IO_STACK_LOCATION after its header.

- Most of the IRP parameters are in the IO_STACK_LOCATION (including its IRP major/minor number).

- A driver accesses its IO_STACK_LOCATION using the IoGetCurrent IrpStacLocation routine. Because this routine is forced-inline, you must recognize it through its inlined patterns. It is a common coding pattern to retrieve the IO_STACK_LOCATION in the beginning of an IRP handler.

Lines 15–17 read the IRP structure and write a 0 to a field at offset 0x18. Looking at the IRP structure you see the following:

```
0: kd> dt nt!_IRP
   +0x000 Type             : Int2B
   +0x002 Size             : Uint2B
...
   +0x00c AssociatedIrp    : <unnamed-tag>
...
   +0x018 IoStatus         : _IO_STATUS_BLOCK
      +0x000 Status           : Int4B
      +0x000 Pointer          : Ptr32 Void
      +0x004 Information      : Uint4B
...
   +0x020 RequestorMode    : Char
...
   +0x040 Tail             : <unnamed-tag>
```

An IO_STATUS_BLOCK structure stores status information about an IRP:

```
typedef struct _IO_STATUS_BLOCK {
  union {
    NTSTATUS  Status;
    PVOID   Pointer;
  };
  ULONG_PTR  Information;
} IO_STATUS_BLOCK, *PIO_STATUS_BLOCK;
```

An IRP handler typically sets the Status field to indicate whether the IRP was successful or requires further processing. Information stores request-specific information for the IRP; a driver may use it to store a pointer to a buffer or set the completion status. Pointer is reserved.

Hence, you know that line 17 sets the IRP->IoStatus.Status field to 0 and that the local variable var_4 is of type NTSTATUS. Lines 18–19 access the IRP structure and write a 0 at offset 0x1c, which is the Information field in IoStatus. This is simply setting IRP->IoStatus.Information to 0. Lines 20–22 access offset 0x60 in the IRP structure and save its address in a local variable. The IRP structure is filled with unions in the Tail field (starting at offset 0x40), so it can be somewhat confusing to determine which union field member is accessed. Let's dump some of the unions:

```
0: kd> dt nt_IRP Tail.Overlay.
   +0x040 Tail        :
      +0x000 Overlay     :
         +0x000 DeviceQueueEntry : _KDEVICE_QUEUE_ENTRY
         +0x000 DriverContext : [4] Ptr32 Void
```

```
+0x010 Thread          : Ptr32 _ETHREAD
+0x014 AuxiliaryBuffer : Ptr32 Char
+0x018 ListEntry       : _LIST_ENTRY
+0x020 CurrentStackLocation : Ptr32 _IO_STACK_LOCATION
+0x020 PacketType      : Uint4B
+0x024 OriginalFileObject : Ptr32 _FILE_OBJECT
```

This indicates that offset 0x60 could be either a pointer to an IO_STACK_
LOCATION or an unsigned integer indicating the packet type. We can make an
educated guess that it is the CurrentStackLocation field because of the code
context (occurring at the beginning of an IRP handler). Furthermore, we know
that the inlined routine IoGetCurrentIrpStackLocation is defined as follows:

```
FORCEINLINE
PIO_STACK_LOCATION
IoGetCurrentIrpStackLocation(PIRP Irp)
{
  return Irp->Tail.Overlay.CurrentStackLocation;
}
```

Therefore, lines 20–22 are saving the current IO_STACK_LOCATION to a local
variable. The local variable _var_10 is of the type PIO_STACK_LOCATION.

> **NOTE**   Many of these functions are declared as **FORCEINLINE** and thus
> will never appear as call destinations—i.e., you will never see see the symbol
> **IoGetCurrentIrpStackLocation** in the assembly code. We recommend that you
> write a simple driver using these forced-inline routines so that you can get used to the
> code pattern.

Lines 23–25 access the first byte at offset 0 in the IO_STACK_LOCATION using
the movzx instruction. This indicates that field is of type unsigned char. From
the IRP section, we know that this is the MajorFunction field. Line 5 checks
whether the MajorFunction number is 0xe, i.e., IRP_MJ_DEVICE_CONTROL.
You can now decompile the first block of IRP_ReadCloseIo as follows:

```
NTSTATUS IRP_ReadCloseIo(PDEVICE_OBJECT devobj, PIRP Irp)
{
  NTSTATUS status = STATUS_SUCCESS;
  PIO_STACK_LOCATION isl;
  Irp->IoStatus.Status = status;
  Irp->IoStatus.Information = 0;

  isl = IoGetCurrentIrpStackLocation(Irp);
  if (isl->MajorFunction != IRP_MJ_DEVICE_CONTROL) {
    ... // loc_1037D
  }
  ... // .text:00010334
}
```

Next, we analyze block `0x10334`, which executes if major code is `IRP_MJ_DEVICE_CONTROL`:

```
01: .text:00010334    mov     ecx, [ebp+var_10]
02: .text:00010337    mov     edx, [ecx+0Ch]
03: .text:0001033A    mov     [ebp+var_C], edx
04: .text:0001033D    mov     eax, [ebp+Irp]
05: .text:00010340    mov     ecx, [eax+0Ch]
06: .text:00010343    mov     [ebp+var_8], ecx
07: .text:00010346    mov     edx, [ebp+Irp]
08: .text:00010349    mov     dword ptr [edx+1Ch], 644h
09: .text:00010350    mov     eax, [ebp+var_C]
10: .text:00010353    mov     [ebp+var_14], eax
11: .text:00010356    cmp     [ebp+var_14], 22C004h
12: .text:0001035D    jz      short loc_10361
```

In the previous paragraph, we deduced that `var_10` is of type `PIO_STACK_LOCATION`. Lines 1–2 access offset `0xC` of the `IO_STACK_LOCATION`. Again, recall that an `IO_STACK_LOCATION` contains the I/O request parameters, which are all stored in unions. How do you determine which union to use? We know that it will use the `DeviceIoControl` field because we are processing an `IRP_MJ_DEVICE_CONTROL` request. Also, the `IoControlField` is at offset `0xC` from the base of `IO_STACK_LOCATION`:

```
1: kd> dt nt!_IO_STACK_LOCATION Parameters.
   +0x004 Parameters  :
      +0x000 Create        : <unnamed-tag>
      +0x000 CreatePipe    : <unnamed-tag>
      +0x000 CreateMailslot : <unnamed-tag>
      +0x000 Read          : <unnamed-tag>
      +0x000 Write         : <unnamed-tag>
      +0x000 QueryDirectory : <unnamed-tag>
...
      +0x000 DeviceIoControl : <unnamed-tag>
...
1: kd> dt nt!_IO_STACK_LOCATION Parameters.DeviceIoControl.
   +0x004 Parameters                :
      +0x000 DeviceIoControl        :
         +0x000 OutputBufferLength          : Uint4B
         +0x004 InputBufferLength           : Uint4B
         +0x008 IoControlCode               : Uint4B
         +0x00c Type3InputBuffer            : Ptr32 Void
```

Therefore, lines 1–3 retrieve the `IoControlCode` field and save it in `var_C`, which we now know is of type `ULONG`.

Lines 4–6 access offset `0xC` in an IRP and save the pointer to a local variable `var_8`. From the previous section, we know that at offset `0xC` is the `AssociatedIrp` union:

```
1: kd> dt nt!_IRP AssociatedIrp.
   +0x00c AssociatedIrp  :
```

```
+0x000 MasterIrp       : Ptr32 _IRP
+0x000 IrpCount        : Int4B
+0x000 SystemBuffer    : Ptr32 Void
```

Which of the three fields should you use? Given the current information, you cannot tell. The context required to determine the proper field is in lines 9–12, which retrieve the saved IOCTL code (var_c) and compare it against 0x22c004. You know that an IOCTL code encodes device type, function code, access, and buffering method. Hence, after decoding 0x22c004, you know the following:

▪ Device type is FILE_DEVICE_UNKNOWN (0x22).

▪ The IOCTL code is 0x1.

▪ Access is (FILE_READ_DATA | FILE_WRITE_DATA).

▪ Buffering method is METHOD_BUFFERED.

Recall that we are in an IOCTL handler and that drivers must specify a buffering method when defining the IOCTL code. For buffered I/O, the SystemBuffer field points to a non-paged pool buffer storing the user input. We can now say that lines 4–6 access the SystemBuffer field.

Lines 7–8 write 0x644 to offset 0x1c inside an IRP, which is the IRP->IoStatus. Information field. It is unclear why the author chose this value.

Given this information, you know that the control code must have been constructed this way:

```
#define IOCTL_1 CTL_CODE(FILE_DEVICE_UNKNOWN, 1, METHOD_BUFFERED, \
                         FILE_READ_DATA | FILE_WRITE_DATA)
```

Because we have not fully analyzed or understood the IOCTL operation, we gave it the generic IOCTL_1 name. This block can now be decompiled as follows:

```
PVOID userinput = Irp->AssociatedIrp.SystemBuffer;
Irp->IoStatus.Information = (ULONG_PTR) 0x644;
if (isl->Parameters.DeviceIoControl.IoControlCode == IOCTL_1)
{
  ... // loc_10361
}
... // 0001035F
```

To understand what the IOCTL does, we need to analyze loc_10361 and the function sub_103B0. However, before doing that, let's finish the nearby blocks first (as they are simpler):

```
// remember var_4 is status local variable (type NTSTATUS)
01: .text:0001035F   jmp     short loc_1036C
02: .text:00010361 loc_10361:
03: .text:00010361   mov     ecx, [ebp+var_8]  ;
04: .text:00010364   push    ecx
```

```
05: .text:00010365    call     IOCTL_1_handler
06: .text:0001036A    jmp      short loc_1037D
07: .text:0001036C loc_1036C:
08: .text:0001036C    mov      [ebp+var_4], 0C0000010h
09: .text:00010373    mov      edx, [ebp+Irp]
10: .text:00010376    mov      dword ptr [edx+1Ch], 0
11: .text:0001037D loc_1037D:
12: .text:0001037D    cmp      [ebp+var_4], 103h
13: .text:00010384    jz       short loc_1039A
14: .text:00010386    xor      dl, dl                      ; PriorityBoost
15: .text:00010388    mov      ecx, [ebp+Irp]              ; Irp
16: .text:0001038B    call     ds:IofCompleteRequest
17: .text:00010391    mov      eax, [ebp+Irp]
18: .text:00010394    mov      ecx, [ebp+var_4]
19: .text:00010397    mov      [eax+18h], ecx
20: .text:0001039A loc_1039A:
21: .text:0001039A    mov      eax, [ebp+var_4]
22: .text:0001039D    mov      esp, ebp
23: .text:0001039F    pop      ebp
24: .text:000103A0    retn     8
25: .text:000103A0 IRP_ReadCloseDeviceIO endp
```

You enter 0x1035F if the IOCTL code does not match up. It immediately
jumps to line 7, which sets the local status variable to 0xC0000010, which is
STATUS_INVALID_OPERATION; and Irp->IoStatus.Information to 0. Next, in
line 11, it checks whether the local status is 0x103 (STATUS_PENDING); this block
is actually redundant because the status variable in this function can only have
two values (STATUS_SUCCESS or STATUS_INVALID_OPERATION). When an IRP is
marked with STATUS_PENDING, it means that the operation is incomplete and
is awaiting completion from another driver. This occurs often in drivers so it is
wise to remember the magic constant 0x103. If the status is STATUS_PENDING,
the handler immediately returns with that status (line 13 and 20). Otherwise,
it calls IoCompleteRequest to mark the IRP completed and saves the status in
IRP->IoStatus.Status (line 19) and returns it. This is actually a bug because a
driver should set the IoStatusBlock field *before* completing the request; once an
IRP is completed, it should not be touched again. These blocks can be decompiled as follows:

```
status = STATUS_INVALID_OPERATION;
Irp->IoStatus.Information = 0;
if (status == STATUS_PENDING) {
  return status;
}
IoCompleteRequest(Irp, IO_NO_INCREMENT);
Irp->IoStatus.Status = status;
return status;
```

Returning to the `IOCTL_1_handler` routine, note that it calls only two other functions: `sub_10460` and `sub_10550`. `sub_10550` is a small leaf routine so we will analyze that first:

```
01: .text:00010550 ; void __stdcall sub_10550(PMDL Mdl, PVOID BaseAddress)
02: .text:00010550 sub_10550 proc near
03: .text:00010550    push    ebp
04: .text:00010551    mov     ebp, esp
05: .text:00010553    mov     eax, [ebp+Mdl]
06: .text:00010556    push    eax                     ; MemoryDescriptorList
07: .text:00010557    mov     ecx, [ebp+BaseAddress]
08: .text:0001055A    push    ecx                     ; BaseAddress
09: .text:0001055B    call    ds:MmUnmapLockedPages
10: .text:00010561    mov     edx, [ebp+Mdl]
11: .text:00010564    push    edx                     ; MemoryDescriptorList
12: .text:00010565    call    ds:MmUnlockPages
13: .text:0001056B    mov     eax, [ebp+Mdl]
14: .text:0001056E    push    eax                     ; Mdl
15: .text:0001056F    call    ds:IoFreeMdl
16: .text:00010575    pop     ebp
17: .text:00010576    retn    8
18: .text:00010576 sub_10550 endp
```

This function unmaps, unlocks, and frees an MDL. It is unclear what the MDLs describe because we have not analyzed the other routines. This function can be decompiled as follows:

```
void UnmapMdl(PMDL mdl, PVOID baseaddr)
{
  MmUnmapLockedPages(baseaddr, mdl);
  MmUnlockPages(mdl);
  IoFreeMdl(mdl);
}
```

`sub_10460` is another leaf routine involving MDLs; its main functionality is to create, lock, and map an MDL for a given buffer and length. Its prototype is as follows:

```
PVOID MapMdl(PMDL *mdl, PVOID VirtualAddress, ULONG Length);
```

By default, the disassembler was not able to infer the first parameter's type. You can tell that it is a `PMDL *` because of instruction at `0x1049D`. The assembly listing is shown here but without line-by-line commentary, as it is very simple:

```
01: .text:00010460 ; PVOID __stdcall MapMdl(PMDL *mdl,
                                 PVOID VirtualAddress, ULONG Length)
02: .text:00010460 MapMdl proc near
03: .text:00010460    push    ebp
04: .text:00010461    mov     ebp, esp
05: .text:00010463    push    0FFFFFFFFh
06: .text:00010465    push    offset unk_10748
07: .text:0001046A    push    offset _except_handler3
```

```
08: .text:0001046F    mov     eax, large fs:0
09: .text:00010475    push    eax
10: .text:00010476    mov     large fs:0, esp
11: .text:0001047D    add     esp, 0FFFFFFF0h
12: .text:00010480    push    ebx
13: .text:00010481    push    esi
14: .text:00010482    push    edi
15: .text:00010483    mov     [ebp+var_18], esp
16: .text:00010486    push    0                       ; Irp
17: .text:00010488    push    0                       ; ChargeQuota
18: .text:0001048A    push    0                       ; SecondaryBuffer
19: .text:0001048C    mov     eax, [ebp+Length]
20: .text:0001048F    push    eax                     ; Length
21: .text:00010490    mov     ecx, [ebp+VirtualAddress]
22: .text:00010493    push    ecx                     ; VirtualAddress
23: .text:00010494    call    ds:IoAllocateMdl
24: .text:0001049A    mov     edx, [ebp+mdl]
25: .text:0001049D    mov     [edx], eax
26: .text:0001049F    mov     eax, [ebp+mdl]
27: .text:000104A2    cmp     dword ptr [eax], 0
28: .text:000104A5    jnz     short loc_104AE
29: .text:000104A7    xor     eax, eax
30: .text:000104A9    jmp     loc_10534
31: .text:000104AE loc_104AE:
32: .text:000104AE    mov     [ebp+var_4], 0
33: .text:000104B5    push    1                       ; Operation
34: .text:000104B7    push    0                       ; AccessMode
35: .text:000104B9    mov     ecx, [ebp+mdl]
36: .text:000104BC    mov     edx, [ecx]
37: .text:000104BE    push    edx                     ; MemoryDescriptorList
38: .text:000104BF    call    ds:MmProbeAndLockPages
39: .text:000104C5    mov     [ebp+var_4], 0FFFFFFFFh
40: .text:000104CC    jmp     short loc_104F6
41: .text:000104CE loc_104CE:
42: .text:000104CE    mov     eax, 1
43: .text:000104D3    retn
44: .text:000104D4 loc_104D4:
45: .text:000104D4    mov     esp, [ebp+var_18]
46: .text:000104D7    mov     eax, [ebp+mdl]
47: .text:000104DA    mov     ecx, [eax]
48: .text:000104DC    push    ecx                     ; Mdl
49: .text:000104DD    call    ds:IoFreeMdl
50: .text:000104E3    mov     [ebp+var_20], 0
51: .text:000104EA    mov     [ebp+var_4], 0FFFFFFFFh
52: .text:000104F1    mov     eax, [ebp+var_20]
53: .text:000104F4    jmp     short loc_10534
54: .text:000104F6 loc_104F6:
55: .text:000104F6    push    10h                     ; Priority
56: .text:000104F8    push    0                       ; BugCheckOnFailure
57: .text:000104FA    push    0                       ; BaseAddress
```

```
58: .text:000104FC    push    0                           ; CacheType
59: .text:000104FE    push    0                           ; AccessMode
60: .text:00010500    mov     edx, [ebp+mdl]
61: .text:00010503    mov     eax, [edx]
62: .text:00010505    push    eax                         ; MemoryDescriptorList
63: .text:00010506    call    ds:MmMapLockedPagesSpecifyCache
64: .text:0001050C    mov     [ebp+var_1C], eax
65: .text:0001050F    cmp     [ebp+var_1C], 0
66: .text:00010513    jnz     short loc_10531
67: .text:00010515    mov     ecx, [ebp+mdl]
68: .text:00010518    mov     edx, [ecx]
69: .text:0001051A    push    edx                         ; MemoryDescriptorList
70: .text:0001051B    call    ds:MmUnlockPages
71: .text:00010521    mov     eax, [ebp+mdl]
72: .text:00010524    mov     ecx, [eax]
73: .text:00010526    push    ecx                         ; Mdl
74: .text:00010527    call    ds:IoFreeMdl
75: .text:0001052D    xor     eax, eax
76: .text:0001052F    jmp     short loc_10534
77: .text:00010531 loc_10531:
78: .text:00010531    mov     eax, [ebp+var_1C]
79: .text:00010534 loc_10534:
80: .text:00010534    mov     ecx, [ebp+var_10]
81: .text:00010537    mov     large fs:0, ecx
82: .text:0001053E    pop     edi
83: .text:0001053F    pop     esi
84: .text:00010540    pop     ebx
85: .text:00010541    mov     esp, ebp
86: .text:00010543    pop     ebp
87: .text:00010544    retn    0Ch
88: .text:00010544 MapMdl endp
```

Although this function seems long and complicated, it is not difficult to understand if you see how the APIs are used together. IoAllocateMdl, MmProbeAndLockPages, and MmMapLockedPagesSpecifyCache are routines used to create, lock, and map MDLs; MmProbeAndLockPages must be done inside a try/except block so there is extra code generated in the beginning to set up the exception handler (i.e., the lines involving fs:0). This routine effectively maps a buffer into kernel space as writable and returns the address of a new mapping for this buffer. The whole routine can be roughly decompiled as follows:

```
PVOID MapMdl(PMDL *mdl, PVOID VirtualAddress, ULONG Length)
{
  PVOID addr; // virtual address of the mapped MDL

  *mdl = IoAllocateMdl(VirtualAddress, Length, FALSE, FALSE, NULL);
  if (*mdl == NULL) return NULL;
  __try {
    MmProbeAndLockPages(*mdl, KernelMode, IoWriteAccess);
    addr = MmMapLockedPagesSpecifyCache(
```

```
                    *mdl,
                    KernelMode,
                    MmNonCached,
                    NULL,
                    FALSE,
                    NormalPagePriority);
      if (addr == NULL) {
        MmUnlockPages(*mdl);
        IoFreeMdl(*mdl);
      }
    } __except (EXCEPTION_EXECUTE_HANDLER) {
      IoFreeMdl(*mdl);
    }
    return addr;
  }
```

With an understanding of these two routines, we can now approach the handler. Note that it takes one parameter, Irp->AssociatedIrp.SystemBuffer. Recall that the content of this buffer may be copied back to user mode once the IRP is completed:

```
01: .text:000103B0 ; void __stdcall IOCTL_1_handler(PVOID buffer)
02: .text:000103B0 IOCTL_1_handler proc near
03: .text:000103B0    push    ebp
04: .text:000103B1    mov     ebp, esp
05: .text:000103B3    sub     esp, 10h
06: .text:000103B6    push    esi
07: .text:000103B7    call    ds:KeRaiseIrqlToDpcLevel
08: .text:000103BD    mov     [ebp+NewIrql], al
09: .text:000103C0    mov     eax, ds:KeServiceDescriptorTable
10: .text:000103C5    mov     ecx, [eax+8]
11: .text:000103C8    shl     ecx, 2
12: .text:000103CB    push    ecx                     ; Length
13: .text:000103CC    mov     edx, ds:KeServiceDescriptorTable
14: .text:000103D2    mov     eax, [edx]
15: .text:000103D4    push    eax                     ; VirtualAddress
16: .text:000103D5    lea     ecx, [ebp+Mdl]
17: .text:000103D8    push    ecx                     ; mdl
18: .text:000103D9    call    MapMdl
19: .text:000103DE    mov     [ebp+BaseAddress], eax
20: .text:000103E1    cmp     [ebp+BaseAddress], 0
21: .text:000103E5    jz      short loc_10449
22: .text:000103E7    mov     [ebp+var_8], 0
23: .text:000103EE    jmp     short loc_103F9
24: .text:000103F0 loc_103F0:
25: .text:000103F0    mov     edx, [ebp+var_8]
26: .text:000103F3    add     edx, 1
27: .text:000103F6    mov     [ebp+var_8], edx
28: .text:000103F9 loc_103F9:
29: .text:000103F9    mov     eax, [ebp+buffer]
```

```
30: .text:000103FC    mov     ecx, [ebp+var_8]
31: .text:000103FF    cmp     ecx, [eax]
32: .text:00010401    jnb     short loc_1043C
33: .text:00010403    mov     edx, [ebp+var_8]
34: .text:00010406    mov     eax, [ebp+buffer]
35: .text:00010409    cmp     dword ptr [eax+edx*4+4], 0
36: .text:0001040E    jz      short loc_1043A
37: .text:00010410    mov     ecx, [ebp+var_8]
38: .text:00010413    mov     edx, [ebp+BaseAddress]
39: .text:00010416    mov     eax, [ebp+var_8]
40: .text:00010419    mov     esi, [ebp+buffer]
41: .text:0001041C    mov     ecx, [edx+ecx*4]
42: .text:0001041F    cmp     ecx, [esi+eax*4+4]
43: .text:00010423    jz      short loc_1043A
44: .text:00010425    mov     edx, [ebp+var_8]
45: .text:00010428    mov     eax, [ebp+buffer]
46: .text:0001042B    mov     ecx, [eax+edx*4+4]
47: .text:0001042F    mov     edx, [ebp+var_8]
48: .text:00010432    mov     eax, [ebp+BaseAddress]
49: .text:00010435    lea     edx, [eax+edx*4]
50: .text:00010438    xchg    ecx, [edx]
51: .text:0001043A loc_1043A:
52: .text:0001043A    jmp     short loc_103F0
53: .text:0001043C loc_1043C:
54: .text:0001043C    mov     eax, [ebp+BaseAddress]
55: .text:0001043F    push    eax                 ; BaseAddress
56: .text:00010440    mov     ecx, [ebp+Mdl]
57: .text:00010443    push    ecx                 ; Mdl
58: .text:00010444    call    UnmapMdl
59: .text:00010449 loc_10449:
60: .text:00010449    mov     cl, [ebp+NewIrql]   ; NewIrql
61: .text:0001044C    call    ds:KfLowerIrql
62: .text:00010452    pop     esi
63: .text:00010453    mov     esp, ebp
64: .text:00010455    pop     ebp
65: .text:00010456    retn    4
66: .text:00010456 IOCTL_1_handler endp
```

This function first raises the IRQL to DISPATCH_LEVEL (line 7), which effectively suspends the thread dispatcher on the current processor. Whatever this function does, it cannot wait or take a pagefault; otherwise, the machine will bugcheck. The same effect can be achieved with KeRaiseIrql. Line 8 saves the previous IRQL so that it can be restored later (see line 61). Lines 9–11 retrieve the undocumented KeServiceDescriptorTable entry field and multiply it by 4. Lines 12–18 pass KiServiceTable, a length (four times the size of the syscall table), and an MDL pointer to MapMdl. Because we already analyzed MapMdl, we know that this simply maps a buffer starting from KiServiceTable to KiService Table+(NumberOfSyscalls*4). Line 12 saves the virtual address of the newly mapped buffer. Lines 20–22 check the mapping status; if it was not successful, the IRQL is lowered and the code returns (lines 60–65), otherwise, a loop is entered whose counter is determined by the user input (lines 29–31). The loop body is from lines 33–50 and can be understood as follows:

```
DWORD *userbuffer = Irp->AssociatedIrp.SystemBuffer;
DWORD *mappedKiServiceTable = MapMdl(mdl, KiServiceTable, nsyscalls*4);
for (i=0; i < userbuffer[0] ; i++)
{
  if ( userbuffer[i+1] != 0) {
    if ( userbuffer[i+1] != mappedKiServiceTable[i]) {
      swap(mappedKiServiceTable[i], userbuffer[i+1]);
    }
  }
}
...
UnmapMdl(mdl);
KeLowerIrql(oldirql);
```

After many pages of explanations and decompiling the entire driver, you can now understand the sample's goal. For whatever reason, the developer of this driver wanted to use an IOCTL to overwrite the NT native system calls table with custom addresses. The user-mode buffer is a structure in this format:

```
[# of system calls]
[syscall 1 replacement address]
[syscall 2 replacement address]
...
[syscall n replacement address]
```

While the developer may have achieved his or her goals, the driver has several critical issues that can lead to system instability and security vulnerabilities. Some were mentioned during the walk-through, but you should be able to identify many others. Here are some questions to start your quest:

- Will this driver work on a multi-core system? Explain your reasoning.

- Why does the author think the IRQL needs to be raised to DISPATCH_LEVEL? Is it really necessary?

- How can a normal user use this driver to execute arbitrary code in ring 0 context?

- Suppose the author wanted to replace some system calls with a custom implementation in user space. What problems might be encountered?

This driver is very small and simple, but it has most of the important constructs typically found in software drivers: dispatch routines, device I/O control from user mode, buffering methods, symbolic links, raising and lowering IRQL levels, MDL management, IO_STACK_LOCATIONs, and so on. You can apply the same analytical techniques shown here to other drivers. Just don't imitate its development techniques in real life.

An x64 Rootkit

This section analyzes Sample B, an x64 driver. Because it is quite large and complex, we will focus only on areas related to callbacks. We will not paste every line of this function, so you will need to follow it in a disassembler.

Note that this driver specifies process creation and image load notifications using the documented APIs. 0x4045F8 is the start of the process creation callback routine. First, it clears a LARGE_INTEGER structure to zero. A LARGE_INTEGER structure is typically used to represent file size or time (note that it is later used at 0x4046FF as an argument to KeDelayExecutionThread). Next, it gets the current process id with PsGetCurrentProcessId. Does this get the process id of the newly created process? Not necessarily. The process creation callback prototype is as follows:

```
VOID
(*PCREATE_PROCESS_NOTIFY_ROUTINE) (
    IN HANDLE   ParentId,
    IN HANDLE   ProcessId, // processId of the created/terminated proc
    IN BOOLEAN  Create // TRUE=creation FALSE=termination
    );
```

The Creation parameter is saved and tested at 0x404604 and 0x404631, respectively; if it is TRUE, then the callback simply returns. Hence, we know that this callback tracks only process termination. In the case of process termination, the callback executes in the context of the dying process. After gathering the terminating process id (which is not used at all), it retrieves the EPROCESS object for the current process through IoGetCurrentProcess (0x40461C and 0x404622). It is not clear why IoGetCurrentProcess is called twice (it could be a typo in the original source code). Next, it retrieves and saves the process image filename string through PsGetProcessImageFileName (0x404633). While this routine is not documented, it is simple, exported, and frequently used by the kernel. Then it tries to acquire a resource lock previously initialized in DriverEntry (0x4025EB); it enters a critical region before acquiring a resource lock because KeAcquireResourceExclusiveLite requires normal kernel APCs to be disabled (which is what KeEnterCriticalRegion does). Next, it gets a pointer to a linked list and checks the terminating process image name against each entry in the list (offset 0x20). You know that this is a linked list because the loop iterates by pointers (0x404679) and terminates when two pointers are the same (0x40465F). If there is no match, it releases the resource lock and pauses the current thread (0x4046FF) one second from the current time. If the terminating process filename matches one of those in the list, then it unmaps, unlocks, and frees an MDL stored in the list entry (offset 0x1070). If the buffer at offset 0x10b0 in the list entry is NULL, then it is freed; otherwise, the entry is freed from the list by the RemoveEntryList macro:

```
01: .text:00000000004046CA loc_4046CA:
02: .text:00000000004046CA    mov     rax, [rbx+8]
03: .text:00000000004046CE    mov     r8, [rbx]
04: .text:00000000004046D1    mov     edx, edi      ; Tag
05: .text:00000000004046D3    mov     [rax], r8
06: .text:00000000004046D6    mov     rcx, rbx      ; P
07: .text:00000000004046D9    mov     [r8+8], rax
08: .text:00000000004046DD    call    cs:ExFreePoolWithTag
```

Again, we can recognize the list operation because of the Flink (offset 0x0) and Blink (offset 0x8) manipulation pattern. In fact, we can now say that qword_40A590 is of type LIST_ENTRY.

Even though this callback is only one piece of the puzzle, you can apply the previous facts to indirectly understand other components of the rootkit. For example, you can tell that the rootkit either maps or injects code into processes and tracks them in a large linked list (using process name as the key). When the process dies, they have to unmap those MDLs because the system will bugcheck if a dead process still has locked pages. The original MDL mappings were most likely done through the image load callback routine (0x406494).

Another interesting routine in this file is 0x4038F0. We will do a line-by-line analysis of this routine because it uses constructs that you will frequently see in other drivers. Furthermore, it teaches some valuable lessons about analyzing optimized x64 code:

```
01: ; NTSTATUS __cdecl sub_4038F0(PFILE_OBJECT FileObject, \
                          HANDLE Handle, BOOLEAN flag)
02: sub_4038F0 proc near
03:    push    rbx
04:    push    rbp
05:    push    rsi
06:    push    rdi
07:    push    r12
08:    sub     rsp, 60h
09:    mov     bpl, r8b
10:    mov     r12, rdx
11:    mov     rdi, rcx
12:    call    cs:IoGetRelatedDeviceObject
13:    mov     [rsp+88h+arg_18], 1
14:    xor     edx, edx       ; ChargeQuota
15:    mov     cl, [rax+4Ch]  ; StackSize
16:    mov     rsi, rax
17:    call    cs:IoAllocateIrp
18:    test    rax, rax
19:    mov     rbx, rax
20:    jnz     short loc_403932
21:    mov     eax, 0C0000017h
22:    jmp     loc_403A0C
23: loc_403932:
24:    lea     rax, [rsp+88h+arg_18]
25:    xor     r8d, r8d       ; State
```

```
26:    lea      rcx, [rsp+88h+Event] ; Event
27:    mov      [rbx+18h], rax ; IRP.AssociatedIrp.SystemBuffer
28:    lea      rax, [rsp+88h+Event]
29:    lea      edx, [r8+1]     ; Type
30:    mov      [rbx+50h], rax ; IRP.UserEvent
31:    lea      rax, [rsp+88h+var_58]
32:    mov      [rbx+48h], rax ; IRP.UserIosb
33:    mov      rax, gs:+188h   ; KPCR.Prcb.CurrentThread
34:    mov      [rbx+0C0h], rdi ; IRP.Tail.Overlay.OriginalFileObject
35:    mov      [rbx+98h], rax ; IRP.Tail.Overlay.Thread
36:    mov      byte ptr [rbx+40h], 0 ; IRP.RequestorMode
37:    call     cs:KeInitializeEvent
38:    test     bpl, bpl
39:    mov      rcx, [rbx+0B8h]
40:    mov      byte ptr [rcx-48h], 6 ; IRP_MJ_SET_INFORMATION
41:    mov      [rcx-20h], rsi ; IO_STACK_LOCATION.DeviceObject
42:    mov      [rcx-18h], rdi ; IO_STACK_LOCATION.FileObject
43:    jz       short loc_4039A6
44:    mov      rax, [rdi+28h] ; FILE_OBJECT.SectionObjectPointer
45:    test     rax, rax
46:    jz       short loc_4039A6
47:    mov      [rax+10h], 0 ; SECTION_OBJECT_POINTERS.ImageSectionObject
48: loc_4039A6:
49:    mov      [rcx-28h], r12
                ; IO_STACK_LOCATION.Parameters.SetFile.DeleteHandle
50:    mov      [rcx-30h], rdi
                ; IO_STACK_LOCATION.Parameters.SetFile.FileObject
51:    mov      dword ptr [rcx-38h], 0Dh ; FileDispositionInformation
                ; IO_STACK_LOCATION.Parameters.SetFile.FileInformationClass
52:    mov      dword ptr [rcx-40h], 1
                ; IO_STACK_LOCATION.Parameters.SetFile.Length
53:    mov      rax, [rbx+0B8h] ; CurrentIrpStackLocation
54:    lea      rcx, sub_4038B4 ; completionroutine
55:    mov      [rax-10h], rcx  ; IO_STACK_LOCATION.CompletionRoutine
56:    mov      rcx, rsi        ; DeviceObject
57:    mov      rdx, rbx        ; Irp
58:    mov      qword ptr [rax-8], 0
59:    mov      byte ptr [rax-45h], 0E0h ; flag
60:    call     cs:IofCallDriver
61:    cmp      eax, 103h ; STATUS_PENDING
62:    jnz      short loc_403A09
63:    lea      rcx, [rsp+88h+Event] ; Object
64:    mov      r9b, 1          ; Alertable
65:    xor      r8d, r8d        ; WaitMode
66:    xor      edx, edx        ; WaitReason
67:    mov      [rsp+88h+var_68], 0
68:    call     cs:KeWaitForSingleObject
69: loc_403A09:
70:    mov      eax, [rbx+30h] ; IRP.IoStatus.Status
71: loc_403A0C:
72:    add      rsp, 60h
73:    pop      r12
74:    pop      rdi
```

```
75:    pop    rsi
76:    pop    rbp
77:    pop    rbx
78:    retn
79: sub_4038F0 endp
```

First, we recover the function prototype by noting that the function's caller uses three registers: RCX, RDX, R8 (see 0x404AC8 to 0x404ADB). Even though the disassembler marks CDECL as the function's calling convention, it is not really correct. Recall that Windows on the x64 platform only uses one calling convention which specifies that the first four arguments are passed via registers (RCX, RDX, R8, and R9) and the rest are pushed on the stack. Line 12 calls IoGetRelatedDeviceObject using FileObject as the parameter; this API returns the device object associated with the file object. The associated device object is saved in RSI. Lines 14–17 allocate an IRP from scratch with IoAllocateIrp; the device object's StackSize field is used as the new IRP's IO_STACK_LOCATION size. If the IRP allocation somehow fails, the routine returns STATUS_NO_MEMORY (lines 20–22). Otherwise, the new IRP is saved in RBX (line 19) and we continue to line 24. Lines 24–37 initialize basic fields of an IRP and call KeInitializeEvent. Line 33 may look strange because of the GS:188h parameter. Recall that on x64 Windows, the kernel stores a pointer to the PCR in GS, which contains the PRCB that stores scheduling information. In fact, this routine is simply the inlined form of KeGetCurrentThread. Line 39 accesses a field at offset 0xb8 in the IRP structure. What is this field?

```
0: kd> dt nt!_IRP Tail.Overlay.
   +0x078 Tail          :
      +0x000 Overlay       :
         +0x000 DeviceQueueEntry : _KDEVICE_QUEUE_ENTRY
         +0x000 DriverContext : [4] Ptr64 Void
         +0x020 Thread        : Ptr64 _ETHREAD
         +0x028 AuxiliaryBuffer : Ptr64 Char
         +0x030 ListEntry      : _LIST_ENTRY
         +0x040 CurrentStackLocation : Ptr64 _IO_STACK_LOCATION
         +0x040 PacketType     : Uint4B
         +0x048 OriginalFileObject : Ptr64 _FILE_OBJECT
```

It is accessing the CurrentStackLocation pointer in the Overlay union. Does this sound familiar? Line 39 is actually just IoGetCurrentIrpStackLocation. Lines 40–42 set some fields using negative offsets from the current stack location. Recall that the dynamic part of an IRP is an array of IO_STACK_LOCATION structures and the "next" stack location is actually the element above the current one. Review this structure and its size:

```
0: kd> sizeof(_IO_STACK_LOCATION)
unsigned int64 0x48
0: kd> dt _IO_STACK_LOCATION
nt!_IO_STACK_LOCATION
```

```
+0x000 MajorFunction       : UChar
+0x001 MinorFunction       : UChar
+0x002 Flags               : UChar
+0x003 Control             : UChar
+0x008 Parameters          : <unnamed-tag>
+0x028 DeviceObject        : Ptr64 _DEVICE_OBJECT
+0x030 FileObject          : Ptr64 _FILE_OBJECT
+0x038 CompletionRoutine   : Ptr64     long
+0x040 Context             : Ptr64 Void
```

The size of an IRP on x64 Windows is 0x48. Hence, line 40 must be accessing the "next" IO_STACK_LOCATION because it is subtracting 0x48 bytes from the current location; it is setting the MajorFunction field to 0x6 (IRP_MJ_SET_INFORMATION). This tells you that the parameters for this request will be described using the SetFile union member. Line 41 accesses the "next" IRP with negative offsets 0x20 and 0x18, which corresponds to the DeviceObject and FileObject fields, respectively. What is happening here is that the developer used IoGetNextIrpStackLocation and then filled out the field, and the aggressive Microsoft x64 compiler optimized the code that way. The optimizer decided that because we are operating on an array of structures, it is cheaper (in terms of space) to directly access the previous element using negative offsets; the alternative would have been to calculate a new base pointer for the previous element and access its fields using positive offsets. You will run into this optimization quite often in x64 binaries.

Line 43 tests a flag to determine whether additional checks should be performed for section objects. Lines 44–47 set the ImageSectionObject field accordingly. Lines 48–52 initialize various fields in the "next" IRP stack location using negative offsets again. These offsets are inside the Parameters union; as we already know the IRP major function (IRP_MJ_SET_INFORMATION), we know that it will use the SetFile union member:

```
1: kd> dt nt!_IO_STACK_LOCATION Parameters.SetFile.
   +0x008 Parameters          :
      +0x000 SetFile                :
         +0x000 Length                  : Uint4B
         +0x008 FileInformationClass : _FILE_INFORMATION_CLASS
         +0x010 FileObject              : Ptr64 _FILE_OBJECT
         +0x018 ReplaceIfExists         : UChar
         +0x019 AdvanceOnly             : UChar
         +0x018 ClusterCount            : Uint4B
         +0x018 DeleteHandle            : Ptr64 Void
```

After calculating the offsets, we know that line 49 sets the DeleteHandle field with the second parameter, line 50 sets the FileObject field, line 51 sets the FileInformationClass field (0xD is FileDispositionInformation), and line 52 sets the Length field. The documentation for the FileDispositionInformation class says that it will take a structure with a one-byte field; if it is 1, then the file handle is marked for deletion. Hence, we now know why lines 13 and 27 set the `IRP.AssociatedIrp.SystemBuffer` to 1. Lines 53–55 set `sub_4038B4` as this IRP's completion routine. Line 60 passes the newly filled IRP to another driver (taken from line 16) for processing (most likely the file system driver). Line 61 checks status with `STATUS_PENDING` to see if the operation is done; if yes, the IRP's status is returned in `EAX`; if not, `KeWaitForSingleObject` is called to wait on the event initialized in line 37. The completion routine will set the event and free the IRP when it's done:

```
01: sub_4038B4 proc near
02:    push    rbx
03:    sub     rsp, 20h
04:    movdqu  xmm0, xmmword ptr [rdx+30h]
05:    mov     rax, [rdx+48h]
06:    mov     rbx, rdx
07:    xor     r8d, r8d        ; Wait
08:    xor     edx, edx        ; Increment
09:    movdqu  xmmword ptr [rax], xmm0
10:    mov     rcx, [rbx+50h] ; Event
11:    call    cs:KeSetEvent
12:    mov     rcx, rbx        ; Irp
13:    call    cs:IoFreeIrp
14:    mov     eax, 0C0000016h
15:    add     rsp, 20h
16:    pop     rbx
17:    retn
18: sub_4038B4 endp
```

The entire routine can be decompiled as follows:

```
NTSTATUS sub_4038F0(PFILE_OBJECT FileObj, HANDLE hdelete, BOOLEAN flag)
{
  NTSTATUS status;
  PIO_STACK_LOCATION iosl;
  PIRP Irp;
  PDEVICE_OBJECT devobj;
  KEVENT event;
  IO_STATUS_BLOCK iosb;
  CHAR buf = 1;

  devobj = IoGetRelatedDeviceObject(FileObj);
  Irp = IoAllocateIrp(devobj->StackSize, FALSE);
  if (Irp == NULL) { return STATUS_NO_MEMORY; }
  Irp->AssociatedIrp.SystemBuffer = &buf;
  Irp->UserEvent = &event;
  Irp->UserIosb = &iosb;
  Irp->Tail.Overlay.Thread = KeGetCurrentThread();
  Irp->Tail.Overlay.OriginalFileObject = FileObj;
  Irp->RequestorMode = KernelMode;
  KeInitializeEvent(&event, SynchronizationEvent, FALSE);
```

```
iosl = IoGetNextIrpStackLocation(Irp);
iosl->DeviceObject = devobj;
iosl->FileObject = FileObj;
if (!flag && FileObj->SectionObjectPointer != NULL) {
  FileObj->SectionObjectPointer.ImageSectionObject = NULL;
}
iosl->Parameters.SetFile.FileObject = FileObj;
iosl->Parameters.SetFile.DeleteHandle = hdelete;
iosl->Parameters.SetFile.FileInformationClass = \
                                  FileDispositionInformation;
iosl->Parameters.SetFile.Length = 1;
IoSkipCurrentIrpStackLocation(Irp);
IoSetCompletionRoutine(Irp, sub_4038B4, NULL, TRUE, TRUE, TRUE);
if (IoCallDriver(devobj, Irp) == STATUS_PENDING) {
  KeWaitForSingleObject(&event, Executive, KernelMode, TRUE, NULL);
}
return Irp->IoStatus.Status;
}
```

Now you can see that the driver uses this function to delete a file from the system without using the file deletion API (ZwDeleteFile). It achieves this by crafting its own IRP to describe the file deletion operation and passes it down to a lower driver (presumably the file system). Also, it uses a completion routine to be notified when the IRP is complete (either success, failed, or somehow cancelled). While somewhat esoteric, this method is very useful because it can bypass security software that tries to detect file deletion through system call hooking.

This walk-through demonstrated two main points. First, if you know and understand the objects and mechanisms drivers used to interact with the kernel, your analytical task becomes easier. Second, you must be prepared to deal with code that seems strange due to an aggressive optimizer. This is especially true for x64 code. The only way to improve is to practice.

Next Steps

We have covered most of the important domain-specific concepts relevant to kernel-mode code in Windows. This knowledge can be immediately applied to driver reverse engineering tasks. To be more effective, however, it is instructive to understand what normal drivers look like in source form. The best way to learn that is to study driver samples included in the WDK and/or develop your own drivers. While they are not rootkits, they demonstrate the proper structure and constructs used by drivers.

Where do you go from here? Our advice is as follows (in order):

- Read the WDK manual thoroughly. You can start with the "Kernel-Mode Driver Architecture" section. It is confusing at first, but if you read this chapter it will be much easier because we bypassed all the non-essential topics.

- Read *Windows NT Device Driver Development* by Peter G. Viscarola and W. Anthony Mason from cover to cover (you can skip the chapter on DMA and programmed I/O).

- Write a few small, simple drivers. Then analyze them in a disassembler without looking at the source code. Be sure you do this for both x86 and x64.

- Review the Recon 2011 presentation *Decompiling kernel drivers and IDA plugins,* by Bruce Dang and Rolf Rolles.

- Read the Microsoft debugger documentation for useful kernel extensions (e.g., !process, !thread, !pcr, !devobj, !drvobj, etc.)

- Read all articles published in *The NT Insider* and kernel-related articles in *Uninformed.* The former is probably the most useful resource for Windows kernel driver development in general. The latter is more geared toward security enthusiasts.

- Do all the exercises at the end of this chapter. All of them. Some may take a substantial amount of time because you will need to read up on undocumented areas not covered in the book. Reading and exploring are steps in the learning process.

- Open the Windows kernel binary in a disassembler and try to understand how some of the common APIs work.

- Read the http://kernel-mode.info forums.

- Analyze as many rootkits as you can. While analyzing, think about why and how the rootkit author chose to use certain objects/mechanisms and assess whether they are appropriate.

- Find and read open-source Windows drivers.

- After you think you have a good understanding of the basic concepts, you can explore other areas of the kernel such as the network and storage stacks. These are two highly complex areas so you will need a lot of time and patience.

- Subscribe to the NTDEV and NTFSD mailing lists to read about other developers' problems and how they solved them.

Keep reading, practicing, and learning! There is a steep learning curve, but once you pass that, it is smooth sailing. Remember: Without failure, it is difficult to appreciate success. Happy bugchecking.

Exercises

We believe that the best way to learn is through a combination of concept discussion, hands-on tutorials, and independent exercises. The first two items have been covered in the previous sections. The following independent exercises have been designed to help you build confidence, solidify your understanding of Windows kernel concepts, explore and extend knowledge into areas not covered in the book, and continue to analyze real-world drivers. As with other chapters, all exercises are taken from real-world scenarios. We reference files as (Sample A, B, C, etc.). The SHA1 hash for each sample is listed in the Appendix.

Building Confidence and Solidifying Your Knowledge

Each of these exercises can usually be answered within 30 minutes. Some may require additional reading/thinking, so they might take longer.

1. Explain why code running at `DISPATCH_LEVEL` cannot take a page fault. There can be multiple explanations for this. You should be able to come up with at least two.

2. Suppose you read an article on the Internet about the Windows kernel and it claims that kernel-mode threads always have higher priority than user-mode threads; hence, if you write everything in kernel mode, it will be faster. Assess the validity of this claim using your knowledge of IRQL, thread dispatching, and thread priority.

3. Write a driver for Windows 7/8 that prints out the base address of every newly loaded image. Repeat the same for processes and threads. This driver does not need to set up any IRP handler because it does not need to process requests from users or other drivers.

4. Explain the security implications of using `METHOD_NEITHER` and what driver developers do to mitigate them.

5. Given a kernel-mode virtual address, manually convert it to a physical address. Verify your answer using the `!vtop` extension in the kernel debugger.

6. Develop a driver that uses all the list operations and identify all the inlined list routines in assembly form. Is there a generic pattern for each routine? If so, explain them. If not, explain why.

7. You learned about linked lists, but the kernel also supports hash tables, search trees, and bitmaps. Investigate their usage and develop a driver using all of them.

8. Explain how the `FIELD_OFFSET` macro works.

9. The exported function `ExGetCurrentProcessorCpuUsage` is undocumented, but a documented NDIS API `NdisGetCurrentProcessorCpuUsage` uses it internally. Explain how `ExGetCurrentProcessorCpuUsage` works on x64 and x86 Windows.

10. Explain how `KeGetCurrentIrql` works on x86 and x64.

11. Explain how the following APIs work in Windows 7/8 on x86/x64/ARM:

    ■ `IoThreadToProcess`

    ■ `PsGetThreadProcessId`

    ■ `PsIsSystemThread`

    ■ `PsGetCurrentThreadId`

    ■ `PsGetCurrentThreadPreviousMode`

    ■ `PsGetCurrentThreadProcess`

    ■ `PsGetCurrentThreadStackBase`

    ■ `PsGetCurrentThreadWin32Thread`

    ■ `PsGetThreadId`

    ■ `PsGetThreadSessionId`

    ■ `PsIsSystemProcess`

    ■ `PsGetProcessImageFileName`

12. The PCR, PRCB, EPROCESS, KPROCESS, ETHREAD, and KTHREAD structures store a lot of useful information. Unfortunately, all of them are opaque structures and can change from one version of Windows to the next. Hence, many rootkits hardcode offsets into these structures. Investigate these structures on Windows XP, 2003, Vista, and 7 and note the differences. Can you devise ways to generically get the offsets of some useful fields without hardcoding? If so, can you do it such that it will work on all the listed platforms? (Hint: You can use a disassembler, pattern matching and relative distance.)

13. The `MmGetPhysicalAddress` API takes a virtual address and returns the physical address for it. Sometimes the returned physical address contains junk data. Explain why this may happen and how to mitigate it.

14. Set up test-signing on your 32- and 64-bit machines and test-sign your driver. Validate that it works.

15. Explain how `AuxKlibGetImageExportDirectory` works. After that, explain how `RtlImageNtHeader` and `RtlImageDirectoryEntryToData` work.

16. Suppose you want to track the life and death of processes. What data structure would you use and what are some properties you can use to uniquely identify a process?

17. Where is the page directory table (CR3 in x86 and TTBR in ARM) stored in a process?

Investigating and Extending Your Knowledge

These exercises require that you to do more background research. You may need to develop drivers using undocumented APIs or access undocumented structures. You should use the knowledge from the experiments only for good.

1. Many modern operating systems support a feature called Data Execution Prevent (DEP). Sometimes it is called Never Execute (NX) or Execute Never (XN). This feature simply blocks code execution in memory pages that are not marked executable. Investigate how this feature is implemented in hardware (x86, x64, and ARM) and how the operating system supports it. After that, investigate how this feature would be implemented without any hardware support.

2. Although we covered the basic idea behind APCs, we did not explain how to use them. Investigate the (undocumented) APIs related to kernel-mode APCs and how they are used. Write a driver that uses them.

3. Devise and implement at least two methods to execute a user-mode process from a kernel-mode driver. Assess the advantages and disadvantages of each method.

4. Suppose that you are on an SMP system with four processors and you want to modify a shared global resource. The global resource is in non-paged pool and it can be modified at any time by any processor. Devise a synchronization mechanism to safely modify this resource. (Hint: Think about IRQL and the thread dispatcher.)

5. Write a driver that blocks all future drivers with the name "bda.sys" from loading.

6. Investigate how the Windows input stack works and implement a keyboard logger. The keylogger can be implemented in several different ways (with and without hooking). Assess the advantages and disadvantages of each keylogging method. Is it possible to get the application receiving the keystrokes?

7. Implement a function that takes a virtual address and change its page protection to readable, writable, and executable. Repeat the same task for a virtual address that is in session space (e.g., win32k.sys).

8. We explained that DriverEntry is the first function to be called in a driver. Explain which function actually calls this routine. How did you figure it out?

9. The Microsoft kernel debugger provides a mechanism that breaks into the debugger when a driver is loaded. This is done through the `"sxe ld:drivername"` command. Build a simple driver and experiment with this command. Explain how it works. Enumerate all the different ways that it may fail.

10. User-mode debuggers can easily "freeze" threads in a process; however, the kernel debugger does not have a facility to do so. Devise a way to freeze and unfreeze a user-mode thread from the kernel.

11. Periodic timers are used by drivers to execute something on a regular basis. Develop a driver that will print a "hello" every 10 minutes. Then devise a way to modify the timer expiration *after* it has been queued. You can use a debugger to do this.

12. Implement a driver that installs its own interrupt handler and validate that it is triggerable from user mode. On x64 Windows, you will run into PatchGuard so be sure to test it only in debug mode.

13. Process privileges are defined using tokens. The highest privilege is LocalSystem (the SYSTEM process runs in this context). Develop a driver that changes a running process privilege such that it runs with LocalSystem privilege.

14. Windows Vista and higher support cryptographic operations in kernel mode through the KSECDD driver. While it is not documented in the official WDK, it is on MSDN under the user-mode bcrypt library. Develop a driver that uses AES, RSA, MD5, SHA1, and a random number generator.

15. Develop a driver that enumerates the address and name of all exported symbols in NTDLL, KERNEL32, and KERNELBASE. Repeat the same for USER32 and GDI32. Did you run into any difficulties? If so, how did you fix them?

16. Develop a driver that hooks an exported function in NTDLL in the `"explorer.exe"` process. Assess the merit of your method. Investigate and evaluate other methods.

17. Develop a driver that attaches to the SMSS.EXE process and patch a win32k system call while in that process context. Explain the problems you encountered and how you solved them.

18. Suppose someone tells you that user-mode exceptions do not ever go into the kernel. Research how user-mode exception handling works in x86 and x64 Windows and assess the aforementioned claim.

19. Suppose you have a malicious driver on the system that hooks INT 1 and INT 3 to make debugging/tracing more difficult. Devise a way to get an

execution trace (or debug code) even with these hooks in place. You have no restrictions. What are some of the corner cases that you must handle?

20. The instruction INT 3 can be represented in two forms. The one-byte version, 0xCC, is the most common. The less common two-byte form is 0xCD03. Explain what happens when you use the two-byte form in Windows.

Analysis of Real-Life Drivers

These exercises are meant for you to practice your analytical skills on a real driver. We provide the file hashes and ask you questions about them. Most (if not all) questions can be answered through static analysis, but you are welcome to run the sample if needed.

1. (Sample D) Analyze and explain what the function 0x10001277 does. Where does the second argument come from and can it ever be invalid? What do the functions at offset 0x100012B0 and 0x100012BC do?

2. (Sample E) This file is fairly large and complex; some of its structures are massive (nearly 4,000 bytes in size). However, it does contain functions performing interesting tasks that were covered in the chapter, so several of the exercises are taken from it. For this exercise, recover the prototype for the functions 0x40400D, 0x403ECC, 0x403FAD, 0x403F48, 0x404088, 0x4057B8, 0x404102, and 0x405C7C, and explain the differences and relationships between them (if any); explain how you arrived at the solution. Next, explain the significance of the 0x30-byte non-paged pool allocation in functions 0x403F48, 0x403ECC, and 0x403FA; while you're at it, recover its type as well. Also, explain why in some of the previous routines there is a pool freeing operation at the beginning. These routines use undocumented functions, so you may need to search the Internet for the prototype.

3. (Sample E) In DriverEntry, identify all the system worker threads. At offset 0x402C12, a system thread is created to do something mundane using an interesting technique. Analyze and explain the goal of function 0x405775 and all functions called by it. In particular, explain the mechanism used in function 0x403D65. When you understand the mechanism, write a driver to do the same trick (but applied to a different I/O request). Complete the exercise by decompiling all four routines. This exercise is very instructive and you will benefit greatly from it.

4. (Sample E) The function 0x402CEC takes the device object associated with \Device\Disk\DR0 as one of its parameters and sends a request to it using IoBuildDeviceIoControlRequest. This device object describes the first partition of your boot drive. Decode the IOCTL it uses and find the meaningful name for it. (Hint: Search all the included files in the WDK, including user-mode files.) Identify the structure associated with this request.

Next, beautify the IDA output such that each local variable has a type and meaningful name. Finally, decompile the routine back to C and explain what it does (perhaps even write another driver that uses this method).

5. (Sample E) Decompile the function 0x401031 and give it a meaningful name. Unless you are familiar with how SCSI works, it is recommended that you read the *SCSI Commands Reference Manual*.

6. (Sample F) Explain what the function 0x100051D2 does and why. What's so special about offset 0x38 in the device extension structure? Recover as many types as possible and decompile this routine. Finally, identify all the timers, DPCs, and work items used by the driver.

Debugging and Automation

Debuggers are programs that leverage support from the processor and operating system to enable tracing of other programs so that one can discover bugs or simply understand the logic of the debugged program. Debuggers are an essential tool for reverse engineers because, unlike disassemblers, they allow runtime inspection of the program's state.

The purpose of this chapter is to familiarize you with the free debugging tools from Microsoft. It is not intended to teach you debugging techniques or how to troubleshoot memory leaks, deadlocks, and so forth. Instead, it focuses on the most important commands and automation/scripting facilities, and how to write debugger extensions for the sole purpose of aiding you in reverse engineering tasks.

The chapter covers the following topics:

- **The debugging tools and basic commands**—This section covers the basics of debugging, various commands, expression evaluations and operators, process and thread-related commands, and memory manipulation.

- **Scripting**—The scripting language of the debugger engine is not very user friendly. This section explains the language in a structured and easy to follow manner, with various examples and a set of scripts to illustrate each topic. After reading this section, you will start leveraging the power of scripting in the debugger.

- **Using the SDK**—When scripts are not enough, you can always write extensions in C or C++. This section outlines the basics of extension writing in C/C++.

The Debugging Tools and Basic Commands

The Debugging Tools for Windows package is a set of debugging utilities that you can download for free from Microsoft's website. The toolset ships with four debuggers that are all based on the same debugger engine (DbgEng).

The DbgEng is a COM object that enables other programs to use advanced debugging APIs rather than just the plain Windows Debugging APIs. In fact, the Debugging Tools package comes with an SDK that illustrates how to write extensions for the DbgEng or host it in your own programs.

The Debugging Tools for Windows package includes the following debuggers:

- **NTSD/CDB**—Microsoft NT Symbolic Debugger (NTSD) and Microsoft Console Debugger (CDB) are both identical except that the former creates a new console window when started, whereas the latter inherits the console window that was used to launch it.

- **WinDbg**—This a graphical interface for the DbgEng. It supports source-level debugging and saving workspaces.

- **KD**—Kernel Debugger (KD) is used to debug the kernel.

The debuggers have a rich set of command-line switches. One particularly useful switch is -z, which is used to analyze crash dumps (*.dmp), cab files (*.cab) containing a crash dump file. Another use of the -z switch is to analyze PE files (executables or DLLs) by having the DbgEng map them as though they were in a crash dump.

The following example runs the cdb debugger with the -z switch in order to map calc.exe in the debugger:

```
C:\>cdb -z c:\windows\syswow64\calc.exe

Microsoft (R) Windows Debugger Version 6.13.0009.1140 X86
Copyright (c) Microsoft Corporation. All rights reserved.

Loading Dump File [c:\windows\syswow64\calc.exe]
Symbol search path is: SRV*C:\cache*http://msdl.microsoft.com/download/
symbols
```

```
Executable search path is:
ModLoad: 00400000 004c7000   c:\windows\syswow64\calc.exe
eax=00000000 ebx=00000000 ecx=00000000 edx=00000000 esi=00000000 edi=00000000
eip=0041a592 esp=00000000 ebp=00000000 iopl=0         nv up di pl nz na po nc
cs=0000  ss=0000  ds=0000  es=0000  fs=0000  gs=0000              efl=00000000
calc!WinMainCRTStartup:
0041a592 e84bf0ffff      call    calc!__security_init_cookie (004195e2)
0:000>
```

Please note two things:

- ▪ `Calc.exe` was mapped into the debugger, and `EIP` points to its entry point (unlike live targets, which point inside `ntdll.dll`).

- ▪ Many debugger commands won't be present, especially the process control commands (because the program is mapped for analysis/inspection, not for dynamic tracing/debugging).

Using the `-z` switch, you can write powerful scripts to analyze programs and extract information.

> **NOTE** You can configure WinDbg to act as the just-in-time (JIT) debugger (for the purposes of postmortem debugging) by running `Windbg.exe  -I` once as a privileged user.

The following sections explain various debugger commands, providing examples along the way.

Setting the Symbol Path

Before launching any of the debuggers (WinDbg, CDB, NTSD, or KD), let's set up the `_NT_SYMBOL_PATH` environment variable:

`_NT_SYMBOL_PATH`=SRV*c:\ cache*http://msdl.microsoft.com/download/symbols

You can also set that up from inside the debugger using the `.sympath` command:

> **NOTE** Setting the symbol path is important so that you can inspect some basic OS structures as you debug the programs in question. For instance, the `!peb` extension command will not function without symbols loaded for NTDLL.

Debugger Windows

The following windows, including their hotkeys when applicable, are exposed in WinDbg:

- ▪ **Command/output window** (Alt+1)—This window enables you to type commands and see the output of operations. While it is possible to debug using other windows and menu items, the command window enables you to make use of the full power of DbgEng's built-in commands and the available extensions.

- **Registers window** (Alt+4)—Displays the configured registers. It is possible to customize this view to control which registers are displayed or hidden.

- **Memory** (Alt+5)—Memory dump window. This window enables you to see the contents of memory, and to scroll, copy, and even edit the memory contents.

- **Calls** (Alt+6)—Displays the call stack information.

- **Disassembly** (Alt+7)—Whereas the command window will display the current instruction disassembly listing, the disassembly window displays a page worth of disassembled code. In this window it is also possible to carry out actions with hotkeys:

  - Add or delete breakpoints on the selected line (F9)

  - Process control (stepping/F11, resuming/F5, etc.)

  - Navigation (Page up/Page down to explore disassembled code)

NOTE WinDbg supports workspaces to enable the window configuration to be saved or restored.

Evaluating Expressions

The debugger understands two syntaxes for expression evaluation: Microsoft Macro Assembler (MASM) and C++.

To determine the default expression evaluator, use .expr without any arguments:

```
0:000> .expr
Current expression evaluator: MASM - Microsoft Assembler expressions
```

To change the current expression evaluation syntax, use

```
0:000> .expr /s c++
Current expression evaluator: C++ - C++ source expressions
```

or

```
0:000> .expr /s masm
Current expression evaluator: MASM - Microsoft Assembler expressions
```

Use the ? command to evaluate expressions (using the default syntax).

The ?? command is used to evaluate a C++ expression (disregarding the default selected syntax).

> **NOTE** The C++ syntax is preferable when type/symbol information is present and you need to access structure members or simply leverage the C++ operators.

Numbers, if not prefixed with a base specifier, are interpreted using the default radix setting. Use the n command to display the current number base, or `n base_value` to set the new default base.

When using MASM syntax, you can express a number in a base of your choice, use the following prefixes:

- **0n**123 for decimal
- **0x**123 for hex
- **0t**123 for octal
- **0y**10101 for binary

Unlike evaluating with the MASM syntax, when using `??` to evaluate commands, it is not possible to override the radix:

```
? 0y101  -> works
?? 0y101 -> does not work.
```

> **NOTE** When the default radix is 16 and you try to evaluate an expression such as abc, it can be confused between a symbol named abc or the hexadecimal number abc (2748 decimal). To resolve the symbol instead, prepend ! before the variable name: ? !abc.

As in the C++ language, the C++ evaluator syntax only permits the 0x prefix for hex and the 0 prefix for octal numbers. If no prefix is specified, base 10 is used.

To mix and match various types of expression, use the `@@c++(expression)` or `@@masm(expression)`:

```
0:000> .expr
Current expression evaluator: MASM - Microsoft Assembler expressions
0:000> ? @@c++(@$peb->ImageSubsystemMajorVersion) + @@masm(0y1)
Evaluate expression: 7 = 00000007
```

The `@@` prefix is a shorthand prefix that can be used to denote the alternative expression evaluation syntax (not the currently set syntax):

```
0:000> .expr
Current expression evaluator: MASM - Microsoft Assembler expressions
0:000> ? @@(@$peb->ImageSubsystemMajorVersion) + @@masm(0y1)
Evaluate expression: 7 = 00000007
```

You do not have to specify `@@c++(...)` because when MASM is the default, `@@(...)` will use the C++ syntax and vice versa.

Useful Operators

This section illustrates various useful operators that can be used in expressions. For the sake of demonstration, we use the predefined pseudo-registers $ip and $peb, which denote the current instruction pointer and the _PEB * of the current process, respectively. Other pseudo-registers are mentioned later in the chapter.

The notation used is "operator (expression syntax)", where the expression syntax will be either C++ or MASM. Note that in the following examples the MASM expression evaluator is set by default.

- Pointer->Field (C++)—As in the preceding example, you use the arrow operator to access the field value pointed at by $peb and the offset of the ImageSubsystemMajorVersion field.

- sizeof(type) (C++)—This operator returns the size of the structure. This can come in handy when you are trying to parse data structures or write powerful conditional breakpoints:

```
0:000> ? @@c++(sizeof(_PEB))
Evaluate expression: 592 = 00000250
```

- #FIELD_OFFSET(Type, Field) (C++)—This macro returns the byte offset of the field in the type:

```
0:000> ? #FIELD_OFFSET(_PEB, ImageSubsystemMajorVersion)
Evaluate expression: 184 = 000000b8
```

- The ternary operator (C++)—This operator behaves like it does in the C++ language:

```
0:000> ? @@c++(@$peb->ImageSubsystemMajorVersion >= 6 ? 1 : 0)
Evaluate expression: 1 = 00000001
```

- (type) Value (C++)—Type casting enables you to cast from one type to another:

```
0:000> ? #FIELD_OFFSET(_PEB, BeingDebugged)
Evaluate expression: 2 = 00000002
0:000> ? @$peb
Evaluate expression: 2118967296 = 7e4ce000
0:000> ? #FIELD_OFFSET(_PEB, BeingDebugged) + (char *)@$peb
Evaluate expression: 2118967298 = 7e4ce002
```

  Note that you cast @$peb to (char*) before adding to it the offset of BeingDebugged.

- *(pointer) (C++)—Dereferencing operator:

```
0:000> dd @$ip L 4
012a9615  2ec048a3 8b5e5f01 90c35de5 90909090
0:000> ? *( (unsigned long *)0x12a9615 )
Evaluate expression: 784353443 = 2ec048a3
```

Note that before dereferencing the pointer you have to give it a proper type (by casting it).

■ poi(address) (MASM)—Pointer dereferencing:

```
0:000> ? @@masm(poi(0x12a9615))
Evaluate expression: 784353443 = 2ec048a3
```

■ hi|low(number) (MASM)—Returns the high or low 16-bit value of a number:

```
0:000> ? hi(0x11223344)
Evaluate expression: 4386 = 00001122
0:000> ? low(0x11223344)
Evaluate expression: 13124 = 00003344
```

■ by/wo/dwo(address) (MASM)—Returns the byte/word/dword value when the address is dereferenced:

```
0:000> db @$ip L 4
012a9615  a3 48 00 00
0:000> ? by(@$ip)
Evaluate expression: 163 = 000000a3
0:000> ? wo(@$ip)
Evaluate expression: 18595 = 000048a3
0:000> ? dwo(@$ip)
Evaluate expression: 18595 = 000048a3
```

■ pointer[index] (C++)—The array subscript operator enables you to dereference memory using indices:

```
0:000> db @$ip L 10
012a9615  a3 48 c0 2e 01 5f 5e 8b e5 5d
0:000> ? @@c++(((unsigned char *)@$ip)[3])
Evaluate expression: 46 = 0000002e
```

The same thing can be achieved using MASM syntax and poi() or by():

```
0:000> ? poi(@$ip+3) & 0xff
Evaluate expression: 46 = 0000002e
0:000> ? by(@$ip+3)
Evaluate expression: 46 = 0000002e
```

NOTE When the pointer[index] is used, the base type size will be taken into consideration (unlike poi(), for which one has to take the type size into consideration).

■ $scmp("string1", "string2")/$sicmp("String1", "String2") (MASM)—String comparison (case sensitive/case insensitive). Returns -1, 0, or 1, as in C's strcmp() / stricmp():

```
0:000> ? $scmp("practical", "practica")
Evaluate expression: 1 = 00000001
```

```
0:000> ? $scmp("practical", "practical")
Evaluate expression: 0 = 00000000
0:000> ? $scmp("practica", "practical")
Evaluate expression: -1 = ffffffff
0:000> ? $scmp("Practical", "practical")
Evaluate expression: -1 = ffffffff
0:000> ? $sicmp("Practical", "practical")
Evaluate expression: 0 = 00000000
```

▪ $iment(address) (MASM)—Returns the image entry point for the image existing in that address. The PE header is parsed and used:

```
0:000> lmvm ole32
start     end         module name
74b70000 74c79000    ole32
...
0:000> ? $iment(74b70000)
Evaluate expression: 1958154432 = 74b710c0
0:000> u $iment(74b70000)
ole32!_DllMainCRTStartup:
74b710c0 8bff            mov     edi,edi
74b710c2 55              push    ebp
74b710c3 8bec            mov     ebp,esp
```

▪ $vvalid(address, length) (MASM)—Checks if the memory pointed at by the address until address + length is accessible (returns 1) or inaccessible (returns 0):

```
0:000> ? @@masm($vvalid(@$ip, 100))
Evaluate expression: 1 = 00000001
0:000> ? @@masm($vvalid(0x0, 100))
Evaluate expression: 0 = 00000000
```

▪ $spat("string", "pattern") (MASM)—Uses pattern matching to determine if the pattern exists in the string, and returns true or false.

Process Control and Debut Events

This section introduces the basic process control commands (such as single stepping, stepping over, etc.) and the commands that can be used to change how the debugger reacts to certain debug events.

Process and Thread Control

These are some commands that allow you control the flow of the debugger:

▪ t (F11)—Step into.

▪ gu (Shift+F11)—Go up. Steps out of the current function and back to the caller.

- p (F10)—Step over.
- g (F5)—Go. Resumes program execution.
- Ctrl+Break—When the debuggee is running, use this hotkey to suspend it.

Note that the preceding commands work only with live targets.

There are useful variations to the "resume," "step into," and "step over" instructions, including the following:

- [t|p]a Address—Step into. Steps over until the specified address is reached.
- gc—This is used to resume execution when a conditional breakpoint suspends execution.
- g[h|n]—This is used to resume execution as handled or unhandled when an exception occurs.

Another set of tracing/stepping commands are useful to discover basic blocks:

- [p|t]c—Step over/into until a CALL instruction is encountered.
- [p|t]h—Step over/into until a branching instruction is encountered (all kinds of jump, return, or call instructions).
- [p|t]t—Step over/into until a RET instruction is encountered.
- [p|t]ct—Step over/into until a CALL or RET instruction is encountered.

Most of the preceding commands (tracing and stepping over) are implicitly operating within the context of the current thread.

To list all threads, use the ~ command:

```
0:004> ~
   0  Id: 1224.13d8 Suspend: 1 Teb: ff4ab000 Unfrozen
   1  Id: 1224.1758 Suspend: 1 Teb: ff4a5000 Unfrozen
   2  Id: 1224.2920 Suspend: 1 Teb: ff37f000 Unfrozen
   3  Id: 1224.1514 Suspend: 1 Teb: ff37c000 Unfrozen
.  4  Id: 1224.b0 Suspend: 1 Teb: ff2f7000 Unfrozen
```

The first column is the thread number (decided by DbgEng), followed by a pair of SystemProcessId.SystemThreadId in hexadecimal format.

The DbgEng commands work with DbgEng IDs, rather than the operating system's process/thread IDs.

To switch to another thread, use the ~Ns command, where N is the thread number you want to switch to:

```
0:004> ~1s
eax=00000000 ebx=00bb1ab0 ecx=00000000 edx=00000000 esi=02faf9ec edi=00b2ec00
eip=7712c46c esp=02faf8a4 ebp=02fafa44 iopl=0         nv up ei pl nz na po nc
cs=0023  ss=002b  ds=002b  es=002b  fs=0053  gs=002b            efl=00000202
```

```
ntdll!NtWaitForWorkViaWorkerFactory+0xc:
7712c46c c21400          ret     14h
0:001>
```

The debugger prompt also shows the selected thread ID in the prompt
`ProcessID:ThreadId>`.

You don't have to switch to threads before issuing a command; for instance,
to display registers of thread ID 3, use the ~3 prefix followed by the desired
debugger command (in this case the r) command:

```
0:001> ~3r
eax=00000000 ebx=00000000 ecx=00000000 edx=00000000 esi=00000001 edi=00000001
eip=7712af2c esp=031afb38 ebp=031afcb8 iopl=0         nv up ei pl nz na po nc
cs=0023  ss=002b  ds=002b  es=002b  fs=0053  gs=002b             efl=00000202
ntdll!NtWaitForMultipleObjects+0xc:
7712af2c c21400          ret     14h
0:001> ~3t
eax=00000000 ebx=00000000 ecx=77072772 edx=00000000 esi=00000001 edi=00000001
eip=758c11b5 esp=031afb50 ebp=031afcb8 iopl=0         nv up ei pl nz na po nc
cs=0023  ss=002b  ds=002b  es=002b  fs=0053  gs=002b             efl=00000202
KERNELBASE!WaitForMultipleObjectsEx+0xdc:
758c11b5 8bf8           mov     edi,eax
```

To display the register values of all the threads, simply pass ∗ as the thread
number.

> **NOTE** Not all debugger commands can be prefixed with ~N cmd so that they yield
> information about thread N. Instead, use the thread-specific command ~eN cmd.

If you are debugging various user mode processes (i.e., when the debugger is
launched with the -o switch), it is possible to switch from one process to another
using the | command. The following example uses Internet Explorer because
it normally spawns various child processes (with different integrity levels and
for various purposes):

```
C:\ dbg64>windbg -o "c:\Program Files (x86)\Internet Explorer\iexplore.exe"
```

Let it run, open a few tabs, and then let the debugger resume with g and then
suspend it and type |:

```
0:030> |
.  0   id: 1818    child  name: iexplore.exe
   1   id: 1384    child  name: iexplore.exe
```

To switch from one process to another, type |Ns, where N is the process number:

```
0:030> |1s
1:083> |
#  0   id: 1818    child  name: iexplore.exe
.  1   id: 1384    child  name: iexplore.exe
```

Once you switch to a new process, future commands will apply to this process. Breakpoints you set for a process will not be present in the other process.

NOTE Aliases and pseudo-registers will be common to all the processes being debugged.

Monitoring Debugging Events and Exceptions

It is possible to capture certain debugging events and exceptions as they occur and let the debugger suspend, display, handle, leave unhandled, or just ignore the event altogether.

The DbgEng may suspend the target and give the user a chance to decide what action to take in the follow two circumstances:

- **Exceptions**—These events happen when an exception triggers in the context of the application (Access Violation, Divide By Zero, Single Step Exception, etc.).

- **Events**—These events are not errors, they are triggered by the operating system to notify the debugger about certain activities taking place (a new thread has been created or terminated, a module has been loaded or unloaded, a new process has been created or terminated, etc.).

To list all the events, use the sx command. Equally, if you are using WinDbg, you can navigate to the Debug/Event Filters menu to graphically configure the events, as shown in Figure 4-1.

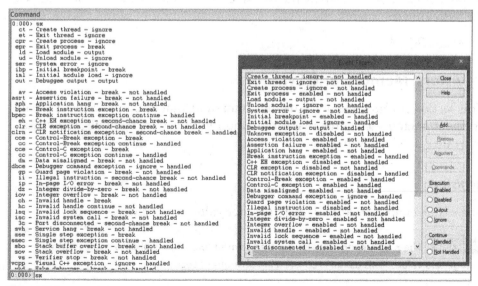

Figure 4-1

The screenshot shows two sets of configuration to control events:

- **Execution**—Dictates what to do when that event takes place.
- **Continue**—Decides how to resume from the event or exception.
  - **Handled**—Marks the exception as being handled (the application's exception handler will not trigger). This is useful when the debugger breaks and you manually fix the situation and then resume the application with the gh command.
  - **Not Handled**—Lets the application's exception handler take care of the exception. Use the gn command to resume.

Use the following commands to control how events/exceptions are handled:

- sxe event—Enables breaking for an event
- sxd event—Disables breaking for an event
- sxr event—Enables output only for an event
- sxi event—Ignores the event (do not event output anything)

The event parameter can be an exception code number, event short code name, or * for any event.

A rather useful application of the sxe or the sxd commands is to catch module loading or unloading. For example, when kernel debugging, to stop the debugger when a certain driver is loaded, use the following command:

```
sxe ld:driver_name.sys
```

To associate a command with an event, use the sx- -c command event command. For example, to display the call stack each time a module is loaded, use the following command:

```
sx- -c "k" ld
```

Registers, Memory, and Symbols

This section covers some of the useful commands that deal with registers management, memory contents inspection and modification, symbols, structures, and other handy commands.

Registers

The r command is used to display register values or to change them.

> **NOTE** The r command can also be used to alter fixed-name aliases and pseudo-registers values. This usage is covered in subsequent sections.

The general syntax of the r command is as follows:

```
r[M Mask|F|X] [RegisterName_Or_FlagName[:[Num]Type] [=[Expression_Or_Value]]]
```

Here is the simplest syntax of the r command:

```
r RegisterName|FlagName [= Expression_Or_Value ]
```

If the expression or value is omitted, then r will display the current value of the register:

```
0:001> r eax
eax=7ffda000
0:001> r eax = 2
0:001> r eax
eax=00000002
```

To display the registers involved in the current instruction, use the r. command:

```
0:000> u rip L1
00007ff6`f54d6470 48895c2420       mov     qword ptr [rsp+20h],rbx
0:000> r.
rsp=000000c9`e256fbb8  rbx=00000000`00000000
0:000> u eip L1
user32!MessageBoxA+0x3:
773922c5 8bec            mov     ebp,esp
0:000> r.
ebp=0018ff98  esp=0018ff78
```

Register Masks

The r command can be suffixed with the M character followed by a 32-bit mask value. The mask designates which registers to display when r is typed without parameters. Table 4-1 shows a short list of the mask values:

Table 4-1: Register Mask Values

REGISTER MASK VALUE	DESCRIPTION
2	General registers
4	Floating-point registers
8	Segment registers
0x10	MMX
0x20	Debug registers
0x40	SSE XMM
0x80	Kernel mode: Control registers
0x100	Kernel mode: TSS

> **NOTE** Use the OR operator (|) to combine various masks.

To see the current mask, type rm:

```
0:000> rm
Register output mask is a:
        2 - Integer state (64-bit)
        8 - Segment registers
```

Now if you execute r, you should see only general-purpose registers and the segment registers:

```
eax=025ad9d4 ebx=00000000 ecx=7c91056d edx=00ba0000 esi=7c810976 edi=10000080
eip=7c810978 esp=025ad780 ebp=025adbec iopl=0         nv up ei pl nz na po nc
cs=001b  ss=0023  ds=0023  es=0023  fs=003b  gs=0000              efl=00000202
```

To display all possible registers, set all the bits to one in the mask parameter (mask 0x1ff):

```
kd> rM1ff
eax=025ad9d4 ebx=00000000 ecx=7c91056d edx=00ba0000 esi=7c810976 edi=10000080
eip=7c810978 esp=025ad780 ebp=025adbec iopl=0         nv up ei pl nz na po nc
cs=001b  ss=0023  ds=0023  es=0023  fs=003b  gs=0000              efl=00000202
fpcw=027F: rn 53 puozdi  fpsw=0000: top=0 cc=0000 -------- fptw=FFFF
fopcode=0000  fpip=0000:00000000  fpdp=0000:00000000
st0= 0.000000000000000000000e+0000   st1= 0.303405511757512497160e-4933
st2=-3.685298464319287816590e-4320   st3= 0.000000015933281407050e-4357
st4=-0.008610620845784322250e-4310   st5= 0.000000125598791309870e-4184
st6=-0.008011795206688037930e+0474   st7=-1.#QNAN0000000000000000e+0000
mm0=0000000000000000  mm1=0127b52000584c8e
mm2=2390ccb400318a24  mm3=000000057c910732
mm4=003187cc00000000  mm5=000000117c910732
mm6=003187ec00000000  mm7=7c9107387c90ee18
xmm0=1.79366e-043 0 6.02419e+036 6.02657e+036
xmm1=0 3.08237e-038 3.08148e-038 0
xmm2=3.30832e-029 5.69433e-039 0 3.08147e-038
xmm3=5.6938e-039 0 9.62692e-043 5.69433e-039
xmm4=3.04894e-038 2.12997e-042 3.07319e-038 5.69433e-039
xmm5=5.69528e-039 6.02651e+036 4.54966e-039 1.16728e-042
xmm6=5.69567e-039 0 5.69509e-039 6.02419e+036
xmm7=4.54901e-039 5.69575e-039 0 5.69559e-039
cr0=8001003b cr2=7c99a3d8 cr3=07f40280
dr0=00000000 dr1=00000000 dr2=00000000
dr3=00000000 dr6=ffff4ff0 dr7=00000400 cr4=000006f9
gdtr=8003f000  gdtl=03ff idtr=8003f400  idtl=07ff tr=0028  ldtr=0000
```

> **NOTE** Some processor registers (GDT, IDT, control registers, etc.) can be displayed in kernel mode debugging only.

To set the default mask, use the `rm` command followed by the desired mask value:

```
0:000> rm 2|4|8
0:000> rm
Register output mask is f:
        2 - Integer state (64-bit)
        4 - Floating-point state
        8 - Segment registers
```

The DbgEng provides shorthand flags for certain masks—namely, the floating-point and the MMX registers.

To display floating-point registers, use `rF`; and to display XMM registers, use `rX`:

```
0:000> rF
fpcw=027F: rn 53 puozdi  fpsw=4020: top=0 cc=1000 --p----- fptw=FFFF
fopcode=0000  fpip=0023:74b785bc  fpdp=002b:00020a84
st0= 0.000000000000000000000e+0000  st1= 0.000000000000000000000e+0000
...
0:000> rX
xmm0=0  0  0  0
xmm1=0  0  0  0
xmm2=0  0  0  0
...
```

Register Display Format

It is possible to specify how the registers should be displayed. This is very useful in many cases, as illustrated in the following examples.

Displaying Registers in Floating-Point Formats

Suppose you're debugging and notice that register eax holds a floating-point value:

```
0:000> r eax
eax=3f8ccccd
```

To display it properly, use the following:

```
0:000> r eax:f
eax=1.1
```

To display the contents of `rax` in double-precision, floating-point value, use this:

```
0:000> r rax
rax=4014666666666666
0:000> r rax:d
rax=5.1
```

Displaying Registers in Bytes/Word/Dword/Qword Formats

When registers are involved in data transfer, it is useful to see the register's individual bytes:

```
msvcrt!memcpy+0x220:
00007ff9`5f671a5d f30f7f40f0      movdqu  xmmword ptr [rax-10h],xmm0
0:000> r xmm0
xmm0=            0 1.05612e-038 1.01939e-038 1.00102e-038
0:000> r xmm0:ub
xmm0=00 00 00 00 00 73 00 6c 00 6f 00 62 00 6d 00 79
0:000> rX xmm0:uw
xmm0=0000 0000 0073 006c 006f 0062 006d 0079
0:000> rX xmm0:ud
xmm0=00000000 0073006c 006f0062 006d0079
0:000> rX xmm0:uq
xmm0=000000000073006c 006f0062006d0079
```

In the preceding example, memcpy() uses the XMM registers to transfer 16 bytes at a time. You use the ub format to display the contents of xmm0 in unsigned bytes format, uw for word format, ud for double-word format, and uq for quad-word format. To display in signed format, use the i prefix instead of u.

Display Selector Command

The display selector command has the following syntax:

```
dg FirstSelector [LastSelector]
```

It displays information about a given selector (or range of selectors). In this case, you are interested in selector values that are currently set in one of the x86/x64 registers—namely, the cs, ds, ss, gs, and fs registers.

Selectors are used in the segment part of an address in protected mode.

The following example executes the dg command for cs, ds, ss, gs, and fs, respectively:

```
0:001> .foreach /s (sel "cs ds ss gs fs") { dg sel; }
(cs Selector)
                                   P Si Gr Pr Lo
Sel    Base     Limit     Type    l ze an es ng Flags
----   -------- --------  ------------ - -- -- -- -- --------
0023 00000000 ffffffff Code RE Ac 3 Bg Pg P  Nl 00000cfb
(ds Selector)
                                   P Si Gr Pr Lo
Sel    Base     Limit     Type    l ze an es ng Flags
----   -------- --------  ------------ - -- -- -- -- --------
002B 00000000 ffffffff Data RW Ac 3 Bg Pg P  Nl 00000cf3
(ss Selector)
```

```
                            P  Si Gr Pr Lo
 Sel    Base     Limit     Type      l  ze an es ng Flags
 ----  --------  --------  ----------  -  -- -- -- --  --------
 002B  00000000  ffffffff  Data RW Ac  3  Bg Pg P  Nl  00000cf3
 (gs Selector)
                            P  Si Gr Pr Lo
 Sel    Base     Limit     Type      l  ze an es ng Flags
 ----  --------  --------  ----------  -  -- -- -- --  --------
 002B  00000000  ffffffff  Data RW Ac  3  Bg Pg P  Nl  00000cf3
 (fs Selector)
                            P  Si Gr Pr Lo
 Sel    Base     Limit     Type      l  ze an es ng Flags
 ----  --------  --------  ----------  -  -- -- -- --  --------
 0053  7ffda000  00000fff  Data RW Ac  3  Bg By P  Nl  000004f3
```

In MS Windows/user-mode applications, the cs, ds, es, ss, and gs selectors have a base value of zero, thus the linear address is the same as the virtual address.

Conversely, the fs register is variable, changing its value from thread to thread. The fs segment in user-mode processes points to the TEB (Thread Environment Block) structure:

```
0:003> dg fs
 Sel    Base     Limit     Type      l  ze an es ng Flags
 ----  --------  --------  ----------  -  -- -- -- --  --------
 0053  ff306000  00000fff  Data RW Ac  3  Bg By P  Nl  000004f3

(Switch to another thread)
0:003> ~2s
0:002> dg fs
 Sel    Base     Limit     Type      l  ze an es ng Flags
 ----  --------  --------  ----------  -  -- -- -- --  --------
 0053  ff4a5000  00000fff  Data RW Ac  3  Bg By P  Nl  000004f3
```

Memory

Before describing memory-related commands, it is important to explain the address and range notations because they are passed as arguments to most commands that require a memory address and count.

The Address parameter can be any value, expression, or symbol that resolves to a numeric value that can be interpreted as an address. The number 0x401000 can be treated as an address if the address is mapped in memory. The name kernel32 will resolve to the image base of the module:

```
0:000> lmm kernel32
start     end          module name
75830000 75970000     KERNEL32
0:000> ? kernel32
Evaluate expression: 1971519488 = 75830000
```

A symbol such as `module_name!SymbolName` can be used as an address as long as it resolves:

```
0:000> ? kernel32!GetProcAddress
Couldn't resolve error at 'kernel32!GetProcAddress'
0:000> ? kernelbase!GetProcAddress
Evaluate expression: 1979722334 = 76002a5e
```

It is possible to use any expression as an address (notwithstanding whether the value resolves to a valid address or not):

```
0:000> ? (kernelbase!GetProcAddress - kernel32) / 0n4096
Evaluate expression: 2002 = 000007d2
```

The `Range` parameter can be specified in two ways. The first method is with a pair of starting and ending addresses:

```
0:000> db 02c0000 02c0005
002c0000  23 01 00 00 00 00                                #.....
```

The second method is by using an address followed by the `L` character and an expression (`address L Expression_Or_Value`) that designs a count.

If the count is a positive value, then the starting address will be the specified address, and the ending address is implied and equal to `address + count`:

```
0:000> db 02c0000 L5
002c0000  23 01 00 00 00                                   #....
```

If the count is a negative value, then the ending address becomes the specified address, and the starting address becomes `address - count`:

```
0:000> db 02c0005 L-5
002c0000  23 01 00 00 00                                   #....
```

By default, the expression or the value passed after `L` cannot exceed 256MB. This is to prevent accidentally passing very large values. To overwrite this limitation, use `L?` instead of just `L`. For example, notice how the DbgEng will complain about this big size:

```
0:000> db @$ip L0xffffffff
                          ^ Range error in 'db @$ip l0xffffffff
```

When `L?` is used, the DbgEng will be happy to comply:

```
0:000> db @$ip L?0xffffffff
760039c2  83 e4 f8 83 ec 18 8b 4d-1c 8b c1 25 b7 7f 00 00  .......M...%....
...
```

Dumping Memory Contents

The d command is used to dump memory contents. The general syntax is as follows:

```
d[a|b|c|d|D|f|p|q|u|w|W] [Options] [Range]
```

Various formats can be used to display memory contents. The most common formats are as follows:

- b, w, d, q—For byte, word, double-word, and quad-word format, respectively
- f, D—For single and double-precision floating-point values, respectively
- a, u—To display ASCII or Unicode memory contents, respectively
- p—For pointer values (the size varies according to the current pointer size of the target)

When the dp, dd, or dq are suffixed with s, the symbols corresponding to the addresses will be displayed. This can be handy to discover function pointers that are defined in an array or a virtual table:

```
(1)
0:011> bp combase!CoCreateInstance
(2)
0:024> g
Breakpoint 0 hit
combase!CoCreateInstance:
7526aeb0 8bff            mov     edi,edi
0:011> ? poi(esp+4*5)
Evaluate expression: 112323728 = 06b1ec90
0:011> ? poi(poi(esp+4*5))
Evaluate expression: 0 = 00000000
(3)
0:011> g poi(esp)
combase!CustomUnmarshalInterface+0x15d:
752743e7 fe8ef0000000    dec     byte ptr [esi+0F0h]
ds:002b:08664160=01
0:011> ? poi(06b1ec90)
Evaluate expression: 141774136 = 08734d38
(4)
0:011> dps 08734d38 L1
08734d38  752c9688 combase!CErrorObject::`vftable'
0:011> dps 752c9688 L3
752c9688  752f6bdf combase![thunk]:CErrorObject::QueryInterface`adjustor{8}'
752c968c  752f6bd0 combase![thunk]:CErrorObject::AddRef`adjustor{8}'
752c9690  752a9b91 combase![thunk]:CErrorObject::Release`adjustor{8}'
```

Marker 1 adds a breakpoint on the following function:

```
HRESULT CoCreateInstance(
  REFCLSID rclsid,
```

```
LPUNKNOWN pUnkOuter,
DWORD dwClsContext,
REFIID riid,
LPVOID *ppv)
```

We are interested in determining the pointer value (parameter 5) of the newly created interface after the function returns. On marker 2, we resume execution. The program later breaks on the breakpoint and gets suspended. We then inspect the fifth pointer location and dereference it. Its dereferenced value should be NULL and initialized properly only if the function returns successfully. On marker 3, we let the debugger run the CoCreateInstance function and return to the caller. We then dereference the output pointer again. Finally, on marker 4, we use the dps command to display the address of the vftable, and then use dps once more to display three pointers at the vftable.

NOTE   dps is equivalent to dds on 32-bits targets, and to dqs on 64-bits targets.

Editing Memory Contents

To edit the memory contents, use the e command. The general syntax is as follows:

```
e[b|d|D|f|p|q|w] Address [Values]
```

NOTE   If no suffix is specified after the e command, the last suffix that was previously used with e will be used. For instance, if ed were used the first time, then the next time e alone is used, it will act as if it were ed.

Use the b, w, d, or q format specifiers to set byte, word, dword, or qword values, respectively, at the specified memory address:

```
0:000> eb 0x1b0000 11 22 33 44; db 0x1b0000 L 4
001b0000   11 22 33 44
0:000> ed 0x1b0000 0xdeadbeef 0xdeadc0de; dd 0x1b0000 L 2
001b0000   deadbeef deadc0de
```

It is possible to use single quotes to enter character values when using either of the w/d or q formats. The DbgEng will respect the "endianness" of the target:

```
0:000> ed 1b0000 'TAG1'
0:000> db 1b0000 'TAG1' L 4
001b0000   31 47 41 54                                    1GAT
```

Apart from editing the memory with integer values, the e command has other format specifiers that allow you to enter other types:

- e[f|D] (address values)—Sets a single or double-precision floating-pointer number:

```
0:000> eD @$t0 1999.99
0:000> dD @$t0 L 1
000000c9`e2450000                    1999.99
```

- ep (address values)—Sets pointer-sized values. This command knows how big a pointer is based on the currently debugged target.

- e[a|u] (address string)—Enters an ASCII or Unicode string at the given address. The entered string will not be zero terminated:

```
0:000> f 0x1b0000 L0x40 0x21 0x22 0x23; db 0x1b0000 L0x20;
Filled 0x40 bytes
001b0000  21 22 23 21 22 23 21 22-23 21 22 23 21 22 23 21  !"#!"#!"#!"#!"#!
001b0010  22 23 21 22 23 21 22 23-21 22 23 21 22 23 21 22  "#!"#!"#!"#!"#!
0:000> ea 0x1b0000 "Hello world"; db 0x1b0000 L0x20
001b0000  48 65 6c 6c 6f 20 77 6f-72 6c 64 23 21 22 23 21  Hello
world#!"#!
001b0010  22 23 21 22 23 21 22 23-21 22 23 21 22 23 21 22  "#!"#!"#!"#!"#!
```

- e[za|zu] (address string)—As opposed to e[a|u], this command will enter the zero character termination at the end of the string.

To fill a memory area with a given pattern, use the f command:

```
f Address L Count Values
```

For example:

```
0:000> f @eax L0x40 0x21 0x22 0x23; db @eax L0x20
Filled 0x40 bytes
001b0000  21 22 23 21 22 23 21 22-23 21 22 23 21 22 23 21  !"#!"#!"#!"#!"#!
001b0010  22 23 21 22 23 21 22 23-21 22 23 21 22 23 21 22  "#!"#!"#!"#!"#!"
```

Miscellaneous Memory Commands

Following is another set of memory-related commands that come in handy:

- s [-[flags]type] Range Pattern—Searches the memory for a given pattern

- c Range_For_Address1 Address2—Compares two memory regions

- .dvalloc [Options] Size—Allocates memory in the process space of the debugger:

```
0:000> .dvalloc 0x2000
Allocated 2000 bytes starting at 001c0000
```

- .dvfree [Options] BaseAddress Size—Frees the memory previously allocated by .dvalloc

■ `.readmem FileName Range`—Reads a file from disk to the debuggee's memory:

```
kd> .readmem file.bin @eax L3
Reading 3 bytes.
```

■ `.writemem FileName Range`—Writes the debuggee's memory to a file on disk

Symbols

The following commands enable you to inspect symbols and structured data:

■ `dt [type] [address]`—A very handy command to display the type of an item at the given address:

```
$$ Display the type of the structure UNICODE_STRING
0:000> dt UNICODE_STRING
ole32!UNICODE_STRING
   +0x000 Length            : Uint2B
   +0x002 MaximumLength     : Uint2B
   +0x004 Buffer            : Ptr32 Wchar


$$ Display type information and values in a type at a given address
0:000> dt _UNICODE_STRING 0x18fef4
ntdll!_UNICODE_STRING
  "KERNEL32.DLL"
   +0x000 Length            : 0x18
   +0x002 MaximumLength     : 0x1a
   +0x004 Buffer            : 0x00590168   "KERNEL32.DLL"
```

■ `dv [flags] [pattern]`—Displays information about local variables

■ `x [options] [module_pattern]![symbol_pattern]`—Displays symbol(s) in a given module or modules

■ `!dh [options] Address`—Dumps PE image headers

■ `!drvobj DriverObjectPtr [Flags]`—Displays information about a `DRIVER_OBJECT` object.

■ `!heap`—Displays heap information

■ `!pool`—Displays kernel pool information

Breakpoints

On the x86/x64 architecture, the DbgEng supports two types of breakpoints:

■ **Software breakpoints**—These breakpoints are created by saving the byte at the breakpoint address then replacing it with a 0xCC byte (on x64/x64). The debugger implements the underlying logic to handle the breakpoint magic.

■ **Hardware breakpoints**—Also known as processor or data breakpoints, these breakpoints may or may not be present depending on the hardware running the target. They are limited in count and can be set up to trigger on read, write, or execute.

The simple syntax to create a software breakpoint is as follows:

```
bp Address ["CommandString"]
bu Address "CommandString"
bm SymbolPattern ["CommandString"]
```

NOTE Please refer to the debugger documentation for the full syntax of the b* commands.

To list breakpoints, simply use the `bl` command:

```
0:001> bl
 0 e 771175c9     0001 (0001)  0:**** ntdll!RtlInitString+0x9
 1 e 77117668     0001 (0001)  0:**** ntdll!RtlInitUnicodeString+0x38
 2 e 771176be     0001 (0001)  0:**** ntdll!_sin_default+0x26
 3 e 7711777e     0001 (0001)  0:**** ntdll!sqrt+0x2a
 4 e 771177c0     0001 (0001)  0:**** ntdll!sqrt+0x6a
```

To disable breakpoints, use the `bd` command. Similarly, use the `be` command to enable breakpoints, and the `bc` command to clear (delete) breakpoints.

You can specify a series of breakpoint IDs to enable, disable, or clear them:

```
be 0 2 4
```

Or a range:

```
be 1-3
```

Or simply all breakpoints:

```
be *
```

Unresolved Breakpoints

The `bu` command creates a breakpoint whose address is still unknown/unresolved or whose address may change if it belongs to a module (that is ASLR aware) that is loaded and unloaded many times at different base addresses.

The debugger will try to reevaluate the breakpoint address when a new module is loaded and if the symbol is matched the breakpoint becomes active. When the module is unloaded, the breakpoint becomes inactive until the symbol can be resolved again.

In short, the address of the breakpoint is not fixed and will automatically be adjusted by the debugger.

Software Breakpoints

Software breakpoints can be created using the bp command. If the address can be resolved when the breakpoint is created, then the breakpoint becomes active. If the breakpoint cannot be resolved, the breakpoint will act like an unresolved breakpoint and become active once the address can be resolved. If the module at the breakpoint address is unloaded and then loaded again, the previously resolved breakpoint address will remain fixed (as opposed to the unresolved breakpoints).

Hardware Breakpoints

Hardware breakpoints can be created using the ba command. These breakpoints are assisted by the hardware. To create a hardware breakpoint you need to specify the address, access type, and size. The access type designates whether to break on read (read/write), write (write only), or execute. The size designates how big the item you are breaking on access for is. For instance, to break on "word access," specify the size 2.

NOTE There is an architectural limit on the number of hardware breakpoints you can have.

Conditional Breakpoints

Conditional breakpoints can be any type of breakpoint just described. In fact, each breakpoint can be associated with a command. When a conditional command is associated with a breakpoint, the breakpoint can be considered a conditional breakpoint.

The following example creates a conditional breakpoint such that when eax has the value of 5, the breakpoint will suspend execution; otherwise, the breakpoint will continue resuming execution:

```
0:000> uf kernelbase!GetLastError
KERNELBASE!GetLastError:
7661d0d6 64a118000000    mov     eax,dword ptr fs:[00000018h]
7661d0dc 8b4034          mov     eax,dword ptr [eax+34h]
7661d0df c3              ret

0:000> bp 7661d0df ".if @eax!=5 { gc; }"
0:000> bl
0 e 7661d0df 0001 (0001) 0:*** KERNELBASE!GetLastError+0x9 ".if @eax!=5
{gc;}"
```

It is possible to associate a more elaborate condition with a breakpoint. This is covered in the section "Scripting with the Debugging Tools," later in this chapter.

Inspecting Processes and Modules

The DbgEng enables you to inspect running processes, loaded/unloaded modules, or loaded kernel mode drivers.

To get the list of loaded and unloaded modules, use `lm`:

```
0:001> lm n
start     end        module name
00400000 00405000    image00400000
5ca40000 5cb44000    MFC42
733a0000 733b9000    dwmapi
73890000 73928000    apphelp
...
```

Similarly, in kernel mode debugging, the `lm` command will display the list of loaded device drivers:

```
kd> lm n
start     end        module name
804d7000 806cd280    nt       ntkrnlpa.exe
806ce000 806ee380    hal      halaacpi.dll
b205e000 b2081000    Fastfat  Fastfat.SYS
b2121000 b2161380    HTTP     HTTP.sys
b2d2b000 b2d4cd00    afd      afd.sys
b2d4d000 b2d74c00    netbt    netbt.sys
b2d75000 b2dcca80    tcpip    tcpip.sys
bf800000 bf9c0380    win32k   win32k.sys
f83e6000 f8472480    Ntfs     Ntfs.sys
f86ca000 f86d6c80    VolSnap  VolSnap.sys
f8aaa000 f8aad000    BOOTVID  BOOTVID.dll

...
```

> **NOTE** The n option was passed to minimize the default output of the `lm` command.

To view module information (version, size, base, etc.), use the `v` switch for verbose mode and `m` to specify a module name to match:

```
kd> lm v m *volsnap*
start     end        module name
f86ca000 f86d6c80    VolSnap
    Loaded symbol image file: VolSnap.sys
    Image path: VolSnap.sys
    Image name: VolSnap.sys
    Timestamp:        Tue Aug 03 23:00:14 2004 (41107B6E)
```

```
CheckSum:        00017B61
ImageSize:       0000CC80
Translations:    0000.04b0 0000.04e4 0409.04b0 0409.04e4
```

When in kernel mode, you have a full view of all running processes. Use the !process extension command with the 0 0 flags to list all running processes:

```
kd> !process 0 0
**** NT ACTIVE PROCESS DUMP ****
PROCESS 823c8830  SessionId: none  Cid: 0004    Peb: 00000000  ParentCid:
0000
    DirBase: 00334000  ObjectTable: e1000c90  HandleCount: 246.
    Image: System
PROCESS 820ed020  SessionId: none  Cid: 017c    Peb: 7ffdd000  ParentCid:
0004
    DirBase: 07f40020  ObjectTable: e14f9c60  HandleCount:  21.
    Image: smss.exe
PROCESS 81e98740  SessionId: 0  Cid: 0278    Peb: 7ffde000  ParentCid: 017c
    DirBase: 07f40060  ObjectTable: e1010ac8  HandleCount: 517.
    Image: winlogon.exe
PROCESS 81e865c0  SessionId: 0  Cid: 02a4    Peb: 7ffde000  ParentCid: 0278
    DirBase: 07f40080  ObjectTable: e1a7a450  HandleCount: 265.
    Image: services.exe
PROCESS 821139f0  SessionId: 0  Cid: 0354    Peb: 7ffd9000  ParentCid: 02a4
    DirBase: 07f400e0  ObjectTable: e1a78ce0  HandleCount: 201.
    Image: svchost.exe
PROCESS 81e68558  SessionId: 0  Cid: 0678    Peb: 7ffdd000  ParentCid: 0658
    DirBase: 07f401e0  ObjectTable: e177aa70  HandleCount: 336.
    Image: explorer.exe
```

NOTE   This is equivalent to using the !for_each_process **extension command without any parameters.**

It is possible to set breakpoints in user-mode processes using the kernel debugger. First you need to switch to the correct process context, and for that you need the EPROCESS value:

```
kd> !process 0 0 explorer.exe
PROCESS 81e68558  SessionId: 0  Cid: 0678    Peb: 7ffdd000  ParentCid: 0658
    DirBase: 07f401e0  ObjectTable: e177aa70  HandleCount: 336.
    Image: explorer.exe
```

Then use the .process /r /p EPROCESS command to switch to the context of the desired process:

```
kd> .process /r /p 81e68558
Implicit process is now 81e68558
.cache forcedecodeuser done
Loading User Symbols........
```

At this point, after the context switch, use lm to not only list the loaded kernel drivers but also the user-mode modules.

The next example sets a breakpoint at kernel32!CreateFileW for that EPROCESS:

```
(1)
kd> bp /p 81e68558 kernel32!CreateFileW
(2)
kd> bl
 0 e 7c810976     0001 (0001) kernel32!CreateFileW
     Match process data 81e68558
(3)
kd> g
Breakpoint 0 hit
kernel32!CreateFileW:
001b:7c810976 8bff                mov     edi,edi
(4)
kd> .printf "%mu\n", poi(@esp+4);
C:\Temp\desktop.ini
```

In marker 1, we set an EPROCESS filter with the bp /p EPROCESS command so that only the explore.exe process triggers the breakpoint. Marker 2 lists the breakpoints. Note that it will only match for a certain EPROCESS. At marker 3 we resume execution and wait until the breakpoint triggers. At marker 4, we display the filename that was accessed. Marker 4 will become much clearer after you read the "Language" section later in this chapter.

Now suppose you want to display all processes that called the CreateFileW API and display which filename was referenced:

```
kd> bp kernel32!CreateFileW "!process @$proc 0;.printf "%mu\n",poi(@esp+4);gc;"
```

This will break whenever any user-mode process hits the breakpoint, and then the breakpoint command will invoke !process with the current EPROCESS (set in the pre-defined pseudo-register $proc) to display the current process context information, display the filename, and finally resume execution with gc.

> **NOTE** !process @$proc 0 **is equivalent to** !process -1 0.

When execution is resumed, you see this redacted output:

```
kd> g

PROCESS 82067020  SessionId: 0  Cid: 0138    Peb: 7ffdf000  ParentCid: 02a4
    DirBase: 07f40260  ObjectTable: e1b66ef8  HandleCount: 251.
    Image: vmtoolsd.exe

C:\WINDOWS\SoftwareDistribution\DataStore\DataStore.edb
PROCESS 81dc0da0  SessionId: 0  Cid: 0204    Peb: 7ffd5000  ParentCid: 03fc
```

```
    DirBase: 07f40280  ObjectTable: e1ba8ea8  HandleCount: 177.
    Image: wuauclt.exe

PROCESS 81e68558  SessionId: 0  Cid: 0678    Peb: 7ffdd000  ParentCid: 0658
    DirBase: 07f401e0  ObjectTable: e177aa70  HandleCount: 362.
    Image: explorer.exe

C:\WINDOWS\media\Windows XP Start.wav
PROCESS 81e68558  SessionId: 0  Cid: 0678    Peb: 7ffdd000  ParentCid: 0658
    DirBase: 07f401e0  ObjectTable: e177aa70  HandleCount: 351.
    Image: explorer.exe

C:\WINDOWS\WinSxS\Policies\x86_Policy.6.0.Microsoft.Windows.Common-Controls
_6595b64144ccf1df_x-ww_5ddad775\6.0.2600.2180.Policy
PROCESS 820f0020  SessionId: 0  Cid: 0260    Peb: 7ffdf000  ParentCid: 017c
    DirBase: 07f40040  ObjectTable: e1503128  HandleCount: 343.
    Image: csrss.exe
```

Miscellaneous Commands

This section introduces several miscellaneous debugger commands, the `.printf` command, along with the format specifiers it supports, and describes how to use the Debugger Markup Language (DML) with `.printf` or other commands that support DML.

The .printf Command

The `.printf` command is one of the most useful commands to help display information from scripts or commands. As in the C language, this command takes format specifiers. Following are a few important ones:

- ▪ `%p` (pointer value)—Displays a pointer value.

- ▪ `%d`, `%x`, `%u` (number value)—Displays integer values. The syntax is very similar to C's format specifiers.

- ▪ `%ma` / `%mu` (pointer value)—Displays the ASCII/Unicode string at the specified pointer.

- ▪ `%msa` / `%msu` (pointer value)—Displays the ANSI_STRING / UNICODE_STRING value at the specified pointer.

- ▪ `%y` (pointer value)—Displays the symbol name (and displacement if any) at the specified pointer.

Here is a simple example:

```
0:000> .printf "t0=%d t1=%d eax=%x ebx=%d\n", @$t0, @$t1, @eax, @ebx
t0=0 t1=0 eax=5 ebx=8323228
```

There is no %s specifier to expand string arguments. The following example expands the value of the user-defined alias by embedding it in the format parameter:

```
0:000> aS STR "TheValue"
0:000> al
  Alias           Value
  -------         -------
STR             TheValue

0:000> .printf "This value of string is ${STR}\n"
```

The .printf command can make use of the Debugger Markup Language (DML). To use DML with .printf, specify the /D switch.

NOTE DML works only in WinDbg.

To display with strings with colors, use the col markup:

```
0:000> .printf /D "<col fg=\"emphfg\">Hello</col> world\n"
Hello world
```

It is also possible to use the u, i, and b tags for underline, italic, and bold, respectively:

```
0:000> .printf /D "<u>underline</u> <b>bold</b> <i>italics</i>\n";
underline bold italics
```

A very useful markup is the link because it makes the output clickable and associated with a command:

```
0:000> .printf /D "Click <link cmd=\"u 0x401000\">here</link>\n"
Click here
```

Some debugger commands also take the /D switch. For example, lm /D will list the modules, and each module is clickable. When a module is clicked, the command lmvm modulename will be issued.

NOTE Use the .prefer_dml 1 command to toggle a global setting that tells commands that support DML to prefer DML when applicable.

For more information, check `dml.doc` in the debugging tools distribution.

Other Commands

Before ending our discussion about debugger commands, we list a few more useful commands:

- `#`—Searches for a disassembly pattern.
- `!gle`—Returns the last error code.
- `.logopen`/`.logfile`/`.logappend`/`.logclose`—Commands to manage logging of output from the command window to text files.
- `.load`—Loads a debugger extension.
- `.cls`—Clears the debugger's output window. (This command does not work in scripts because it is not part of the DbgEng scripting language.)
- `.effmach`—Changes or displays the processor mode that the debugger uses. It is useful when debugging WOW64 processes. This command is also similar to the extension command `!wow64exts.sw`.

Scripting with the Debugging Tools

This section illustrates important scripting features in the DbgEng that are useful for automating reverse engineering and debugging tasks.

Pseudo-Registers

The DbgEng supports pseudo-registers to hold certain values. All of the pseudo-registers start with the $ sign. Prefixing a pseudo-register or a register with the @ sign tells the interpreter that the identifier is not a symbol, thus no exhaustive, sometimes slow, symbol lookup will take place.

Predefined Pseudo-Registers

In this section we introduce some useful predefined pseudo-registers. They can be used in expressions or as parameters to debugger commands or scripts. Please note that some pseudo-registers may or may not be defined, depending on the debugged target.

- `$csp`—The current call stack pointer. This is useful because you don't have to guess if you should use `esp` or `rsp`.
- `$ip`—The current instruction pointer. Similarly, a dot (.) can be used to denote the current instruction pointer.

▪ $retreg/$retreg64—The return registers (typically eax, edx:eax, or rax).

▪ $p—The first value that the last d? command displayed:

```
0:000> dd @$ip L 1
012aa5e5  012ec188
0:000> ? @$p
Evaluate expression: 19841416 = 012ec188
0:000> dw @$ip+2 L 1
012aa5e5  c188
0:000> ? @$p
Evaluate expression: 49544 = 0000c188
0:000> db @$ip+2 L 1
012aa5e5  88
0:000> ? @$p
Evaluate expression: 136 = 00000088
```

▪ $ra—The current return address. This is equivalent to poi(@$csp).

▪ $exentry—The entry point address of the first executable of the current process. This is very useful when debugging a program from the beginning because DbgEng does not break on the entry point but in the kernel.

▪ $peb—Process Environment Block. This pseudo-register has the following type: ntdll!_PEB *.

▪ $proc—The EPROCESS* address of the current process in kernel mode. In user-mode it equates to $peb.

▪ $teb—Thread Environment Block of the current thread. It has the following type: ntdll!_TEB*.

▪ $thread—ETHREAD* in kernel mode. In user-mode it is same as $teb.

▪ $tpid—The current process id.

▪ $tid—The current thread id.

▪ $ptrsize—The pointer size from the point of view of the debuggee. If your host OS is 64-bit and you are debugging a 32-bit process, then $ptrsize=4. In kernel mode it returns the pointer size of the target machine.

▪ $pagesize—The number of bytes per memory page (usually 4,096).

▪ $dbgtime—The current time (based on the computer running the debugger).

▪ $bpNUM—The address associated with the breakpoint number:

```
0:000> bl
  0 e 012aa597     0001 (0001)  0:****  calc!WinMainCRTStartup+0xf
  1 e 012aa5ab     0001 (0001)  0:****  calc!WinMainCRTStartup+0x23
0:000> ? @$bp0
Evaluate expression: 19572119 = 012aa597
0:000> ? @$bp1
Evaluate expression: 19572139 = 012aa5ab
```

▪ $exp—The value of the last expression evaluated:

```
0:000> r $t0 = 1 + 4
0:000> ? @$exp
Evaluate expression: 5 = 00000005
```

or

```
0:000> ? Esp
Evaluate expression: 1637096 = 0018fae8
0:000> ? @$exp
Evaluate expression: 1637096 = 0018fae8
```

The first example assigns a value into a pseudo-register after it was evaluated. You can see how $exp returns the last value. The same is true for the second example, which evaluates the value of the esp register.

User-Defined Pseudo-Registers

In addition to the pre-defined pseudo-registers, DbgEng enables users to define their own set of pseudo-registers. DbgEng provides 20 user-defined pseudo-registers (UDPRs) for use and to store integer values. They are $t0 to $t19.

The r command is used to assign values to those registers:

```
0:000> r $t0 = 1234
0:000> ? @$t0
Evaluate expression: 4660 = 00001234
```

Because numbers can be pointers, it is possible to store typed pointers into those pseudo-registers using the r? command:

```
(1)
0:000> ? poi(@$ip)
Evaluate expression: 409491562 = 1868586a
(2)
0:000> r? $t0 = @@c++((unsigned long *)@$ip)
(3)
0:000> ? @@c++(*@$t0)
Evaluate expression: 409491562 = 1868586a
```

On marker 1, we dereference and evaluate the value pointed to by $ip. On marker 2, we use r? to assign a C++ expression to $t0; the cast operator is used to return a typed pointer (of type unsigned long *) into $t0. Finally, on marker 3 we use the C++ dereferencing operator to dereference $t0. (This would have not been possible without having a previously typed $t0 or without preceding the expression by a cast.)

Here's another example:

```
0:000> r? $t0 = @@c++(@$peb->ProcessParameters->ImagePathName)
0:000> ? $t0
```

```
Evaluate expression: 0 = 00000000
0:000> ?? @$t0
struct _UNICODE_STRING
 "c:\windows\syswow64\calc.exe"
   +0x000 Length         : 0x38
   +0x002 MaximumLength  : 0x3a
   +0x004 Buffer         : 0x0098189e   "c:\windows\syswow64\calc.exe"
```

Note that when you evaluate $t0 with ?, you get zero. When you use the C++ evaluation syntax ??, however, you get the actual typed value.

Symbols, all kinds of pseudo-registers, or aliases can also be used in expressions.

Aliases

An alias is a mechanism that enables you to create equivalence between a value and a symbolic name. By evaluating the alias you get the value that was assigned to the alias.

The DbgEng supports three kinds of aliases:

- **User-named aliases**—As the name implies, these aliases are chosen by the user.

- **Fixed-name aliases**—There are ten of them, named $u0 .. $u9.

- **Automatic aliases**—These are pre-defined aliases that expand to certain values.

User-Named Aliases

This section describes how to create and manage user-defined aliases and explains how they are interpreted.

Creating and Managing User-Named Aliases

The following commands are used to create user-named aliases:

- as AliasName Alias_Equivalence—Creates a line equivalence for the given alias:

  ```
  as MyAlias lm;vertarget
  ```

  This will create an alias for two commands: lm and then vertarget. You can execute both commands by invoking MyAlias.

- aS AliasName Alias_Equivalence—Creates a phrase equivalence for the given alias. That means a semicolon will terminate the alias equivalence (unless the equivalence was enclosed in quotes) and start a new command.

  ```
  aS MyAlias lm;vertarget
  aS MyAlias "lm;vertarget"
  ```

The first line will execute two things: create an alias with value 1m and then execute the vertarget command. The second line (because the equivalence is enclosed in quotes) defines the alias with value 1m;vertarget.

NOTE   User-defined alias names cannot contain the space character.

Other alias commands include the following:

■ al—Lists already defined aliases.

■ ad [/q] AliasName|*—Deletes an alias by name or all aliases. The /q switch will not show error messages if the alias name was not found.

The as command can used to create aliases that equate to environment variables values, expressions, file contents, command output, or even string contents from the debuggee's memory:

■ aS /f AliasName FileName—Assigns the contents of a file to the alias:

```
0:000> aS /f AliasName c:\temp\lines.txt
0:000> al
  Alias           Value
  -------         -------
  AliasName       line1
line2
line3
line4
line5
```

■ aS /x AliasName Expression64—Assigns the 64-bit value of an expression to the alias. This is useful in many ways, especially when assigning the value of an automatic alias to a user-named alias:

```
0:000> r $t0 = 0x123
0:000> as /x AliasName @$t0
0:000> al
  Alias           Value
  -------         -------
  AliasName       0x123
0:000> as IncorrectAlias @$t0
0:000> al
  Alias           Value
  -------         -------
  AliasName       0x123
  IncorrectAlias  @$t0
```

Note that the first `as /x` usage correctly assigned the value `0x123` to the alias, whereas the second `as` assignment took the literal value of `@$t0` (because of the missing `/x` switch).

▪ `as /e AliasName EnvVarName`—Sets the `AliasName` alias to the value of the environment variable called `EnvVarName`:

```
0:000> as /e CmdPath COMSPEC
0:000> al
  Alias            Value
  -------          -------
  CmdPath          C:\Windows\system32\cmd.exe
```

▪ `as /ma AliasName Address`—Sets the content of the null-terminated ASCII string pointed to by the address in the alias:

```
0:000> db 0x40600C
0040600c  54 6f 6f 6c 62 61 72 57-69 6e 64 6f 77 33 32 00  ToolbarWin-
dow32.
0:000> as /ma Str1 0x40600C
0:000> al
  Alias            Value
  -------          -------
  Str1             ToolbarWindow32
```

▪ `as /mu AliasName Address`—Sets the content of the null-terminated Unicode string pointed to by the address in the alias

▪ `as /ms[a|u] AliasName Address`—Sets the contents of an `ASCII_STRING` (structure defined in the DDK) or `UNICODE_STRING` in the alias:

```
(1)
0:000> dt _UNICODE_STRING
ntdll!_UNICODuE_STRING
   +0x000 Length           : Uint2B
   +0x002 MaximumLength    : Uint2B
   +0x004 Buffer           : Ptr32 Uint2B

(2)
0:000> ?? sizeof(_UNICODE_STRING)
unsigned int 8

(3)
0:000> ?? @@c++(@$peb->ProcessParameters->DllPath)
struct _UNICODE_STRING
 "C:\Windows\system32\NV"
   +0x000 Length           : 0x2c
   +0x002 MaximumLength    : 0x2e
   +0x004 Buffer           : 0x001f1880   "C:\Windows\system32\NV"
```

```
(4)
0:000> dd @@c++(&(@$peb->ProcessParameters->DllPath)) L2
001f1408  002e002c  001f1880


(5)
0:000> db 001f1880 L2e
001f1880  43 00 3a 00 5c 00 57 00-69 00 6e 00 64 00 6f 00   C.:.\.W.i.n.d.o.
001f1890  77 00 73 00 5c 00 73 00-79 00 73 00 74 00 65 00   w.s.\.s.y.s.t.e.
001f18a0  6d 00 33 00 32 00 5c 00-4e 00 56 00 00 00         m.3.2.\.N.V...


(6)
0:000> as /msu DllPath @@c++(&(@$peb->ProcessParameters->DllPath))
0:000> al
  Alias              Value
  -------            -------
  DllPath            C:\Windows\system32\NV
```

At marker 1, we display the fields of the _UNICODE_STRING structure, and
at marker 2 we display the structure's size using the C++ evaluator. Similarly,
marker 3 uses the C++ typed evaluation to dump the value of DllPath field.
Marker 4 uses the & operator to dump the _UNICODE_STRING field contents, and
marker 5 dumps the Buffer address. Finally, marker 6 uses the as command to
create an alias with its contents read from a _UNICODE_STRING pointer.

Interpreting User-Named Aliases

User-named aliases can be interpreted using the basic syntax ${AliasName} or
by simply typing the alias name. The former should be used when the alias is
embedded in a string and not surrounded by space characters:

```
0:000> aS AliasName "Alias value"
0:000> .printf "The value is >${AliasName}<\n"
The value is >Alias value<
```

When an alias is not defined, alias evaluation syntax remains unevaluated:

```
0:000> .printf "The value is >${UnkAliasName}<\n"
The value is >${UnkAliasName}<
```

The following switches control how the aliases are interpreted:

■ ${/d:AliasName}—Evaluates to 1 if the alias is defined, and 0 if the alias
  is not defined. This switch comes in handy when used in a script to determine whether an alias is defined or not:

```
0:000> .printf ">${/d:AliasName}<\n"
>1<
```

```
0:000> .printf ">${/d:UnkAliasName}<\n"
>0<
```

- ■ `${/f:AliasName}`—When this switch is used, an undefined alias will evaluate to an empty string or to the actual value if the alias was defined:

```
0:000> .printf ">${/f:DefinedAliasName}<\n"
>Alias value<
0:000> .printf ">${/f:UndefinedAliasName}<\n"
><
```

- ■ `${/n:AliasName}`—Evaluates to the alias name or remains unevaluated if the alias is not defined:

```
0:000> .printf ">${/n:AliasName}<\n"
>AliasName<
0:000> .printf ">${/n:AliasName2}<\n"
>${/n:AliasName2}<
0:000> .printf ">${/n:UnkAliasName}<\n"
>${/n:UnkAliasName}<
```

- ■ `${/v:AliasName}`—This switch prevents any alias evaluation:

```
0:000> .printf ">${/v:AliasName}<\n"
>${/v:AliasName}<
0:000> .printf ">${/v:UnkAliasName}<\n"
>${/v:UnkAliasName}<
```

After an alias is defined, it can be used in any subsequent command (as a command or a parameter to a command):

```
0:000> aS my_printf .printf
0:000> al
  Alias           Value
  -------         -------
  my_printf       .printf
```

When used as a command:

```
0:000> ${my_printf} "Hello world\n"
Hello world
0:000> my_printf "Hello world\n"
Hello world
```

When used as a parameter to a command:

```
0:000> .printf "The command to display strings is >${my_printf}<\n"
The command to display strings is >.printf
```

```
0:000> .printf "The command to display strings is my_printf \n"
The command to display strings is  printf
```

When reassigning values to user-defined aliases, note the following:

▪ Using the aS command as follows produces an error:

```
0:000> aS MyVar 0n123;.printf "v=%d", ${MyVar}
v=Couldn't resolve error at '${MyVar}'
```

The reason for this error is because aliases are expanded in new blocks only. This can be remedied with the following:

```
0:000> aS MyVar 0n123;.block { .printf "v=%d", ${MyVar}; }
v=123
```

▪ The /v: switch behaves like the /n: switch when used with aS, as, and ad. The reason we mention this is illustrated in the following example:

```
0:000> aS MyVar 0n123;.block { aS /x MyVar ${MyVar}+1 }
0:000> al
  Alias           Value
  -------         -------

  0n123           0x7c
  MyVar           0n123
```

The first command creates the MyVar alias and increments its value by one; however, a new alias named 0n123 is created. That's because the MyVar alias has been replaced by its equivalent instead of being used as an alias name.

What you instead need to do is let the aS command know that MyVar is the alias name, and its value should not be expanded or evaluated. This is where the /v: switch, when used with the aS or the as command, should be used:

```
0:000> aS MyVar 123;.block { aS /x ${/v:MyVar} ${MyVar}+1 };al
  Alias           Value
  -------         -------
  MyVar           0x124
```

Notice that now, when ${/v:MyVar} is used in conjunction with aS, it evaluates to the alias name (like the ${/n:AliasName} would).

Fixed-Name Aliases

As mentioned earlier, there are 10 fixed-name aliases named $u0 through $u9. While the fixed-name aliases look like registers or pseudo-registers, they are not. To assign values to them, use the r command followed by $. and the alias name, like this:

```
(1)
0:000> r $.u0 = .printf
(2)
0:000> r $.u1 = 0x123
(3)
0:000> r $.u2 = Hello world
(4)
0:000> $u0 "$u2\n"
Hello world
(5)
0:000> $u0 "$u2, u1=%x", $u1
Hello world, u1=123
```

Marker 1 aliases $u0 to the .printf command. Note the $. prefix and that the .printf command is purposely not enclosed with quotes in the equivalence. Marker 2 defines $u1 with a numeric value, and marker 3 defines $u2 with a string value. Marker 4 uses $u0 as an equivalent to the .printf command and prints $u2, which is enclosed in quotes and resolves to "Hello world." Finally, marker 5 prints the value $u1 in a similar fashion to marker 4.

> **NOTE** Always use $. when defining the alias; however, when using the alias you do not need to use $. or even the @ sign as you do for pseudo-registers or aliases.

Fixed-name alias replacement has a higher precedence than user-named aliases.

Automatic Aliases

The DbgEng defines a few aliases when the debugging session starts. The automatic aliases are similar to the pre-defined pseudo-registers except that they can also be used with the ${} syntax (like user-named aliases).

The following registers are defined:

- $ntnsym
- $ntwsym
- $ntsym
- $CurrentDumpFile

- `$CurrentDumpPath`

- `$CurrentDumpArchiveFile`

- `$CurrentDumpArchivePath`

To illustrate this, the following invokes the `cdb` command-line debugger with the `-z` switch to open a crash dump file, and uses `-cf script.wds` to execute a series of commands from a text file:

```
c:\Tools\dbg>cdb -cf av.wds -z m:\xp_kmem.dmp
```

The contents of the script file is as follows:

```
.printf "Script started\n"
.logopen @"${$CurrentDumpFile}.log"
!analyze -v
.logclose
.printf "Script finished, quitting\n"
q
```

When the debugger starts, it will interpret each line in `av.wds`:

1. Print a startup message.

2. Open a log file that has the name of the current crash dump file with `.log` appended to it. Note how you expand to automatic alias with the `${}` syntax.

3. Issue the `!analyze -v` command.

4. Close the log file, print a quit message, and exit the debugger with the `q` command.

NOTE   The @ sign is used to define a literal (or raw) string. See the upcoming "Characters and Strings" section.

Language

In this section, we discuss the scripting language, tokens, and commands.

Comments

Use the `$$` command to specify comments. For instance:

```
$$ This is a comment
$$ This is another comment
```

To use more than one comment on a line with multiple statements, use the semicolon character to terminate the comment:

```
r eax = 0; $$ clear EAX ; r ebx = ebx + 1; $$ increment EBX;
```

The asterisk (*) can also be used to create comments; however, the entire line after the asterisk will be ignored even if a semicolon delimiter is used:

```
r eax = 0; * clear EAX ; r ebx = ebx + 1;
```

The preceding command will just clear EAX; it won't increment EBX by one.

There is a slight difference between the $$ comment specifier and the .echo command. The .echo command displays the line instead of just ignoring it.

Characters and Strings

Characters are specified when enclosed in single quotes:

```
0:000> @dvalloc 1
0:000> eb @$t0 'a' 'b' 'c' 'd' 'f' 'g'
0:000> db @$t0 L 6
02250000   61 62 63 64 66 67
```

Strings are specified with double quotes:

```
0:000> ea @$t0 "Practical reverse engineering";
0:000> db @$t0 L20
02250000   50 72 61 63 74 69 63 61-6c 20 72 65 76 65 72 73   Practical revers
02250010   65 20 65 6e 67 69 6e 65-65 72 69 6e 67 00 00 00   e engineering...
```

As in C, the string may contain escape sequences; therefore, you need to escape the sequence in order to get the correct result:

```
(1)
0:000> .printf "c:\\tools\\dbg\\windbg.exe\n"
c:\tools\dbg\windbg.exe
(2)
0:000> .printf "a\tb\tc\n1\t2\t3\n"
a       b       c
1       2       3
```

The first command escaped the backslash with the escape character. The second example uses the horizontal tab escape sequence (\t).

The DbgEng allows the use of raw strings; such strings will be interpreted literally without taking into consideration the escape sequence. To specify a literal string, precede the string with the at sign (@):

```
(1)
0:000> .printf @"c:\tools\dbg\windbg.exe\n";.printf "\n";
c:\tools\dbg\windbg.exe\n
(2)
0:000> .printf @"a\tb\tc\n1\t2\t3\n"
a\tb\tc\n1\t2\t3\n
```

Notice how the escape sequences remained as specified without being interpreted. Similarly, if you have a user-named alias that was created from memory contents and you want to evaluate it literally, also prefix the ${ } with @:

```
(1)
0:000> aS /mu STR 0x3cba030
0:000> al
  Alias               Value
  -------             -------
STR                   C:\Temp\file.txt
(2)
0:000> .printf "${STR}\n";
C:Tempfile.txt
(3)
0:000> .printf @"${STR}";.printf "\n";
C:\Temp\file.txt
```

Marker 1 creates a user-named alias from the zero-terminated Unicode string at the specified memory address and displays the list of aliases. Marker 2 prints the alias value. (Notice that the output is not as intended.) At marker 3, after prefixing the string with @, the output is correct.

Blocks

A block can be created via the .block command followed by opening and closing curly braces ({ }):

```
.block
{
      $$ Inside a block ...
      .block
      {
            $$ Nested block ...
      }
}
```

When a user-named alias is created in a script, its value won't be evaluated/interpreted as intended unless a new block is created:

```
aS MyAlias (@eax + @edx)
.block
{
      $$ Inside a block ...
```

```
        .printf "The value of my alias is %X\n", ${MyAlias}
}
```

Conditional Statements

The .if, .elsif, and .else command tokens are used to write conditional statements.

The usage of .if and .elsif is similar to other languages where they take a condition. The condition can be any expression that evaluates to zero (treated as false) or a non-zero value (treated as true):

```
r $t0 = 3;
.if (@$t0==1)
{
        .printf "one\n";
}
.elsif @$t0==2
{
        .printf "two\n";
}
.elsif (@$t0==3)
{
        .printf "three\n";
}
.else
{
        .printf "unknown\n";
}
```

> **NOTE**   The use of parentheses around the condition is optional.

All the built-in repetition structures and conditional statements require the use of the curly braces ({ and }) and thus create a block, which results in the proper evaluation of aliases:

```
aS MyAlias (@eax + @edx)
.if (1)
{
        $$ Inside a block ...
        .printf "The value of my alias is %X\n", ${MyAlias}
}
```

You can also compare strings with .if using a few different methods:

```
$$ By enclosing the strings to be compared in single quotes:
.if '${my_alias}'=='value'
{
        .printf "equal\n";
}
```

```
.else
{
        .printf "not equal!\n";
}

$$ By using the MASM operator scmp (or sicmp):
.if $scmp("${my_alias}", "value")
{
        .printf "equal\n";
}

$$ By using the MASM operator spat:
.if $spat("${my_alias}", "value")
{
        .printf "equal\n";
}
.else
{
        .printf "not equal!\n";
}
```

The DbgEng also provides the j command, which can be compared to C's ternary operator (cond ? true-expr: false-expr), except that it runs commands instead of returning expressions:

```
j Expression ['] Command-True['] ; ['] Command-False[']
```

The following is a very simple example with one command being executed in both cases (true or false):

```
0:000> r $t0 = -1
0:000> j (@$t0 < 0) r $t0 = @$t0-1 ; r $t0 = @$t0+1
0:000> ? $t0
Evaluate expression: -2 = fffffffe
```

The single quotes are optional in most cases; specify them if more than one command is to be executed:

```
0:000> r $t0 = 2
0:000> j (@$t0 < 0) 'r $t0 = @$t0-1;.echo Negative value' ;
                    'r $t0 = @$t0+1;.echo Positive value'
Positive value
0:000> ? $t0
Evaluate expression: 3 = 00000003
```

It is common to use the j command as part of breakpoint commands to form conditional breakpoints.

The following example suspends the debugger (note the empty single quotes that specify that no command should be executed when the expression evaluates to True) only when the return address matches a certain value:

```
0:000> bp user32!MessageBoxA "j (@$ra=0x401058) '';'gc;'"
0:000> g
user32!MessageBoxA:
756e22c2 8bff                 mov     edi,edi
0:000> ? $ra
Evaluate expression: 4198488 = 00401058
```

The next example suspends the debugger whenever the GetLastError function is called and it returns ACCESS_DENIED (value 5):

```
0:014> bp kernelbase!GetLastError "g @$ra;j @eax==5 '';'gc'"
0:014> g
uxtheme!ThemePreWndProc+0xd8:
00007ff8`484915e8 33c9            xor     ecx,ecx
0:000> !gle
LastErrorValue: (Win32) 0x5 (5) - Access is denied.
LastStatusValue: (NTSTATUS) 0xc0000034 - Object Name not found.
```

This is not the optimal way to achieve that. The public symbols of NTDLL, when loaded, expose a symbol called g_dwLastErrorToBreakOn. Editing this value in memory and passing the desired error value to break on is the better approach:

```
0:000> ep ntdll!g_dwLastErrorToBreakOn 5
0:000> g
(2a0.2228): Break instruction exception - code 80000003 (first chance)
ntdll!RtlSetLastWin32Error+0x21:
00007ff8`4c444df1 cc              int     3
0:000> !gle
LastErrorValue: (Win32) 0 (0) - The operation completed successfully.
LastStatusValue: (NTSTATUS) 0xc0000034 - Object Name not found.
```

Script Errors

If an error is encountered when a debugger script is executing, then the entire script will be aborted after the error message is displayed. Consider a script file with the following contents:

```
.printf "Script started\n";
invalid command;
.printf "Script ending\n";
```

When this script is executed, it will produce an error:

```
Script started
Script started

    ^ Syntax error in '.printf "Script started
'
0:000>
```

To prevent the script from aborting, you can use the `.catch` command token:

```
.printf "Script started\n";
.catch
{
        invalid command;
        .printf "!! will not be reached !!\n";
}
.printf "After catch\n";
```

The error will cause the script to break out of the `.catch` block and display the error, but continue executing the script after that block:

```
Script started
                ^ Syntax error in ';     invalid command; '
After catch
```

When inside a `.catch` block, one can explicitly exit it with the `.leave` command token.

Interestingly, `.leave` can be used to emulate a "break," like in a loop:

```
r $t0=0;
.catch
{
      .if (by(@$ip) == 0xb9)
      {
            .printf "found MOV ECX, ...\n";
            r $t0 = dwo(@$ip+1);
            .leave;
      }
      .elsif (by(@$ip) == 0xb8)
      {
            .printf "found MOV EAX, ...\n";
            r $t0 = dwo(@$ip+1);
            .leave;
      }
      $$ do some other analysis ...
      .printf "Could not find the right opcode\n";
      $$ do more stuff...
}
$$ Reached after the catch block is over, an error has
$$ occurred or a .leave is used
```

Repetition Structures

The DbgEng supports four repetition structures, which are described in the following sections.

The .break command can be used to break out of a loop. Similarly, the .continue command can be used to go to the next iteration within the encapsulating repetition structure.

> **NOTE** In the case of an erroneous repetition condition (the script or command executes endlessly), you can interrupt it by pressing Ctrl+C in any of the console debuggers (kd, cdb, ntsd) or Ctrl+PauseBreak in WinDbg.

The for Loop

The .for command token has the following syntax:

```
.for (InitialCommand ; Condition ; IncrementCommands) { Commands }
```

The following example script dumps the interrupt descriptor table (IDT) handlers using a for loop. First, we run the dt command to inspect the structure of an IDTENTRY on a 32-bit system in a kernel-mode debug session:

```
kd> dt _KIDTENTRY
ntdll!_KIDTENTRY
   +0x000 Offset          : Uint2B
   +0x002 Selector        : Uint2B
   +0x004 Access          : Uint2B
   +0x006 ExtendedOffset  : Uint2B
```

The script is as follows:

```
.for (r $t0=0; 1;r $t0=@$t0+1)
{
        $$ Take a typed pointer to the next IDT entry
        r? $t1 = @@c++(((_KIDTENTRY *)@idtr) + @$t0);

        $$ Last entry?
        .if (@@c++(@$t1->Selector) == 0)
        {
             $$ Break out
             .break;
        }

        $$ Resolve the full address
        r $t2  = @@c++((long)(((unsigned long)@$t1->ExtendedOffset << 0x10) +
                         (unsigned long)@$t1->Offset));

        .printf "IDT[%02x] @ %p\n", @$t0, @$t2
        $$ .printf "IDT[%02x] @ %p\n", @$t2
}
```

Some important aspects of the script to note:

- The `for` loop's condition is set to 1 so it loops indefinitely. We will break out conditionally from inside the loop's body with the `.break` command.

- The `r?` is used to assign a typed value to $t1.

- The pseudo-register $t1 is a pointer to _KIDTENTRY. When $t0 is added to it, this will advance to the appropriate memory location (taking into consideration the size of _KIDTENTRY).

- You determine the end of the IDT entries by examining the `Selector` field and breaking out of the loop accordingly.

- The full base address of the IDT handler is computed by combining the `ExtendedOffset` and `Offset` fields.

- You cast $t2 to `long` so that it is properly sign extended (as pseudo-registers are always 64-bit values).

- Display the result.

If you find using pseudo-registers like $t0 as a `for` loop counter a bit unusual and instead want to use a name like `i`, `j`, or `k`, for example, then create a user-named alias called `i` that is equivalent to @$t0:

```
aS i @$t0;

.block
{
        .for (r ${i} = 1; ${i} <= 5; r ${i} = ${i}+1)
        {
                .printf "i=%d\n", ${i}
        }
}
```

The while Loop

The `while` loop is a simplified form of a `for` loop that has neither an initial command nor an increment command:

```
.while (Condition) { Commands }
```

Depending on the condition expression, the `while` loop's body may not execute at all. Here's a sample script that traces 200 instructions in a newly started process:

```
$$ Go to entry point (skip NT process initialization)
.printf "Going to entry point\n";
```

```
g @$exentry;

.printf "Started tracing...\n";

$$ Reset the counter
r $t0 = 0;

.while (@$t0 <= 0n200)
{
        .printf "ip -> %p; ntrace=%d\n", @$ip, @$t0;
        r $t0 = @$t0 + 1;
        tr;
}

.printf "Condition satisfied\n";
u @$ip L1;
```

Note that this is not the ideal way to do conditional tracing. The t and j commands used together are a better approach.

The do-while Loop

The do-while loop has the following syntax:

```
.do { Commands } (Condition)
```

Unlike the while loop, the do loop's body will execute at least once before the condition is evaluated:

```
.do
{
        .if (by(@$ip) == 0xb8)
        {
                .printf "Found MOV EAX, ...\n";
                .break;
        }
        $$ do other things
        $$ ....
        $$ ....
} (0);
.printf "Continue doing something else...\n";
```

The DbgEng also provides the z command to execute commands while a certain condition holds true:

```
Command [ Command ; [Command ...;] ]; z( Expression )
```

In the following example, $t0 is used as a counter to trace five (5) branching instructions:

```
0:000> r $t0=1
0:000> th;r $t0=@$t0 + 1; z (@$t0 <= 5);
redo [1] th;r $t0=@$t0 + 1; z (@$t0 <= 5);
redo [1] th;r $t0=@$t0 + 1; z (@$t0 <= 5);
redo [1] th;r $t0=@$t0 + 1; z (@$t0 <= 5);
redo [1] th;r $t0=@$t0 + 1; z (@$t0 <= 5);
0:000> ? @$t0
Evaluate expression: 6 = 00000006
```

As in the preceding example, one or more commands can be specified to the left of the z command.

The foreach Loop

The foreach loop is very useful and can be used to enumerate tokens read from a file, from the output of a command or from a user-provided string.

Two common options can be passed (separately or together) as first parameters to the .foreach command token:

- /pS ExpressionValue—Initial number of tokens to skip when the loop starts. This is equivalent to initializing the counter to a non-zero value in a for loop.

- /ps ExpressionValue—The number of tokens to skip after each iteration. This is equivalent to the for loop increment part where the programmer can specify the counter increment value.

Tokenizing from a String

The general syntax is as follows:

```
.foreach [Options] /s (TokenVariableName "InString" ) { OutCommands }
```

For example, assume you are looking for *CreateFile*-related symbols in the following three modules: ntdll, kernelbase, and kernel32. This is one way to do it:

```
.foreach /s (token "ntdll kernel32 kernelbase") { x ${token}!*CreateFile*; }
```

In the next example, suppose you want to tokenize the contents of a given ASCII string in memory:

```
aS /mu STR 0x8905e8
r $t0 = 0;
.block
{
    .foreach /s (token "${STR}")
    {
```

```
        .printf "token_i=%d, token_val=${token}\n", @$t0;
        r $t0 = @$t0 + 1;
    }
}
```

The $\{ \}$ is used to evaluate the token variable's value. This is only necessary only if the token is not surrounded by the space character at the time of evaluation. The .block was used in order to cause the alias STR to be evaluated.

Tokenizing from the Output of a Command

The general syntax is as follows:

```
.foreach [Options] ( Variable { InCommands } ) { OutCommands }
```

This use of .foreach is the most common because it enables extracting information from a command's output and using it in your script.

For the sake of demonstration, imagine a script that needs to allocate memory in the process space of the debuggee and then uses that memory to read a file's contents to it.

First, examine the output of the memory allocation command .dvalloc:

```
0:000> .dvalloc 0n4096
Allocated 1000 bytes starting at 00620000
```

The output can be tokenized into six tokens; thus, the foreach loop should use the /pS flag to skip the first five tokens and directly start with the last token (which is the newly allocated memory address):

```
0:000> .foreach /pS 5 (token {.dvalloc 0x1000 }) { r $t0 = ${token}; .break; }
0:000> ? @$t0
Evaluate expression: 8323072 = 007f0000
```

The full script becomes the following:

```
$$ Set the image file name
aS fileName @"c:\temp\shellcode.bin"
.catch
{
        $$ Set the allocation size to be equal to the file we want to read
        r $t0 = 0n880;

        .foreach /pS 5 (token {.dvalloc @$t0; })
        {
                r $t1 = token;
                .break;
        }

        $$ Read the file
        .readmem "${fileName}" @$t1 L@$t0;
```

```
                .printf "Loaded ${fileName} @ %p\n", @$t1
}
```

NOTE   Remember to free the memory with the `.dvfree` command.

The next example parses the output of `lm1m` (which, by design, returns simplified output for use with `.foreach`):

```
0:000> lm1m
image00400000
SHCORE
KERNEL32
comctl32
user32
Ntdll
```

The `foreach` loop should look like this:

```
0:000> .foreach (modulename { lm1m; }) { .printf "Module name: modulename \n";}
```

Tokenizing from a File

The general syntax is as follows:

```
.foreach [Options] /f ( Variable  "InFile" ) { OutCommands }
```

Assume a file called `lines.txt` with the following contents:

```
This is line 1
This is line 2
This is line 3
```

It will be tokenized as follows:

```
0:000> .foreach /f (line "c:\\temp\\lines.txt") { .printf ">${line}<\n" }
>This<
>is<
>line<
>1<
>This<
>is<
>line<
>2<
>This<
>is<
>line<
>3<
```

Extension-Provided foreach Loops

There are a few other `foreach` commands provided by extensions that are not part of the scripting language. These `foreach` commands are implemented inside various DbgEng extensions:

- `!for_each_frame`—Executes a command for each frame in the stack of the current thread

- `!for_each_function`—Executes a command for each function in a given module that matches the search pattern

- `!for_each_local`—Executes a command for each local variable in the current frame

- `!for_each_module`—Executes a command for each loaded module

- `!for_each_process`—Executes a command for each process (this extension works in kernel debugging only)

- `!for_each_thread`—Executes a command for each thread (kernel debugging only)

> **NOTE** Use the `.extmatch *for_each*` command to enumerate all the `foreach` extension commands.

Each of those extension commands exposes special variables to the command they execute. Please refer to the debugger manual to learn what variables are exposed for each specific extension command.

The following example lists all modules and displays some information about them:

```
!for_each_module .printf /D "%16p %16p: ${@#ModuleName}
@<link cmd=\"u %p\">%p</link>\n", ${@#Base},${@#End},
$iment(0x${@#Base}), $iment(0x${@#Base})
          400000          408000: image00400000 @00406800
         74b70000        74c78000: gdi32 @74b7afc5
         75130000        75270000: KERNEL32 @7514a5cf
         755d0000        75656000: comctl32 @755d1e15
         75670000        757bf000: user32 @75685422
         759b0000        76b28000: shell32 @759b108d
         76c00000        76cbe000: msvcrt @76c0a9ed
         76fa0000        77017000: ADVAPI32 @76fa1005
```

The entry point was computed with the `$iment()` operator. Also, the Debugger Markup Language (DML) was used to make the entry point clickable. When clicked it will unassemble the instructions at the entry point.

The next example scans for all functions in `ntdll` that contain the `File` substring in their name:

```
!for_each_function -m:ntdll -p:*File* -c:.echo @#SymbolName
```

> **NOTE**   To run more commands, enclose them in quotes or just use one of the commands that run script files.

Script Files

Various commands can be used to instruct the DbgEng to run scripts. These commands are split into two main categories:

- Commands that open the script file, replace all new lines with a semicolon (the command separator), and concatenate the whole contents into a single command block. These commands have the following form: `$><`.

- Commands that open the script file and interpret each line separately. These commands have the following form: `$<`.

The former is very handy when using a debugger command that accepts other commands as its arguments. For example, the `bp` command takes a breakpoint action, which can be a simple command or a command that runs a script file (that contains various commands inside of it).

The latter interprets the contents of the script file line by line; each line could contain various commands separated by a semicolon. Each command executed will also be echoed in the debugger output.

Some debugger commands interpret the whole line, disregarding whether there is a semicolon (;) or not. This means that using the `$><`-related commands will not work for such scripts. Consider the following example script:

```
r eax;r ebx
r $.u0 = This is just a line
.printf "$u0"
r ecx;r edx
```

Running this script with `$><` does not work as intended:

```
0:000> $><test.wds
eax=00000000
ebx=00000000
0:000> ? $u0

Couldn't resolve error at 'This is just a line;.printf "";r ecx;r edx'
```

Conversely, running this particular script with $< works just fine:

```
0:000> $<test.wds
0:000> r eax;r ebx
eax=00000000
ebx=00000000
0:000> r $.u0 = This is just a line
0:000> .printf "$u0"
This is just a line0:000> r ecx;r edx
ecx=f7fc0000
edx=00000000
```

The reason for this behavior is that when assigning a value to a fixed-name alias, semicolons will also be part of the assignment. This explains why in the first output, the script seems to have been suddenly stopped; it's because $>< will concatenate all lines and separate them with a semicolon.

For the same reason, if you use a command that creates blocks and the curly braces ({ and }) are used on separate lines in the script file, $< will not work properly:

```
.if (1 == 2)
{
        .printf "No way!\n";
}
.else
{
        .printf "That's what I thought";
}
```

When executed, the preceding returns the following error:

```
(1)
0:000> $<blocktest.wds
0:000> .if (1 == 2)
                   ^ Syntax error in '.if (1 == 2)'
0:000> {
       ^ Syntax error in '{'
0:000>          .printf "No way!";
No way!0:000> }
       ^ Syntax error in '}'
0:000> .else
             ^ Syntax error in '.else'
0:000> {
       ^ Syntax error in '{'
0:000>          .printf "That's what I thought";
That's what I thought0:000> }
       ^ Syntax error in '}'
(2)
0:000> $><p:\book\scripts\t_blocktest.wds
That's what I thought
```

NOTE When the run script commands are prefixed with an extra $, the script file name/path can no longer contain semicolons. When a semicolon is found after $$>< or $$<, then whatever comes after it is interpreted as another set of commands.

To run a script file with its contents concatenated into a single command block, use $>< or $$><:

```
$$><path_to\the_script.wds; r eax; al; bl;
```

Because $$>< is used, the semicolon allows the subsequent commands to be executed.

Passing Arguments to Script Files

It is possible to pass arguments to scripts using the $$>a< command:

```
$$>a<path_to\the_script.wds arg1 arg2 …
```

The arguments can then be accessed in the script via the $argN aliases. The alias $arg0 contains the script name (as in C's argv[0]).

If you pass UDPRs as arguments, then they will not be expanded or evaluated before being passed to the script. This is a tricky situation and can lead to various unexpected behaviors. For example, suppose you call a script like this:

```
$$>a<script.wds @$t1 @$t2
```

The preceding script will be passed the values @$t1 and @$t2 as ${$arg1} and ${$arg2}, respectively. To solve this problem, assign the pseudo-registers to a user-named alias and then call the script from a .block. This will guarantee expansion of the alias values before they are passed to the script:

```
aS /x val1 @$t0
aS /x val2 @$t1
.block
{
    $$>a<script.wds ${val1} ${val2}
}
ad /q val1
ad /q val2
```

To check whether an argument is present, use the .if" with "${/d:…}:

```
.catch
{
        .if ${/d:$arg1} == 0 or ${/d:$arg2} == 0
        {
                .printf "Usage: ${$arg0} memory-address len\n";
                .leave;
        }
        r $t0 = ${$arg1};
```

```
.if $vvalid($t0, 1) == 0
{
        .printf "Invalid memory address specified\n";
        .leave;
}
r $t1 = @$t0 + ${$arg2} - 1;
.printf "Summing memory bytes from %x to %x\n", @$t0, @$t1;
.for (r $t3 = 0;@$t0 <= @$t1;r $t0 = @$t1 +1)
{
        r $t3 = @$t3 + by(@$t1);
}
.printf "The result is %x\n", @$t3;
}
```

We used a few tricks worthy of a brief explanation:

- .catch and .leave were used to simulate a function start and "return" like behavior.

- .if and ${/d:$arg1} were used to check if the first argument was defined. Because we did not explicitly switch the evaluator syntax, the scripting engine will evaluate using MASM; thus the operators used should all be valid in MASM syntax. Enclosing an expression with @@c++(expression) will evaluate the expression using C++ syntax.

- The $vvalid() operator is used to check if the passed memory address is valid.

- The .for command token is used to loop through the memory contents, and each byte at that location is dereferenced using MASM's by() operator.

In the following output, the script is passed various arguments:

```
(1)
0:000> $$>a<script.wds
Usage: script.wds memory-address len
(2)
0:000> $$>a<script.wds 0xbadf00d
Invalid memory address specified
(3)
0:000> $$>a<script.wds @eip 2
Summing memory bytes from 76f83bc5 to 76f83bc6
The result is eb
```

At marker 1, the script is executed without any arguments and it successfully showed its arguments. At marker 2, the script is passed an invalid memory address. Finally, at marker 3, the script is called correctly and the sum of the bytes is returned.

NOTE The `.wds` file extension is not necessary. It is just a convention used by various script writers and stands for *WinDbg* Script file.

Using Scripts Like Functions

There is no way to define functions in the DbgEng's scripting language. However, it is possible to use various script files as if they were functions. A script can call itself recursively or call another script with another set of arguments, and those arguments will be different in the context of each script.

UDPRs are very handy when writing a script. When a script calls another script, those UDPRs will be common to all scripts and thus cannot be used exclusively inside each script without disrupting the state of the other caller scripts, unless of course they are saved and restored by the script in its entry and exit points.

NOTE You can think of the need to preserve UDPRs in terms of registers in X86 or AMD64 programs, where the compiler ensures that it emits code that preserves certain general-purpose registers upon the entry and the exit of each function while (depending on the calling convention) dedicating certain registers for input/output of the function.

With that in mind, it is important to devise a mechanism that allows us to easily and seamlessly, and with as little repetition as possible, save/restore certain UDPRs anytime a script is going to call another.

The @call Script File Alias

In the previous section we outlined the necessity of having a way to save/restore UDRPs. For that reason, we devised two simple scripts that do just that. This section illustrates both the `init.wds` and `call.wds` scripts and explains how they work.

The `init.wds` script is used to set up the scripting environment and create the short aliases to act like function names:

```
(1)
ad /q *;
(2)
aS ${/v:SCRIPT_PATH} @"p:\book\scripts";
.block
{
        $$ Callable scripts (using @call) (3)
```

```
        aS ${/v:#sigma}        @"${SCRIPT_PATH}\sigma";
        aS ${/v:#pi}           @"${SCRIPT_PATH}\pi";
        $$ Script call aliases (4)
        aS ${/v:@dvalloc}      @"$$>a<${SCRIPT_PATH}\dvalloc.wds";
        aS ${/v:@call}         @"$$>a<${SCRIPT_PATH}\call.wds";
}

r $t19 = 0; (5)
r $t18 = 1; (6)
```

The `init.wds` script devises two user-named alias naming conventions:

- Names prefixed with @ denote aliases to the $$>a< command (run a script with arguments). Normally those are scripts that are self-sufficient. (They do not need to preserve UDPRs and do not necessarily call themselves or other scripts.)

- Names prefixed with # designate an alias that can be called with the @call alias. Those scripts can be recursive and can safely assume that all the UDPRs other than those designated as return values will be saved/restored before/after a script is called/returns.

Marker 1 deletes all previously defined aliases. At marker 2, the script's base path is defined. (Note the use of @ to specify a literal string.) At marker 3, we define two user-named aliases prefixed with # defined. These are callable via the @call alias and evaluate to the full script path without the .wds extension. (The call script will append the extension.) For the sake of demonstration, two callable scripts are defined: sigma and pi. At marker 4, we define two user-named aliases prefixed with @. These aliases simply resolve to $$>a< followed by the full script path. The @call alias is what makes calling scripts as a function possible. The @dvalloc is a wrapper around the .dvalloc command. Marker 5 defines the $t19 UDPR, which is used internally by call.wds script to remember the script calls nesting level. The nesting level is used to form an alias that will save all UDPRs per nest level. At marker 6, we define UDPR $t18, which is used internally by call.wds to determine how many UDPRs starting from $t0 should be skipped while restoring the saved UDPRs after a script call (more on that in the following explanation).

Here is the `call.wds` script:

```
ad /q ${/v:_tn_} (1)
.catch
{
        .if ${/d:$arg1} == 0 (2)
        {
                .printf "No script to call specified";
                .leave;
```

```
        }
        $$ Compute the saved registers alias name of the previous call
        aS /x ${/v:_tn_} @$t19; (3)
        .block
        {
                $$ Delete the saved registers alias name of the previous run
                ad /q _sr_${_tn_};
        }
        r $t19 = @$t19 + 1; $$ Increment the nesting level (4)

        $$ Compute the saved registers alias name for the current run
        aS /x ${/v:_tn_} @$t19; (5)

        $$ Save all pseudo-registers
        .block
        { (6)
                aS /c _sr_${_tn_} "r $t0,$t1,$t2,$t3,$t4,$t5,$t6,$t7,$t8,$t9,
$t10,$t11,$t12,$t13,$t14,$t15,$t16,$t17";
        }

        $$ Call the script
        .catch
        {(7)
                $$>a<"${$arg1}.wds" ${/f:$arg2} ${/f:$arg3} ${/f:$arg4}
${/f:$arg5} ${/f:$arg6} ${/f:$arg7} ${/f:$arg8} ${/f:$arg9} ${/f:$arg10}
${/f:$arg11} ${/f:$arg12} ${/f:$arg13} ${/f:$arg14} ${/f:$arg15}
${/f:$arg16} ${/f:$arg17} ${/f:$arg18} ${/f:$arg19} ${/f:$arg20};
        }

        $$ Restore the registers after calling
        .block
        {
                (8)
                $$ Compute the saved registers alias name
                aS /x ${/v:_tn_} @$t19;
                .block
                {
                        $$ Restore all registers except the first ones that
                        $$ are due to return a value
                        .foreach /pS @$t18 /s (X "_sr_${_tn_}" ) (9)
                        {
                                r ${X}; (10)
                        }
                }

                $$ Delete the saved registers alias name
                ad /q _sr_${_tn_}; (11)

                $$ Decrease the nesting level
                r $t19 = @$t19 - 1; (12)
        }
}
ad /q ${/v:_tn_}; (13)
```

This script needs two UDPRs for special purposes. The first is $t19, which is used to store the call nesting level. It is incremented each time @call is used to run a script, and decremented when the script finishes execution. Because $t19 is incremented and decremented, you can create an alias with a unique name per nesting level to store the UDPR values.

The second UDPR is $t18, which is used to designate the count of UDPRs used to return values (starting from $t0). By default, the value 1 indicates that $t0 is the only register to be used as a return value. If the script returns more than one value (for example, in $t0 and $t1), then the caller has to set $t18 to 2 before calling the script. This guarantees that neither $t0 nor $t1 will be reverted back to their original values (the values before the script was called). The call script takes the script name to be called as the first argument, followed by the rest of the arguments ($arg2 through $argN).

Now we briefly explain how the rest of this script works before putting it into action. At marker 1, we delete the user-named alias _tn_ (used to compute a per-nesting-level alias name) before redefining it. Marker 2 checks if a parameter was passed to the script. At marker 3 and 4, we assign to the _tn_ alias the numeric value of the nesting level (note the use of as /x), and then we increment the nesting level UDPR $t19. At marker 5, we create a temporary alias that has the value of the current nesting level.

At marker 6, we save UDPRs $t0 through $t17 into an alias named _sr_{_tn_} by using as /c followed by the r command and the list of UDPRs to return their values. For instance, if the nesting level is 2, the saved register's alias name will be _sr_2 and will contain the values of all UDPRs in question. _sr_0x2 will equate to $t0=00000003 $t1=00000000 $t2=00000000 ... $t17=00000000.

At markers 7 and 8, the script that was passed into $arg1 is called with the rest of the arguments that were passed. After the script returns, re-compute the _tn_ alias. (The alias could have been overwritten by the called script.)

At markers 9 and 10, we iterate in the current _sr_NESTING_LEVEL alias but skip $t18 tokens (note the /pS switch), and then restore each UDPR with the r command.

At markers 11–13, we clean up the saved registers alias (_sr_NESTING_LEVEL), decrement the nesting level, and delete the temporary name alias.

The next step is to run the init.wds script that will create the appropriate aliases:

```
0:000> ad /q *; $$><p:\book\scripts\init.wds; al;
  Alias              Value
  -------            -------
  #pi                "p:\book\scripts\pi"
  #sigma             "p:\book\scripts\sigma"
  #test              "p:\book\scripts\test"
  @call              $$>a<"p:\book\scripts\call.wds"
  @dvalloc           $$>a<"p:\book\scripts\dvalloc.wds"
  SCRIPT_PATH        p:\book\scripts
```

Another way to do that is to run WinDbg (or cdb) with the `-c` command-line switch:

```
c:\dbg\windbg.exe -c "ad /q *;$$><p:\book\scripts\init.wds;al;" p:\test.exe
```

You can now tell that you have two aliases for `@call` and `@dvalloc` that are scripts that do not require automatic save/restore of UDPRs, and three other scripts that rely on `@call` to automatically save/restore UDPRs, and they act like "functions."

The `sigma.wds` script takes two numeric parameters and returns the sum of terms between the first and second argument, returning the result in `$t0`:

```
.for (r $t0=0, $t1=${$arg1}, $t2=${$arg2}; @$t1 <= @$t2; r $t1 = @$t1 + 1)
{
        r $t0 = @$t0 + @$t1;
}
```

To execute `sigma.wds`, use `@call #sigma start_num end_num`, as follows:

```
0:000> @call #sigma 1 4;.printf "The result is %d\n", @$t0
The result is 10
```

Similarly, the script `pi.wds` returns the multiplication result of the terms between the first and second argument:

```
.for (r $t0=1, $t1=${$arg1}, $t2=${$arg2}; @$t1 <= @$t2; r $t1 = @$t1 + 1)
{
        r $t0 = @$t0 * @$t1;
}
```

The `dvalloc.wds` script is a wrapper around the `.dvalloc` command. When `@dvalloc` is called, the result is returned in `$t0` so it can be used in scripts:

```
.catch
{
        r $t0 = -1; $$ Set invalid result
        .if ${/d:$arg1} == 0
        {
                .printf "Usage: dvalloc.wds memory-size\n";
                .printf "The allocated memory is returned in t0\n";
                .leave;
        }

        $$ Allocate memory and set result into $t0
        .foreach /pS 5 (t {.dvalloc ${$arg1}})
        {
                .if $vvalid(${t}, 1) == 1
                {
                        r $t0 = ${t};
                        .leave;
```

```
          }
        }
  }
```

After allocating memory with .dvalloc, we tokenize the result and parse out the memory address into $t0.

Both sigma.wds and pi.wds are sample functions that use the $t1 and $t2 UDPRs. That means if a script calls sigma or pi, then $t1 and $t2 should not be modified in any way upon returning from both the functions back to the caller.

You can verify this behavior with the following simple test.wds script:

```
r $t1 = 0x123;
r $t2 = 0x456;

.printf "Before calling sigma: t1=%x, t2=%x\n", @$t1, @$t2
@call #sigma 1 3
.printf "After calling sigma: the result is t0=%x, t1=%x, t2=%x\n",
     @$t0, @$t1, @$t2
```

The preceding script assigns values to UDPRs $t1 and $t2 and then calls #sigma 1 3, which will modify $t1 and $t2. If @call works as expected, then those UDPRs are restored just after the call:

```
0:000> @call #test
Before calling sigma: t1=123, t2=456
After calling sigma: the result is t0=6, t1=123, t2=456
```

Example Debug Scripts

In this section you will make use of various helpful scripts, putting into practice all that you have learned so far.

Getting the Image Base of a Specified Module

One quick way to get the image base of a module is to use the lm (list modules) command with the m switch to list modules matching the specified pattern:

```
0:000> lm m kernel32
start      end          module name
749e0000 74b20000    KERNEL32    (deferred)
```

From the output, you can tell that at the fifth token you have the image base. Thus, the image base can be easily parsed with .foreach by skipping the first tokens, extracting the value of the fifth token, and breaking out of the loop:

```
r $t0 = -1;
.foreach /pS 4 ( imgbase { lmm ${$arg1}; } )
{
```

```
        r @$t0 = ${imgbase};
        .break;
    }
```

Writing a Basic UPX Unpacker

Writing a UPX unpacker is pretty simple, and there are many ways to do it.
The method used here is elaborate in order to exercise various debugger commands. It is assumed that you have basic PE file format knowledge to properly
understand the script.

The idea behind the script is as follows:

1. UPX packs the program and moves the original entry point (OEP) away
   from the .text section, which is the first section.

2. The script calculates the bounds of the first section and starts tracing.

3. If instruction pointer (EIP) is outside of the program image, then the script
   issues a gu to return to the caller.

4. Tracing continues until EIP is inside the first section. At that point, it is
   assumed that the program has been unpacked.

Here is the script:

```
$$ Get image base
$$ Get image base
aS /x IMG_BASE @@c++(@$peb->ImageBaseAddress); (1)
$$ Declare some user-named aliases that equate to UDPRs
aS SEC_START    @$t19; (2)
aS SEC_END      @$t18;
aS IMG_START    @$t17;
aS IMG_END      @$t16;

$$ Go to the program entrypoint
g @$exentry

.catch
{
    $$ Get pointer to NT headers
(3)
r $t0 = ${IMG_BASE} + @@c++(((_IMAGE_DOS_HEADER *)${IMG_BASE})->e_lfanew)

    $$ Now from the IMAGE_NT_HEADERS.FileHeader, get the size of optional
header
(4)
r $t1 = @@c++( ((_IMAGE_NT_HEADERS*)@$t0)->FileHeader.SizeOfOptionalHeader )

    $$ Compute the address to the first section
    $$ skip signature, size of file headers and size of optional headers
    r $t2 = @$t0 + 4 + @@c++(sizeof(ole32!_IMAGE_FILE_HEADER)) + @$t1; (5)
```

```
$$ (6) Get first section boundaries
r ${SEC_START} = IMG_BASE +
              @@c++(((_IMAGE_SECTION_HEADER *)@$t2)->VirtualAddress);
r ${SEC_END} = IMG_BASE +
              @@c++(((_IMAGE_SECTION_HEADER *)@$t2)->Misc.VirtualSize);

$$ Compute the image bounds (7)
r ${IMG_START} = IMG_BASE;
r ${IMG_END} = IMG_START +
              @@c++(((_IMAGE_NT_HEADERS *)@$t0)->OptionalHeader.SizeOfIm-
age);

$$ The logic is as follows:
$$ 1. Trace
$$ 2. If IP is outside of image then "gu"
.for (r $t0=0; 1; r $t0 = @$t0 + 1) (8)
{
  $$ Trace once more to see where it leads (9)
  t;

  $$ IP outside image boundaries?
  .if (@$ip < ${IMG_START}) or (@$ip > ${IMG_END}) (10)
  {
     gu;
     .continue;
  }

  $$ IP within the first section?
  .if (@$ip >= ${SEC_START}) and (@$ip <= ${SEC_END}) (11)
  {
     .printf "--- Reach first section ---\n";
     u;
     .break;
  }
 }
}
```

At marker 1, we take the image base of the current running program from the $peb typed pseudo-register by accessing its ImageBaseAddress field using the C++ evaluator, and then store it in an alias called IMG_BASE.

At marker 2, we create a bunch of user-named aliases that correspond to some UDPRs. This is a nice trick to give names to those UDPRs. At marker 3, we assign the address of the _IMAGE_NT_HEADERS to the $t0 UDPR by adding the image base to the value of the field in IMAGE_DOS_HEADER.e_lfanew.

At marker 4, we retrieve the size of the optional headers into the $t1 UDPR. This will be useful to skip over all the PE headers and land in the first image section header.

At marker 5, we compute the address of first image section into the $t2 UDPR. At marker 6, we parse from the IMAGE_SECTION_HEADER both the section virtual address (section start) and the section end (section start + section size).

At marker 7, we compute the program's start and end addresses. The start address is the image base, and the end address is the image base plus the contents of the IMAGE_OPTIONAL_HEADER.SizeOfImage field.

At marker 8, we start looping infinitely using a for loop, $t0 as the counter, and the value 1 as the condition.

At markers 9–11, we use the t command to trace a single instruction. Don't trace if EIP is not within the image's boundaries and stop tracing if the EIP is within the first section's boundaries.

Although this method is too long, it illustrates how to write a more complex tracing script and logic in case the unpacking process is more sophisticated.

The following is a simpler version of the unpacker that searches for a code pattern that is executed just before the program is about to transition to the original entry point (OEP):

```
$$ UPX unpack w/ pattern
$$ UPX1:0107D7F5 39 C4              cmp      esp, eax
$$ UPX1:0107D7F7 75 FA              jnz      short loc_107D7F3
$$ UPX1:0107D7F9 83 EC 80           sub      esp, -80h
$$ UPX1:0107D7FC E9 ?? ?? ??        jmp      near ptr word_103FC62

$$ Go to program entry point (not the original entry point, but the packed
one)
$$ only if no arguments were specified
.if ${/d:$arg1} == 0
{
        g @$exentry;
}

$$ Pattern not found!
r $t0 = 0; (1)
.foreach (addr { s -[1]b @$ip L200 39 c4 75 fa 83 EC}) (2)
{
        $$ Pattern found!
        r $t0 = 1;
        r $t1 = ${addr} + 7; (3)
        .printf /D "The JMP to OEP @<link cmd=\"u %x\">%x</link>\n",@$t1,@$t1;
        (4)
        ga @$t1;
        (5)
        t; u;
        .break;
}

.if $t0 == 0
{
    .printf "Could not find OEP jump pattern. Is the program packed by
UPX?\n";
}
```

At marker 1, we use the $t0 UDPR as a `Boolean` variable to indicate whether the pattern was found.

At marker 2, we search for the pattern starting from the entry point and for at most 200 bytes using the 1 flag with the search command `s`. This will return just the address where the match occurred. If no match is found, an empty string is returned and thus the `.foreach` has nothing to tokenize.

At marker 3, we skip seven bytes past the matched pattern location to point to the long relative jump (which jumps back to the OEP). Store that address into $t1.

At markers 4 and 5, we run the program until the `JMP OEP` instruction is reached (the `ga` command was used, so a hardware breakpoint is used rather than a software breakpoint), and then we trace once over the `JMP OEP` instruction and thus reach the first instruction of the unpacked program.

Writing a Basic File Monitor

This example creates a script that illustrates how to use scripts in combination with conditional breakpoints to track all calls to ASCII and Unicode versions of various file I/O API functions: `CreateFile, DeleteFile, GetFileAttributes, CopyFile`, and so on.

The script is designed to be called once with the `init` parameter to initialize it and then multiple times as a command to the breakpoints it creates when it initializes.

The following parameters are passed when the script is called from the breakpoint:

- `ApiName`—Used for display purposes only.

- `IsUnicode`—Pass zero to specify that this is the ASCII version of the API, and pass one to specify that it is the Unicode version.

- `FileNamePointerIndex`—The parameter number on the stack that contains the pointer to the filename buffer

- `ApiID`—An ID of your choice, this parameter is optional. This is helpful if you want to add extra logic when this breakpoint occurs. In this script, `CreateFile[A|W]` is given the ID 5. Later you check whether this API is triggered, and then check what filename is accessed and act accordingly.

Here is the contents of the `bp_displayfn.wds` script:

```
.catch
{
    .if '${$arg1}' == 'init' (1)
    {
```

```
    (2)
    bp kernelbase!CreateFileA @"$$>a<${$arg0} CreateFileA 0 1 5";
    bp kernelbase!CreateFileW @"$$>a<${$arg0} CreateFileW 1 1 5";

    (3)
    bp kernelbase!DeleteFileA @"$$>a<${$arg0} DeleteFileW 0 1";
    bp kernelbase!DeleteFileW @"$$>a<${$arg0} DeleteFileW 1 1";
    bp kernelbase!FindFirstFileA @"$$>a<${$arg0} FindFirstFileA 0 1";
    bp kernelbase!FindFirstFileW @"$$>a<${$arg0} FindFirstFileW 1 1";
    bp kernel32!MoveFileA @"$$>a<${$arg0} MoveFileA 0 1";
    bp kernel32!MoveFileW @"$$>a<${$arg0} MoveFileW 1 1";
    bp kernelbase!GetFileAttributesA
            @"$$>a<${$arg0} GetFileAttributesA 0 1";
    bp kernelbase!GetFileAttributesExA
            @"$$>a<${$arg0} GetFileAttributesExA 0 1";
    bp kernelbase!GetFileAttributesExW
            @"$$>a<${$arg0} GetFileAttributesExW 1 1";
    bp kernel32!CopyFileA @"$$>a<${$arg0} CopyFileA 0 1";
    bp kernel32!CopyFileW @"$$>a<${$arg0} CopyFileW 1 1";

    $$ Ignore some debug events (to lessen output pollution)
    sxi ld;

    $$ Display the list of the newly installed breakpoints
    bl;
    (4)
    .leave;
}
(5)
$$ Display API name
.printf "${$arg1}: >";
(6)
$$ Fetch the file name pointer
r $t0 = poi(@$csp + 4 * ${$arg3});
(7)
$$ Is it a unicode string pointer?
.if ${$arg2} == 1
{
    (8)
    .printf "%mu<\n", @$t0;
}
.else
{
    $$ Display as ASCII SZ (9)
    .printf "%ma<\n", @$t0;
}

$$ ApiID parameter set? (10)
.if ${/d:$arg4} == 1
{
    $$ ID of CreateFile API? (11)
    .if ${$arg4} == 5
```

```
        {
                $$ Grab the name of the file so we compare it
                aS /mu ${/v:FILE_NAME} @$t0;  (12)
                .block
                {
                    (13)
                    .if $sicmp(@"${FILE_NAME}", @"c:\temp\eb.txt") == 0
                    {
                            .leave;  (14)
                    }
                }
                ad /q ${/v:FILE_NAME};
        }
    }

    $$ Continue after breakpoint
    gc;  (15)
}
```

At marker 1, we check whether the script is called with init; if so, then initialize the script (markers 2–4) and exit the script. At marker 2, we create two breakpoints for CreateFileA/W and set the condition to be the script itself, and pass ApiID = 5.

At markers 3 and 4, we add breakpoints for the rest of the APIs without passing the ApiID argument, and then return from the script. At markers 5 and 6, we print the API name then assign into $t0 the pointer of the filename (using the passed parameter index). At markers 7–9, we check if the script is called for the ASCII or Unicode version of the API and then appropriately use the %mu or the %ma format specifier. At markers 10–12, we check if an ApiID was passed and is the CreateFile ApiID.

At markers 12–14, we extract the filename into an alias called FILE_NAME, create a block so that the alias is expanded properly, and then compare the FILE_NAME alias against a desired file path. (Notice the use of @ to indicate literal string expansion.) If the path matches what we are looking for, the script terminates and suspends execution. Finally, at marker 15, the script will resume execution after any of the defined breakpoint is reached.

To use this script, run it with the init parameter first:

```
0:000> $$>a<P:\book\scripts\bp_displayfn.wds init; g;
```

Writing a Basic String Descrambler

This script implements a simple descrambling routine. Imagine the C scrambling routine is as follows:

```
void descramble(unsigned char *p, size_t sz)
{
  for (size_t i=0;i<sz;i++, ++p)
```

```
    {
        *p = *p ^ (235 + (i & 1));
    }
}
```

NOTE The descrambling routine can be more sophisticated. If the routine involves the use of tables and whatnot, remember that you have access to those tables because the script has full access to the debuggee's memory.

The following is the same routine implemented using the DbgEng's scripting language. Note how it makes use of the `@@c++` evaluator to easily mimic the original algorithm:

```
.catch
{
        $$ Take the Source
        r $t0 = ${$arg1};

        $$ Take the Destination
        r $t1 = ${$arg2};

        $$ Take the Size
        r $t2 = ${$arg3};

        .for (r $t3=0; @$t3<@$t2; r $t3 = @$t3 + 1, $t0 = @$t0+1, $t1=@$t1+1)
        {
                r $t4 = @@c++((*(unsigned char *)@$t0) ^ (235 + (@$t3 & 1)));
                eb @$t1 @$t4;
        }
        $$ Display the descrambled result
        db ${$arg2} L ${$arg3};
}
```

The scrambled memory contents is as follows:

```
0:000> db 0x4180a4 L 30
004180a4  bb 9e 8a 8f 9f 85 88 8d-87 cc 99 89 9d 89 99 9f  ................
004180b4  8e cc 8e 82 8c 85 85 89-8e 9e 82 82 8c ec eb ec  ................
004180c4  eb ec eb ec eb ec eb ec-eb ec eb ec eb ec eb ec  ................
```

To descramble, run the script:

```
0:000> @dvalloc 1; ? $t0
Evaluate expression: 131072 = 00020000
0:000> $$>a<descramble.wds 0x4180a4 0x20000 30
00020000  50 72 61 63 74 69 63 61-6c 20 72 65 76 65 72 73  Practical revers
00020010  65 20 65 6e 67 69 6e 65-65 72 69 6e 67 00 00 00  e engineering...
00020020  00 00 00 00 00 00 00 00-00 00 00 00 00 00 00 00  ................
```

Using the SDK

So far we have covered how to automate tasks using the scripting facilities provided by the debugging tools. The SDK that ships with the debugging tools provides another way to automate or extend the debugger. It ships with header files, library files to link your extension with, and various examples that show you how to use the DbgEng programmatically.

The SDK is found in the sdk subdirectory where the debugging tools are installed. It has the following directory structure:

- Help—Contains references to the DbgHelp library.

- Inc—Contains the includes needed when using the SDK.

- Lib—Contains the appropriate library files used during the linking build stage. It contains libraries for WOA (Windows on ARM), AMD64, and i386.

- Samples—Contains samples of various examples written using the different frameworks that can be used to write debugger extensions. There are also samples on how to use the DbgEng instead of writing an extension for it.

Although covering the SDK is beyond the scope of this chapter, the following sections briefly discuss how to use the SDK to write DbgEng extensions for the debugger. The material covered should be just enough to give you a head start, making it easy for you to understand the sample extensions and start learning and writing your own.

To begin, you should know that the SDK provides three frameworks with which you can write extensions:

- **WdbgExts extension framework**—These are the original WinDbg extensions. To interact with the DbgEng, they require exporting a few callbacks in order to work with the WinDbg Extension APIs instead of the debugger client interface. The programmer can later acquire a debugger client interface or other interfaces on demand if more functionality is required.

- **DbgEng extension framework**—These newer types of extensions can provide extra functionality to the extension writer. The extension commands have access to a debugger client interface instance that enables them to acquire other interfaces and interact further with the DbgEng.

- **EngExtCpp extensions**—Built on top of the DbgEng extension framework, these extensions are created by subclassing the ExtExtension base class. The ExtExtension class provides a variety of utility functions that enable the extension to perform complex tasks.

The following sections briefly illustrate how to write extensions using the WdbgExts extension framework. Please note that writing extensions using either of the other frameworks is fairly straightforward and can be done by following the SDK samples that ship with the Debugging Tools package.

Concepts

This section describes two methods for accessing the DbgEng APIs:

- Via the debugger interfaces, which can be retrieved using a debug client object instance.

- Via a structure passed to the WbgExts extension initialization callback. The structure contains a set of API function pointers that can be used by the extension.

The Debugger Interfaces

The DbgEng provides seven base interfaces to be used by the programmer. Over time, more functionality has been added, and in order to preserve backward compatibility, new versions of those interfaces have been introduced. For example, at the time of writing, IDebugControl is the first interface version and IDebugControl4 is the latest version of this interface.

Following is the list of interfaces and a brief explanation of their purpose and some of the functions they provide:

- IDebugClient5—This interface provides various useful functions to start or stop a debugging session and set the necessary DbgEng callbacks (input/output/events). In addition, its QueryInterface method is used to retrieve interfaces of the remaining interfaces.

  - CreateProcess/AttachProcess—Creates a new process or attaches to an existing one:

  - AttachKernel—Attaches to a live kernel debugger.

  - GetExitCode—Returns the exit code of a process.

  - OpenDumpFile—Starts a debugging session from a dump file.

  - SetInputCallbacks/SetEventCallbacks—Sets the input/output callbacks.

- IDebugControl4—This interface provides process-control-related functions:

  - AddBreakpoint—Adds a breakpoint.

  - Execute—Executes a debugger command.

- ■ `SetInterrupt`—Signals the DbgEng to break into the target.
- ■ `WaitForEvent`—Waits until a debugger event occurs. This is similar to the `WaitForDebugEvent()` Win32 API.
- ■ `SetExecutionStatus`—Sets the DbgEng's status. This allows the programmer to resume execution, request a step into or step over, etc.
- ■ `IDebugDataSpaces4`—This interface provides memory and data-related functionality:
  - ■ `ReadVirtual`—Reads memory from the target's virtual memory.
  - ■ `QueryVirtual`—Equivalent to Win32's `VirtualQuery()`, this function queries the virtual memory of the target's virtual address space.
  - ■ `ReadMsr`—Reads the model-specific register value.
  - ■ `WritePhysical`—Writes physical memory.
- ■ `IDebugRegisters2`—Provides register introspection (enumeration, information query) and set/get functionality. The DbgEng assigns registers an index. To work with a named register you have to first figure out its index:
  - ■ `GetDescription`—Returns a description of the register (size, name, type, etc.).
  - ■ `SetValue`/`GetValue`—Sets/gets the value of a register.
  - ■ `GetIndexByName`—Finds a register index given its name.
- ■ `IDebugSymbols3`—Provides functionality to deal with debugging symbols, source line information, querying types, etc:
  - ■ `GetImagePath`—Returns the executable image path.
  - ■ `GetFieldName`—Returns the name of a field within a structure.
- ■ `IDebugSystemObjects4`—Provides functionality to query information from the debugged target(s) and the system it runs on:
  - ■ `GetCurrentProcessId`—Returns the DbgEng process id of the currently debugged process.
  - ■ `GetCurrentProcessHandle`—Returns the system handle of the current process.
  - ■ `SetCurrentThreadId`—Switches the current thread given its DbgEng id. This is equivalent to the ~Nk command.
- ■ `IDebugAdvanced4`—Provides more functionality not necessarily present in the other interfaces:
  - ■ `GetThreadContext`/`SetThreadContext`—Gets/sets the thread context.
  - ■ `GetSystemObjectInformation`—Returns information about the desired system object.

In order to use the APIs via the interfaces, you need to have an instance of the IDebugClient (debugger client) interface or any of its derived interfaces. In the following code snippet, the IDebugClient5 interface instance is passed to the CreateInterfaces utility function. The latter then calls QueryInterface repetitively to retrieve the needed interfaces:

```
bool CreateInterfaces(IDebugClient5 *Client)
{
  // Interfaces already created?
  if (Control != NULL)
    return true;

  // Get the debug client interface
  if (Client == NULL)
  {
    m_LastHr=m_pDebugCreate(__uuidof(IDebugClient5),(void**)&Client);
    if (m_LastHr != S_OK)
      return false;
  }

  // Query for some other interfaces that we'll need.
  do
  {
    m_LastHr = Client->QueryInterface(
      __uuidof(IDebugControl4),
      (void**)&Control);
    if (m_LastHr != S_OK)
      break;
    m_LastHr = Client->QueryInterface(
      __uuidof(IDebugSymbols3),
      (void**)&Symbols);
    if (m_LastHr != S_OK)
      break;
    m_LastHr = Client->QueryInterface(
      __uuidof(IDebugRegisters2),
      (void**)&Registers);
    if (m_LastHr != S_OK)
      break;
    m_LastHr = Client->QueryInterface(
      __uuidof(IDebugSystemObjects4),
      (void**)&SystemObjects);
    if (m_LastHr != S_OK)
      break;
    m_LastHr = Client->QueryInterface(
      __uuidof(IDebugAdvanced3),
      (void**)&Advanced);
    if (m_LastHr != S_OK)
      break;
    m_LastHr = Client->QueryInterface(
      __uuidof(IDebugDataSpaces4),
      (void**)&DataSpace);
  } while ( false);
```

```
    return SUCCEEDED(m_LastHr);
}
```

The interface variables are defined like this:

```
IDebugDataSpaces4    *DataSpace;
IDebugRegisters2     *Registers;
IDebugSymbols3       *Symbols;
IDebugControl4       *Control;
IDebugSystemObjects4 *SystemObjects;
IDebugAdvanced3      *Advanced;
```

To acquire a debugger client interface (IDebugClient), use either the DebugCreate function or the DebugConnect (connect to a remote host) function. The following example acquires a debugger client interface using DebugCreate:

```
HRESULT Status;
IDebugClient *Client;
if ((Status = DebugCreate(__uuidof(IDebugClient),
                          (void**)&Client)) != S_OK)
{
    printf("DebugCreate failed, 0x%X\n", Status);
    return -1;
}
// Okay, now ready to query for other interfaces...
```

WinDbg Extension APIs

Debugger extensions receive a pointer to a WINDBG_EXTENSION_APIS structure via the WinDbgExtensionDllInit extension initialization callback routine. The structure has the following API pointers:

```
// wdbgexts.h
typedef struct _WINDBG_EXTENSION_APIS {
    ULONG                                   nSize;
    PWINDBG_OUTPUT_ROUTINE                  lpOutputRoutine;
    PWINDBG_GET_EXPRESSION                  lpGetExpressionRoutine;
    PWINDBG_GET_SYMBOL                      lpGetSymbolRoutine;
    PWINDBG_DISASM                          lpDisasmRoutine;
    PWINDBG_CHECK_CONTROL_C                 lpCheckControlCRoutine;
    PWINDBG_READ_PROCESS_MEMORY_ROUTINE     lpReadProcessMemoryRoutine;
    PWINDBG_WRITE_PROCESS_MEMORY_ROUTINE    lpWriteProcessMemoryRoutine;
    PWINDBG_GET_THREAD_CONTEXT_ROUTINE      lpGetThreadContextRoutine;
    PWINDBG_SET_THREAD_CONTEXT_ROUTINE      lpSetThreadContextRoutine;
    PWINDBG_IOCTL_ROUTINE                   lpIoctlRoutine;
    PWINDBG_STACKTRACE_ROUTINE              lpStackTraceRoutine;
} WINDBG_EXTENSION_APIS, *PWINDBG_EXTENSION_APIS;
```

When the extension receives this structure, it should copy and store it in a global variable, preferably named `ExtensionApis`. The reason to choose this particular variable name is because the header file `wdbgexts.h` defines some macros that refer to `ExtensionApis` to access the API pointers:

```
extern WINDBG_EXTENSION_APIS ExtensionApis;

#define dprintf          (ExtensionApis.lpOutputRoutine)
#define GetExpression    (ExtensionApis.lpGetExpressionRoutine)
#define CheckControlC    (ExtensionApis.lpCheckControlCRoutine)
#define GetContext       (ExtensionApis.lpGetThreadContextRoutine)
...
#define ReadMemory       (ExtensionApis.lpReadProcessMemoryRoutine)
#define WriteMemory      (ExtensionApis.lpWriteProcessMemoryRoutine)
#define StackTrace       (ExtensionApis.lpStackTraceRoutine)
```

These macros enable extension writers to directly call `StackTrace` or `WriteMemory`, for instance, instead of using `pExtension.lpStackTraceRoutine` or `pExtension.WriteMemory`.

Apart from being able to use only the functions declared in the `WINDBG_EXTENSION_APIS` structure, it is also possible to use a whole range of other functions that are based on the `ExtensionApis.lpIoctlRoutine` function. For example, `ReadPhysical()` is an inline function that calls `IoCtl()` with the `IG_READ_PHYSICAL` control code while passing it the appropriate parameters.

Please refer to the DbgEng help file for a list of functions that you can use inside WdbgExts extensions.

Writing Debugging Tools Extensions

In the previous section you learned the concepts behind the SDK; now you are ready to delve into more details about what a WdbgExts extension looks like and how to write a very basic extension.

A debugger extension is simply a Microsoft Windows DLL. The DLL has to export two mandatory functions needed by the DbgEng and then export as many functions as the extension is providing to the debugger.

The first function that should be exported is `WinDbgExtensionDllInit`. It is called when the debugger loads your extension:

```
VOID WinDbgExtensionDllInit(
    PWINDBG_EXTENSION_APIS lpExtensionApis,
    USHORT MajorVersion,
    USHORT MinorVersion)
{
    ExtensionApis = *lpExtensionApis; // Take a copy

    // Optionally also save the version information
    SavedMajorVersion = MajorVersion;
```

```
SavedMinorVersion = MinorVersion;

return;
}
```

Notice that you save the passed `lpExtensionApis` pointer contents. The passed version information variables denote the Microsoft Windows build type and build number, respectively. Optionally save those variables if you want to check their values in the extension commands later.

The second function that should be exported is `ExtensionApiVersion`. It is called by the DbgEng when it wants to query the version information from your extension:

```
EXT_API_VERSION ApiVersion =
{
  5, // Major
  1, // Minor
  EXT_API_VERSION_NUMBER64,  // Revision
  0 // Reserved
};

LPEXT_API_VERSION ExtensionApiVersion(VOID)
{
  return &ApiVersion;
}
```

Now that the mandatory functions (or callbacks) have been defined, you proceed by declaring the extension commands.

An extension command has the following declaration:

```
CPPMOD VOID myextension(
    HANDLE              hCurrentProcess,
    HANDLE              hCurrentThread,
    ULONG              dwCurrentPc,
    ULONG              dwProcessor,
    PCSTR              args)
```

The most notable passed arguments are as follows:

- `dwProcessor`—The index of the current processor
- `dwCurrentPc`—The current instruction pointer
- `args`—The arguments passed (if any)

Another preferred way to declare an extension function is to use the DECLARE_API(api_s) macro:

```
DECLARE_API( test )
{
  dprintf("This is a test extension routine");
}
```

> **NOTE**   At any time, any extension command can call `DebugCreate()` and then get any interface it wants in order to gain extra functionality.

The final step is to export the two mandatory functions and the extension commands that you plan to expose to the DbgEng. The usual way is to create a `.def` file and call the linker with an additional `/DEF:filename.def` switch. This is what the DEF file for the test extension we wrote looks like:

```
EXPORTS

    ; Callbacks provided for the debugger
    WinDbgExtensionDllInit
    ExtensionApiVersion

    ; Command callbacks
    test
```

Place the resulting DLL in the debugging tools directory (or in the `winext` subdirectory) or in the Windows system directory. Use `!load extname` to load your compiled extension and then `!extension_command` or `!extname.ext_command` to execute the extension command.

Useful Extensions, Tools, and Resources

Following is a short list of useful extensions, tools, and resources that can enhance your debugging experience:

- **narly** (`https://code.google.com/p/narly/`)—A handy extension that lists `/SAFESEH` handlers, displays information about `/GS` and DEP, searches for ROP gadgets, and provides other miscellaneous commands.

- **SOS**—This extension, which ships with the Windows Driver Kit (WDK), facilitates managed code debugging.

- **!analyze**—A very useful extension (ships with the DbgEng) that displays information about the current exception or bugcheck.

- **VirtualKd** (`http://virtualkd.sysprogs.org/`)—This is a tool that improves the kernel debugging speed when used with VMWare or VirtualBox.

- **windbg.info**—This website provides a very comprehensive WinDbg/DbgEng command reference and a discussion forum for users.

- **kdext.com**—This website provides a pair of DbgEng extensions. A notable extension is the assembly syntax highlighting and UI enhancements extension.

- **SysecLabs WinDbg Scripts** (`www.laboskopia.com/download/SysecLabs-Windbg-Script.zip`)—A set of scripts that help you inspect the kernel. Especially useful for rootkit hunting.

- **!exploitable** (`http://msecdbg.codeplex.com/`)—An extension that provides automated crash analysis and security risk assessment.

- **Qb-Sync** (`https://github.com/quarkslab/qb-sync`)—A nifty WinDbg extension by Quarkslab that enables synchronizing IDA Pro's disassembly or graph view with WinDbg.

- **Pykd** (`http://pykd.codeplex.com/`)—A Python extension to access the DbgEng.

Obfuscation

Reverse engineering compiler-generated code is a difficult and time-consuming process. The situation gets even worse when the code has been hardened, deliberately constructed to resist analysis. We refer to such techniques for hardening programs under the general umbrella of *obfuscation*. Some examples of situations in which obfuscation might be applied are as follows:

- **Malware**—Avoiding the scrutiny of both antivirus detection engines and reverse engineers is a primary motive of the criminals who employ malware in their operations, and therefore this has been a traditional application of obfuscation for many years now.

- **Protection of intellectual property**—Many commercial programs have some sort of protection against unauthorized duplication. Some systems employ further obfuscation for the purpose of obscuring the implementation details of certain parts of the system. Good examples include Skype, Apple's IMessage, or even the Dropbox client, which protect their communication protocol formats with obfuscation and cryptography.

- **Digital Rights Management**—DRM schemes commonly protect certain crucial pieces of information (e.g., cryptographic keys and protocols) using obfuscation. Apple's FairPlay, Microsoft's Media Foundation Platform and its PlayReader DRM, to cite only two, are examples of obfuscation application. Currently, this is the leading contemporary application of obfuscation.

Speaking in the abstract, "obfuscation" can be viewed in terms of *program transformations*. The goal of such methods is to take as input a program, and produce as output a new program that has the same computational effect as the original program (formally speaking, this property is called *semantic equivalence* or *computational equivalence*), but at the same time it is "more difficult" to analyze.

The notion of "difficulty of analysis" has long been defined informally, without any backing mathematical rigor. For example, it is widely believed that—insofar as a human analyst is concerned—a program's size is an indicator of the difficulty in analyzing it. A program that consumes 20,000 instructions in performing a single operation might be thought to be "more difficult" to analyze than one that takes one instruction to perform the same operation. Such assumptions are dubious and have attracted the scrutiny of theoreticians (such as that by Mila Dalla Preda[17] and Barak et al.[2]).

Several models have been proposed to represent an obfuscator, and (in a dual way) a deobfuscator. These models are useful to improve the design of obfuscation tools and to reason about their robustness, through adapted criteria. Among them, two models are of special interest.

The first model is suited for the analysis of cryptographic mechanisms, in the so-called *white box attack context*. This model defines an attacker as a probabilistic algorithm that tries to deduce a pertinent property from a protected program. More precisely, it tries to extract information other than what can be trivially deduced from the analysis of the program's inputs and outputs. This information is pertinent in the sense that it enables the attacker to bypass a security function or represents itself as critical data of the protected program. In a dual way, an obfuscator is defined in this model as a virtual black box's probabilistic generator, an ideal obfuscator ensuring that the protected program analysis does not provide more information than the analysis of its input and output distributions.

Another way to formalize an attacker is to define the reverse engineering action as an abstract interpretation of the concrete semantics of the protected program. Such a definition is naturally suited to the static analysis of the program's data flow, which is a first step before the application of optimization transformations. In a dual way, an obfuscator is defined in the abstract interpretation model as a specialized compiler, parameterized by some semantic properties that are not preserved.

The goal of these modeling attempts is to get some objective criteria relative to the effective robustness of obfuscation transformations. Indeed, many problems that were once thought to be difficult can be efficiently attacked via judicious application of code analysis techniques. Many methods that have arisen in the context of more conventional topics in programming language theory (such as compilers and formal verification) can be repurposed for the sake of defeating obfuscation.

This chapter begins with a survey of existing obfuscation techniques as commonly found in real-world situations. It then covers the various available methods and tools developed to analyze and possibly break obfuscation code. Finally, it provides an example of a difficult, modern obfuscation scheme, and details its circumvention using state-of-the-art analysis techniques.

A Survey of Obfuscation Techniques

For simplicity of presentation, we begin by dividing obfuscations into two categories: data-based obfuscation and control-based obfuscation. You will see later that the two combine in complex and difficult ways and are, in fact, inseparable. Before wandering deeply down these paths, however, we begin with a representative example of the types of code that one might encounter in real-world obfuscation. Note that the example is particularly simple because it involves only data-based obfuscations, not control-based ones.

The Nature of Obfuscation: A Motivating Example

When targeting the x86 processor, compilers tend to generate instructions drawn from a particular, tiny subset of the available instruction set, and the control structure of the generated program follows predictable conventions. Over time, the reverse engineer develops a style of analysis tailored to these patterns of structured code. When confronted by nonconformant code, the speed of one's analysis can suffer tremendously.

This phenomenon can be illustrated simply by a concrete example. Because one of the goals of a compiler optimizer is to reduce the amount of computational resources involved in performing a task, and 50 years' worth of research have imbued them with formidable capabilities toward this pursuit, one does not commonly spot obvious inefficiencies in the translation of the original source code into assembly language. For example, if the source code were to dictate that some variable be incremented by five (e.g., due to a statement such as `x += 5;`), a compiler would likely generate assembly code akin to one of the following:

```
01: add eax, 5
02: add dword ptr [ebp-10h], 5
03: lea ebx, [ecx+5]
```

In obfuscated code, one might instead encounter code such as the following, assuming that EAX corresponds to the variable x, and that the value of EBX is free to be overwritten (or "clobbered"):

```
01: xor ebx, eax
02: xor eax, ebx
03: xor ebx, eax
04: inc eax
05: neg ebx
06: add ebx, 0A6098326h
07: cmp eax, esp
08: mov eax, 59F67CD5h
09: xor eax, 0FFFFFFFFh
10: sub ebx, eax
11: rcl eax, cl
12: push 0F9CBE47Ah
13: add dword ptr [esp], 6341B86h
14: sbb eax, ebp
15: sub dword [esp], ebx
16: pushf
17: pushad
18: pop eax
19: add esp, 20h
20: test ebx, eax
21: pop eax
```

You can see a variety of obfuscation techniques at work in this example:

- Lines 1–3 use the "XOR *swap trick*" for exchanging the contents of two locations—in this case, the EAX and EBX registers.

- Line 4 shows an assignment to the EAX register that is actually "junk" (as EAX is overwritten with a constant on line 8).

- On lines 5–6, the EBX register is negated and added to the constant 0A6098326h: EBX = - EAX + 0A6098326h.

- On line 7, EAX is compared with ESP. The CMP instruction modifies only the flags, and the flags are overwritten on subsequent lines before being used again, so this code is junk.

- Lines 8–9 move the constant 59F67CD5h into the EAX register and XOR it with -1h (which, in binary, is all one bits). XORing with all ones is equivalent to the NOT operation; therefore, the effect of this sequence is to move the constant 0A609832Ah into EAX.

- Line 10 subtracts the constant in EAX from EBX: EBX = - EAX + 0A6098326h - 0A609832Ah, or EBX = - EAX - 5, or EBX = -(EAX + 5).

- Line 11 modifies EAX through use of the RCL instruction. This instruction is junk because EAX is overwritten on line 18.

- Lines 12–13 push the constant 0F9CBE47Ah and then add the constant 6341B86h to it, resulting in the value 0h on the bottom of the stack.

- Line 14 modifies EAX through use of the SBB instruction, involving the extraneous register EBP. This instruction is junk, as EAX is overwritten on line 18.

- Line 15 subtracts EBX from the value currently on the bottom of the stack (which is 0h). Therefore, dword ptr [ESP] = 0 - -(EAX + 5), or dword ptr [ESP] = EAX + 5.

- Lines 16–19 demonstrate operations involving the stack: nine dwords are pushed, one is popped into EAX, and the stack pointer is then adjusted to point to the same location that it pointed to before the sequence executed.

- Line 20 tests EBX against the EAX register and sets the flags accordingly. If the flags are redefined before their next use, then this instruction is dead.

- Line 21 pops the value on the bottom of the stack (which holds EAX + 5) into the EAX register.

In summary, the code computes EAX = EAX + 5.

Needless to say, the obfuscated code does not at all resemble the compiler-generated code, and one faces considerable difficulty in ascertaining the functionality of the snippet. Several obfuscation techniques are present in this example:

- Pattern-based obfuscation

- Constant unfolding

- Junk code insertion

- Stack-based obfuscation

- The use of uncommon instructions, such as RCL, SBB, PUSHF, and PUSHAD

Correspondingly, a variety of existing compiler transformations can be used to render the code into a form that is closer to the original:

- Peephole optimization

- Constant folding

- Dead statement elimination

- Stack optimization

The Interplay Between Data Flow and Control Flow

Consider the following instruction sequence:

```
01: mov eax, dword ptr [ebp-10h]
02: jmp eax
```

Suppose you wish to construct a "correct," classical control-flow graph for a program containing sequences like this one. In order to determine what the next instruction will be after line 2 has executed—or, perhaps the set of potential successor instructions—you need to determine the set of possible value(s) for the EAX register at that location. In other words, the control flow for this snippet is dependent upon the data flow as it pertains to the location [EBP-10h] at the program point l1 (line 1). However, in order to determine the data flow with respect to [EBP-10h], you need to determine the control flow with respect to the line 1 location: You must know all possible control transfer instructions (and the associated data flow leading to those locations) that could possibly target the line 1 location. It is not meaningful to talk about control flow without simultaneously talking about data flow, or vice versa.

The situation is even more difficult than it might appear on the surface. Program analysis tries to answer questions such as "What values might the location [EBP-10h] assume under any possible circumstance?" To combat intractability and undecidability, many forms of program analysis employ approximations of the state space. Some approximations are *fine* (e.g., approximating the set {1,3} by {1,2,3}), and some are *coarse* (e.g., approximating that same set by $\{0,1,...,2^{32}-1\}$). (*Fine* and *coarse* are not technical terms in this paragraph.) If you cannot finely approximate the set of potential values of the [EBP-10h] location (for example, if you must assume that the location could take on any possible value), then you do not know where the jump will point, so you must assume that it could target any location within the address space. Then, the data flow facts from the line 2 location must be propagated into those at every other location. In practical settings, such a decision will severely impact the analysis, most likely causing it to conservatively conclude that all states are possible at all locations, which is correct but useless.

Worse yet, if you ever must assume that a jump could target any location, then due to variable-length instruction encoding on x86, many of these transfers will be into locations that do not correspond to the beginning of a proper instruction. Such bogus instructions are likely to wreak havoc on any analysis, especially when combined with the observations in the previous paragraph.

Academic work in this area, such as that by Kinder[30] and Thakur et al.[41], seeks to construct systems that can return correct answers for all possible inputs. These systems prefer to tell users that they cannot determine precise information, return correct but grossly imprecise results, or die trying (e.g., by exhausting all available memory or failing to terminate due to tractability issues), rather than give an answer that is not fully justified. This goal is laudable, given the motivation from whence these disciplines were founded: to ensure absolute correctness of programs and analyses. However, it is not in line with our motivations as obfuscation researchers.

Deobfuscation is a creature of a different sort than formal verification or program analysis, even if we prefer to use techniques developed in those contexts. Whereas an obfuscator transforms a program P_{orig} into a program P_{obf}, we seek either a translator from P_{obf} into P_{orig} or enough information about P_{obf} to answer questions proximate to some reverse engineering effort. We hesitate to use unsound methods, but we prefer actual results when the day is finished, so we may employ such methods, albeit consciously and grudgingly.

Data-Based Obfuscations

We begin by looking at obfuscation techniques that can be best described in terms of their effect on data values and noncontrol computations. In particular, assume that the presented snippets occur within a single basic block of the program's control-flow graph. The discussions of control-based obfuscations, and their combination with data-based obfuscations, are deferred to later sections.

Constant Unfolding

Constant folding is one of the earliest and most basic compiler optimizations. The goal of this optimization is to replace computations whose results are known at compile-time with those results. For example, in the C statement x = 4 * 5;, the expression 4 * 5 consists of a binary arithmetic operator (*) that is supplied with two operands whose values are statically known (4 and 5, respectively). It would be wasteful for the compiler to generate code that computed this result at run-time, as it can deduce what the result will be during compilation. The compiler can simply replace the assignment with x = 20;.

Constant unfolding is an obfuscation that performs the inverse operation. Given a constant value that is used somewhere in the input program, the obfuscator can replace the constant by some computation process that produces the constant. You have already encountered this obfuscation in the motivating example:

```
01: push 0F9CBE47Ah
02: add dword ptr [esp], 6341B86h
```

Neglecting the modifications that this sequence has upon the flags, this was found to be equivalent to push 0h.

Data-Encoding Schemes

The fundamental flaw of this technique is that constants have to be dynamically decoded (thus exposed, as well as the decode function) at run-time before being processed. We have the encoding function $f(x) = x - 6341B86h$, whose result $f(x)$ is pushed on the stack, and then the decoded function is applied: $f_{-1}(x) = x + 6341B86h$.

This construct is trivial; deobfuscation is done by simply applying the standard compiler's constant folding optimization.

Efforts have been made to harden these statements and propose more resilient encoding schemes. Some techniques, such as polynomial encoding and residue encoding, have been described in patent US6594761 B1 by Chow, Johnson and Gu[11]. Affine maps are also commonly used.

What if one could find an encoding such that it is not mandatory to decode variables to manipulate them (an equivalent operation can be defined on the encoded variables)? This property, called *homomorphism*, has been discussed in an obfuscation-oriented view, as well as a refinement of the residue coding technique in works such as those of Zhu and Thomborson.[44]

In abstract algebra, a homomorphism is an *operation-preserving mapping* between two algebraic structures. Consider, for example, two groups, G and H, equipped respectively with operations $+_g$ and $+_h$. We want to construct a mapping f between the sets underlying G and H, and we want your mapping to respect the operations $+_g$ and $+_h$. In particular, we must have that $f(x +_g y) = f(x) +_h f(y)$.

The notion of a homomorphism can be generalized beyond groups to arbitrary algebraic structures. For example, you can consider ring homomorphisms that simultaneously preserve both the addition and the multiplication operators. In contrast to mappings that preserve only one of the ring's operations and not the other, or induce restrictions upon the operators or their usage, unrestricted mappings are considered *fully homomorphic*.

Fully homomorphic mappings have a natural application to obfuscation. If the source algebra is the unencoded domain, and the target algebra is the encoded one, then a homomorphic mapping enables us to perform computations directly upon the encoded data without having to decode it beforehand and re-encode it afterward.

At the time of writing, the topic of homomorphic cryptography is still in its infancy. Fully homomorphic cryptosystems have been shown to exist, and they enable the computation of *encrypted programs* upon *encrypted data*. That is to say, rigorous statements can be made concerning the hardness of determining specifics about the program being executed, and which data it is operating upon. At present, the schemes are too inefficient for practical usage, and how to best apply the technology to arbitrary computer programs is an open question.

Dead Code Insertion

Another common compiler optimization is known as *dead code elimination*, which is responsible for removing program statements that do not have any effect on the program's operation. For example, consider the following C function:

```c
int f()
{
    int x, y;
```

```
x = 1;    // this assignment to x is dead
y = 2;    // y is not used again, so it is dead
x = 3;    // x above here is not live
return x; // x is live
}
```

Ultimately, the function returns the number 3. It does so after several meaningless computations that do not affect the function's output. The first assignments to x and y are said to be *dead*, as they have no effect on live computations.

Obfuscators perform the inverse of this operation by inserting dead code for the purpose of making the code harder to follow—the reverse engineer has to manually decide whether a given instruction participates in the computation of some meaningful result. The ability to insert "dead" code requires the obfuscator to know which registers are "live" at every given program point; for example, if EAX contains an important value (it's *live*), and EBX does not (it's *dead*), then you can insert statements that modify EBX.

Deobfuscation of this construct is done by simply applying the standard compiler's dead statement elimination optimization, which can be done either on a single basic block or across an entire control-flow graph.

Arithmetic Substitution via Identities

Mathematical statements can be made relating the results of certain operators to the results of combinations of other operators. You have already seen an instance of this general phenomenon in the motivating example, when you encountered the instruction XOR EAX, 0FFFFFFFFh (where the binary representation of 0FFFFFFFFh is all one bits). Because 0 XOR 1 = 1, and 1 XOR 1 = 0, this instruction actually flips each of the bits in EAX; in other words, it is synonymous with the NOT operator. Similarly, you can make the following statements:

- -x = ~x + 1 (by definition of two's complement)
- rotate left(x,y) = (x << y) | (x >> (bits(x)-y))
- rotate right(x,y) = (x >> y) | (x << (bits(x)-y))
- x-1 = ~-x
- x+1 = - ~x

Pattern-Based Obfuscation

Pattern-based obfuscation, a staple of many contemporary protections, has a simple underlying concept. The protection author manually constructs transformations that map one or more adjacent instructions into a more complicated sequence of instructions that has the same semantic effect. For example, a pattern might convert the sequence

```
01: push reg32
```

into this sequence (which we will call #1):

```
01: push imm32
02: mov dword ptr [esp], reg32
```

Or, it might convert that same sequence into this sequence (#2):

```
01: lea esp, [esp-4]
02: mov dword ptr [esp], reg32
```

Or this one (#3):

```
01: sub esp, 4
02: mov dword ptr [esp], reg32
```

Patterns can be arbitrarily complicated. A more complex example might substitute the pattern:

```
01: sub esp, 4
```

for this pattern (#4):

```
01: push reg32
02: mov reg32, esp
03: xchg [esp], reg32
04: pop esp
```

Some protections have hundreds of patterns. Most protections apply patterns randomly to the input sequence, such that two obfuscations of the same piece of code result in a different output. Also, the patterns are applied iteratively. Consider the following input:

```
01: push ecx
```

Imagine that it is transformed via substitution #3:

```
01: sub esp, 4
02: mov dword ptr [esp], ecx
```

Now suppose that the obfuscator is run a second time, and the first instruction is replaced according to pattern #4:

```
01: push ebx
02: mov ebx, esp
03: xchg [esp], ebx
04: pop esp
05: mov dword ptr [esp], ecx
```

This process can be applied indefinitely, resulting in an arbitrarily large output sequence. With enough patterns, one can transform one instruction into millions of instructions.

Note a few things about these substitutions. #1 and #2 preserve semantic equivalence: After those sequences execute, the CPU will be in the same state that it would have been if the original one were executed instead. #3 does not preserve semantic equivalence, because it uses the sub-instruction that changes the flags, whereas the original push does not. As for sequence #4, the original does change the flags, whereas the substitution does not; also, whereas the original does not modify memory at all, the substitution writes the value of ESP onto the bottom of the stack (hence, you could also consider this as being equal to the PUSH ESP instruction).

These considerations illustrate the difficulty of obfuscating assembly code post-compilation. The protection is only safe to execute substitution #3 if it is known that the flags modified by the instruction are not used before the next modification to those flags. Substitution #4 is similarly safe if the flags are dead, and if the resultant code is indifferent to the contents of [ESP] after the original SUB ESP, 4 operation. Ensuring flag liveness requires building the function's control-flow graph, which can be difficult due to indirect branches. Ensuring that the stack memory modification is safe would be extremely difficult due to memory aliasing. These specific concerns are unlikely to affect normal functions generated by a compiler for which control-flow graphs can be generated, but it is hoped that they illustrate the perils of applying semantically non-equivalent transformations to compiled code.

Owing to the complexities of obfuscating compiled assembly language, protections most commonly apply these transformations against the code corresponding to the protection itself, rather than the target's code. This way, the protection authors can guarantee that the input code will be oblivious to those transformations that do not preserve strict semantic equivalence.

Deobfuscation of this type of obfuscation is simple, although it can be time-consuming to write the deobfuscator. One can construct inverse pattern substitutions, which instead map the target sequences into the original ones. In fact, this corresponds to a routine compiler optimization known as *peephole optimization*. Academic works, such as that by Jacob et al.[25] or Bansal,[1] have discussed the automated construction of both pattern-obfuscators and peephole optimizers.

This brings us back to the question of practical results versus academic ones. Suppose you are dealing with a pattern-based obfuscator that contains errors (e.g., erroneous pattern substitutions that do not preserve semantic equivalence). Suppose further that you, as a deobfuscation researcher, are aware of the errors and are able to correct them at deobfuscation time. This means that your deobfuscator will similarly not preserve semantic equivalence and is therefore "incorrect" in absolute terms as far as transformation goes, but it actually produces "correct" results with respect to the pre-obfuscated code. Should you make the substitution? The formal correctness crowd would say no; we would answer in the affirmative.

Control-Based Obfuscation

When reverse engineering compiler-generated code, reverse engineers are able to rely on the predictability of the compiler's translations of control flow constructs. In doing so, they can quickly ascertain the control flow structure of the original code at a level of abstraction higher than assembly language. Along the way, the reverse engineer relies upon a host of assumptions about how compilers generate code. In a pure compiled program, all code in a basic block will be most often sequentially located (heavy compiler optimizations can possibly render this basic premise null and void). Temporally related blocks usually will, too. A CALL instruction always corresponds to the invocation of some function. The RET instruction, too, will almost always signify the end of some function and its return to its caller. Indirect jumps, such as for implementing switch statements, appear infrequently and follow standard schemas.

Control-based obfuscation attacks these planks of standard reverse engineering, in a way that complicates both static and dynamic analyses. Standard static analysis tools make similar assumptions as human reverse engineers, in particular:

- The CALL instruction is only used to invoke functions, and a function begins at the address targeted by a call.

- Most calls return, and if they do, they return to the location immediately following the CALL instruction; ret and RETN statements connote function boundaries.

- Upon encountering a conditional jump, disassemblers assume that it was placed into the code "in good faith"—in particular that:

  - Both sides of the branch could feasibly be taken.

  - Code, not data, is located down each side of the branch.

- They will be able to easily ascertain the targets of indirect jumps.

- Indirect jumps and calls will only be generated for standard constructs such as switches and function pointer invocations.

- All control transfers target code locations, not data locations.

- Exceptions will be used in predictable ways.

With respect to control transfers, disassemblers assume a model of "normality" based around the patterns of standard compiled code. They explicitly create functions at call targets, end them at return statements, continue disassembling after a call instruction, traverse both sides of all conditional branches, assume all branch targets are code, use syntactic pattern-matching to resolve indirect jump schema, and generally ignore exceptional control flow. Violating the assumptions laid out previously leads to very poor disassembly. This is a consistent thorn in the side of obfuscation researchers, and an open research topic (as discussed previously) in verification.

Dynamic analysis has an easier time with respect to indirect control transfers, since it can explicitly follow execution flow. However, the attacker still faces questions involving determining the targets of indirect transfers, and suffers from the lack of sequential locality induced by so-called *spaghetti code*. The following sections elaborate upon what happens when these assumptions are challenged.

Functions In/Out-Lining

The call graph of a program carries a lot of its high-level logic. Playing with the notion of a function can break some of the reverser's assumptions. It's possible to:

- **Inline functions**—The code of a subfunction is merged into the code of its caller. Code size can grow quickly if the subfunction is called multiple times.

- **Outline functions**—A subpart of a function is extracted and transformed into an independent function and replaced by a call to the newly created functions.

Combining these two operations over a program leads to a degenerated call graph with no apparent logic. It goes without saying that functions' prototypes can also be toyed with to reorder arguments, add extra, fake arguments, and so on, to contribute to logic obscurity.

Destruction of Sequential and Temporal Locality

As stated, and as understood intrinsically by those who reverse engineer compiled code, the instructions within a single, compiled basic block lie in one straight-line sequence. This property is called *sequential locality*. Furthermore, compiler optimizers attempt to put basic blocks that are related to one another (for example, a block and its successors) nearby, for the purpose of maximizing instruction cache locality and reducing the number of branches in the compiled output. We call this property *the sequential locality of temporally related code*. When you reverse engineer compiled code, these properties customarily hold true. One learns in analyzing such code that all of the code responsible for a single unit of functionality will be neatly contained in a single region, and that the proximate control-flow neighbors will be nearby and similarly sequentially located.

A very old technique in program obfuscation is to introduce unconditional branches to destroy this aspect of familiarity that reverse engineers organically obtain through typical endeavors. Here is a simple example:

```
01: instr_1:
02:    push offset caption
03:    jmp instr_4
```

```
04:
05: instr_2:
06:     call MessageBoxA
07:     jmp instr_5
08:
09: instr_3:
10:     push 0
11:     jmp instr_2
12:
13: start:
14:     push 0
15:     jmp instr_1
16:
17: instr_4:
18:     push offset dlgtxt
19     jmp instr_3
20:
21: instr_5:
22: ; ...
```

This example shows the lack of sequential locality for instructions within a basic block, and not temporal locality of multiple basic blocks. In practice, large amounts of the program's code will be intertwined in such a fashion (usually with more than one instruction on a given basic block, unlike the preceding example).

From a formal perspective, this technique does not even deserve to be called "trivial," as it has no semantic effect whatsoever on the program. Constructing a control-flow graph and removing spurious unconditional branches will defeat this scheme entirely. However, in terms of analysis performed manually by a human, the ability to follow the code has been dramatically slowed.

Processor-Based Control Indirection

For most processors, two essential displacement primitives are the JMP-like branch and the CALL-like save instruction pointer and branch. These primitives can be obfuscated by using dynamically computed branch addresses or by emulating them. One of the most basic techniques is the couple PUSH-RET used as a JMP instruction:

```
01: push target_addr
02: ret
```

That's (almost) semantically equivalent to the following:

```
01: jmp target_addr
```

The CALL instruction is an easy target for obfuscators because most disassemblers assume the following about its high-level semantics:

■ The target address is a subfunction entry point.

■ A call returns (i.e., the instruction after the CALL is executed).

It is actually easy to break these assumptions. Consider the following example:

```
01: call target_addr
02: <junk code>
03: target_addr:
04: add esp, 4
```

The CALL is used as a JMP; it will never return to line 2. The stack is fixed (the return address is discarded from the stack) on line 3. Next consider, these two elements:

```
01: basic_block_a:
02: add [esp], 9
03: ret
```

and

```
01: basic_block_b:
02: call basic_block_a
03: <junk code>
04: true_return_addr:
05: nop
```

basic_block_b's line 2 CALL instruction points to basic_block_a, which actually is only a stub that updates (see basic_block_a's line 2) the return address stored onto the top of the stack before the RET instruction uses it (basic_block_a's line 3). In these two examples the result is an interval between CALL's natural (expected) and effective return addresses; an obfuscator can (and will) take advantage to insert code that thwarts disassemblers and creates confusion.

The following example is an interesting enrichment of the standard PUSH-RET used as JMP previously:

```
01: push addr_branch_default
02: push ebx
03: push edx
04: mov ebx, [esp+8]
05: mov edx, addr_branch_jmp
06: cmovz ebx, edx
07: mov [esp+8], ebx
08: pop edx
09: pop ebx
10: ret
```

The basis of this construction actually is a PUSH-RET. Line 7 writes the target address onto the stack; it is used by the RET at line 10. The pushed address comes from EBX (line 7), which is conditionally updated by the CMOVZX instruction at line 6. If the condition is satisfied (the z flag is tested), then the instruction acts like a standard MOV (EBX is overwritten by EDX, which contains the branch target address), otherwise it acts like a NOP (thus EBX contains the default branch address). In the end, one can clearly see this pattern stands for a conditional jump (JZ).

Operating System–Based Control Indirection

The program can make use of operating system primitives (even though it may imply a loss of portability). The Structured Exception Handler (SEH), Vectored Exception Handler (VEH), and Unhandled Exception Handler, in Windows, and signal handlers and setjmp/longjmp functions, in Unix, are commonly used to obfuscate the control flow.

The basic algorithm can be decomposed as follows:

1. Obfuscated code triggers an exception (using invalid pointer, invalid operation, invalid instruction, etc.).

2. The operating system calls the registered exception handler(s).

3. The exception handler dispatches the instruction flow according to its internal logic and sets back the program in a clean state.

The following example has been seen billions of times within x86 binaries:

```
01: push addr_seh_handler
02: push fs:[0]
03: mov fs:[0], esp
04: xor eax, eax
05: mov [eax], 1234h
06: <junk code>
07: addr_seh_handler:
08: <continue execution here>
09: pop fs:[0]
10: add esp, 4
```

Lines 1–3 set up the SEH. An exception is then triggered in the form of an access violation as line 5 attempts to write at 0x0. Assuming the program is not debugged, the operating system will transfer execution to the SEH handler. Please also note that when a SEH handler is called, it receives a copy of the thread's context as one of its arguments, and the instruction pointer register value can be modified to further obfuscate the control flow redirection.

NOTE This technique also efficiently acts as an anti-debugger. Basically, the job of a debugger is to handle exceptions. These exceptions have to be passed to the debug target; otherwise, the target's behavior will be modified and tampering detected.

More interesting, the concept can also be reversed. What if a protection inserts exceptions in the original program and catches them with its own attached debugger? The protected program consists of a debuggee and debugger. A well-known example of this is the namomites feature from Armadillo. Namomites actually replace (conditional) jumps by INT 3 instruction. The exception is caught by the protection's debugger, which updates the debuggee's context appropriately to emulate the (conditional) jumps. One cannot simply detach the debugger from the debuggee; otherwise, exceptions would not be handled and the program would crash. An implementation of this concept has been proposed by Deroko.[19]

Opaque Predicates

An *opaque predicate* (introduced by Collberg in "A Taxonomy of Obfuscating Transformations"[12] and "Manufacturing Cheap, Resilient, and Stealthy Opaque Constructs"[13]) is a special conditional construct (Boolean expression) that always evaluates to either true or false (respectively noted P^T and P^F). Its value is known only at compilation/obfuscation time and should be unknown to an attacker as well as computationally hard to prove, to meet a sufficient degree of resilience. Used in combination with a conditional jump instruction, it introduces an additional, spurious branch—i.e., an additional edge in the control-flow graph (CFG). This dead branch can be used to insert junk code or special properties like cycles in the CFG to harden the analysis. However, the spurious branch has to look real enough to escape simple detection by a human attacker (for example, only one of the two branches contains necessary variable initializations).

It has the appearance of a conditional jump but its semantics are that of an unconditional jump. Computationally complex mathematical problems can be used to implement opaque predicates. You can also use some environmental variables whose values are constant and known at compilation/obfuscation time. This last technique may be less resilient because there is a limited, finite set of candidate variables, thus limiting the potential diversity.

Designing resilient opaque predicates is a tough job. They are superfluous pieces of code mixed with existing code that has its own logic/style; if no special care is taken they are easily detectable. A good practice is to create dependencies between the predicate and the program's state/variables. A human attacker (you) is usually quite efficient at detecting dubious patterns. Using an absurdly complex predicate may effectively thwart a static analysis tool but it will probably be easily detected by a human attacker.

An interesting variation on the original concept uses a predicate that randomly returns either true or false (noted $P^?$). As both branches are potentially executed at run-time, they have to be semantically equivalent. In most cases that amounts to cloning (and possibly diversifying) a basic block (or a larger piece of code), producing a "diamond-like" construct.

Simultaneous Control-Flow and Data-Flow Obfuscation

For the sake of clarity, we have dissociated control-flow and data-flow obfuscation so far. In practice, however, both are intimately linked. This section presents techniques based on this interplay.

Inserting Junk Code

This technique is intimately tied to control flow obfuscation. It basically consists of inserting a dead (that is, never executed) code block between two valid code blocks. The objective is to totally thwart a disassembler that has already been tricked into following an invalid path (typically a case of opaque predicates). Instructions contained within the junk code may be partially invalid, or may create branches to invalid addresses (such as in the middle of valid instructions) to over-complicate the CFG.

The most trivial example of junk code insertion could be as follows:

```
01: jmp label
02: <junk>
03: label:
04: <real code>
```

Here is something a bit more elaborate, using a dummy opaque predicate:

```
01: push eax
02: xor eax, eax
03: jz 9
04: <junk code start>
05: jg 4
06: inc esp
07: ret
08: <junk code end>
09: pop eax
```

The conditional jump at (address) line 3 is always true because the EAX register is zeroed by the XOR instruction at line 1. That means you have six bytes of junk code. This junk block uses instructions that will influence the disassembler, creating a new branch and seemingly inserting a function end (the RET instruction at line 9).

When generated appropriately, junk code blocks may be quite difficult to spot at first sight. Most often they will be removed from the disassembler's reach as a side effect of control flow deobfuscation (see http://www.openrce.org/blog/ view/1672/Control_Flow_Deobfuscation_ via_Abstract_Interpretation). In the last example, if the opaque predicate is detected as such, then no more paths lead to the junk code block. Like all the other techniques, if it is not differentiated sufficiently—for example, using a limited database of static patterns—its resilience and strength tend to be minimal.

Control-Flow Graph Flattening

The basic idea behind graph flattening is to replace all control structures with a unique switch statement, known as the *dispatcher*. A subgraph of the program's control-flow graph is selected (implementations often work at the level of functions) and transformed, at which time basic blocks may be reworked (split or merged). Each basic block is then responsible for updating the dispatcher's context (i.e., the subprogram's state) so that the dispatcher can link to the next basic block (see Figure 5-1). Relationships between basic blocks are now "hidden" within the dispatcher context's manipulation operations. Conditional jumps (as in block d) can easily be emulated using flags testing and IMUL instructions, or simple CMOV instructions.

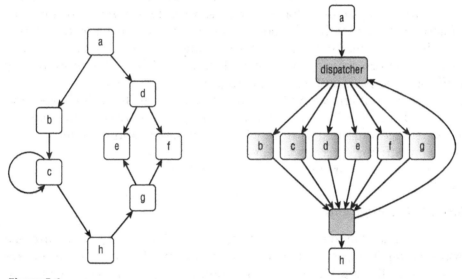

Figure 5-1

It goes without saying that a large part of this technique's resilience against static analysis rests on the ability to obfuscate the context's manipulations and transitions. Various features can be implemented to harden the problem, such as inter-procedural relationships, pointer aliasing, inserting dummy states, and so on.

In the same fashion as opaque predicates, CFG flattening can also be used to insert dead code paths and spurious basic blocks. A lot can be said about graph flattening and how to harden an implementation. The resulting graph offers no clues about the structure of the algorithm, and dispatch and context manipulation code also add an overhead that contributes to hiding the protected code. This technique is conceptually the same as code virtualization (virtual machine); it can be seen as partial virtualization that targets (virtualizes) only the control flow (not the data flow).

Should you want to see flattened code yourself, just grab a copy of a Flash plugin (such as NPSWF32.dll), disassemble the file, and look for functions with the biggest size. Flattened functions are easily recognizable.

Virtual Machines

Virtual machines (VMs) are a potent class of software protection and an especially complex transformation. A VM basically consists of an interpreter and some bytecode. The language supported by the interpreter is at the discretion of the protection. At compile-time, selected parts of code are compiled with respect to the VM's target architecture (they are retargeted) and then inserted into the protected program alongside the associated interpreter. At run-time, the interpreter assumes the bytecode execution (i.e., the translation from target architecture to original architecture). VMs usually come with sizeable overhead in terms of performance (particularly CPU time), which is why typically only specific, selected parts of the original program are virtualized.

Examples of well-known, VM-centered protections include VMProtect and CodeVirtualizer. We will later delve into the delightful activity of VM analysis. For now, suffice it to say that an attacker has to understand the interpreter in order to analyze the bytecode and eventually to create a compiler from target architecture to native architecture (unvirtualization).

White Box Cryptography

When the application to be protected cannot base its security on the use of a hardware component, or on a network server, you must hypothesize an attacker able to execute the application in an environment that he or she perfectly controls. The attacker model matching this situation, called the *white-box attack context* (WBAC), imposes a particular software implementation of classical cryptographic primitives.

Such mechanisms are tailor-made to ensure confidentiality of a secret key within an algorithm. Such a transformation (hiding a key in an encryption algorithm, with or without the help of environment interaction) can be formalized as an obfuscation transformation.

This section describes some negative and positive results concerning code obfuscation, and their impact on this key management problem.

A probabilistic algorithm O is an obfuscator if it satisfies the following properties, given by Barak et al.[2]:

- P and $O(P)$ compute the same function.
- The growth of execution time and space of $O(P)$ is at most polynomial in regard to execution time and space of program P.

- For any polynomial time probabilistic algorithm A, there exists a polynomial time probabilistic algorithm S and a negligible function m (a negligible function is a function that grows much slower than the inverse of any polynomial), such as the following: for all programs P,

$$| \, p[A(O(P))=1] - p[S^P(1^{|P|})=1] \, | \; \leq m(|P|)$$

The *virtual black box property* expresses the fact that the outputs distribution of any probabilistic analysis algorithm A applied to the obfuscated program $O(P)$ is almost everywhere equal to the outputs distribution of a simulator S making oracle access to program P. (Program S does not have access to the description of program P, but for any entry x, it is given access to $P(x)$ in polynomial time in regard to the size of P. An oracle access to program P is equivalent to an access to sole inputs/outputs of the program P.)

Intuitively, the virtual black box property simply stipulates that everything that can be calculated from the obfuscated version $O(P)$ can also be calculated via oracle access to P.

One of the main points about such an ideal obfuscator is that it does not exist. The proof is based on the construction of a program that cannot be obfuscated. This impossibility result demonstrates that a virtual black box generator—which could protect the code of any program by preventing it from revealing more information than is revealed by its inputs/outputs—does not exist. This impossibility result naturally leads to important outcomes for designers of obfuscation mechanisms (adapted to WBAC context).

Consider a practical application of obfuscation that consists of transforming a symmetric encryption into an asymmetric encryption, by obfuscating the private key encryption scheme. An unobfuscatable private key encryption scheme does exist if a private key encryption scheme exists. This clearly indicates that private key encryption schemes are not all well suited for obfuscation.

Note that this result does not prove that there is not some private key encryption scheme such that we can give to the attacker a circuit calculating the encryption algorithm without security loss. It does prove, however, that there is no general method enabling the transformation of any private key encryption scheme into a public key encryption system by obfuscating the encryption algorithm.

The problem of constructing a private key encryption scheme verifying the virtual black box property (thus resilient in the WBAC context) remains of interest for cryptography researchers, even if the impossibility result concerning a generic way to manage it may seem discouraging. White box DES and AES implementations proposals illustrate this interest.

Obfuscation by using a network of encoded lookup tables makes it possible to obtain from DES and AES algorithm versions that are more resilient in the white box attack context. However, effective cryptanalysis of DES (such as the one done by Goubin[24]) and AES (by Billet[5]) white box implementations has established that the problem of constructing a private key encryption scheme verifying the virtual black box property remains unsolved.

The ideal model of an obfuscator able to transform any program into a virtual black box cannot be implemented. In particular, there is no general transformation that enables, starting from an encryption algorithm and a key, obtaining an obfuscated version of this algorithm that could be published without leaking information about the key it contains.

However, this formalism does not establish that it is impossible to hide a key in an algorithm in order to transform a private key algorithm into public key encryption.

A method has been published (by Chow[9]) to make the extraction of the key difficult in the white box context. The principle is to implement a specialized version of the DES algorithm that embeds the key K, and which is able to do only one of the two operations, encrypt or decrypt. This implementation is resilient in a white box context because it is difficult to extract the key K by observing the operations carried out by the program and because it is difficult to forge the decryption function starting from the implementation of the encryption function, and inversely.

The main idea is to express the algorithm as a sequence (or a network) of lookup tables, and to obfuscate these tables by encoding their input/output. All the operations of the block cipher, such as the addition modulo 2 of the round key, are embedded in these lookup tables. These tables are randomized, in order to obfuscate their functioning.

Obfuscation of AES (described by Chow[10]) is done in a similar way as DES. The goal is still to embed the round keys in algorithm code, in order to avoid storing the key in static memory or loading it in dynamic memory at the time of execution. The technique used to securely embed these keys is (as for DES) to represent AES as a network of lookup tables, and to apply input/output encodings in order to hide the keys.

Achieving Security by Obscurity

So far, you have seen a great number of obfuscation techniques. Most of them are simple transformations that seem quite weak at first sight—and they are actually weak considered individually. How one can build security or trust from such primitives? The strength of an obfuscation system (or obfuscator) comes from the iterative and combined applications of a set of these techniques. Each successive application of a simple technique accrues into a strong indiscernible global transformation (well, at least that is the objective). An interesting analogy has been proposed by Jakubowski et al.[26] between round-based cryptography and iterated obfuscation. A cryptographic algorithm's round is made of basic arithmetic operations (addition, exclusive or, etc.) that perform trivial transformations on the inputs. Considered individually, a round is weak and prone to multiple forms of attacks. Nevertheless, applying a set of rounds multiple times can result in a somewhat secure algorithm. That is the objective of an obfuscator. The objective of the attacker is to discern the rounds from the global obfuscated form and to attack them at their weakest points.

Keep in mind that even if the obfuscator is not perfect, as soon as it raises the bar required to break into the protected code by a sufficient amount, this may be sufficient for the defender. For example, if a few weeks or months are required to break into a new version of software, the defender can take advantage of that period to work on new protections, protocol updates, and so on, and thus always be ahead of the game.

A Survey of Deobfuscation Techniques

Now that you have a better understanding of code obfuscation, the question is how can you, as a reverse engineer, take up the challenge? What means and tools are at your disposal to break into obfuscated code? Manual analysis of obfuscated code is a tedious, if not impossible, task; you'll want to boil down the problem to clean code analysis.

Because a manual approach using standard program analysis tools is fastidious, and considering the wide variety of obfuscation mechanisms that an analyst may face, it is necessary to find some models and criteria to design and evaluate deobfuscation algorithms. This section provides a brief overview of the problem from a more theoretical perspective, and describes some well-studied formal methods that can be used to design more generic deobfuscation tools and automate as much as possible the tasks undertaken by an analyst.

The Nature of Deobfuscation: Transformation Inversion

In order to undo obfuscation transformation, several software analysis techniques are available. This section covers the following:

- The notion of decidable approximation
- Some methods, either static or dynamic, that can be used, and advantages that can be gained from hybrid static dynamic methods (some of them are presented later through the use of specialized tools)
- Some criteria that can always been applied to evaluate an analysis algorithm and from which it is possible to derive some security criteria about obfuscation robustness (and in a dual way a deobfuscation transformation efficiency)
- Open problems and new trends concerning hybrid dynamic/static analysis and formalization of deobfuscation

The subject is vast, and there is still no consensus about the terminology for the various specialized areas of research in the literature. The goal of this section is thus to provide readers with some keywords to enable a global view, and some useful references for interested readers who want to supplement their knowledge in this domain.

You can observe several dichotomies in the field of software analysis. Some analysis techniques are described as *static* or *dynamic,* even if this distinction sometimes seems quite artificial. (This distinction is discussed by Yannis Smaragdakis and Christoph Csallner[38].) Otherwise, analysis algorithms are qualified as *sound* or *complete*, but these important characteristics may have different meanings in the literature. Finally, program analyses are described as *over-approximation* or *under-approximation,* but this distinction also seems somewhat artificial because some analysis methods appear to use both over- and under-approximation.

The remainder of this section discusses both the "synergy" and "duality" of static and dynamic analysis (also discussed by Michael D. Ernst[20]), first introducing the formal model of abstract interpretation and then providing several analysis examples in relation to deobfuscation.

Finding a Decidable Approximation of the Concrete Semantics

The purpose of any program analysis is to check whether the program satisfies a certain property. Unfortunately, the question is generally *undecidable* for any non-trivial property—that is to say, you cannot design an algorithm to determine whether the property holds for the program. To overcome this difficulty, one solution is to abstract the concrete behaviors of the program into a decidable approximation. The purpose of *abstract interpretation* is to formalize this idea of approximation in a unified framework. (Readers can refer to the paper by Patrick Cousot and Radia Cousot.[14])

The *semantics* of a program represent all of its possible concrete behavior, including its interaction with any possible computer system environment. Among the most precise (concrete) semantics are the so-called *trace semantics.* This semantics includes all finite and infinite sequences of states and transitions. Where X is the set of execution traces (finite and infinite), you can express the trace semantics as the least solution (for the *computational partial ordering*) of a fixpoint equation X=F(X).

An *abstract domain* is an abstraction of a concrete semantics. The goal of abstract interpretation is to provide computable, fixpoint approximations of abstract domains, thus defining computable *abstract semantics*. Obviously, the coarser the abstract semantics, the fewer questions it can answer.

All abstractions of a semantics can be organized in a hierarchy (described by Cousot[16]), from the most precise to the coarsest. More precisely, abstract semantics can be placed on a lattice, and the *approximation partial ordering* of this lattice can be used to characterize the concreteness (or precision) of abstract semantics, and thus the sets of questions they are able to answer.

Abstract interpretation generally applies to static analysis, through an over-approximation of the concrete semantics. You might notice that, in a dual way and according to the "dual principle" of lattice theory, it should also apply to dynamic analysis, even if there are not currently many works on this subject. You will see in the next section that relations and synergy between static and dynamic analysis lead to practical hybrid dynamic/static methods, making it possible both for a dynamic approach to gain in coverage and for a static approach to gain in precision.

Dynamic and Static Analyses Form a Continuum

Static analysis is the discipline of automatically inferring information about computer programs without running them (it thus applies to a "static" representation of the program). Static analysis tries to derive properties (invariants) that hold for all executions of the program, through a conservative over-approximation of its concrete semantics.

An example of such static analysis is the *constant propagation* algorithm, which aims to determine for each program instruction whether a variable has a constant value whenever the control flow reaches that instruction. Information about constants is useful in the context of program compilation, optimization, and recompilation. It is used, for example, for dead code and dead execution path deletion (by replacing all uses of constant variables by their constant values, you may be able to identify constant conditional branches, which are conditioned by constant predicates).

Among the many optimization techniques, *partial evaluation* techniques (described by Beckman et al.[3]) must be kept in mind in the context of reverse engineering. A partial evaluator specializes a program with regard to part of its input data. You expect the program's concrete semantics to be preserved by the specialization process and the resulting program's syntactic representation to be optimized for the class of inputs used, and as a result simpler to understand.

Another important class of optimization techniques includes *slicing* techniques (described by Weiser[42]), which also aim to simplify the program under consideration, but in this case by deleting those parts of the program that are irrelevant according to a criterion provided by the analyst. A *static slicing criterion* includes a set of variables and a chosen point of interest. A *dynamic slicing criterion* completes a static criterion with the information corresponding to some concrete execution. Slicing is of great interest in the reverse engineering context, because it is representative of the way a reverser mentally slices a program when attempting to understand its inner working.

In contrast to static analysis, *dynamic analysis* is the discipline of automatically inferring information about a running computer program. Dynamic analysis derives properties that hold for one or more executions of a program, through a precise under-approximation.

A common method of dynamic analysis is *dynamic testing*, which executes a program with several inputs and checks the program's response. Generally, test cases explore only a subset of the possible executions of the program.

In order to enlarge the coverage of dynamic testing, the principle of *symbolic execution* (described by Boyer[6]) uses symbolic values rather than concrete inputs. At any point during symbolic execution, a *symbolic state* of the program is updated. This symbolic state consists of a *symbolic store* and a *path constraint*. The symbolic store contains the symbolic values, and the path constraint is a formula that records the history of all conditional branches taken until the current instruction.

At a given instruction of the program, you can use a *constraint solver* (SMT or SAT solver) to determine the corresponding path constraint. A satisfying assignment provides concrete inputs with which the program reaches the program instruction. By generating new tests and exploring new paths, you can increase the coverage of dynamic testing.

Unfortunately, constraints generated during symbolic execution may be too complex for the constraint solver. If the constraint solver is unable to compute a satisfying assignment, you cannot determine whether a path is feasible or not.

Concolic execution (described by Godefroid[23] and Sen[37]) provides a solution to this problem in many situations. The idea is to perform both symbolic execution and concrete execution of a program. When the path constraint is too complex for the constraint solver, you can use the concrete information to simplify the constraint (typically by replacing some of the symbolic values with concrete values). You can then expect to find a satisfying assignment of this simplified constraint.

Because symbolic execution is unable to handle an unbounded loop, which results in infinite symbolic execution paths, it must under-approximate the concrete semantics of the program. You can perform this simplification by fixing some arbitrary loop limit. Another solution is to use symbolic execution in conjunction with a static analysis inferring loop invariants.

It appears that dynamic and static analysis approaches form a continuum. As an illustration, dynamic testing, symbolic execution, and abstract interpretation are three ways of approximating the concrete semantics of a program. Dynamic analysis uses concrete values and explores a subset of concrete transitions. Symbolic execution clearly lies between dynamic testing and static analysis. It rests on a more abstract semantics, but also an under-approximation. An abstract interpreter over-approximates the concrete semantics of the program.

However, the borderline between those analysis approaches is not so easy to define. For example, symbolic execution can be defined as a logical abstract interpreter, operating over the abstract domain of logical formulas.

In conclusion, many static analysis methods are improved by the use of a dynamic analysis–based refinement. Conversely, the coverage of many dynamic analysis methods can be increased by using traditional static analysis methods. Thus, the investigation of hybrid dynamic/static approaches is of great interest, especially in the context of reverse engineering. The soundness and completeness criteria can be used to capture this synergy.

Soundness and Completeness

You can formulate any program analysis problem as verification that the program satisfies a property. Two fundamental concepts can be used to characterize an analysis algorithm: its *soundness* and its *completeness*. These concepts, traditionally applied to logical systems, can also be applied to program analysis. Unfortunately, because of their dual natures (soundness and completeness correspond to converse implications in logic), there is still no consensus regarding their application to the various specialized areas of research in the literature.

Given a property, a *sound* program analysis identifies all violations of the property. However, because it over-approximates the behaviors of the program, it may also report violations of the property that cannot occur. For example, a sound error detection algorithm detects every possible error, though some of them may not occur at run-time.

A sound partial evaluation algorithm preserves the original program's concrete semantics, in the sense that the specialized program does not produce any output value that is not produced by the original program (even if it may not be able to produce all of them).

A sound symbolic execution guarantees that because a symbolic constraint path is satisfiable, there must be a concrete execution path that reaches the corresponding concrete state (even if some reachable concrete state does not have a corresponding symbolic state).

A sound abstract interpreter preserves the program's concrete semantics. If it claims that an optimization transformation is possible for a program, then the optimization can be applied without breaking the program semantics. Observe, however, that it may be unable to answer the question for some optimizations. It can claim that an optimization is unsafe even if it is in fact possible to apply the transformation (without any destructive effect). Some potential optimizations will not be applied. The soundness of the abstract interpreter is relative to which questions it can answer correctly, despite the loss of information. In that sense, it is conservative. Technically, the least fixpoints computed by an abstract interpreter represent at least all occurring run-time concrete states.

For example, a constant propagation algorithm is sound when any constant it detects is indeed a constant. However, some constants may be not detected. Given a property, a *complete* analysis algorithm reports a violation of the property only if there is a concrete violation of the property. However, because it under-approximates the behaviors of the program, some concrete violations of the property may not be reported.

A complete partial evaluation algorithm results in the generation of a specialized program that is able to produce the same output values as the original program for the intended input values. If unsound, it may produce unexpected output values (i.e., not produced by the original program).

A complete symbolic execution covers all concrete transitions. It guarantees that if a concrete execution state is reachable, then there must be a corresponding symbolic state. Because symbolic execution is unable to handle an unbounded loop, which results in infinite symbolic execution paths, it must under-approximate the concrete semantics of the program (typically by providing some loop limit). Therefore, symbolic execution algorithms are most often incomplete.

A complete abstract interpreter is the most precise for answering a given set of questions. Technically, this means that every state represented by the least fixpoint is reachable for some concrete input. For example, a complete constant propagation algorithm would be able to detect every constant in a program.

We have presented some criteria (soundness and completeness) that can always be applied to evaluate an analysis algorithm. It is possible to derive from them some security criteria about obfuscation robustness (and, in a dual way, deobfuscation transformation efficiency).

Abstract interpretation can be used for modeling any program transformation (refer to the paper by Patrick and Radia Cousot[15]). By considering the syntax of a program as an abstraction of its concrete semantics, we can formalize any syntactic program transformation as an abstract interpretation of the corresponding semantic transformation.

A particular application of this concerns obfuscation and deobfuscation transformations modeling. Mila Dalla Preda and Roberto Giacobazzi[18] investigate the semantic transformations corresponding to opaque predicate insertion. By modeling deobfuscation as an abstraction interpretation, they observe that breaking opaque predicates corresponds to having complete abstraction. The completeness criterion turns out to be of special interest in terms of qualifying both deobfuscator effectiveness and opaque predicate robustness.

In conclusion, many methods already used in program analysis and compilation are of interest in the context of reverse engineering. As demonstrated earlier, the frontier between static and dynamic analysis is not so obvious. Currently, the abstract interpretation model seems to be sufficiently general to apply to both types of analyses. The soundness and completeness criteria are of special interest when modeling obfuscation and deobfuscation transformations in the abstract interpretation framework. You have seen that both the soundness and the completeness of an algorithm can be defined for static and dynamic analyses (data flow analyses, partial evaluation, slicing, symbolic execution), which are good candidates to represent the actions conducted by reversers when they try to simplify the representation of an obfuscated program. Using the abstract interpretation model, static and dynamic analyses appear to be dual in nature. This duality and the gain that can be obtained from a synergy between static and dynamic methods lead to new possibilities that must be investigated in the future, through the study of hybrid methods.

This section presented some academic models and criteria, as well as dynamic and static analysis methods, that can be useful for designing and evaluating deobfuscation algorithms. It also stressed the importance of hybrid methods. The next section presents some of the tools currently available to assist in undoing obfuscation transformations.

Deobfuscation Tools

In this section we discuss some of the tools that you can use to reverse engineer obfuscated code and especially the features they offer to ease your job. Please note that this list is not meant to be exhaustive in any way; it is based on the experience of some of the authors and seeks to present different categories of tools.

IDA

IDA is the state-of-the-art tool for reverse engineering binary code. Throwing the binary one wants to analyze into IDA is a common reflex, so there's probably no need to introduce this tool here; otherwise, readers can refer to the *The IDA Pro Book* by Chris Eagle (No Starch Press, 2011). Regarding the specific topic that interests us here, dealing with obfuscated code using IDA is problematic (although not impossible) for a few reasons:

- That's not the purpose for which IDA is primarily intended. Obfuscated code is a very particular case, and handling every specific situation/trick would be an endless job; thus it's better not to start on this path.

- We have very little control over the disassembler, a point that greatly impedes us when encountering obfuscation schemes that break/disrupt/destroy the control-flow graph. IDA's disassembler is really easy to confuse and one often ends up with the chicken-and-egg problem: To recover the control flow one needs to clean the data flow, but to clean the data flow one needs the control flow.

- IDA itself doesn't offer any sort of intermediate representation (IR) or at least instruction semantics, so advanced analysis of its output is not trivial.

In 2008 at the ICAR workshop (`http://www.hex-rays.com/ products/ida/ support/ppt/caro_obfuscation.ppt`), Ilfak Guilfanov offered some useful tips on how to use specific features of IDA:

- Graph-level block merging to simplify the CFG
- Event-driven, on-the-fly modification of the graph using hooks like `grcode_changed_graph` (see `graph.hpp` in the SDK)
- Develop specific plugins

IDA can be extended using scripts (either `IDC` or `IDAPython`) or plugins (see IDA's SDK). If you were to implement some advanced analysis, that's where you would be able to interact.

To that end, some plugins have been developed as deobfuscation frameworks (for example, Branko Spasojevic's Optimice plugin, `http://optimice. googlecode.com`). Trying to address some of the issues previously mentioned, including instruction semantics—based on the x86 Opcode and Instruction Reference (`http://ref.x86asm.net/`)—the plugin offers CFG reduction, peephole optimizations, and dead code removal.

Metasm

Metasm (`http://metasm.cr0.org`) is open source framework (released under the GNU Lesser GPL v2) developed by Yoann Guillot. It defines itself as an assembly manipulation suite. The framework, written in Ruby, actually offers cross-architecture assembler, disassembler, compiler, linker, and debugger features. Currently supported processors are Intel x86/x64, MIPS, PPC, Sh4, and ARCompact. Most common file formats are supported as well, such as MZ, PE/ COFF, ELF, Mach-O, and so on.

Disassembler Callbacks

The behavior of the disassemblery can be dynamically modified using a set of exported callbacks of the `Disassembler` class. The two most useful for deobfuscation are as follows:

- `callback_newaddr`—This is called each time a path is discovered and is about to be disassembled. At this point you can inspect the path backward or forward for unseemliness; most important, you can modify the behavior of the disassembly engine—removing a spurious control transfer, thwarting a disassembler trap, etc.
- `callback_newinstr`—As its name suggests, your callback is called each time a new instruction is disassembled.

Instruction Semantics

One of the framework's key features is *backtracking* (think of it as program slicing). This feature is at the heart of its disassembly engine. It enables very precise control flow recovery, at the cost of performance. Built on top of this feature, the framework's API also offers a method to compute the semantics of a basic block. Metasm does not use a strict intermediate language, however; it relies on a description of the semantics of each instruction. The associated terminology in the framework is `binding`. Metasm separates control flow and data flow semantics encoding. Four types are used to describe the semantics of an instruction:

- ▪ Numerical value
- ▪ `Symbol`—Whatever is not a numerical value, based on Ruby's symbol type
- ▪ `Expression`: `Expression[operand1, (operator), (operand2)]`—An operand can be any of the four types.
- ▪ `Indirection`—Memory indirection `Indirection[target, size, origin]`

The following snippet will introduce you to the Metasm instructions' binding:

```
# encoding: ASCII-8BIT
#!/usr/bin/env ruby
require "metasm"
include Metasm

# produce x86 code
sc = Metasm::Shellcode.assemble(Metasm::Ia32.new, <<EOS)
add eax, 0x1234
mov [eax], 0x1234
ret
EOS

dasm = sc.init_disassembler

# disassemble handler code
dasm.disassemble(0)

# get decoded instruction at address 0
# then its basic block
bb = dasm.di_at(0).block

# display disassembled code
puts "\n[+] generated code:"
puts bb.list

# run though the basic block's list of decoded instruction
bb.list.each{|di|
    puts "\n[+] #{di.instruction}"
    sem = di.backtrace_binding()
```

```
puts " data flow:"
sem.each{|key, value| puts   * #{key} => #{value}"}

# does instruction modify the instruction pointer ?
if di.opcode.props[:setip]
    puts " control flow:"
    # then display control flow semantics
    puts "  * #{dasm.get_xrefs_x(di)}"
end
}
```

For each `DecodedInstruction`, you call the `backtrace_binding` method.
It returns a hash. Each key/value pair represents an assignment of the key
according to the value and expresses outputs with respect to inputs. Running
the scripts produces the following result:

```
[+] generated code:
0 add eax, 1234h
5 mov dword ptr [eax], 1234h
0bh ret ; endsub entrypoint_0

[+] add eax, 1234h
  data flow:
    * eax => eax+1234h
    * eflag_z => ((eax+1234h)&0ffffffffh)==0
    * eflag_s => (((eax+1234h)>>1fh)&1)!=0
    * eflag_c => ((eax&0ffffffffh)+1234h)>0ffffffffh
    * eflag_o => (((eax>>1fh)&1)==0)&&((((eax+1234h)>>1fh)&1)!=0)!=
                 ((((eax+1234h)>>1fh)&1)!=0))

[+] mov dword ptr [eax], 1234h
  data flow:
    * dword ptr [eax] => 4660

[+] ret
  data flow:
    * esp => esp+4+0
  control flow:
    * [Indirection[Expression[:esp], 4, 0xb]]
```

The RET instruction is quite representative of the distinction between data
flow and control flow. The `get_xrefs_x` method provided by the disassembler
object returns a list (a Ruby `Array` object) of possible values for the instruction
pointer. For that specific instruction, it is an indirection whose target is the ESP
register and whose size is 4 (for the Ia32 architecture)—i.e., `dword ptr [ESP]`;
`0xb` is the address in the program where the indirection occurs.

Backtracking and Slicing

So far, you have seen how the semantics are described for each isolated instruction. Now consider instructions within a control flow and how an instruction's

binding can be used. For this purpose, the following example demonstrates a typical dynamic jump computation pattern:

```
# encoding: ASCII-8BIT
#!/usr/bin/env ruby
require "metasm"
include Metasm

# produce handler's x86 code
sc = Metasm::Shellcode.assemble(Metasm::Ia32.new, <<EOS)
entry:
    mov ecx, 1
    shl ecx, 0xA
    add edx, 0xBADC0FFE
    mov eax, 0x100000
    lea eax, [ecx+eax]
    add ecx, 0xBADC0FFE
    jmp eax
EOS

# disassemble handler code
dasm = sc.init_disassembler
dasm.disassemble(0)

# get basic block
bb = dasm.block_at(0)
target = dasm.get_xrefs_x(bb.list.last).first
puts "[+] jmp target: #{target}"

# backtrace
values = dasm.backtrace(target, bb.list.last.address,
    {:log => bt_log = [], :include_start => true})
```

get_xrefs_x tells you which target is the final jump instruction. Then the backtrace method is used to *walk back* through the control flow, following variable dependencies, until it reaches variable assignations or simply hits its complexity limit. Each step of the backtracker is stored within the array bt_log. The following adds a few more lines to nicely output the record:

```
bt_log.each{|entry|
    case type = entry.first
    when :start
        entry, expr, addr = entry
        puts "[start] backtacking expr #{expr} from 0x#{addr.to_s(16)}"

    when :di
        entry, to, from, instr = entry
        puts "[update] instr #{instr},\n  -> update expr from #{from} to
#{to}\n"

    when :found
        entry, final = entry
```

```
       puts "[found] possible value: #{final.first}\n"

    when :up
        entry, to, from, addr_down, addr_up = entry
        puts "[up] addr 0x#{addr_down.to_s(16)} -> 0x#{addr_up.to_s(16)}"
    end
}
```

Here is the output from the sample:

```
[+] jmp target: eax
[start] backtacking expr eax from 0x1c
[update] instr 13h lea eax, [ecx+eax],
  -> update expr from eax to ecx+eax
[update] instr 0eh mov eax, 100000h,
  -> update expr from ecx+eax to ecx+100000h
[update] instr 5 shl ecx, 0ah,
  -> update expr from ecx+100000h to (ecx<<0ah)+100000h
[update] instr 0 mov ecx, 1,
  -> update expr from (ecx<<0ah)+100000h to 100400h
[found] possible value: 100400h
```

The backtracking engine has been able to *walk back* the instruction flow to compute the final value of the backtracked expression. A simplification engine enables solving (or at least reducing) expressions at both the symbolic and numerical levels.

From the log record it is even possible to extract a slice—that is, the minimal subset of the original program that produces the studied effect (the slicing criterion). In this case the slice will contain all the instructions involved in the computation of the JMP destination:

```
# DecodedInstruction object is the 3rd item of :id entry
slice = bt_log.select{|e| e.first==:di}.map{|e| e[3]}.reverse
puts slice
```

The slice is as follows:

```
0 mov ecx, 1
5 shl ecx, 0ah
0eh mov eax, 100000h
13h lea eax, [ecx+eax]
```

Note how nonsignificant computations/assignations (e.g., the ones using the constant 0BADC0FFEh) have been eliminated from this list.

That sample is an ideal case: The expression can statically be reduced/solved into a numerical value. Now, imagine you remove the first assembly line (MOV ECX, 1)—within the basic block scope ECX is undefined—and then redo the analysis:

```
[+] jmp target: eax
[start] backtacking expr eax from 0x17
[update] instr 0eh lea eax, [ecx+eax],
  -> update expr from eax to ecx+eax
```

```
[update] instr 9 mov eax, 100000h,
  -> update expr from ecx+eax to ecx+100000h
[update] instr 0 shl ecx, 0ah,
  -> update expr from ecx+100000h to (ecx<<0ah)+100000h
```

The return value is an object of type `Expression` whose value is `(ECX<<0Ah)+100000h`.

This example is fairly trivial. The capacity of the backtracker goes far beyond that. The following modifies the preceding sample to include a more complex control-flow graph:

```
# produce handler's x86 code
sc = Metasm::Shellcode.assemble(Metasm::Ia32.new, <<EOS)
entry:
    mov ecx, 1
    test edx, edx
    jnz label inc cl
label:
    shl ecx, 0xA
    add edx, 0xBADC0FFE
    mov eax, 0x100000
    lea eax, [ecx+eax]
    add ecx, 0xBADC0FFE
    jmp eax
EOS


# disassemble handler code
dasm = sc.init_disassembler
dasm.disassemble(0)


# get last basic block
bblist = dasm.instructionblocks.sort{|b1, b2| b1.address <=> b2.address}
bblist.each{|bb| puts "-\n", bb.list}
bb = bblist.last
```

Basically, this has inserted an instruction (TEST EDX, EDX) controlling a conditional jump; in one case ECX is incremented, in the other it is not. The updated output is as follows:

```
[+] jmp target: eax
[start] backtacking expr eax from 0x21
[update] instr 18h lea eax, [ecx+eax],
  -> update expr from eax to ecx+eax
[update] instr 13h mov eax, 100000h,
  -> update expr from ecx+eax to ecx+100000h
[update] instr 0ah shl ecx, 0ah,
  -> update expr from ecx+100000h to (ecx<<0ah)+100000h
[up]    addr 0xa -> 0x9
[up]    addr 0xa -> 0x7
[update] instr 0 mov ecx, 1,
  -> update expr from (ecx<<0ah)+100000h to 100400h
[found] possible value: 100400h
```

```
[update] instr 9 inc ecx,
  -> update expr from (ecx<<0ah)+100000h to ((ecx+1)<<0ah)+100000h
[up]     addr 0x9 -> 0x7
[update] instr 0 mov ecx, 1,
  -> update expr from ((ecx+1)<<0ah)+100000h to 100800h
[found] possible value: 100800h
```

The backtracker returns an array of two possible values: 100400h or 100800h.
Note how it has followed the control flow over the CFG. (Both branches of the
conditional have been followed.) An [up] tag indicates a basic block's crossing.
Backtracking really is at the heart of the disassembler and produces a more
accurate disassembly. Obviously, this feature comes with severe performance
penalties (remember the trade-off between computability and precision).

Code Binding

You know how to obtain the semantics of an isolated instruction, and you know
how to backtrack a value and compute a slice for that particular value. What if
you could generalize this process and compute the semantics of a basic block?
This is another very powerful feature of Metasm: the code_binding method,
provided by the disassembler object. It totally relies on the backtracking feature.
Here is its usage on the last basic block of the previous example:

```
# compute basic block's semantics
bbsem = dasm.code_binding(bb.list.first.address, bb.list.last.address)
puts "\n[+] basic block semantics"
bbsem.each{|key, value| puts "    * #{key} => #{value}"}
```

Its output is as follows:

```
[+] basic block semantics
    * eax => ((ecx<<0ah)+100000h)
    * ecx => ((ecx<<0ah)+badc0ffeh)
    * edx => (edx+badc0ffeh)
```

Miasm

Miasm (http://code.google.com/p/smiasm) is a reverse engineering framework
developed by Fabrice Desclaux that offers PE/ELF manipulation, assembling,
and disassembling (currently supports Ia32, ARM, PPC, and Java bytecode).
Like Metasm, Miasm is open source and released under the GNU Lesser GPL
v2, so you can delve into its engine to customize specific needs. The examples
provided in this section are based on the latest revision of MIASM available at
the time of writing (changeset:270:6ee8e9a58648).

The framework relies on an intermediate language. That means most common instructions have their semantics encoded as a list of expressions. "List"
is to be understood in its Python meaning (i.e., an ordered set of objects).

The grammar of Miasm's IR makes use of nine basic expression types, the most important of which are as follows:

- ExprInt—Numerical value
- ExprId—Identifier/symbol, whatever is not a numerical value; for example, registers are defined as ExprId
- ExprAff—Affectation a = b
- ExprCond—Ternary/conditional operator a ? b : c
- ExprMem—Memory indirection
- ExprOp—Operation op(a,b,...)

It also provides full support for slices (think of it as an object to represent bitfields) and slice composition. The IR allows symbolic computations and is equipped with an expression simplification engine.

For each supported processor, a "sem" suffixed file describes the semantics of most common instructions. See, for example, the ADD semantics as defined in "miasm/arch/ia32 sem.py":

```
def add(info, a, b):
    e= []
    c = ExprOp('+', a, b)
    e+=update_flag_arith(c)
    e+=update_flag_af(c)
    e+=update_flag_add(a, b, c)
    e.append(ExprAff(a, c))
    return e
```

This function builds the semantics of the instructions based on its two operands (a and b). One can easily write a piece of script to demonstrate these features:

```
#! /usr/bin/env python

from miasm.arch.ia32_arch import *
from miasm.tools.emul_helper import *

# assemble instruction asm at given address

def instr_sem(instr, address):
    print "\n[+] instruction %s @ 0x%x" % (instr, address)
    binary = x86_mn.asm(instr)
    di = x86_mn.dis(binary[0])
    semantics = get_instr_expr(di, address)
    for expr in semantics:
        print "  %s" % expr
```

```
instr_sem("add eax, 0x1234", 0)
instr_sem("mov [eax], 0x1234", 0)
instr_sem("ret", 0)
instr_sem("je 0x1000", 0)
```

Here is the output:

```
[+] instruction add eax, 0x1234 @ 0x0
  zf = ((eax + 0x1234) == 0x0)
  nf = ((0x1 == ((eax + 0x1234) >> 0x1F)) & 0x1)
  pf = (parity (eax + 0x1234)) af = (((eax + 0x1234) & 0x10) == 0x10)
  cf = ((0x1 == (((eax ^ 0x1234) ^ (eax + 0x1234)) >> 0x1F)) ^
        (0x1 == ((((eax + 0x1234)) & (! (eax ^ 0x1234))) >> 0x1F)))
  of = (0x1 == (((eax ^ (eax + 0x1234)) & (! (eax ^ 0x1234))) >> 0x1F))
  eax = (eax + 0x1234)

[+] instruction mov [eax], 0x1234 @ 0x0
  @32[eax] = 0x1234

[+] instruction ret @ 0x0
  esp = (esp + (0x4 + 0x0))
  eip = @32[esp]

[+] instruction je 0x1000 @ 0x0
  eip = (zf == 0x1)?(0x1000,0)
```

The ADD instruction's semantics seem the most complex, due to the flags update. Here is the MOV instruction's semantics with an explicit typing of object:

```
[+] instruction mov [eax], 0x1234 @ 0x0
  ExprAff( ExprMem(@32[ExprId(eax)]) = ExprInt(0x1234) )
```

This is a very appreciable and powerful feature. Built upon the IR, there is a *just-in-time (JIT)* compilation feature whereby code is first disassembled, translated into IR, then regenerated as native code for execution. The documentation and samples provide use cases of Miasm for packer/VM analysis as well as binary instrumentation.

VxStripper

VxStripper is a binary rewriting tool, developed by Sébastien Josse. Designed for analysis of protected and potentially hostile binary programs, it dynamically extracts an intermediate representation of a binary executable and all the necessary information to apply certain simplifications, making the binary inner workings easier to understand for the analyst.

One of the main motivations behind the design and implementation options of this tool is to circumvent current limitations of existing malware and binary programs analysis solutions. (Many tools come with their own intermediate representation—non-exportable, sometimes proprietary—making difficult their integration. Moreover, many of them are not suitable for analysis of hostile or protected code.) The goal is to get as much information as possible from a binary program that uses all available techniques and tools to protect this information. The idea is to instrument a virtual computer processing unit and a guest operating system in a non-intrusive way to dynamically get information required to rebuild the program and simplify its representation. This tool is based on the dynamic binary translator engine of QEMU and on the LLVM compilation chain.

LLVM (Low Level Virtual Machine) is a compilation chain that comes with a consequent set of optimizations that can be applied across the entire lifetime of a program. LLVM uses a strongly typed RISC-like instruction set and a static single assignment (SSA) representation (using this representation, each temporary variable is assigned only once). LLVM includes many binary back-ends (x86, x86-64, SPARC, PowerPC, ARM, MIPS, CellSPU, XCore, MSP430, MicroBlaze, PTX) and some source code back-ends (C, C++). Readers can refer to the paper by Lattner[31] for further details about LLVM.

The QEMU (Quick EMUlator) Dynamic Binary Translator (DBT) is used to dynamically translate the binary code from the guest CPU architecture to the host CPU architecture, through the use of an IR called TCG (Tiny Code Generator). This language consists of simple RISC-like instructions called *micro-operations*. The binary translation consists of two stages. The guest binary code is first translated in sequences of TCG instructions, called *translation blocks* (DBT front end). Then, the translation blocks are converted into code executable by the host CPU (DBT back end). QEMU's DBT comes with many binary front ends (x86, x86-64, ARM, ETRAX CRIS, MIPS, Micro Blaze, PowerPC, SH4, and SPARC). Readers can refer to the paper from Bellard[4] for further details about QEMU.

VxStripper inherits from QEMU the many binary front ends, and from LLVM the many back ends, providing at reasonable cost a complete binary rewriting framework. The rewriting functions are implemented as LLVM passes.

Its current design builds upon work already done to convert TCG IR to LLVM IR (LLVM-QEMU, described by Scheller[36], and S2E, described by Chipounov[8]), as well as upon design algorithms presented by Josse.[27, 28]

One of the goals of this tool is collaboration with the many software analysis tools based on the LLVM compilation chain, through an "exported" representation of the malware program. This binary analysis tool is especially designed to solve the problem of hostile programs analysis. The goal is to automate the often fastidious and repetitive tasks driven by an analyst.

This compilation chain is based on a modular and evolutionary architecture, making it possible to apply the same transformations to a wide variety of software and hardware architectures. It is based on a modern compilation chain, providing efficient intermediate representation and functionalities.

Vellvm (Verified LLVM), described by Zhao,[43] provides formal tools to reason on transformations that operate on LLVM's intermediate representation. Vellvm can be used to extract formally verified implementations of deobfuscation passes implemented in VxStripper.

QEMU DBT Extension

You have seen that the QEMU DBT engine performs the dynamic translation of the binary code from the guest processor architecture to the host processor architecture by using the TCG intermediate representation.

Using a simple example, the following instruction demonstrates what this language looks like:

```
0x0040104c:  push   0xa
```

The preceding instruction is translated as follows in the QEMU TCG representation:

```
(1)     movi_i32 tmp0,$0xa
(2)     mov_i32 tmp2,esp
(3)     movi_i32 tmp13,$0xfffffffc
(4)     add_i32 tmp2,tmp2,tmp13
(5)     qemu_st32 tmp0,tmp2,$0x1
(6)     mov_i32 esp,tmp2
(7)     movi_i32 tmp4,$0x40104e
(8)     st_i32 tmp4,env,$0x30
(9)     exit_tb $0x0
```

This TCG instructions block emulates the execution of the push instruction on the software CPU. The performed operations are as follows: The integer `0xa` is stored in the variable `tmp0` (line 1). This variable is then stored on the stack (lines 2–6). The address of the instruction following the current instruction is stored in `tmp4` (line 7) and then stored in the QEMU VPU register `cc_op`. The last instruction (line 9) indicates the end of the TCG block.

The tool modifies the DBT mechanism in such a way that the instrumentation function of the virtual CPU is systematically invoked before the execution of a translation block. To achieve this, you add an extra micro operation (`op_callback`) that takes as operand the address of the instrumentation function (`vpu_callback`). The resulting TCG code is as follows:

```
(1)     op_callback @vpu_callback
(2      movi_i32 tmp0,$0xa
(3)     mov_i32 tmp2,esp
(4)     movi_i32 tmp13,$0xfffffffc
(5)     add_i32 tmp2,tmp2,tmp13
(6)     qemu_st32 tmp0,tmp2,$0x1
(7)     mov_i32 esp,tmp2
(8)     movi_i32 tmp4,$0x40104e
(9)     st_i32 tmp4,env,$0x30
(10)    exit_tb $0x0
```

This mechanism enables you to execute your instrumentation code at each execution cycle of the virtual CPU. With access to VPU registers and to the virtual PC memory, you can acquire a process context and extract information about its interactions with the guest operating system.

By also instrumenting the load and storing TCG instructions, you can extract information about the interactions of the target process with the memory of the guest system. Thanks to this information, you can recover the relocation information of the process.

Now that you have seen how to modify the QEMU virtual CPU to enable the systematic invocation of your instrumentation function, let's examine the translation of TCG intermediate representation to LLVM representation. The result of translating the preceding TCG block is as follows:

```
(1)   %esp_v.i = load i32* @esp_ptr
(2)   %tmp2_v.i = add i32 %esp_v.i, -4
(3)   %4 = inttoptr i32 %tmp2_v.i to i32*
(4)   store i32 10, i32* %4
(5)   store i32 %tmp2_v.i, i32* @esp_ptr
(6)   store i32 4198478, i32* %next.i
(7)   store i32 0, i32* %ret.i
```

The integer 0xa is stored at the address pointed to by the variable %4, which is equivalent to storing it on the stack (lines 1–4). The address of the instruction following the current instruction is stored in the variable %next.i (line 6). The last instruction (line 7) finishes the LLVM block.

After the normalization process, this LLVM block is compiled to the following assembly code:

```
401269!  mov dword ptr [esp-14h], 0ah
```

Now that you have an overview of the main modifications applied to the QEMU emulator, as shown schematically in Figure 5-2, the following section describes the general architecture of the tool.

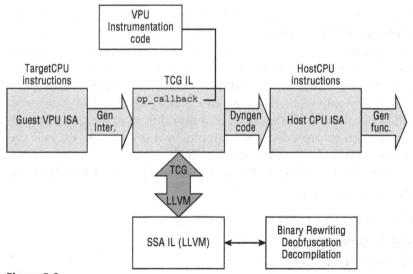

Figure 5-2

Architecture of VxStripper

VxStripper implements an extended DBT engine and several specialized analysis functions (see Figure 5-3) to observe the target program and its execution environment.

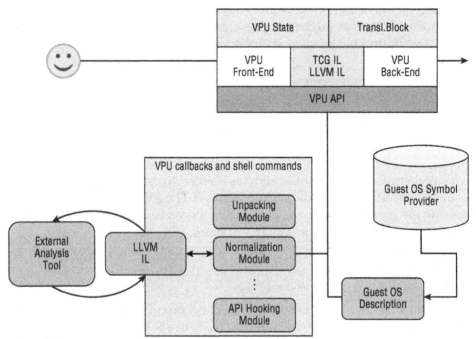

Figure 5-3

A module manager handles activation and collaboration between these analysis functions, implemented as plugins.

These analysis functions extract semantic information from the target program. This information can be the trace of its interactions with APIs of the guest operating system, or the way it handles objects and structures of the guest operating system's executive or kernel, or more simply its machine code trace.

The extraction of this information rests on a description of the guest operating system, which can be provided, for example, by a symbol server, as is the case for the family of Windows operating systems.

Among the modules already implemented, you notably find the following:

- An API hooking module
- A forensics analysis module
- An unpacking module
- A normalization module

API Hooking

The native and Windows API hooking module of VxStripper is based on forensic analysis of the guest operating system's memory, without any interaction with the guest operating system.

The Windows executive maintains a set of structures that contains information about the loaded modules for a given process inside its memory space. These data structures can be recovered by using the process environment block (PEB), which can itself be accessed as an offset of segment register FS. The native and Windows API hooking modules of VxStripper use this information to locate and instrument Windows API.

Forensics/Root-Kit Analysis

The forensics module of VxStripper comes with additional features to monitor and check the integrity of many locations within the guest platform where a hook can be installed. It walks through executive structures of the operating system in order to identify potential targets of a root-kit attack and monitor hardware components that could be corrupted by a root-kit. This information is crucial for the analyst to understand low-level viral attacks.

For the purposes of this chapter, you can consider these features to be similar to those expected from a kernel debugger. You can attach a process, view its CPU state and disassembled code, and trace the interaction of the target program with the operating system API. This inspection is done in a safe and controlled environment, without any intrusive interaction with the guest operating system.

The following two sections take a closer look at the working of Vxstripper's two most important analysis modules: the unpacking module and the normalization module.

Unpacking Module

The unpacking module locates the original entry point (OEP) of the target executable, gets information relative to its interactions with the operating system API, and extracts the relocation information.

The underlying idea is a simple integrity check of the target program's executable code: For each translation block of the program, a comparison between its value in virtual memory and its value on the host file system is made. As long as the values are identical, nothing is done. As soon as a difference is identified, the current translation block is written into the raw file in place of the old translation block. The first instruction of the newly generated translation block is identified as the OEP of the protected program. At the end of the analysis, data sections are written into the raw file in place of original data sections.

The same monitoring algorithm is applied for each translation block. The protection loader of the packed executable can have several deciphering layers. As soon as the last deciphered translation block has been reached, the only thing to be done is to repair the target executable. In order to recover the PE (Portable Executable) structure of an unprotected executable, several tasks have to be carried out: Set the original entry point, rebuild the imports and relocations tables, and consistency check the PE header.

The method used by the unpacking engine in order to reconstruct the Import Address Table (IAT) and relocations is based on Win32 and native API hooking. During the unpacking process, all API calls are traced. A sorted table of API calls is initialized at load-time, by walking NT executive structures.

Next, after process execution has resumed, each API call is traced. This table is updated regularly during the target process execution, and is used to dynamically resolve API function names. Finally, after a dump of the target process memory space is completed, this table is used to fix the IAT in the PE executable.

Thanks to the load and store TCG instructions instrumentation, you can dynamically extract the program's relocation information, which can also be added to a new section of the executable.

For example, here is the (useful) information extracted during the unpacking stage of a program that displays a dialog box (function `MessageBoxA`):

```
[INFO]  eip=0x00401000
[RELOC]  value=0x00403000 va=0x00401003
[RELOC]  value=0x0040300f va=0x00401008
[RELOC]  value=0x00402008 va=0x00401010
[APICALL]  api_pc=0x77d8050b api_oep=0x77d8050b
          dll_name=C:\WINDOWS\system32\user32.dll
          func_name=MessageBoxA
          value=0x00402008 va=0x00401010
```

The relocation information consists of pairs (`va`, `value`), providing the virtual address and the value to relocate, respectively. Note that for this packer, the prologue of the function `MessageBoxA` is not emulated by the protection. Otherwise, the external address that is effectively called (`api_pc`) is different from the entry point of the API function (`api_oep`).

Normalization

In most cases, after the unpacking stage, you are able to get (automatically) a binary stripped of its protection loader and without any rewritable code. Unfortunately, some obfuscation mechanisms (control-flow flattening, VM–based obfuscation transformations, etc.) have to be handled now in order to fully understand the inner workings of a malware.

A first attempt to provide a solution to these problems has been implemented in VxStripper, through the use of the LLVM intermediate representation. Rather than try to work on the binary after its memory image has been dumped, the idea is to work on its intermediate representation and increase the amount of information (that has been dynamically collected) by embedding it in the LLVM module. Such a representation is more suitable for further analysis.

The normalization module uses the output of previous analyses to generate the LLVM representation of translation blocks, to which several optimization transformations are applied. Examining this in more detail, during the execution of the target program, the LLVM back end of QEMU TCG outputs the LLVM representation of translated blocks. This LLVM code is linked with an initialization LLVM module (see Figure 5-4).

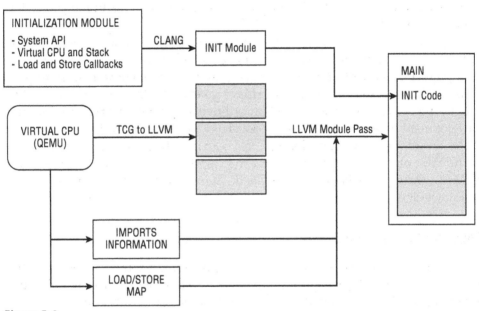

Figure 5-4

This initialization module implements load and store callbacks, declares system API prototypes, and sets a virtual processor unit and its stack.

The normalization module uses the information dynamically collected during target program execution to resolve imports, process relocations, and retrieve data sections. Import table information is used to build LLVM API call instructions. The load/store memory map is used to apply relocations and inject data from the target program into the LLVM module.

When the LLVM module is rebuilt, some additional optimization passes are applied to its representation. The LLVM can next be compiled to the chosen architecture, by using one of available LLVM back ends. It can also be translated to C or C++ code.

First results show that standard optimization used in conjunction with the partial evaluation induced by the dynamic translation of target code to its LLVM representation are sufficient to drastically reduce and simplify the code under analysis.

Final Thoughts

This section has discussed only four tools (and with a bias toward static analysis). Alongside the Metasm and Miasm frameworks, we could have cited the Radare framework (`http://www.radare.org/y/`), for example. Rolf Rolles's efforts to extend IDA with his `idaocaml` interpreter (`https://code.google.com/p/idaocaml/`) merit attention as well. There are plenty of others that we did not mention or only briefly mentioned here, and we encourage you to try them for yourself.

To put these tools into perspective, although IDA is a good disassembler, it cannot help much when it comes to dealing with obfuscated code. The Metasm and Miasm frameworks go a step further, offering more control, an IR to play with, and so on. Tools such as VxStripper go even further. You can probably feel it—there is an arms race going on. A huge amount of effort is put into the development of obfuscators, so our tools have to evolve as well.

As a reverse engineer, developing tools is an investment you make in order to fulfill your objectives; and you expect some sort of return on investment from it. Most advanced tools can take weeks if not months to build and require a lot of knowledge.

Practical Deobfuscation

Now you will see how some of the tools presented earlier can be used for practical deobfuscation. Again, there is no ambition of exhaustiveness in the following sections. Instead, the goal is to illustrate some common use cases of deobfuscation techniques.

Pattern-Based Deobfuscation

This may be the simplest and cheapest deobfuscation, operating at the syntactical level and matching known patterns. Don't forget that early obfuscation patterns were mainly manually crafted and protected code (like some packer code) and exhibited only a limited set of patterns; listing them all was thus "acceptable."

This deobfuscation technique comes down to a search and replace algorithm at the binary (opcode) level (eventually using wildcard searching). The main drawback is that it leaves you with a binary plagued with NOP instructions.

To illustrate this, take a look at the following old OllyDbg script. Packers are a classic example of software using obfuscation techniques (in that case to protect their stubs). For years OllyDbg has been (and probably still is) the favorite tool for unpacking, and many scripts were released to assist in that task. This (random) old script (2004, by loveboom, `http://tuts4you.com/download.php?view.601`) targets ASProtect 2.0x versions (a commonly used packer at that time). It takes advantage of the OllyScript's REPL commands to search and replace a set of patterns. A REPL definition is as follows:

```
repl addr, find, repl, len
Replace find with repl starting att addr for len bytes.
```

All patterns are based on the same technique : an unconditional jump inside its successor instruction is used to confuse disassemblers. The diversity is slightly improved using instruction prefixes (like REP or REPNE). The repl instruction is used to replace these patterns with NOPs:

```
repl eip,#2EEB01??#,#90909090#,1000
repl eip,#65EB01??#,#90909090#,1000
repl eip,#F2EB01??#,#90909090#,1000
repl eip,#F3EB01??#,#90909090#,1000
repl eip,#EB01??#,#909090#,1000
repl eip,#26EB02????#,#9090909090#,1000
repl eip,#3EEB02????#,#9090909090#,1000
```

Here we only operate at the syntactic level. Considering a target with a limited set of patterns, this deobfuscation technique is trivial, however efficient:

- Application cost is limited if not negligible.
- Development cost is also almost null.

Of course, as with virus signatures and AV engines, polymorphism and diversity make it useless. An equivalent script could have been developed using IDA's scripting capabilities. That's typically the kind of script you can create when analyzing trivially obfuscated malware and/or packers, when speed of analysis has priority.

Program-Analysis-Based Deobfuscation

Now consider the following obfuscated code sample (this is only a very small extract; obfuscated code continues like this for thousands of instructions):

```
.text:00405900  loc_405900:
.text:00405900          add edx, 67E37DA7h
.text:00405906          push    esi
.text:00405907          mov esi, 0D0B763Ah
.text:0040590C          push    eax
.text:0040590D          mov eax, 15983FC8h
.text:00405912          neg eax
.text:00405914          inc eax
.text:00405915          inc eax
.text:00405916          jmp loc_4082AD
.text:004082AD  loc_4082AD:
.text:004082AD          not eax
.text:004082AF          and eax, 1D48516Ch
.text:004082B4          sub eax, 0ACE1B37Ah
```

```
.text:004082B9        xor esi, eax
.text:004082BB        pop eax
.text:004082BC        xor edx, esi
.text:004082BE        pop esi
.text:004082BF        and ecx, edx
.text:004082C1  jmp loc_407C54
```

You likely recognize, from the first sections of this chapter, some of the obfuscation techniques used here, especially constant unfolding. Please also note that unconditional jumps are inserted to split code into basic blocks that are then distributed (randomly reordered) across the binary. There is no obvious pattern, at least none you could possibly and effectively match at the syntactical level using signatures.

You need to step up to the semantical level. Based on the output of a disassembler, you could start working on the control flow, merging the basic blocks 405900h and 4082ADh. Then, you could work on the data flow, considering the two instructions:

```
.text:0040590D        mov eax, 15983FC8h
.text:00405912        neg eax
```

Based on the semantics of these instructions, you know that the EAX register is first assigned with a constant value and then negged. You could precompute the NEG instruction and rewrite this in a simpler form, by assigning EAX with the negged value:

```
.text:0040590D        mov eax, EA67C038h
```

Rewriting programs in a simpler form, precomputing values that do not depend on the program's input, removing useless code—that is program optimization, and compilers have done that almost since their creation. You can adapt and reuse these techniques for your own purposes, and an abundant body of literature is available on this topic. Some classical compiler optimization techniques include the following:

- Peephole optimization
- Constant folding/propagation
- Dead store elimination
- Operation folding
- Dead code elimination
- Etc.

This approach is exactly what is proposed by the Optimice deobfuscation plugin for IDA. Some previous works, by Gazet and Guillot[22] and by Josse,[29] have also been presented, respectively as a Metasm plugin and a VxStripper plugin. The idea is to normalize the code in order to get a reduced/optimized/canonical form, which is simpler to analyze and closer to the original, unprotected, code.

These attempts to provide deobfuscation frameworks/utilities are still far from perfect. In addition, not many tools are available to the average reverser to attack obfuscated programs (of course, some private advanced tools exist here and there). The future of deobfuscation will probably take the form of elaborated tools and analysis platforms based on formal IR. Rolf Rolles presented some of his results with his own framework written in OCaml[34]. Other popular frameworks that could be used include LLVM-based SecondWrite (Smithson et al., 2007[39]), S2e/revgen (Chipounov, 2001[7]), or BitBlaze (Song et al., 2008[40] and their works since). Efforts in deobfuscation will have to match those put into obfuscation.

Complex Analysis

This section discusses two of the most impactful obfuscation techniques: code virtualization and code flattening. For these techniques, you clearly need to work at a semantic level.

Simple VM Implementations

There are mainly two forms of VM implementations. The most straightforward form is to develop a simple processor emulator. Algorithmically speaking, it would include the following steps:

1. Loop:
    a. *Fetch* —Read the bytecode stream at the instruction pointer.
    b. *Decode*—Decode the instruction's opcode and its operands.
    c. *Execute*—Call the appropriate opcode handler.
2. Update the instruction pointer or exit the loop.

In this configuration, each instruction handler is responsible for updating the context of the VM. The context represents the underlying emulated architecture. It probably consists of a set registers, and eventually a memory area. Each handler implements a distinctive instruction of the emulated processor (one handler for the ADD, one for the SUB, etc.).

This form is often used by the simpler implementations. Handlers are totally independent of one another, and the instruction pointer is increased by the size of the instruction (except for instructions that directly modify it).

From an attacker's point of view, this type of implementation is easily recognizable. Following is a detailed look at the steps generally required to analyze a VM:

1. Understand how an instruction is decoded from raw bytecode: which part encodes for the operation (handler number), which part encodes the operand(s), and so on.
2. Deduct VM's architecture from instructions' operands: number of registers, memory layout, I/O interfaces, etc.

3. Undertake handler analysis. Once operand decoding is known, you can look at the way each handler manipulates the various operand(s) it possibly takes as argument(s). This step is the essence of VM analysis: Each handler is associated with its own semantics.

With all these pieces of knowledge, you can finally build a disassembler-like tool that enables you to disassemble the bytecode of the VM.

In 2006, Maximus published two great papers about VM reversing: "Reversing a simple virtual machine"[32] and "Virtual machines re-building"[33]. One of the targets he used (*HyperUnpackme2*) was also covered in depth by Rolf Rolles the same year[35].

Although these are useful contributions from talented reversers, VM analysis remains a somewhat manual and repetitive job: One has to develop a new disassembler for each new instance of VM. Moreover, protections authors have also reacted, hardening their implementations of VMs.

Advanced VM Implementations

More advanced VM implementations derive from the simple type but add important features to harden the implementations and make them more resilient to analysis:

- **Loop unrolling**—This classical compiler optimization technique favors the time (speed) aspect of a program's space vs. time trade-off. It replaces the loop structure by the sequential invocations of the loop body (thus unrolled). Applied to a VM, each handler is made responsible for fetching and decoding its own operand(s), and then updates the context accordingly.

- **Code-flattening**—The VM's main execution loop is flattened. That means each handler is responsible for updating the instruction pointer (pointer on the bytecode). Actually, code-flattening and VM-based obfuscation are basically the same thing. Code-flattening only virtualizes/retargets the control flow of the protected code, whereas virtual-machine obfuscation virtualizes/retargets both the control flow and the data flow. You can use almost the same algorithms to follow a code-flatten dispatcher's context and a VM context.

- **Bytecode encoding/encryption**—Each invocation of the VM depends on an encryption key that is passed to the VM as part of its context initialization. Each handler updates that key, resulting in a turning key. The handlers depend on the turning key to decode their operands from encoded bytecode. An attacker cannot start analyzing the VM at a chosen point, as the value of the key at this point would be unknown.

- **Code obfuscation**—The native code of the VM is obfuscated using techniques like the one described at the beginning of this chapter. Simply looking at a handler's code provides no clue about its semantics.

In summary, hardened implementations of VMs are more difficult to analyze statically by an order of magnitude. For each state of the VM, an attacker has to know at least the following mandatory values:

- Bytecode pointer
- Instruction pointer, the value of the next handler to be executed
- Turning encryption key

VMs have reached a new level of complexity, thus necessitating a new level of attack. Handlers are more complex to analyze; moreover, they cannot be analyzed in isolation (one would not know the value of the encryption key, for example). An attacker wants to limit the manual analysis to a minimum. Nevertheless, a manual review is most often required to "capture" the general behavior of a VM and thus infer possible attacks on it.

One of the first places of interest is the VM invocation stub—i.e., the transition between native (nonvirtualized) code and the VM/interpreter. The context initialization indicates the nature of the mapping between the native architecture and the VM's architecture. It may be a carbon copy of native registers to the VM's registers or something more complicated. Also, at this point, it is helpful to distinguish (as much as possible) between mandatory initialization variables (such as a VM's key, handler number, or entry point) for which a numerical value is required, and extra variables that can be kept symbolic.

The second place of major interest is the VM's dispatcher (if it exists). Most often there is a single point of dispatch that basically retrieves the next handler from a handlers table based on an index stored somewhere within the VM's context. A question to answer is, what is the break condition of this execution loop? In this configuration it is possible to consider the VM as a generalization of code-flattening. Code-flattening virtualizes only the control flow, whereas the VM virtualizes both the control and data flows. Moreover, code-flattening most often only operates at single function level, whereas the VM operates at the program level. The other possibility is a distributed dispatch, whereby each handler is responsible for updating the VM's instruction pointer and linking to the next handler.

These are general ideas; each reverser has his or her own tricks and abstractions of the problem.

Using Metasm

The approach we are going to explore is based on the Metasm framework. It relies on symbolic execution to make the VM (i.e., interpreter) process the bytecode (with respect to static data) and compute the residual program. On the one hand, there is a program (the interpreter); on the other hand, there is its static data (the bytecode); we will specialize the program with respect to its static data.

Considering an obfuscated program and its data as a whole would be too complex, the solution is to break this complex problem into multiple, simpler sub-problems. Considering virtual machine's instruction handlers level provides a far more appropriate granularity. From now on, we will consider instruction handlers as the interpreter's smallest unit of semantics.

Based on that basic premise, you can apply the following pseudo algorithm:

1. Capture the current context (VM's bytecode, static parameters, known environment, etc.).

2. Disassemble the current handler.

3. Deobfuscate code, if necessary.

4. Compute its semantics (i.e., transfer function).

5. Generate output from solved semantics.

6. Compute next state (i.e., apply the transfer function to the current context).

7. If the handler's dispatcher doesn't reach a break/exit condition, repeat from step 1.

Optionally, you may be able to regenerate native code from the transfer function computed at step 4. As expressed by Futamura[21], given an interpreter of $L_{interpreted}$ written in a given native language L_{native}, it is possible to automatically compute a compiler from $L_{interpreted}$ to L_{native}.

This is suitable for the theoretical concepts. Now suppose that you face an instance of a VM. Where do you start? Let's take a practical example.

The following script makes use of Metasm to compile and then disassemble what could be a handler from a VM. For the sake of simplicity, this example deals only with the VM's part (thus, code is not obfuscated). The handler's code is located in `10000000h`, while a data section containing the handler's bytecode is located in `1a000000h`:

```ruby
# encoding: ASCII-8BIT
#!/usr/bin/env ruby

require "metasm"
include Metasm

$SPAWN_GUI = false
CODE_BASE_ADDR = 0x10000000
HTABLE_BASE_ADDR = 0x18000000
DATA_BASE_ADDR = 0x1A000000
INJECT_MAX_ITER = 0x20

NATIVE_REGS = [:eax, :edx, :ecx, :ebx, :esp, :ebp, :esi, :edi]

def display(bd)
  bd.each{|key,value| puts "  #{Expression[key]} => #{Expression[value]}"}
end
```

```
# produce handler's x86 code
sc = Metasm::Shellcode.assemble(Metasm::Ia32.new, <<EOS)
lodsd
mov ecx, eax
xor ecx, ebp
movzx eax, cl
push eax
mov eax, [edi+eax]

movzx edx, ch
mov edx, [edi+edx]
xor eax, edx

pop edx
mov [edi+edx], eax

lodsd xor ebp, 0x35ef6a14
xor eax, ebp
jmp [#{HTABLE_BASE_ADDR}+eax*4]
EOS

handler = sc.encode_string

# data section hex
data_section_hex = "\xA3\xCB\xDB\x5F\x60\xBD\x34\x6A"

# add a code section
dasm = sc.init_disassembler
dasm.add_section(EncodedData.new(handler), CODE_BASE_ADDR)

# add a data section
dasm.add_section(EncodedData.new(data_section_hex), DATA_BASE_ADDR)

# disassemble handler code
dasm.disassemble_fast_deep(CODE_BASE_ADDR)
```

The first thing to do is automatically get the semantics of that handler. As mentioned previously, Metasm offers a method called code_binding that computes the function transfer (Metasm's terminology is binding) of a set of instructions. Thus, you can write the following:

```
# compute handler's semantics
bb = dasm.di_at(CODE_BASE_ADDR).block
start_addr = bb.list.first.address
end_addr = bb.list.last.address
puts "[+] from 0x#{start_addr.to_s(16)}, to 0x#{end_addr.to_s(16)}"
binding = dasm.code_binding(start_addr, end_addr)
display(binding)
```

The preceding produces the following output:

```
[+] from 0x10000000, to address 10000021
  dword ptr [esp] => (dword ptr [esi]^ebp)&0ffh
  dword ptr [edi+((dword ptr [esi]^ebp)&0ffh)] =>
```

```
      dword ptr [edi+((dword ptr[esi]^ebp)&0ffh)] ^
      dword ptr [edi+(((dword ptr[esi]>>8)^(ebp>>8))&0ffh)]
  eax => (dword ptr [esi+4]^(ebp^35ef6a14h))&0ffffffffh
  ecx => (dword ptr [esi]^ebp)&0ffffffffh
  edx => (dword ptr [esi]^ebp)&0ffh
  ebp => (ebp^35ef6a14h)&0ffffffffh
  esi => (esi+8)&0ffffffffh
```

From both the assembly and the binding, you can say the following about
the VM:

■ It seems to use a turning key store in EBP. (Note how it is used to decrypt
the instruction's operands from bytecode.)

■ Its context seems to be pointed to by EDI.

That's a good start, but you are still far from the objective. You are still stuck
at the assembly level, so let's step back and consider the VM initialization, which
we have identified as follows:

```
pushad
pop [edi]
pop [edi+0x4]
pop [edi+0x8]
pop [edi+0xC]
pop [edi+0x10]
pop [edi+0x14]
pop [edi+0x18]
pop [edi+0x1C]
```

First, native registers are pushed onto the stack, and then they are read from
the stack into a memory area pointed to by EDI, which in turn is responsible for
pointing at the VM's context. This information enables you to create a mapping
between the VM's symbolic internals and assembly expression:

```
vm_symbolism = {
    :eax => :nhandler,
    :ebp => :vmkey,
    :esi => :bytecode_ptr,
    Indirection[[:edi], 4, nil] => :vm_edi,
    Indirection[[:edi, :+, 4], 4, nil] => :vm_esi,
    Indirection[[:edi, :+, 8], 4, nil] => :vm_ebp,
    Indirection[[:edi, :+, 0xC], 4, nil] => :vm_esp,
    Indirection[[:edi, :+, 0x10], 4, nil] => :vm_ebx,
    Indirection[[:edi, :+, 0x14], 4, nil] => :vm_edx,
    Indirection[[:edi, :+, 0x18], 4, nil] => :vm_ecx,
    Indirection[[:edi, :+, 0x1c], 4, nil] => :vm_eax,
}
```

This symbolism is injected into the binding (each occurrence of a left value
is replaced by its associated right value). Expressions have a special method
named bind that does exactly that. The following example first defines a symbolic

expression: the addition of two terms, one of them being an indirection; and two symbols are involved, :a and :b. Next, symbol :a is associated (bound) with the value 1000h:

```
expr = Expression[[:a, 4], :+, :b]
sym = {:a => 0x1000}

puts expr
>> dword ptr [a]+b

puts expr.bind(sym)
>> dword ptr [1000h]+b
```

You can generalize this for each expression of the binding. This mapping is the key that enables abstracting VM's code from its implementation level up to the VM semantics level. Moreover, a positive side effect of this step is often a significant reduction of the binding's complexity. The new binding is as follows:

```
[+] symbolic binding
  dword ptr [esp] => (dword ptr [bytecode_ptr]^vmkey)&0ffh
  dword ptr [edi+((dword ptr [bytecode_ptr]^vmkey)&0ffh)] =>
  dword ptr [edi+dword ptr [bytecode_ptr]^vmkey)&0ffh)]^
  dword ptr[edi+(((dword ptr [bytecode_ptr]>>8)^(vmkey>>8))&0ffh)]
  nhandler => (dword ptr [bytecode_ptr+4]^(vmkey^35ef6a14h))&0ffffffffh
  vmkey => (vmkey^35ef6a14h)&0ffffffffh
  bytecode_ptr => (bytecode_ptr+8)&0ffffffffh
```

We have made progress, but the encryption is still problematic and we cannot go further if the VM's context at the execution time of this handler is unknown: bytecode pointer, turning key, and optionally the handler number are all required values. Assuming you know these values (you are at the VM's entry point or you have dynamically traced the VM up to that point), you can define a pseudo-context:

```
context = {
    :nhandler => 0x84,
    :vmkey => 0x5fdbd7b7,
    :bytecode_ptr => DATA_BASE_ADDR,
    :virt_eax => 0xffeeffee,
    :virt_ecx => 0,
    :virt_edx => 0x41414141,
    :virt_ebx => 1,
    :virt_edi => :virt_edi,
}
```

Note that the context contains both symbolic and numerical values. For example, nhandler is defined as equal to 84h, while the VM's register virt_edi is symbolic.

The context is then injected within the binding, as well as the symbolism defined previously. In practice that's an iterative process, but let's not get overloaded with implementation details. Expressions are progressively solved and reduced with respect to all known values, which include the current context and the program's data (i.e., the bytecode). At the end you have a solved binding, which actually represents the context of the VM after the execution of the handler. We call that step *symbolic execution*:

```
[+] binding solver
  [+] key: dword ptr [esp]
    => solved key: dword ptr [esp]

  [+] value: (dword ptr [bytecode_ptr]^vmkey)&0ffh
    [+] solved memory read at 0x1a000000, size 4
    [+] value 5fdbcba3h
    => solved value: 14h

  [+] key: dword ptr [edi+((dword ptr [bytecode_ptr]^vmkey)&0ffh)]
    [+] solved memory read at 0x1a000000, size 4
    [+] value 5fdbcba3h
    => solved key: virt_edx

  [+] value: dword ptr [edi+((dword ptr [bytecode_ptr]^vmkey)&0ffh)]^
        dword ptr [edi+(((dword ptr [bytecode_ptr]>>8)^(vmkey>>8))&0ffh)]
    [+] solved memory read at 0x1a000000, size 4
    [+] value 5fdbcba3h
    [+] solved memory read at 0x1a000000, size 4
    [+] value 5fdbcba3h
    => solved value: 0beafbeafh

  [+] key: nhandler
    => solved key: nhandler

  [+] value: (dword ptr [bytecode_ptr+4]^(vmkey^35ef6a14h))&0ffffffffh
    [+] solved memory read at 0x1a000004, size 4
    [+] value 6a34bd60h
    => solved value: 0c3h

  [+] key: vmkey
    => solved key: vmkey
    [+] value: (vmkey^35ef6a14h)&0ffffffffh
    => solved value: 6a34bda3h

  [+] key: bytecode_ptr
    => solved key: bytecode_ptr
    [+] value: (bytecode_ptr+8)&0ffffffffh
    => solved value: 1a000008h

[+] solved binding
  virt_edx => 0beafbeafh
  nhandler => 0c3h
  vmkey => 6a34bda3h
  bytecode_ptr => 1a000008h
```

The expression solver helps to compute the final values of the first handler's binding: the next handler to be executed as well as the updated value of the turning key. Updating the context is a trivial operation:

```
updated_context = context.update(solved_binding)

puts "\n[+] updated context"
display(updated_context)

[+] updated context
  nhandler => 0c3h
  vmkey => 6a34bda3h
  bytecode_ptr => 1a000008h
  virt_eax => 0ffeeffeeh
  virt_ecx => 0
  virt_edx => 0beafbeafh
  virt_ebx => 1
  virt_edi => virt_edi
```

You can repeat this process and walk through the whole control-flow graph of the VM. This is a quite appreciable result; nevertheless, pure numerical values somewhat hide the semantics of the handler. Moreover, one of the objectives is to regenerate native assembly code equivalent to the contextualized execution of the handler.

A trick we often use when analyzing a VM with Metasm is to proceed to a double symbolic execution for each handler: one with the full context (mainly numerical values, used to update the context) and another one with an almost purely symbolic context (used to extract the high-level semantics). The next code sample demonstrates the use of a symbolic context:

```
symbolic_context = {
  :nhandler => 0x84,
  :vmkey => 0x5fdbd7b7,
  :bytecode_ptr => DATA_BASE_ADDR,
  :virt_eax => :virt_eax,
  :virt_ecx => :virt_ecx,
  :virt_edx => :virt_edx,
  :virt_ebx => :virt_ebx,
  :virt_edi => :virt_edi,
}

solved_symolic_binding = sym_exec(symbolic_context,
                                  symbolic_binding,
                                  vm_symbolism)
puts "\n[+] solved binding" display(solved_symbolic_binding)
```

This time the output is as follows:

```
[+] binding solver

  [+] key: dword ptr [esp]
    => solved key: dword ptr [esp]
```

```
[+] value: (dword ptr [bytecode_ptr]^vmkey)&0ffh
  [+] solved memory read at 0x1a000000, size 4
  [+] value 5fdbcba3h
 => solved value: 14h

[+] key: dword ptr [edi+((dword ptr [bytecode_ptr]^vmkey)&0ffh)]
  [+] solved memory read at 0x1a000000, size 4
  [+] value 5fdbcba3h
 => solved key: virt_edx

[+] value: dword ptr [edi+((dword ptr [bytecode_ptr]^vmkey)&0ffh)]^
    dword ptr edi+(((dword ptr [bytecode_ptr]>>8)^(vmkey>>8))&0ffh)]
  [+] solved memory read at 0x1a000000, size 4
  [+] value 5fdbcba3h
  [+] solved memory read at 0x1a000000, size 4
  [+] value 5fdbcba3h
 => solved value: virt_edx^virt_eax

[+] key: nhandler
 => solved key: nhandler

[+] value: (dword ptr [bytecode_ptr+4]^(vmkey^35ef6a14h))&0ffffffffh
  [+] solved memory read at 0x1a000004, size 4
  [+] value 6a34bd60h
 => solved value: 0c3h

[+] key: vmkey
 => solved key: vmkey

[+] value: (vmkey^35ef6a14h)&0ffffffffh
 => solved value: 6a34bda3h
[+] key: bytecode_ptr
 => solved key: bytecode_ptr

[+] value: (bytecode_ptr+8)&0ffffffffh
 => solved value: 1a000008h

[+] solved binding
  virt_edx => virt_edx^virt_eax
  nhandler => 0c3h
  vmkey => 6a34bda3h
  bytecode_ptr => 1a000008h
```

Finally, you can simply reject VM control stuff from the solved binding, leaving you with the following:

```
vm_edx => vm_edx^vm_eax
```

From that final result, native code regeneration is pretty straightforward. You iterate this process over the VM's control-flow graph for each handler. As a general observation, when using this technique, a sensitive choice is when to keep symbolic values and when to reduce to numerical values. The first option favors the recovery of high-level semantics, while the second enables an easier VM's control-flow recovery. At the end, it is also possible to further proceed the output. Imagine a VM that looks like a stack-based interpreter:

```
01: push vm_edx
02: add [esp], vm_eax
03: pop vm_edx
```

Using classic deobfuscation methods such as compiler optimizations would rewrite the preceding three lines as follows:

```
01: add vm_eax, vm_eax
```

Please note that the bytecode itself could have been obfuscated.

Code-Flattening Deobfuscation

As previously stated, code-flattening can be viewed as partial virtualization (only the control flow is virtualized). Thus, techniques described for VM analysis, and especially symbolic execution, can also be applied for flattened code analysis.

There are still some difficulties that are specific to this technique:

- Code-flattening transformation is most often applied at the function level and sometimes there may be more than one flattened "node" in the same function. Overall that means there are multiple instances of the techniques; thus a tool has to be bulletproof and fully automatic.

- Discerning between a function's original code and added dispatcher's code is difficult when code-flattening implementation is robust (program and dispatcher data flows are firmly interleaved /interdependent).

- Inverse transformation is not trivial to implement.

Using VxStripper

To illustrate the use of VxStripper on a simple "toy" example, consider the following program (which displays y = 22) after unpacking and reconstruction:

```
......  | entrypoint:
......  |   push    ebp
401001  |   mov     ebp, esp
401003  |   sub     esp, 10h
401006  |   mov     dword ptr [ebp-4], 0
40100d  |   mov     dword ptr [ebp-0ch], 2
401014  |   mov     dword ptr [ebp-8], 0ah
40101b  |
......  | loc_40101b:
......  |   cmp     dword ptr [ebp-0ch], 6
40101f  |   jnl     loc_40108c
401021  |   mov     eax, [ebp-0ch]
401024  |   mov     [ebp-10h], eax
401027  |   mov     ecx, [ebp-10h]
40102a  |   sub     ecx, 2
```

```
40102d |   mov     [ebp-10h], ecx
401030 |   cmp     dword ptr [ebp-10h], 3
401034 |   ja      loc_40108a
401036 |   mov     edx, [ebp-10h]
401039 |   jmp     dword ptr [edx*4+data_4010a4]
401040     mov     dword ptr [ebp-4], 2
401047     mov     dword ptr [ebp-0ch], 3
40104e     jmp     loc_40108a
401050     cmp     dword ptr [ebp-8], 0
401054     jng     40105fh
401056     mov     dword ptr [ebp-0ch], 4
40105d     jmp     401066h
40105f     mov     dword ptr [ebp-0ch], 6
401066     jmp     loc_40108a
401068     mov     eax, [ebp-4]
40106b     add     eax, 2
40106e     mov     [ebp-4], eax
401071     mov     dword ptr [ebp-0ch], 5
401078     jmp     loc_40108a
40107a     mov     ecx, [ebp-8]
40107d     sub     ecx, 1
401080     mov     [ebp-8], ecx
401083     mov     dword ptr [ebp-0ch], 3
40108a |
...... | loc_40108a:
...... |   jmp     loc_40101b
40108c |
...... | loc_40108c:
...... |   mov     edx, [ebp-4]
40108f |   push    edx
401090 |   push    strz_yd_402008
401095 |   call    dword ptr [msvcrt.dll:printf]
40109b |   add     esp, 8
40109e |   xor     eax, eax
4010a0 |   mov     esp, ebp
4010a2 |   pop     ebp
4010a3 |   ret     return 0;
```

The control-flow graph (CFG) of such a program is flattened.

The normalization module's execution produces (when you do not apply all optimizations) the following code:

```
...... |   push    eax
4011f1 |   mov     dword ptr [esp-0ch], 0ah
4011f9 |   mov     dword ptr [esp-8], 4
401201 |   dec     dword ptr [esp-0ch]
401205 |   add     dword ptr [esp-8], 2
40120a |   dec     dword ptr [esp-0ch]
40120e |   add     dword ptr [esp-8], 2
401213 |   dec     dword ptr [esp-0ch]
401217 |   add     dword ptr [esp-8], 2
40121c |   dec     dword ptr [esp-0ch]
401220 |   add     dword ptr [esp-8], 2
```

```
401225 |   dec     dword ptr [esp-0ch]
401229 |   add     dword ptr [esp-8], 2
40122e |   dec     dword ptr [esp-0ch]
401232 |   add     dword ptr [esp-8], 2
401237 |   dec     dword ptr [esp-0ch]
40123b |   add     dword ptr [esp-8], 2
401240 |   dec     dword ptr [esp-0ch]
401244 |   add     dword ptr [esp-8], 2
401249 |   dec     dword ptr [esp-0ch]
40124d |   add     dword ptr [esp-8], 2
401252 |   dec     dword ptr [esp-0ch]
401256 |   mov     eax, [esp-8]
40125a |   mov     [esp-18h], eax
40125e |   mov     dword ptr [esp-1ch], strz_yd_402010
401266 |   mov     ebp, esp
401268 |   lea     eax, [esp-1ch]
40126c |   mov     esp, eax
40126e |   call    crtdll.dll:printf_4012d8
401273 |   mov     esp, ebp
401275 |   mov     ebp, esp
401277 |   lea     eax, [esp+8]
40127b |   mov     esp, eax
40127d |   mov     esp, ebp
40127f |   xor     eax, eax
401281 |   pop     edx
401282 |   ret
```

Note that the dynamic generation of code performed by VxStripper naturally unflattens the flattened code. Applying standard optimization transformations results in a program stripped of this obfuscation:

```
...... |   push    eax
4011f1 |   mov     dword ptr [esp-18h], 16h
4011f9 |   mov     dword ptr [esp-1ch], strz_yd_402010
401201 |   mov     ebp, esp
401203 |   lea     eax, [esp-1ch]
401207 |   mov     esp, eax
401209 |   call    crtdll.dll:printf_401268
40120e |   mov     esp, ebp
401210 |   mov     ebp, esp
401212 |   lea     eax, [esp+8]
401216 |   mov     esp, eax
401218 |   mov     esp, ebp
40121a |   xor     eax, eax
40121c |   pop     edx
40121d |   ret
```

Even if work remains before obtaining software that supports the set of software protection tools usable by malware authors, these first results encourage us to pursue the study of generic methods of unpacking and normalization, with the goal of automating as much as possible the tasks conducted by an analyst.

This tool provides a self-sufficient piece of software for malware analysis. However, one of the future goals of this project is to enable the tool to interact with other analysis tools. By design, this tool may be able to collaborate with any software analysis tool based on the LLVM compilation chain.

The LLVM compilation chain and the many LLVM-based tools already provide a great library of program analyses that can be used together to defeat malware protection mechanisms.

In addition, Vellvm (Verified LLVM) may be used to formally extract verified implementations of deobfuscation passes implemented by VxStripper. In addition to malware threat analysis, other uses of this tool can also be imagined, such as detection scheme extraction, software protections, and antivirus software robustness analysis.

Case Study

The sample we'll use for this case study is actually a crackme originally posted on Crackmes.de by *quetz* in 2007. Even though it is a "only" a crackme, it features most of the concepts that one would find in a professional-grade protection. Among other rejoicings it contains the following:

- Code-flattening
- Variable encoding
- Code virtualization

Here is how the author introduces its challenge:

> **Lately, protection from static analysis becomes more and more popular. Almost every protector employs some kind of obfuscation, virtual machine, etc... This keygenme is an attempt to show what happens if you abuse idea of obfuscation. Can human effectively analyze such code? Maybe with an assistance of a tool?**
>
> *—http://crackmes.de/users/quetz/q_keygenme_1.0/*

Fortunately, we have tools and in this section we will use them. Before starting, we recommend that you *not* look at the symbols section contained within the binary. As an aside, previous versions of IDA Pro (maybe inferior to 6.2) didn't load these symbols and the author of these lines cheerfully failed to look for them.

First Impressions

Launching the executable offers you the opportunity to input a username and a password. After clicking the Check button, a message box appears and displays the validity of your credentials.

If you've carefully read the previous chapters of this book, you have probably already fired up your favorite disassembler and targeted the GUI's `DialogProc` callback function.

Let's first look at the general architecture of the protected code. The control-flow graph is way too messy to be natural compiler-generated code: We have an obfuscated `DialogProc` calling two code-flattened functions (`func1@0x430DB0`, `func2@0x431E00`). These two functions themselves call what seems to be a VM (`vm@0x401360`).

We have already discussed the VM's single dispatch point; this one is pretty straightforward to spot (look for an important jump table in the absence of any other clues):

```
01: .text:00401F20

02: mov     ebp, [esp+13Ch]
03: cmp     ebp, 3E2Dh; switch 15918 cases
04: ja short loc_401F36
05: jmp     ds:off_43D000[ebp*4]; switch jump
```

These are our two first and almost free pieces of knowledge about the VM: It stores its current handler number in [ESP+13Ch] and there are 15,918 entries in the dispatcher (for now, we cannot conclude whether they are all different handlers).

Before getting our hands dirty, we can try to do some black-box analysis of the func1 and func2 functions. We know func1 and func2 call the VM; we simply log every call to the VM and especially the number of the first handler that is called (a sort of entry point in the VM code). That seems quite trivial but one should never disregard low-hanging fruit.

Results are immediately revealing: func2 is called before func1, so we will start with func2. As soon as you look at the logs of the VM's entry point, these patterns stand out:

- 546h-0BFFh-7B2h-9A2h-405h-919h-3B9h—624 times
- 0CF5h-15Eh-184h-39Ch-5B0h-3C0h-0F75h—624 times
- 0A06h-0xA29h-0x268h-0xCB3h—227 times
- 736h-13Ah-1EBh-897h—396 times
- 150h-8ABh-843h-697h-474h—200 times

That's actually already a lot of information. If you look at the .data section, an extra hint is waiting:

```
01: .data:0043CA44  dword_43CA4402: .data:0043CA48  dd 9908B0DFh
```

Where does 9908B0DFh come from? And 624? And 227? Well, either you are really familiar with random number generators or you look for these values; they identify a Mersenne twister pseudo-random generator algorithm. 624 and 397 are the period parameters, while 9908B0DFh is a constant used during number generation.

We have identified a critical weakness of the protection: Virtualized code leaks some information about the structure of the protected algorithm, making it trivial to recover loop iterations. Nevertheless, do we have nicely crafted virtualized code nullified with one breakpoint? Not yet. We have an algorithm candidate but it needs to be confirmed.

Again, one should never reverse engineer some code when it is possible to guess (and validate) information! In this case, a black-box analysis reveals a lot simply by looking at the inputs/outputs of functions `func1` and `func2`. A basic strategy like this or differential analysis of VM execution can sometimes be of great help. Let's refine our analysis of these two functions:

- `func2`

  - **Input**—Two arguments: an address on the stack that seems to be an array of integers, and a 32-bit value that seems to depend on the length of the name.

  - **Output**—Nothing remarkable except that the integers array has been updated.

  - **Occurrence**—Called a single time, at the beginning and before `func1`.

  - **Guess**—Mersenne twister initialization, the array is actually the state of the PNRG. The 32-bit value is the initialization seed. This can be further validated by matching loop parameters (learned from the logs) with a standard initialization function.

- `func1`

  - **Input**—Two arguments: the address of the (supposed) PRNG state and a 32-bit value that seems to be a letter from the username.

  - **Output**—Returns a 32-bit random value.

  - **Occurrence**—Called 100 times.

  - **Guess**—Mersenne twister rand32-like function.

Analyzing Handlers Semantics

It is now time to analyze the VM. The main dispatcher has already been found at [ESP+13ch]. It is often a good idea to manually check a few handlers to see how they access the VM's context, how they update the program counter and/ or bytecode pointer, and so on.

This process can be applied on a random handler—for example, the one starting at 0x41836c:

```
01: .text:0041836C loc_41836C:
02:         ; DATA XREF: .rdata:off_43D000
03:         ; jumptable 00401F2F cases 2815,4091
04: .text:0041836C  movzx ecx, [esp+3D8h+var_2A2]
```

```
05: .text:00418374  mov    esi, 97Fh
06: .text:00418379  mov    ebx, [esp+3D8h+var_3C8]
07: .text:0041837D  movzx  edi, [esp+3D8h+var_29E]
08: .text:00418385  add    [esp+3D8h+var_3C0], 94Eh
09: .text:0041838D  imul   eax, ecx, 1Ch
10: .text:00418390  sub    [esp+3D8h+var_3C4], 0FF0h
11: .text:00418398  imul   ecx, edi, 5DDh
12: .text:0041839E  mov    [esp+3D8h+var_37C], esi
13: .text:004183A2  lea    edx, [eax+ebx+5C8h]
14: .text:004183A9  mov    ebx, 97Fh
15: .text:004183AE  mov    [esp+3D8h+var_3C8], edx
16: .text:004183B2  sub    ebx, ecx
17: .text:004183B4  lea    edx, [ebp+ebx+29Dh+var_8BC]
18: .text:004183BB  mov    [esp+3D8h+var_378], ebx
19: .text:004183BF  mov    [esp+3D8h+var_380], ebx
20: .text:004183C3  mov    [esp+3D8h+var_29D+1], edx
21: .text:004183CA  jmp    loc_401F20
```

Let's get some help from Metasm. As shown previously, we can use the code-binding method to compute the semantics of a chunk of code:

```
dword ptr [esp+10h] => 1ch*byte ptr [esp+136h]+dword ptr [esp+10h]+5c8h
dword ptr [esp+14h] => dword ptr [esp+14h]-0ff0h
dword ptr [esp+18h] => dword ptr [esp+18h]+94eh
dword ptr [esp+58h] => -5ddh*byte ptr [esp+13ah]+97fh
dword ptr [esp+5ch] => 97fh
dword ptr [esp+60h] => -5ddh*byte ptr [esp+13ah]+97fh
dword ptr [esp+13ch] => ebp-5ddh*byte ptr [esp+13ah]+360h
eax => (1ch*byte ptr [esp+136h])&0ffffffffh
ecx => (5ddh*byte ptr [esp+13ah])&0ffffffffh
edx => (ebp-5ddh*byte ptr [esp+13ah]+360h)&0ffffffffh
ebx => (-5ddh*byte ptr [esp+13ah]+97fh)&0ffffffffh
esi => 97fh
edi => byte ptr [esp+13ah]&0ffffffffh
```

The VM's context is stored on the stack and no values are passed by registers between handlers; that means all register modification can be dropped to get a clearer view:

```
dword ptr [esp+10h] => 1ch*byte ptr [esp+136h]+dword ptr [esp+10h]+5c8h
dword ptr [esp+14h] => dword ptr [esp+14h]-0ff0h
dword ptr [esp+18h] => dword ptr [esp+18h]+94eh
dword ptr [esp+58h] => -5ddh*byte ptr [esp+13ah]+97fh
dword ptr [esp+5ch] => 97fh
dword ptr [esp+60h] => -5ddh*byte ptr [esp+13ah]+97fh
dword ptr [esp+13ch] => ebp-5ddh*byte ptr [esp+13ah]+360h
```

We already know that the handler number is stored at [ESP+13Ch]. It is updated by the handler. Its final value depends on the value of byte ptr [ESP+13ah]. By analyzing a few other handlers, we can guess it is a Boolean value, and a few other Booleans are stored in the context. This one is stored in second position, and it will be named flag2.

[ESP+58h], [ESP +5Ch], and [ESP +60h] are firmly tied with the handler number computation. They respectively contain the delta between the old and new handler number in case the condition (here flag2) is true or false.

[ESP +10h], [ESP +14h], and [ESP +18h] are also of high interest. They are updated by almost every handler and are supposed to decrypt the bytecode: They access the large undefined constants table stored in the .data section). They are actually like a running key; they'll be named respectively key_a, key_b, and key_c.

The following is an example of key usage taken from handler 0xa0a at address 0x427b17:

```
nHandler => dword ptr [4*key_c+436010h] ^
            dword ptr [4*key_b+436010h] ^
            dword ptr [4*key_a+436010h]
```

The names can be injected within the handler's binding, making it more understandable (even if that's not our main objective here) and easy to manipulate:

```
key_a => 1ch*flag6+key_a+5c8h
key_b => key_b-0ff0h
key_c => key_c+94eh
delta_true => -5ddh*flag2+97fh
delta_false => 97fh
delta => -5ddh*flag2+97fh
nHandler => ebp-5ddh*flag2+360h
```

This handler has almost the semantics of a conditional jump. By analyzing a few other handlers, it is possible to recover and validate a mapping of the VM's symbolic variables, which will be represented by a hash object:

```
SYMBOLIC_VM = {
    Indirection[Expression[ :esp, :+, 0x10], 4, nil] => :key_a,
    Indirection[Expression[ :esp, :+, 0x14], 4, nil] => :key_b,
    Indirection[Expression[ :esp, :+, 0x18], 4, nil] => :key_c,
    Indirection[Expression[ :esp, :+, 0x58], 4, nil] => :delta,
    Indirection[Expression[ :esp, :+, 0x5c], 4, nil] => :delta_false,
    Indirection[Expression[ :esp, :+, 0x60], 4, nil] => :delta_true,
    Indirection[Expression[ :esp, :+, 0x134], 1, nil] => :flag8,
    Indirection[Expression[ :esp, :+, 0x135], 1, nil] => :flag7,
    Indirection[Expression[ :esp, :+, 0x136], 1, nil] => :flag6,
    Indirection[Expression[ :esp, :+, 0x137], 1, nil] => :flag5,
    Indirection[Expression[ :esp, :+, 0x138], 1, nil] => :flag4,
    Indirection[Expression[ :esp, :+, 0x139], 1, nil] => :flag3,
    Indirection[Expression[ :esp, :+, 0x13a], 1, nil] => :flag2,
    Indirection[Expression[ :esp, :+, 0x13b], 1, nil] => :flag1,
    Indirection[Expression[ :esp, :+, 0x13c], 4, nil] => :nHandler
}
```

Other memory locations do not seem to have a dedicated purpose; they can be considered/mapped as general-purpose registers. With this mapping, we have all we need to process a symbolic execution of the VM (i.e., step-by-step execution of handler's semantics).

Symbolic Execution

In order to process a symbolic execution, you must have some clues about the initialization context of the VM; recall the initial value of the turning key or the value of the program counter (handler number). In our case, calls to the VM are themselves obfuscated (remember the previously discussed graph-flattened functions), making the initialization context quite hard to recover statically. In that situation, one can simply take the best of the two worlds and use a compromise between static and dynamic analysis, sometimes referred to as *concolic execution*.

Basically that means you debug the target and catch (break at) every call to the VM; within the callback, you switch from dynamic to static analysis and proceed to the following actions:

1. Dump target's memory.

2. Initialize the symbolic analysis context with the memory dump. Actually, a kind of lazy loading can be used. All access to the uninitialized context will be solved and cached using the memory dump.

3. Compute the VM's symbolic execution.

Using concolic execution, it becomes quite easy to follow the execution flow of the VM (i.e., a succession of handlers). The process of handler analysis and tracing is fully automated.

Here is an example of output of the tool for one handler. The extensive use of the turning key (consisting of key_a, key_b, and key_c) clearly appears; in this situation, the key is used to obfuscate access to the VM's context:

```
[+] disasm handler 2be at 42c2cdh
[+] analyzing handler at 0x42c2cd
[+] considering code from 0x42c2cd to 0x42c3b3
[+] cached handler binding

dword ptr [dword ptr [esp+4*(dword ptr [4*key_b+436000h]^
   (dword ptr [4*key_c+436000h]^dword ptr [4*key_a+436000h]))+140h]] =>
   dword ptr [dword ptr [esp+4*(dword ptr [4*key_b+436004h]^
   (dword ptr [4*key_c+436004h]^dword ptr [4*key_a+436004h]))+140h]]

key_c => key_c+5
key_b => key_b+5
key_a => key_a+5

nHandler => (dword ptr [4*key_b+43600ch]^
   (dword ptr [4*key_c+43600ch]^dword ptr [4*key_a+43600ch]))+
   (((dword ptr [4*key_c+436010h]^(dword ptr [4*key_b+436010h]^
   dword ptr [4*key_a+436010h]))*(byte ptr [dword ptr [esp+4*
```

```
           (dword ptr [4*key_b+436008h]^(dword ptr [4*key_c+436008h]^
           dword ptr [4*key_a+436008h]))+140h]]&0ffh))&0ffffffffh)

   [+] symbolic binding

   dword ptr [esp+0a8h] => dword ptr [esp+0ach]
   key_c => 0d6h
   key_b => 1f6h
   key_a => 126ah
   nHandler => ((21eh*(flag4&0ffh))&0ffffffffh)+0ac6h

   [+] solved binding
   dword ptr [esp+0a8h] => 4f3de0b9h
   key_c => 0d6h
   key_b => 1f6h
   key_a => 126ah n
   Handler => 0ac6h
```

Solving the Challenge

What we have designed so far is equivalent to a VM's level-tracing tool. Handling branching statements—(un)conditional jumps, calls—would be required to get a disassembling-oriented tool. We could build a more complex tool, a sort of compiler, based on a bytecode disassembler and be able to regenerate native code. Using a previous example, the tool would process the input:

```
dword ptr [ESP+0a8h] => dword ptr [ESP+0ach]
```

to a C-like source:

```
vm_ctx.reg_2ah = vm_ctx.reg_2bh;
```

For this sample, we will rely on the tracing feature only. The strategy is straightforward. We have a good idea of the algorithm implemented by the VM, so we will use black-box/differential analysis to identify divergence between a standard Mersenne twister (MT) algorithm and the VM's. When a divergence is identified, we will check the trace output.

Let's again take an example to illustrate this: state initialization of the MT algorithm. The initialization is implemented by function func2. We will only look at its inputs/outputs. The state is an array of 624 dwords. Using standard implementations and the same seed used by the program for a name of six characters, (3961821h), we get the following:

- **Standard implementation**—state[1] = 0x968bff6d

- **VM's implementation**—state[1] = 0x968e4c84

We look for these values in the trace:

```
[+] disasm handler 2c2 at 41f056h
[+] analyzing handler at 0x41f056
[+] considering code from 0x41f056 to 0x41f165
```

```
[+] cached handler binding

byte ptr [esp+0dh] => byte ptr [dword ptr [esp+4*(dword ptr
   [4*key_b+43600ch]^(dword ptr [4*key_c+43600ch]^dword ptr
   [4*key_a+43600ch]))+140h]]&0ffh
dword ptr [dword ptr [esp+4*(dword ptr [4*key_b+436000h]^(dword ptr
   [4*key_c+436000h]^dword ptr [4*key_a+436000h]))+140h]] => dword ptr [dword
ptr
   [esp+4*(dword ptr [4*key_b+436004h]^(dword ptr [4*key_c+436004h]^dword ptr
   [4*key_a+436004h]))+140h]]^dword ptr [dword ptr [esp+4*(dword ptr
   [4*key_b+436008h]^(dword ptr [4*key_c+436008h]^dword ptr
   [4*key_a+436008h]))+140h]]
key_c => key_c+6
key_a => key_a+6
key_b => key_b+6
nHandler => (dword ptr [4*key_b+436010h]^(dword ptr [4*key_c+436010h]^dword
ptr
   [4*key_a+436010h]))+(((dword ptr [4*key_c+436014h]^(dword ptr
   [4*key_b+436014h]^dword ptr [4*key_a+436014h]))*(byte ptr [dword ptr
   [esp+4*(dword ptr [4*key_b+43600ch]^(dword ptr [4*key_c+43600ch]^dword ptr
   [4*key_a+43600ch]))+140h]]&0ffh))&0ffffffffh)

[+] symbolic binding
byte ptr [esp+0dh] => flag2&0ffh
dword ptr [esp+100h] => dword ptr [esp+9ch]^dword ptr [esp+10ch]
key_c => 10e2h
key_a => 12b3h
key_b => 0c8ah
nHandler => ((164h*(flag2&0ffh))&0ffffffffh)+0a53h

[+] solved binding
byte ptr [esp+0dh] => 1
dword ptr [esp+100h] => 968e4c84h
key_c => 10e2h
key_a => 12b3h
key_b => 0c8ah
```

We have a XOR operation between `dword ptr [ESP+9ch]` and `dword ptr [ESP+10ch]`. We can check from the context their values:

```
[+] context dump
[...]
dword ptr [esp+9ch] => 968bff6dh
dword ptr [esp+10ch] => 5b3e9h
[...]
```

This handler has a XOR-like semantics and is included within one of the loops previously identified (one with 624 iterations, the size of the MT state). There are a few more steps to recover the full transformation, but this approach is sufficient. Its pseudo-code would be as follows:

```
scramble = 0x5b3e9h
for i in (N-1)
  state[i+1] ^= scramble
```

```
scramble = lcg_rand(scramble)
```

with N being the size of the state: 624. `lcg_rand` is a linear congruential generator $x_{n+1} \equiv (ax_n + c) \pmod{m}$, with a, c, and m respectively equal to `0x159b`, `0x13e8b`, and `0xffffffff`.

The rest of the Mersenne twister algorithm is also lightly modified; each of these tweaks involves the first letter of the username and a simple operation ADD/SUB/XOR. We will not say more about these tweaks; please refer to the following "Exercises" section.

- **Username**—"Hell yeah, we have tools!"
- **Serial number**—"117538a51905ddf6"

Final Thoughts

That sample is a great playground, nicely crafted by its author. We have used an interesting combination of dynamic and static analysis to work through it. The protection implements code-flattening, code virtualization, and data encoding, concepts that can be found in most professional-grade protection systems, and yet it is still accessible. It provides a useful template for sharpening tools and experimenting with new ideas and/or algorithms. The simplicity of the protection scheme and the algorithm enabled us to take many shortcuts for this section.

Exercises

The first exercise we propose to you is to keygen this chapter's case study binary. This is a great starting point:

- The binary is unique, relatively small, and easy to analyze, disassemble, and instrument. Thus, this is an accessible challenge even for beginners.
- Most of the important implemented techniques have been described in the case study. Look for them and ensure that you understand their internals.

After reading this chapter, getting your own hands on the challenge would be an invaluable experience. Your task is as follows:

1. Based on the proposed methodology (or one you come up with), build your own tool to analyze the VM's bytecode.

2. Contact your favorite demo division and package a stunning keygen for this fine crackme.

To familiarize yourself with Metasm, you'll find two exercise scripts with the material shipped with the book: `symbolic-execution-lvl1.rb` and `symbolic-execution-lvl2.rb`. Answering the questions will lead you to a journey in

Metasm internals. You can find the scripts at www.wiley.com/go/practical-reverseengineering.com.

Notes

1. Bansal, Sorav and Aiken, Alex. "Automatic Generation of Peephole Superoptimizers," 2006, http://theory.stanford.edu/~sbansal/pubs/asplos06.pdf.

2. Barak, Boaz et al., "On the (Im)possibility of Obfuscating Programs." Technical report, Electronic Colloquium on Computational Complexity, 2001. http//www.eccc.uni-trier.de/eccc.

3. Beckman, Lennart et al., "A Partial Evaluator, and Its Use as a Programming Tool," *Artificial Intelligence*, Volume 7, Issue 4, pp. 319–357, 1976.

4. Bellard, Fabrice. "QEMU, a Fast and Portable Dynamic Translator." Paper presented at the Proceedings of the USENIX Annual Technical Conference, FREENIX Track, 41–46, 2005.

5. Billet, Olivier, Gilbert, Henri, and Ech-Chatbi, Charaf. "Cryptanalysis of a White Box AES Implementation." In *Selected Areas in Cryptography*, edited by Helena Handschuh and M. Anwar Hasan, 227–240. Springer, 2004.

6. Boyer, R. S., Elspas, B., and Levitt, K. N. SELECT - A Formal System for Testing and Debugging Programs by Symbolic Execution. SIGPLAN Not., 10:234–245, 1975.

7. Chipounov, V. and Candea, G. "Enabling Sophisticated Analyses of x86 Binaries with RevGen." Paper presented at the Dependable Systems and Networks Workshops (DSN-W), 2011 IEEE/IFIP 41st International Conference, 211–216, 2011.

8. Chipounov, V., Kuznetsov, V. and Candea, G. "S2e: A Platform for In-vivo Multi-path Analysis of Software Systems," ACM SIGARCH Computer Architecture News, vol. 39, no. 1, 265–278, 2011.

9. Chow, S., Eisen, P. A., Johnson, H., and van Oorschot, P. C. A White-Box DES Implementation for DRM Applications. In Security and Privacy in *Digital Rights Management*, ACM CCS-9 Workshop, DRM 2002, Washington, DC, USA, November 18, 2002, Revised Papers, volume 2696 of Lecture Notes in Computer Science, 1–15. Springer, 2002.

10. Chow, S., Eisen, P. A., Johnson, H., and van Oorschot, P. C. White-Box Cryptography and an AES Implementation. In *Selected Areas in Cryptography*, volume 2595 of Lecture Notes in Computer Science, 250–270. Springer, 2002.

11. Chow, Stanley T., Johnson, Harold J., and Gu, Yuan. Tamper Resistant Software Encoding, 2003.

12. Collberg, Christian, Thomborson, Clark, and Low, Douglas. A Taxonomy of Obfuscating Transformations. Technical report, 1997.

13. Collberg, Christian S., Thomborson, Clark D., and Low, Douglas. "Manufacturing Cheap, Resilient, and Stealthy Opaque Constructs." In *POPL*, 184–196, 1998.

14. Cousot, P. and Cousot, R. "Abstract Interpretation: A Unified Lattice Model for Static Analysis of Programs by Construction or Approximation of Fixpoints." In Conference Record of the 4th ACM Symp. on Principles of Programming Languages (POPL '77), 238–252. ACM Press, New York, 1977.

15. Cousot, P. and Cousot, R. "Systematic Design of Program Transformation Frameworks by Abstract Interpretation. In Conference Record of the Twenty-Ninth Annual ACM SIGPLAN-SIGACT Symposium on Principles of Programming Languages, 178–190. New York, 2002. ACM Press.

16. Cousot, P. "Constructive Design of a Hierarchy of Semantics of a Transition System by Abstract Interpretation. ENTCS, 6, 1997.

17. Dalla Preda, Mila. "Code Obfuscation and Malware Detection by Abstract Interpretation," (PhD diss.), http://profs.sci.univr.it/~dallapre/MilaDallaPreda_PhD.pdf.

18. Dalla Preda, Mila. and Giacobazzi, Roberto. "Control Code Obfuscation by Abstract Interpretation." In *Third IEEE International Conference on Software Engineering and Formal Methods*, 301–310, 2005.

19. Deroko. Nanomites.w32. http://deroko.phearless.org/nanomites.zip.

20. Ernst, Michael D. Static and Dynamic Analysis: Synergy and Duality." In *Proceedings of WODA 2003: Workshop on Dynamic Analysis*, Portland, Oregon, 24–27, May 2003.

21. Futamura, Yoshihiko. "Partial Evaluation of Computation Process - An Approach to a Compiler-Compiler," 1999. http://cs.au.dk/~hosc/local/HOSC-12-4-pp381-391.pdf.

22. Gazet, Alexandre and Guillot, Yoann. "Defeating Software Protection with Metasm. In *HITB Malaysia, Kuala Lumpur*, 2009. http://metasm.cr0.org/docs/2009-guillot-gazet-hitb-deprotection.pdf.

23. Godefroid, P., Klarlund, N., and Sen, K. "DART: Directed Automated Random Testing." In *PLDI '05*, June 2005.

24. Goubin, L., Masereel, J. M., and Quisquater, M. "Cryptanalysis of White Box DES Implementations." Cryptology ePrint Archive, Report 2007/035, 2007.

25. Jacob, Matthias et al. "The Superdiversifier: Peephole Individualization for Software Protection." 2008. http://research.microsoft.com/apps/pubs/default.aspx?id=77265.

26. Jakubowski, Marius H. et al. "Iterated Transformations and Quantitatives Metrics for Software Protection," 2009. http://research.microsoft.com/apps/pubs/default.aspx?id=81560.

27. Josse, S. "Secure and Advanced Unpacking using Computer Emulation." In Proceedings of the AVAR 2006 Conference, Auckland, New Zealand, December 3–5, 174–190, 2006.

28. Josse, S. "Rootkit Detection from Outside the Matrix." *Journal in Computer Virology*, vol. 3, 113–123. Springer, 2007.

29. Josse, S. "Dynamic Malware Recompilation." In IEEE Proceedings of the 47th HICSS Conference, 2014.

30. Kinder, Johannes, Zuleger, Florian, and Veith, Helmut. "An Abstract Interpretation-Based Framework for Control Flow Reconstruction from Binaries." 2009. http://pure.rhul.ac.uk/portal/files/17558147/vmcai09.pdf.

31. Lattner, C. and Adve, V. "LLVM: A Compilation Framework for Lifelong Program Analysis & Transformation." In International Symposium on Code Generation and Optimization, 75–86, 2004.

32. Maximus. "Reversing a Simple Virtual Machine." 2006. http://tuts4you.com/ download.php?view.210.

33. Maximus. "Virtual Machines Re-building." 2006. http://tuts4you.com/download. php?view.1229.

34. Rolles, Rolf. "Finding Bugs in VMs with a Theorem Prover, Round 1." http://www.openrce.org/blog/view/1963/Finding_Bugs_in_VMs_with_a_heorem_Prover,_Round_1.

35. Rolles, Rolf. "Defeating HyperUnpackMe2 With an IDA Processor Module," 2006. http://www.openrce.org/articles/full_view/28.

36. Scheller, T. "Llvm-qemu, Backend for QEMU using LLVM Components," Google Summer of Code 2007. http://code.google.com/p/llvm-qemu/.

37. Sen, K., Marinov, D., and Agha, G. "CUTE: A Concolic Unit Testing Engine for C." In *ESEC/FSE '05*, Sep 2005.

38. Smaragdakis, Yannis and Csallner, Christoph. "Combining Static and Dynamic Reasoning for Bug Detection." In Proceedings of International Conference on Tests and Proofs (TAP), LNCS vol. 4454, 1–16, Springer, 2007.

39. Smithson, Matt et al. "A Compiler-level Intermediate Representation Based Binary Analysis and Rewriting System." In *MALWARE*, 47–54, 2010.

40. Song, Dawn et al. "BitBlaze: A New Approach to Computer Security via Binary Analysis." In Proceedings of the 4th International Conference on Information Systems Security, Hyderabad, India, 2008.

41. Thakur, A. et al. "Directed Proof Generation for Machine Code." 2010. `http://research.cs.wisc.edu/wpis/papers/cav10-mcveto.pdf`.

42. Weiser, M., "Program Slices: Formal, Psychological, and Practical Investigations of an Automatic Program Abstraction Method (PhD diss., University of Michigan, Ann Arbor, 1979).

43. Zhao, J. et al, "Formalizing the LLVM Intermediate Representation for Verified Program Transformations." In Proceedings of the 39th Annual ACM SIGPLAN-SIGACT Symposium on Principles of Programming Languages, 427–440, 2012.

44. Zhu, William and Thomborson, Clark. "A Provable Scheme for Homomorphic Obfuscation in Software Security." In *CNIS*, 208–212. ACTA Press, 2005.

Sample Names and Corresponding SHA1 Hashes

The following are the real-life malware samples used in the book's walk-throughs and exercises. They are *live malware and may cause damage to your computer*, if not properly handled. Please exercise caution in storing and analyzing them.

REFERENCE NAME	SHA1
Sample A	092e149933584f3e81619454cbd2f404595b9f42
Sample B	bee8225c48b07f35774cb80e6ce2cdfa4cf7e5fb
Sample C	d6e45e5b4bd2c963cf16b40e17cdd7676d886a8a
Sample D	2542ba0e808267f3c35372954ef552fd54859063
Sample E	0e67827e591c77da08b6207f550e476c8c166c98
Sample F	086b05814b9539a6a31622ea1c9f626ba323ef6d
Sample G	531971827c3b8e7b0463170352e677d69f19e649
Sample H	cb3b2403e1d777c250210d4ed4567cb527cab0f4
Sample I	5991d8f4de7127cfc34840f1dbca2d4a8a6f6edf
Sample J	70cb0b4b8e60dfed949a319a9375fac44168ccbb
Sample K	23fffc74cf7737a24a5150fab4768f0d59ca2a5c
Sample L	7679d1aa1f957e4afab97bd0c24c6ae81e23597e

Index